Law, Governance and Technology Series

Volume 22

The *Law-Governance and Technology Series* is intended to attract manuscripts arising from an interdisciplinary approach in law, artificial intelligence and information technologies. The idea is to bridge the gap between research in IT law and IT-applications for lawyers developing a unifying techno-legal perspective. The series will welcome proposals that have a fairly specific focus on problems or projects that will lead to innovative research charting the course for new interdisciplinary developments in law, legal theory, and law and society research as well as in computer technologies, artificial intelligence and cognitive sciences. In broad strokes, manuscripts for this series may be mainly located in the fields of the Internet law (data protection, intellectual property, Internet rights, etc.), Computational models of the legal contents and legal reasoning, Legal Information Retrieval, Electronic Data Discovery, CollaborativeTools (e.g. Online Dispute Resolution platforms), Metadata and XML Technologies (for Semantic Web Services), Technologies in Courtrooms and Judicial Offices (E-Court), Technologies for Governments and Administrations (E-Government), Legal Multimedia, and Legal Electronic Institutions (Multi-Agent Systems and Artificial Societies).

More information about this series at http://www.springer.com/series/8808

Anne Michèle Bardopoulos

eCommerce and the Effects of Technology on Taxation

Could VAT be the eTax Solution?

Springer

Anne Michèle Bardopoulos
University of Cape Town
Western Cape, South Africa

ISSN 2352-1902 ISSN 2352-1910 (electronic)
Law, Governance and Technology Series
ISBN 978-3-319-15448-0 ISBN 978-3-319-15449-7 (eBook)
DOI 10.1007/978-3-319-15449-7

Library of Congress Control Number: 2015935749

Springer Cham Heidelberg New York Dordrecht London

Printed on acid-free paper

Springer International Publishing AG Switzerland is part of Springer Science+Business Media (www.springer.com)

"To accuse others for one's own misfortunes is a sign of want of education. To accuse oneself shows that one's education has begun. To accuse neither oneself nor others shows that one's education is complete."
Epictetus[1]

Plato contended that *"[n]o man should bring children into the world who is unwilling to preserve to the end in their nature and education"*.[2] This manuscript is dedicated to my late grandparents who believed that the greatest legacy that one can bequeath to a child is education. An educated man is an empowered man and *"[i]f a man neglects education, he walks lame to the end of his life"*[3]:

Πλάτων Μπαρδόπουλος (Platon Bardopoulos)

Κωνσταντίνα Παπαμανολοπούλου (Constandina Papamanolopoulos)

---

[1]Epictetus (AD 55 – AD 135). Available at http://www.brainyquote.com/quotes/quotes/e/epictetus149122.html [Accessed 27/01/2011].

[2]Plato (c429 – c347). Available at http://www.brainyquote.com/quotes/quotes/p/plato397319.html [Accessed 27/01/2011].

[3]Plato (c429 – c347). Available at http://www.brainyquote.com/quotes/quotes/p/plato383526.html [Accessed 27/01/2011].

Μανόλης Παπαμανολόπουλος
(Emmanuel Papamanolopoulos)
They sacrificed themselves to educate their children and children's children. They never accused others for their misfortunes and they inspired me to neither accuse myself nor others for my misfortunes.

Preface

The introductory chapter of the paper is a synopsis of salient points at issue cardinal to the intellectual basis of the paper, *id est*, the impact of technology on taxation and is VAT the eTax solution? Indeed, it is submitted that the imposition and implication of an eTax on eCommerce in the cyberworld, the formulation of which tax is at once efficient and compliant, is feasible and possible. It is further submitted that VAT, without reconceptualisation or formulation of a new system, is the most effective (actually usable) and practicable solution.

A critical point at issue is rapidly increasing eCommerce transactions and unconstrained amelioration of technology. The issue of an eTax is a compelling field of study because it is both topical and of historical consequence to the extent that the traditional world of tax, commerce and international trade is witnessing the radical evolution of taxation as it rises to meet the unprecedented challenges of eCommerce.

The paper explores the challenge to tax that has thrown the "*application of tax laws into disarray*".[4] The point at issue is the marking of "*territory in a seamless digital world . . . of mark[ing] nations and tax jurisdictions in a world that is not based on geography...*".[5] It is contended that this challenge pertains primarily to income tax laws to a greater extent than indirect tax laws.

The submission that value-added tax ("VAT") is the eTax solution is supported by a comparative analysis and application of both income tax principles and VAT to practical examples. It is submitted that such a comparison elucidates VAT's superior effectiveness and potentiality as an eTax tool in the virtual world. The current escalation of globalisation which in turn has compounded taxation issues has been expedited by the development of the Internet. With the introduction of the Internet and the advent of eCommerce, the traditional concept of international trade

---

[4]Bird, Richard *Taxing Electronic Commerce: A Revolution in the Making* (September 2003). C.D. Howe Institute Commentary, p4-5. Available at http://www.cdhowe.org/pdf/commentary_187.pdf [Accessed 16/09/2010].

[5]supra.

and commerce can no longer be effectively applied to the new taxing complications and issues manifested by technological amelioration. Unprecedented tax issues in respect of eCommerce transactions in the Internet may be classified as pertaining to the next generation taxing regime. The clumsy attempt to impose "physical world" laws upon a "virtual world" has generated multiple points at issue and has accentuated the impracticability of imposing "physical world" laws on a "virtual world".

Further to a discussion of tax points at issue and solutions proffered in respect of eCommerce, the eCommerce environment itself and the laws pertaining to such an environment should be examined. Indeed, ignorance of the virtual world and its *modus operandi* precludes competent formulation of effective solutions to points at issue in eCommerce. Acknowledgment of the intricacies and complications of electronic transactions, as well as the continuous evolution of the Internet, will assist in the endeavour to develop a flexible and equitable solution to taxing problems inherent to our new "virtual world".

Cardinal to the paper is the contention that taxing solutions should not be rigidly tailored to current technology operations and systems. It is essential that proposed tax solutions to all next generation taxing regime issues take cognizance of the current growth rate of electronic technology, that is, taxing solutions to eCommerce should be considered in conjunction with Moore's Law.[6] The prevailing tax "challenge" is undoubtedly temporary as it is in the nature of tax to be infinitely adaptable. Taxation is an integral part of human history, past and present, and the virtual world is commerce's future. It is essential that any taxing system adopted to be imposed upon the virtual world should have the flexibility to be adapted to unpredictable taxing issues precipitated by technological amelioration.

Attempting to enforce a narrow view of tax principles on technology is proving to be increasingly difficult, especially as traditional taxing precepts have fallen victim to the proverbial generation gap and as such are not congruent with contemporary technological concepts of the Y-Generation, particularly with regard to the concept of "physical presence" in the internet. Tax authorities targeting the virtual tax prize may gratify their predilection by espousing the Y-Generation's philosophy of technology and their concept of being "physically present" in the Internet, which is, furthermore, supported by technology academics.

As the paper is concerned primarily with the analysis and evaluation of VAT as the eTax solution, it is, therefore, imperative to examine some of the inefficiencies of traditional income tax provisions within the eCommerce environment; this relates most significantly to the issues of "residence" and "source" provisions and principles within the income tax analysis. Traditional income tax provisions dismally lack the flexibility to be effectively applied to the virtual world – the

[6]"*The 'law' was adopted after Intel co-founder Gordon Moore wrote in a 1965 article that the number of transistors on a chip would double every 24 months.*" BBC News, Moore's Law on chips marks 40th (18 April 2005). Available at http://news.bbc.co.uk/2/hi/technology/4446285.stm [Accessed 21 July 2009].

theoretical principles upon which traditional income tax is founded are all too often couched in concepts which directly obstruct the necessary adaptability and flexibility of income tax provisions in respect of an ameliorating technological society. The problem of inflexible tax laws is especially pertinent in a society which is still adapting to the concept of being "physically present" within a virtual world. It is, therefore, submitted that current income tax principles are too rigid to adapt sufficiently to the exponentially burgeoning virtual world and technology. Indeed, it may be argued that income tax principles deem that adaptation is the responsibility of technology, the consequences of which are increasingly ineffective application of income tax in eCommerce and increasing loss of tax revenue in respect of government coffers.

The Internet has had a drastic impact on society and, moreover, the economy. It is imperative that we recognise that "*the Internet [is] an important cultural phenomenon... [which has, however,] failed to comply with basic economic laws... [probably because] it was devised by a bunch of hippie anarchists*".[7] Thus, tax authorities should seize the advantage of conceding to the concept that "*[t]o get others to come into our way of thinking, we must go over to theirs; and it is necessary to follow, in order to lead*".[8] Cognizance of the principles and concepts which enmesh the virtual world – the pressing concept of "presence" in the virtual world is a cogent point at issue – is essential to an understanding of the issue of traditional tax principles and virtual world incompatibility. Indeed, a careful scrutiny of the application of income tax principles within the virtual world is significant to the intellectual basis of the paper: "*The impact of technology on taxation*".

The point at issue is taxation, either direct or indirect, in an eCommerce environment, which is subject to technology and technological concepts, and, as such, it may be proposed that tax adjust its principles and perceptions to those of the technology and communication industry and not demand the reverse. The question begs as to whether the continuing attempt to impose "basic economic laws" on an environment which defies such laws is not in itself a futile exercise. It may be argued that the continuing changes and advancements in technology make such an endeavour a futile exercise, and that the only tax that may possibly work within a "virtual world" may be the imposition of an indirect tax like VAT. The focus of the paper is to highlight the current efficiencies of VAT and consumption taxes in contradistinction to the inefficiencies of income tax principles which have possibly been stretched to their finite point of elasticity. It is submitted that the virtual world, engulfed in its own complications and perplexities, may be more amenable to the application of VAT than to the application of "source-based", or other income tax, principles.

The issue of countries not implementing a VAT system in respect of eCommerce is a point at issue which posits the challenge as to whether it is possible for VAT

---

[7]Nolle, Thomas. Available at www.quotegarden.com.internet.html [Accessed 8 May 2008].

[8]Shanahan, John M. (Ed). *The Most Brilliant Thoughts of All Times*; Hazlitt, William (1778–1830); Harper Collins, Inc.; New York, USA (1999). p275.

jurisdictions to effectively interact with non-VAT jurisdictions. The inability of VAT jurisdictions to effectively operate in conjunction with retail sales tax jurisdictions would doubtlessly precipitate problematic imposition of indirect taxation within the virtual world. However, a crucial aspect may be that whether a jurisdiction utilises a retail sales tax system or a VAT system, both are indirect taxes. While sales tax may deviate from the principle of neutrality and may not be considered a "general consumption tax"[9] as is VAT, it is, nevertheless, consumption tax principle based similar to VAT.

While there may be other types of indirect tax systems utilised, VAT and retail sales tax (while the former is more prevalent than the latter) are without a doubt the two prevailing indirect tax systems within the global community. Indeed, 130 jurisdictions currently, as of the year 2010, have adopted and implemented a VAT system. The significant USA jurisdiction utilises a retail sales tax system. Canada, further to this issue, provides a functional example of VAT and retails sales tax co-existing effectively and efficiently in relation to each other, as both VAT and retails sales tax have been implemented in Canada for over 20 years.

eCommerce has not impacted VAT laws to the extent it has income tax laws, but has effectuated an exponential increase in cross-border transactions in respect of which tax laws, depending upon jurisdiction, zero-rate exports and tax imports. Technology has, however, impacted the current retail sales tax systems in effect in the USA instigating an increased urgency to streamline the retail sales tax system. While the paper may not advocate the abandonment of income tax principles in their entirety, comparison of income tax based principles to VAT laws implemented in the various jurisdictions suggests that the virtual world may be more amenable to the application of VAT than to income tax principles. Yet income tax appears to be the primary focus of much research, debate and discussion contingent upon the quantity of tax revenue connected with effective imposition of income tax.

VAT as an effective eTax can be applied to the virtual world in a manner analogous to traditional application precluding administrative difficulties. Inherent to indirect taxes such as VAT, the capacity to expedite eCommerce and facilitate the general operation, management and control of the virtual world is testament to the latter's potential as an effective eTax tool.

Despite the impact of globalisation on international taxation, disputes pertaining to diverse political agendas predominate most specifically in respect of application of income tax principles. It is not to be implied, however, that indirect taxes such as VAT are insusceptible to disputes extant to conflicting political agendas; however,

[9]Tumpel, Michael, Professor *A Hybrid VAT System in the European Union* (Draft 04/24/2007) p31. Available at http://docs.google.com/viewer?a=v&q=cache:g5ZTN7J6sf8J:www.law.nyu.edu/idcplg?IdcService%3DGET_FILE%26dDocName%3DECM_DLV_013830%26RevisionSelectionMethod%3DLatestReleased+The+common+framework+for+VAT+created+in+1967+for+the+EU&hl=en&pid=bl&srcid=ADGEESig8c6y5AwqvxSipGHOW8-aslQcrIqfbzM1dwHa6pTbqOQbLX60f8_nx3d-UlY3vjQQg2BR8zYGevnpGPnM9rt5H2Q4RkiAHe0Pl_tR6xZFjyqhxg0yx3ZcnIdwyatBM51Kdeyp&sig=AHIEtbSZXkC370HMugv4EdOPt6e-bY4eFA&pli=1 [Accessed 14/12/2010].

existing similarities have promoted harmonisation of indirect taxes on account of cross-border transactions. VAT is not without defect and perplexities relative to both the traditional and virtual worlds. VAT is not the "*silver bullet that will solve all the fiscal problems to which the growth of the borderless economy of cyberspace potentially gives rise*".[10] Further taxation problems arise with the proliferation of eCommerce which may not be effectively resolved with the application of VAT. Thus, while the paper's primary focus is to evaluate the effectiveness of VAT in regard to collecting taxes on eTransactions, an examination of these issues in terms of finding or exploring a plausible solution is vital for other spheres of taxation, such as transfer pricing.

The submission that VAT is the eCommerce solution is cardinal to the prevailing discourse of the paper. VAT's attraction is that it is both flexible and adaptable in respect of eCommerce, and in contradistinction to income taxation can be applied to eCommerce without significant change or amendment. However, amendment, radical change and reconceptualisation of income tax provisions are requisite for effective application to the virtual world. Notwithstanding the applicable amendment of relevant general peculiarities of the virtual world which would unequivocally assist in establishing VAT's capacity as an effective eTax, it is submitted that VAT is, not only in the interim, a dependable eTax in respect of eCommerce, but will remain a powerful taxing tool in the virtual world.

University of Cape Town, South Africa Anne Michèle Bardopoulos

[10]op cit Bird, Richard *Taxing Electronic Commerce: A Revolution in the Making*, p2.

Abstract

Technology has impacted taxation and the manner in which it is effectively imposed. While this paper submits that VAT is the eTax solution, income tax issues relating to "residence" versus "source" have been addressed. A comparative analysis is made in respect of the application of income tax and VAT principles to eCommerce transactions.

Application of VAT within the virtual world does not differ significantly from traditional application. The primary difference pertains to determining the place of "supply", but apart from such determination VAT principles and concepts can be applied with relative ease within the virtual world. Income tax laws, however, have deemed certain technology to constitute, for example, permanent establishment, and the conflict in "source" and "resident" based systems implemented globally has generated further points at issue. It is submitted that income tax principles may have to be "reconceptualised" in order to be effectively applied to eCommerce transactions because, in their current form they are not conducive to cross-border eCommerce transactions.

It is submitted that the indirect consumption-based VAT system is the most effective taxation system in respect of cross-border eCommerce transactions. Furthermore, VAT is the most amenable tax system in respect of eCommerce, because VAT's inherently flexible nature enables it to adapt to technical amelioration and the unprecedented and unexplored terrain of a seamless, borderless virtual world. While VAT is not perfect and requires modification if it is to be effectively applied to the virtual world, and although administrative difficulties pertaining to cross-border transactions do require resolution, it is submitted that VAT is, nevertheless, more effective as an eTax than income tax. This assertion is based primarily on the flexibility of VAT principles compared to the inflexible principles of income tax.

Due to the infancy of eCommerce, case studies and data are relatively limited. Nevertheless, case studies of Amazon.com and Second Life are used as examples in an analysis of VAT application in the virtual world, and where possible electronic transactions have been either tested or attempted. A comparative analysis of the application of income tax and VAT principles to practical examples is provided to demonstrate the effectiveness of VAT as the eTax solution.

Contents

Classified Guide to the Paper

1. Abbreviations and Acronyms

ARPA	Advanced Research Project Agency
ATO	Australian Tax Office
AUS	Australia
B2C	Business to Consumer
C2C	Consumer to Consumer
CAN	Canada
CIR	Commissioner of Inland Revenue
CIT	Collector of Income Tax
COT	Commissioner of Tax
CRA	Canadian Revenue Agency
DNS	Domain Name Server
DTA	Double Tax Agreements
EC	European Community
E-Commerce/eCommerce/e-commerce	Electronic Commerce
EU	European Union
GST	Goods and Service Tax (alternative name for VAT. Name and acronym applied in Countries such as Canada, New Zealand and Australia.)
HMRC	Her Majesty's Revenue & Customs
HST	Harmonized Sales Tax (Canada)
IP	Internet Protocol
IRS	Inland Revenue Service
ISP (server)	Internet Service Provider
MC	Model Tax Convention
NBL	Network Load Balancing
NZ	New Zealand
OECD	Organisation for Economic Co-Operation and Development

(continued)

OEEC	Organisation for European Economic Co-Operation
PST	Provincial Sales Tax (Canada)
QST	Quebec Sales Tax (Canada)
RCC	Revenue and Customs Commissioners
RSA/ZAR	Republic of South Africa
SARS	South African Revenue Services
SSTP	Streamlined Sales Tax Program/Project (USA)
SSTP/SSUTA	Streamlined Sales Tax Program (USA)
SSUTA	Streamlined Sales and Use Tax Agreement (USA)
States	As used within the OECD Model Convention, refers to "countries"
TAG	Technical Advisory Group of the OECD
TCP	Transmission Control Protocol
UN	United Nations
UNCITRAL	United Nations Commission on International Trade Law
USA	United States of America
VAT	Value-Added Tax
WWW/the Web	World Wide Web

2. Currency Symbols

£	United Kingdom Pound currency symbol
$	Dollar currency symbol used by USA, Canada, New Zealand and Australia. Distinguished by placing the country abbreviation before the currency symbol
Kr/SEK	Swedish currency symbol
¥	Japanese Yen currency symbol
R	South African Rand currency symbol
€	European Union Euro currency symbol
CHF	Swiss Francs currency symbol/abbreviation

3. Footnote Referencing

et al.	And others
ibid	In the same place
Idem	The same
op cit	In the work cited
loc cit	In the place cited
supra	Above

4. Date Formatting

Unless otherwise stated date formats throughout this paper will be as follows:	
YYYY/MM/DD	Year/Month/Day
DD/MM/YYYY	Day/Month/Year
Day Month Year	The date written out in full

Chapter 1
A Bird's Eye View

It took the Telephone 38 years to reach 50 million users; Television 13 years to reach 50 million users; Internet 4 years to reach 50 million users. (Nellen, Annette *Overview to E-Commerce Taxation – Guide to Understanding the Current Discussions and Debates* (July 2003) 8. Available at www.cob.sjsu.edu/facstaff/NELLEN_A/ECOMM.pdf [Accessed 24/12/2008])

Abstract Globalization and the dominion of the Internet have confounded traditional international tax systems. Unprecedented tax issues flowing from eCommerce, powered by continuously mutating technology represent the central agenda for the next generation taxing regime. The continuing attempt to impose 'basic economic laws' on an environment which defies such laws is a futile exercise.

Critical points at issue are: 'source'; 'residence' and the virtual world; harmonization; internationally equitable and effective imposition of tax in respect of eCommerce; privacy; introduction between VAT and non-VAT jurisdictions and administrative issues. A further problematical point at issue in respect of eCommerce is the question of tax avoidance or tax evasion. The concept of 'presence; in the virtual world is a cogent point at issue as is the concept that being 'here' and 'there' within the context of the virtual world is synchronically possible.

Such challenges demand that taxing solutions should have the flexibility to adept to the impact of currently unimaginable technological amelioration.

It is submitted that VAT's superior efficiency and potency in the virtual world of cyberspace can be demonstrated in a comparative analysis with income tax principles and the application thereof to practical examples.

This paper explores the implications of globalisation consequent to the dominion of the internet for traditional tax systems and the consequent argument that these developments have thrown the "*application of tax laws into disarray*".[1] In brief the challenge to tax is posed by the marking of "*territory in a seamless digital*

[1]Bird, Richard *Taxing Electronic Commerce: A Revolution in the Making* (September 2003). C.D. Howe Institute Commentary, p4–5. Available at http://www.cdhowe.org/pdf/commentary_187.pdf [Accessed 16/09/2010].

A.M. Bardopoulos, *eCommerce and the Effects of Technology on Taxation*, Law, Governance and Technology Series 22, DOI 10.1007/978-3-319-15449-7_1

flagrant tax evasion. *"Legislation governing ... trade that is technology neutral is required. The use of an electronic medium should not affect the laws that would ordinarily govern the transaction."*[10] This principle is pertinent to the various codes of law which have been proposed to govern the virtual world, including methods of taxation.

A narrow conception of 'physical presence' within the virtual world will induce an inflexible taxing system. It is essential that any taxing system within the virtual world should have the flexibility to be adapted to unpredictable taxing issues precipitated by technological amelioration. Therefore, educated cognizance of technological terms, definitions and concepts is essential. Attempting to enforce a narrow view of tax principles on technology has proved increasingly to be difficult, especially as traditional taxing precepts have fallen victim to the proverbial generation gap and as such are not synchronous with contemporary technological concepts of the Y-Generation, particularly with regard to the concept of 'physical presence' in the internet.

Within the context of eCommerce, to impute a *parti pris* definition to 'physical presence' would prejudice the issue of 'physical presence' in the Internet for the purpose of determining taxing rights, imposition of consumption tax as well as enforcing obligation to collect consumption taxes on behalf of revenue authorities.

By adopting a common broad view of 'physical presence' in the virtual world, a more flexible application of real world laws in the virtual world will be possible, especially in the case of the prevalent Functional Equivalence Approach. Furthermore, such a stance may enable the Functional Equivalence Approach to meet the challenge of possible future technological advances such as space ISPs.

Tax authorities who seek to target new sources of revenue and thus pursue the virtual tax honey-pot may espouse the Y-Generation's philosophy of technology and a concept of being 'physically present' in the Internet, which has support from technology academics. Tax authorities should seize the advantage of conceding to Hazlitts'[11] axiom that *"[t]o get others to come into our way of thinking, we must go over to theirs; and it is necessary to follow, in order to lead*".[12]

Furthermore, it should be possible for tax principles to be applied in a manner compatible with the technology and communication industry's perception of 'presence'. The Internet has had a drastic impact on society and, moreover, the economy. It is imperative that we recognise that *"the Internet [is] an important cultural phenomenon... [which has, however,] failed to comply with basic economic*

[10]Contracting and Trade Laws, Green Paper on Electronic Commerce for South Africa, Co-ordinated and complied by the Department of Communications Republic of South Africa (November 2000).

[11]Hazlitt, William (1778–1830). *"English essayist and critic. From about 1812 he wrote many articles on diverse subjects for several periodicals, including the Edinburgh Review and the Morning Chronicle; his essays were collected in Table Talk (1821–2) and The Plain Speaker (1826)"*. **[*The Oxford English Reference Dictionary*, Sec. Ed. (1996), p647]**.

[12]Shanahan, John M. (Ed). *The Most Brilliant Thoughts of All Times*; Hazlitt, William (1778–1830); Harper Collins, Inc.; New York, USA (1999). p275.

laws... [probably because] it was devised by a bunch of hippie anarchists".[13] The point at issue is that taxation, either direct or indirect, in an eCommerce environment, which is subject to technology and technological concepts, will need to adjust its principles and perceptions to those of the technology and communication industry. The further question then follows as to whether the continuing attempt to impose 'basic economic laws' on an environment which defies such laws is not in itself a futile exercise.

Although the primary interest of this paper is not the manner in which 'physical presence' is perceived, 'physical presence' is, nevertheless, a significant issue, the impact of which on sales within the virtual world and the relevance of which to the imposition of VAT in the virtual world cannot be disregarded.

1.1 Key Tax Principles: Source, Residence, Physical Presence

One of the crucial points at issue to be taken into account with regard to the imposition of income tax principles upon eCommerce is the question as to whether income tax principles are flexible enough to be effectively imposed on eCommerce Transactions. Because traditional income tax is founded on theoretical principles, there may be too many criteria which directly obstruct adaptability and flexibility of income tax provisions in a 'virtual world' due to continuously burgeoning technology.

As this paper is concerned primarily with the analysis and evaluation of VAT as the primary solution to the new forms of economic activity, it is imperative to examine some of the inefficiencies of traditional income tax provisions within the eCommerce environment; this relates most significantly to the issues of 'residence' and 'source' provisions and principles within the income tax analysis.

The OECD Commentary, in these circumstances, defines "source" and, therefore, "permanent establishment", by determining the physical location of the server. Such application may now be outdated and redundant in respect of technological development; that is, it has become common technological practice to work off several servers when executing one transaction. This is referred to as "load-shedding" and allows for faster Internet processing and less "bottle-necks" occurring within the Internet environment. Thus, the simple transaction of acquiring one book off Amazon may utilize, for example, six servers located in several jurisdictions in order to complete the transaction.

A critical issue pertaining to source is its practicability within the modern global context. With regard to businesses, several jurisdictions will tax the business profits of an enterprise which is resident of another State if that enterprise is conducting business through a 'permanent establishment', thereby satisfying a fundamental

[13]Nolle, Thomas. Available at www.quotegarden.com.internet.html [Accessed 8 May 2008].

'source' requirement. 'Permanent establishment' has become a topical subject pertinent to 'source-based' taxation systems applied within an eCommerce context.

Traditional income tax provisions dismally lack the flexibility to be applied effectively to the virtual world – the theoretical principles upon which traditional income tax is founded are all too often couched in concepts which directly obstruct the necessary adaptability and flexibility of income tax provisions apropos to a burgeoning technological society. The problem of inflexible tax laws is especially pertinent in a society which is still adapting to the concept of being 'physically present' within a virtual world. The concept of being 'physically present' and having 'residency' in the virtual world is too many "*a riddle wrapped in a mystery inside an enigma*".[14] The acknowledgement of 'physical presence' in the virtual world with the aim of determining jurisdiction of residence illuminates the predicament of electing how to apply provisions for determining residency, a prerequisite of which is geographical location.

Thus, it may be contended that rather than attempting to adapt traditional 'residence' tests to the virtual world for income tax purposes, it may be more expedient to devise provisions more apposite to the virtual world business model.

1.2 The Scope of This Paper

That in turn compels an intelligent comprehension of a continuously evolving technological environment imperative in the endeavour to devise and implement a method of taxation that is at once flexible and intrinsically applicable. It may be argued that the continuing changes and advancements in technology make such an endeavour a futile exercise, and that the only tax that may possibly work within a "virtual world" may intelligibly be the imposition of an indirect tax like VAT.

Although the limitation of the scope of this paper implies only a limited degree of electronic analysis or the operations of the Internet, a brief examination of the Internet and electronic law is necessary for an understanding of the complexities intrinsic to the application of tax principles within an eCommerce environment. Study and understanding of the electronic environment is requisite to determine differing taxing consequences.

Furthermore, the subject matter extends to an examination of diverse taxing consequences of international trade and commerce; consequences pertinent to the understanding of the extent of the effect eCommerce on the taxing world. While the primary interest of this paper is VAT within an ecommerce environment, as

[14]Churchill, Sir Winston (Leonard Spencer) (1874–1965). *"British conservative statesman, Prime Minister 1940–5 . . . [R]eplaced Neville Chamberlain as Prime Minister in May 1940. Serving as war leaser of a coalition government until 1945, Churchill demonstrated rare qualities of leadership and outstanding gifts as an orator"*. **[op cit *Oxford English Reference Dictionary*, 1996, p262]**.

I have argued, a sound understanding of other taxing implications (for example, defining "source", "residence", income taxation implications, etc.) is essential to the understanding of tax and its place within the eCommerce market.

To understand how the current ineffective imposition and collection of tax within the virtual world may be addressed, an understanding of the various problems and issues attendant upon taxing eCommerce transactions is thus imperative. The development of an efficient and effective eCommerce taxing system is an ever increasing global need. Therefore, the submission that VAT may be the eTax solution (at the least until an entirely new taxing system is developed for the purpose of effectively imposing and collecting tax on eCommerce transactions) this study takes place within the context of ineffective applications of traditional income taxing principles within the new virtual world. In turn the latter serves as an overview of the various concerns and problems appertaining to the imposition of income tax principles in the virtual world.

In summary, it is submitted that current income tax principles are too rigid to adapt sufficiently to the exponentially burgeoning virtual world and technology with the consequence of increasingly ineffective application of income tax in eCommerce and a concomitant loss of tax revenue. To this end, cognizance of the principles and concepts which enmesh the virtual world – the pressing concept of 'presence' in the virtual world is a cogent point at issue – is essential to the submission of traditional tax principles and virtual world incompatibility.

Indeed, a careful scrutiny of the application of income tax principles within the virtual world is significant to the intellectual basis of this paper: '*The impact of technology on taxation*'.

This paper falls within a fairly new and unestablished field of study. Comparatively few papers and publications on the subject of taxation within an eCommerce environment and the expanding importance of examining effective eCommerce taxation methods have been published. It is, however, an area of accelerated expansion induced by the rapid evolution of technology and ever increasing transactions within an eCommerce environment. It is indisputably an exciting area of study as the foundation for taxation within an eCommerce environment is currently being posited. Indeed, we are witnessing the evolution and development of taxation as it rises to meet the challenges of eCommerce.

The paper seeks to highlight the current efficiencies of VAT and consumption taxes in contradistinction to the inefficiencies of income tax principles which have possibly been stretched to their finite point of elasticity.[15]

---

[15]This paper is not concerned with an in-depth discussion of the various issues regarding the application of source within an eCommerce environment, and the measures which have to be taken in order to effectively apply a 'source-based' taxing system within the virtual world. Dr Dale Pinto discusses these issues in great detail within his doctoral thesis, *E-Commerce and Source-Based Income Taxation*, and he asserts the need for 'source-based' taxation to be "*reconceptualised*" rather than abandoned in its entirety.

Dr Dale Pinto submitted his thesis, *E-Commerce and Source-Based Income Taxation*, in total fulfilment of the requirements of the degree of Doctor of Philosophy in March 2002 through the

The argument is not about the total abandonment of income tax principles such as 'source-based' tax systems. However, it is submitted that it is crucial for all governments affected by the advent of the Internet to recognise that it may be several years before problematic income taxing provisions are effectively resolved. Indeed, it is submitted that the virtual world, engulfed in its own complications and perplexities, may be more amenable to the application of VAT than to the application of 'source-based', or other income tax, principles. The theoretical application of VAT within the virtual world will be examined in this paper and then the practicality of applying such a system will be examined.

While cloud computing, as well as cloud gaming, is not discussed any further in this paper, it mentioned here as it is an attestation to continuously ameliorating technology in that at the start of this paper in 2010 'cloud gaming' had not yet been launched in the UK, and it emphasizes the urgency of establishing and imposing a flexible taxing system which can be adapted to eCommerce in a continuously evolving cyber-world. The launch of 'cloud gaming'[16] in the United Kingdom has

---

Faculty of Law at the University of Melbourne. Dr Pinto, an Associate Professor and Head of the Taxation Department at Curtin University in Perth, Western Australia, has published extensively and presented papers at several conferences in relation to Taxation.

[16]Cloud gaming was launched by OnLive in the UK on 22 September 2011. OnLive "*is the pioneer of on-demand, instant-play video game services, delivering real-time interactive experiences and rich media through the Internet. With groundbreaking video compression technology, OnLive harnesses cloud computing to provide the power and intelligence needed to instantly deliver the latest, premium game titles to any HDTV via the OnLive Game System or nearly any PC and Mac via a small browser download*"[A].

Wired describes OnLive's cloud gaming as a "*service [which] is all about on-demand gaming, and through a nifty combination of ridiculously powerful servers, a BT-powered infrastructure that's laced over Britain and some on-the-fly video codecs, you can stream full-on PC games over the web*".[B] The BBC News Technology reported the launch as "*[t]he system, which went live in the United States last year, allows users to play games without owning a traditional console. Instead, the applications are all run on remote servers with the video streamed across the internet*"[C].

The Huffington Post further states that "*[t]he OnLive cloud system will revolutionise the way games are bought, played and viewed, doing away with games discs, large demo files and allowing non-gamers to view live games being played. OnLive will also challenge the gaming system where gamers must choose a console or buy a high capacity PC to play games… 'OnLive will be transformative in how people think of video games.'…*"[D].

[A]BT Press Releases (September 22, 2011) *OnLive and BT launch revolutionary cloud gaming*. Available at http://www.btplc.com/news/articles/showarticle.cfm?articleid=%7B323bde77-276a-417e-bf9d-809adc140609%7D [Accessed 26/09/2011].

[B]Brown, Mark. *Cloud gaming platform OnLive will hit the UK on 22 September 2011. Wired*. Available at http://www.wired.co.uk/news/archive/2011-08/11/onlive-launch-date [Accessed 26/09/2011].

[C]BBC News Technology. *OnLive cloud gaming comes to UK*. 22 September 2011. Available at http://www.bbc.co.uk/news/technology-15015335?print=true [Accessed 26/09/2011].

[D]HuffPost Tech, United Kingdom (20 September 2011) *OnLive Cloud Gaming Launches At Eurogamer Expo*. Available at http://www.huffingtonpost.co.uk/2011/09/20/cloud-gaming-at-eurgamer_n_971332.html?view=print [Accessed 26/09/2011].

been internationally proclaimed. Cloud gaming, utilising the principles of cloud computing,[17] allows users to access games anywhere in the world without having to download the game – in other words, cloud gaming is completely used on-line. Cloud gaming is a major achievement for the gaming industry in its battle to combat piracy as users are unable to download the game and, therefore, are unable to copy the game. At this juncture the point at issue in respect of Cloud Gaming is the issue of privacy, that is, the control and security of users' personal information. A very significant point at issue in respect of Cloud Gaming is the tax issue. However, there is an ostensible absence of interest regarding this issue at this point in time.[18] It has been proffered that the loss of tax revenue to governments as a result of eCommerce is not significant enough to cause major concern.[19] However, it may be argued that a vast quantity of eCommerce is disregarded as a prospective and lucrative source of taxation.

---

[17]The Web Techforum describes 'cloud computing' as "*equivalent to using an electricity grid. Instead of maintaining a full IT infrastructure, companies using this model 'plug into' a cloud solution, which is provided by a third party via the Internet, as and when they need to.*"

Joubert, Billy (10 June 2010) *The Tax Implications of Cloud Computing* Web Techforum. Available at http://www.itweb.co.za/index.php?option=com_content&view=article&id=33906%3Athe-tax-implications-of-cloud-computing&catid=355&Itemid=86 [Accessed 26/09/2011].

[18]Cloud computing, as addressed from a United States perspective, has been described as shifting from the downloading of

> *products to internet-based access to applications and data 'in the cloud', [which] has the potential to once again take a large segment of digital transactions outside of the states' taxing reach. At the very least, cloud computing promises to raise a series of new questions, the most basic of which is how states will presumably impose sales tax on digital transactions . . .*
>
> *. . . cloud computing raises numerous and unresolved state sales-tax issues. These issues are likely to be resolved piecemeal on a state-by-state basis. However, as they are being resolved, cloud computing will present vendors and consumers with potential sales-tax planning opportunities. In many cases, cloud computing will make it possible for consumers to obtain many of the benefits that were once associated with taxable purchases of software and digital products, through the purchase of a non-taxable service. In addition, because of the uncertainties regarding the sourcing of cloud computing transactions, vendors and consumers may have opportunities to achieve more advantageous sourcing for transactions by moving them to the cloud. For instance, there may be opportunities to move data processing services from origin-sourcing states that tax such services to the cloud . . .*

While expressed from a USA perspective it, nevertheless, aptly describes the situation jurisdictions across the globe are facing.

ReedSmith *Transcending the Cloud, A Legal Guide to the Risks and Rewards of Cloud Computing, Pennies From Heaven – U.S. State Tax Implications Within Cloud Computing*. Reedsmith.com. Available at http://www.reedsmith.com/_db/_documents/State_Tax_Cloud_Computing_Paper.pdf [Accessed 26/09/2011].

[19]Per the OECD Ottawa Framework, "*[t]here is little tax revenue at stake currently in end-to-end (B2C) [that is, Business to Customer] online downloading*".

OECD *Taxation and Electronic Commerce, Implementing the Ottawa Taxation Framework Conditions* ("*OECD Taxation & eCommerce*") (2001) p74.

The significance of studying diverse countries in respect of the application of tax laws rather than concentrating on disparate thinking is to demonstrate that:

(i) Despite diversity of principles in respect of VAT application by diverse jurisdictions VAT appears to be, nevertheless, "*flexible and technology neutral*"[26];
(ii) It is possible for diverse principles in VAT application to co-exist, for example, Australia in relation to New Zealand and South Africa;
(iii) In respect of countries of economic importance, for example, Brazil and China, even if application varies from other countries they, nevertheless, utilize the indirect consumption-based VAT system;
(iv) It is possible for various countries to harmonize their VAT systems, as demonstrated by the European Union; and
(v) It is possible for the Canadian consumption-based VAT system to co-exist with, and operate efficiently in conjunction with, the consumption-based retail sales tax system as implemented in the USA, a major commercial hub.

The inability of VAT jurisdictions effectively to operate in conjunction with retail sales tax jurisdictions will doubtless precipitate problematic imposition of indirect taxation within the virtual world. Furthermore, the impact of countries which fail to implement a VAT system in respect of eCommerce is a point at issue which posits the challenge as to whether it is possible for VAT jurisdictions to effectively interact with non-VAT jurisdictions.[27]

A crucial aspect may be that whether a jurisdiction utilises a retail sales tax system or a VAT system, both are indirect taxes. While sales tax may deviate from the principle of neutrality and may not be considered a 'general consumption tax'[28] as is VAT, it is, nevertheless, consumption tax principle based similar to VAT. However, while there may be other types of indirect tax systems utilised in the global community, VAT and retail sales tax (while the former is more prevalent than the latter) are without a doubt the two prevailing indirect tax systems within the global community. Indeed, 130 jurisdictions currently, as of the year 2010, have adopted and implemented a VAT system. The significant USA jurisdiction utilises a retail sales tax system. The USA is a major commercial hub and a critical point at issue is whether VAT can co-exist effectively with retail sales tax.

---

[26]op cit Rendahl, p245.

[27]Discussed in Chap. 18 – Jurisdictional Analysis, Part V of this paper [p169].

[28]Tumpel, Michael, Professor, *A Hybrid VAT System in the European Union* (Draft 04/24/2007) p31. Available at http://docs.google.com/viewer?a=v&q=cache:g5ZTN7J6sf8J:www.law.nyu.edu/idcplg?IdcService%3DGET_FILE%26dDocName%3DECM_DLV_013830%26RevisionSelectionMethod%3DLatestReleased+The+common+framework+for+VAT+created+in+1967+for+the+EU&hl=en&pid=bl&srcid=ADGEESig8c6y5AwqvxSipGHOW8-aslQcrIqfbzM1dwHa6pTbqOQbLX60f8_nx3d-UlY3vjQQg2BR8zYGevnpGPnM9rt5H2Q4RkiAHe0Pl_tR6xZFjyqhxg0yx3ZcnIdwyatBM51Kdeyp&sig=AHIEtbSZXkC370HMugv4EdOPt6e-bY4eFA&pli=1 [Accessed 14/12/2010].

While VAT and retail sales tax differ in terms of the principles of neutrality and the manner in which each tax is imposed and effected, the primary discrepancy between the two systems may, arguably, be the contention as to whether the destination or origin principle is applied and the manner in which the place of supply is determined and, furthermore, the interpretation of 'physical presence'. However, this is a conflict which may also exist between VAT jurisdictions. The contemporaneous actuality of the two indirect tax systems and, moreover, additional VAT systems, necessitates a common global recognition of tax and technology definitions and principles.

Although the USA applies an indirect tax system, that is, retail sales tax as opposed to VAT, scrutiny of USA tax law is relevant because of the significance of the USA as a major commercial hub in respect of eCommerce, the virtual world and ameliorating technology. The submission of VAT as an effective eTax solution would be futile if VAT could not co-exist with USA indirect taxing principles. Pertinent to this issue, Canada presents a functional example of VAT and retails sales tax co-existing, effectively and efficiently in relation to each other as both VAT and retails sales tax have been implemented in Canada (the former on a federal level and the latter on provincial levels) for over 20 years.

A study of Canada is relevant to the argument of this paper because Canadian tax law proves that GST/VAT and retail sales tax can co-exist efficiently, thus supporting the assertion that VAT can be an effective eTax solution co-existing with the tax law of the USA, a major commercial hub, especially in respect of eCommerce transactions although the USA operates on a retail sales tax system as opposed to VAT.

Furthermore, the USA provides a clear example of the impact of technology on taxation. In the matter of state tax (distinct from federal tax) the USA has attempted for decades to streamline her retail sales tax, founded on diverse principles and definitions, implemented in different states to no avail. However, with the introduction of the internet and eCommerce transactions interstate transactions increased substantially and within a decade several states entered into a streamlined retail sales tax agreement.

Thus the impact of ameliorating technology wrought a change in USA interstate retail sales tax principles and systems which prior to such impact proved impossible. Furthermore, the USA has demonstrated the ability to overcome obstacles in respect of defining and satisfying presence within an area in order to enforce and impose indirect taxes. Furthermore, a pertinent aspect of retail sales tax is that while it is not VAT it is, nevertheless, indirect tax based on consumption tax principles similar to VAT.

eCommerce has not impacted VAT laws to the extent it has income tax laws, but has effectuated an exponential increase in cross-border transactions in respect of which tax laws, depending upon jurisdiction zero-rate exports and tax imports. Technology has, however, impacted the current retail sales tax systems in effect in the USA instigating an increased urgency to streamline the retail sales tax system.

To reiterate, the substantial impact of technology on VAT has not been in regard to the application of the VAT laws itself, but rather to the determination of the place of supply, enforcement, collection and overall administrative aspect. This is evident from the eCommerce guidelines published by the several jurisdictions and the OECD wherein the issues in respect of the place of supply determination and administrative aspect have been discussed and debated, more so than the need to change the actual laws.

Income tax has been examined and debated in detail, and while 'source-based' taxation has been supported as the best income tax method, the application of the 'source-based' method in its current form carries a wide range of complexities and inefficiencies. The application of the 'residence-based' tax system pertinent to eCommerce remains problematic as the virtual world has enabled manipulation of the place of 'effective management'. Furthermore, as concluded within the Australian Review of International Taxation Arrangements Constitution Paper "*it is clear that legislative reform is the only option*"[29] in regard to applying the 'residence-based' tests for determining income tax.[30]

While this paper does not advocate the abandonment of income tax principles in their entirety, a comparison of income tax based principles to VAT laws implemented in the various jurisdictions, will show that the 'virtual world' may be more amenable to the application of VAT than to income tax principles. Income tax, however, appears to be the primary focus of so much research, debate and discussion contingent upon the quantity of tax revenue connected with effective imposition of income tax. VAT, on the other hand, appears to be regarded as the lesser tax revenue as VAT is generally a much lower tax percentage than income tax. However, the global community may currently find itself in the situation where it may prove more advantageous to collect peanuts rather than attempting to collect walnuts and ending up with nothing.

The argument in favour of VAT should not be over emphasised: VAT is not without defect and perplexities relative to both the traditional and virtual worlds. VAT as an effective eTax can be applied to the virtual world in a manner analogous to traditional application precluding administrative difficulties. Inherent to indirect

---

[29]Dirkis, Michael, *Still a Problem Child: Central Management and Control After RITA* (2005) Available at http://www.austlii.edu.au/au/journals/RevenueLJ/2005/7.pdf [Accessed 14 July 2010].

[30]Application of traditional 'residence' definition is discussed and analysed in Part III of this paper. For the purpose of convenience, the concluding paragraph of Part III of this paper [p103] is recapitulated:

> *...Indeed, it may be argued that legislative reform for determining 'residency' in the virtual world for income tax purposes should presuppose provisions especially structured to accommodate flexibility of application. In the traditional business world, the 'effective management' test is principle based in that an examination of the facts and circumstances of each case is a requisite for determining jurisdiction of residency of a company. However, determining place of 'effective management' within the virtual world has proved to be more rule based than principle driven. Thus, it may be contended that rather than attempting to adapt traditional 'residence' tests to the virtual world for income tax purposes, it may be more expedient to devise provisions more apposite to the virtual world business model.* [Emphasis Added]

taxes such as VAT, the capacity to expedite eCommerce and facilitate the general operation, management and control of the virtual world is testament to the latter's potentiality as an effective eTax.

Harmonization of global tax systems is generally problematic, the primary point at issue being diverse political agendas. However, escalating globalization has impelled the urgency for intensified co-ordination and co-operation between jurisdictions. Despite the impact of globalisation on international taxation, disputes pertaining to diverse political agendas predominate, most specifically in respect of application of income tax principles. To emphasize again: it is not to be implied, however, that indirect taxes such as VAT are insusceptible to disputes extant to conflicting political agendas; however, existing similarities have promoted harmonization of indirect taxes on account of cross-border transactions.

VAT is not the "*silver bullet that will solve all the fiscal problems to which the growth of the borderless economy of cyberspace potentially gives rise*".[31] Further taxation problems arise with the proliferation of eCommerce which may not be effectively resolved with the application of VAT, such as transfer pricing. Thus, while this paper's primary focus is designed to evaluate the effectiveness of VAT in regard to collecting taxes on eTransactions, the issues set out within this paper can neither be discarded nor ignored, as an examination of these issues in terms of finding or exploring a plausible solution is vital for other spheres of taxation, such as transfer pricing. The comparison is essential to the evaluation of VAT as the best practical response to the challenge as set out. From this vantage point it is possible to fully assess the impact of technology on taxation and the urgent necessity to devise an effective tax system relevant to this issue.

The various aspects of the collection and monitoring of the application of eVAT in diverse jurisdictions are discussed. Methods of determining the eCustomer's location have been examined, debated and proposals pertinent to this point at issue have been submitted by, including others, the OECD.

The diverse jurisdictions to be examined all face the urgent need for decisive tax rules. The crucial element concerns commonality of decisive tax rules. This paper will show that in respect of income tax, jurisdictions are not in unanimity regarding the adaptation of income tax to technology and the establishing of common decisive rules in regard to cross-border transactions engendered by technology. However, the principles of VAT, and even sales tax, are more flexible and are more amenable to technology and permutation because the consumer bears the tax. However, this does not imply that administrative problems will not be a point at issue. Intrinsic to administrative difficulties is the establishing of globally accepted common rules, definitions, principles and collection methods. The OECD and EU have made considerable progress in the pursuit of this common goal.

Notwithstanding rigorous debate in respect of radical hypothesis of collection and monitoring of tax in respect of eCommerce, indirect taxes such as VAT persist

[31]Bird, Richard *Taxing Electronic Commerce: A Revolution in the Making* p2 Available at http://www.cdhowe.org/pdf/commentary_187.pdf [Accessed 16/09/2010].

in being the most flexible when applied to eCommerce. Indeed, the submission that VAT is the eCommerce solution is cardinal to the prevailing discourse of this paper. For this reason, VAT's attraction is that it is both flexible and adaptable in respect of eCommerce and, in contradistinction to income taxation, can be applied to eCommerce without significant change or amendment. However, amendment, radical change and reconceptualisation of income tax provisions are requisite for effective application to the virtual world. However, the changes which further the relevant quotidian peculiarities of the virtual world promote VAT's capacity as a powerful taxing tool within the virtual world, administrative difficulties notwithstanding.

Bibliography

Primary Sources

Statutes

Green Paper on Electronic Commerce for South Africa, Coordinated and Compiled by the Department of Communications Republic of South Africa (November 2000).

Secondary Sources

BBC News *Moore's Law on chips marks 40th*. 2005, April 18. Available at http://news.bbc.co.uk/2/hi/technology/4446285.stm [Accessed 21 July 2009] BBC News Technology. *OnLive cloud gaming comes to UK*. 22 September 2011. Available at http://www.bbc.co.uk/news/technology-15015335?print=true. Accessed 26 Sept 2011.

Bird, Richard. 2003, September. *Taxing electronic commerce: A revolution in the making*. Toronto: C.D. Howe Institute Commentary. Available at http://www.cdhowe.org/pdf/commentary_187.pdf. Accessed 16 Nov 2010.

Brown, Mark. *Cloud gaming platform OnLive will hit the UK on 22 September 2011. Wired*. Available at http://www.wired.co.uk/news/archive/2011-08/11/onlive-launch-date. Accessed 26 Sept 2011.

BT Press Releases. 2011, September 22. *OnLive and BT launch revolutionary cloud gaming*. Available at http://www.btplc.com/news/articles/showarticle.cfm?articleid=%7B323bde77-276a-417e-bf9d-809adc140609%7D. Accessed 26 Sept 2011 [Article access reconfirmed via http://www.onlive.com/news/pressreleases/873 12/10/2014].

Chang, Jacqui. 2009, January 13. *Sales tax holiday may be over for Amazon, other e-Tailers*. Available at http://arstechnica.com/tech-policy/news/2009/01/sales-tax-holiday-may-be-over-for-amazon-other-e-tailers.ars. Accessed 22 Mar 2010.

Churchill, Sir Winston (Leonard Spencer) (1874–1965). 1996. *Oxford English reference dictionary*, 2nd ed. New York: Oxford University Press.

Dirkis, Micahel. 2005. *Still a problem child: Central management and control after RITA*. Available at http://www.austlii.edu.au/au/journals/RevenueLJ/2005/7.pdf. Accessed 14 July 2010.

Hazlitt, William (1778–1830). 1996. *Oxford English reference dictionary*, 2nd ed. New York: Oxford University Press.

HuffPost Tech, United Kingdom. 2011, September 20. *OnLive cloud gaming launches at eurogamer expo*. Available at http://www.huffingtonpost.co.uk/2011/09/20/cloud-gaming-at-eurgamer_n_971332.html?view=print. Accessed 26 Sept 2011.

Joubert, Billy. 2010, June 10. *The tax implications of cloud computing*. Web Techforum. Available at http://www.itweb.co.za/index.php?option=com_content&view=article&id=33906%3Athe-tax-implications-of-cloud-computing&catid=355&Itemid=86. Accessed 26 Sept 2011.

Mainelli, Michael, Professor, of the Gresham College. Available at http://www.gresham.ac.uk/printtranscript.asp?EventId=514. Accessed 17 June 2008.

MecroPress, South Atlantic News Agency. *Japan retains position as world' second largest economy*. Available at http://en.mecropress.com/2010/02/15/japan-retains-position-as-world-second-largest-economy. Accessed 27 Dec 2010 [Article access reconfirmed via http://en.mercopress.com/2010/02/15/japan-retains-position-as-world-second-largest-economy 12/10/2014].

Nellen, Annette. *Overview to e-Commerce taxation – Guide to understanding the current discussions and debates (July 2003)*. Available at www.cob.sjsu.edu/facstaff/NELLEN_A/ECOMM.pdf. Accessed 24 Dec 2008.

Nolle, Thomas. Available at www.quotegarden.com.internet.html. Accessed 8 May 2008.

OECD. 2001. *Taxation and electronic commerce, implementing the Ottawa taxation framework conditions*. Paris: OECD Publications.

OECD. *Biography of Arvid Aage Skaar.* Available at http://www.oecd.org/speaker/0,3438,en_21571361_40047302_40414394_1_1_1_1_1,00.html. Accessed 26 July 2010.

OECD Committee on Fiscal Affairs. 2000. *Clarification on the application of the permanent establishment definition in e-Commerce: Changes to the commentary on the model tax convention on article 5*. Paris: OECD Publications.

Olivier, Lynette, and Michael Honiball. 2008. *International tax, a South African perspective 2008*, 4th ed. Cape Town: Siber Ink CC.

Pinto, Dale. 2003. *E-Commerce and source-based income taxation*. Amsterdam: IBFD Publications.

Plato (c429 – c347). 1996. *Oxford English reference dictionary*, 2nd ed. New York: Oxford University Press.

Plato 429BC–347BC. Available at http://www.quotesandpoem.com/quotes/listquotes/subject/taxes. Accessed 22 Jan 2007.

ReedSmith. *Transcending the cloud, a legal guide to the risks and rewards of cloud computing, Pennies From Heaven – U.S. state tax implications within cloud computing*. Reedsmith.com. Available at http://www.reedsmith.com/_db/_documents/State_Tax_Cloud_Computing_Paper.pdf. Accessed 26 Sept 2011 [Article access reconfirmed http://www.reedsmith.com/files/Publication/0e68e0e5-c193-4b9f-bf2d-c9f99bcb00d5/Presentation/PublicationAttachment/607bd5b1-e33f-4db4-be0a-802f4f1712cd/Cloud%20Computing%20white%20paper%20-%20State%20Tax%20Chapter%20ONLY.pdf. 12/10/2014].

Rendahl, Pernilla. 2009. *Cross-border consumption taxation of digital supplies*. Amsterdam: IBFD.

Schenk, Alan, and Oliver Oldman. 2007. *Value added tax, a comparative approach*. New York: Cambridge University Press.

Shanahan, John M. (ed). 1999. *The most brilliant thoughts of all times*, Hazlitt, William (1778–1830). New York: Harper Collins, Inc.

Tumpel, Professor Michael. *A Hybrid VAT System in the European Union* (Draft 04/24/2007). New York University. Available at http://docs.google.com/viewer?a=v&q=cache:g5ZTN7J6sf8J:www.law.nyu.edu/idcplg?IdcService%3DGET_FILE%26dDocName%3DECM_DLV_013830%26RevisionSelectionMethod%3DLatestReleased+The+common+framework+for+VAT+created+in+1967+for+the+EU&hl=en&pid=bl&srcid=ADGEESig8c6y5AwqvxSipGHOW8-aslQcrIqfbzM1dwHa6pTbqOQbLX60f8_nx3d-UlY3vjQQg2BR8zYGevnpGPnM9rt5H2Q4RkiAHe0Pl_tR6xZFjyqhxg0yx3ZcnIdwyatBM51Kdeyp&sig=AHIEtbSZXkC370HMugv4EdOPt6e-bY4eFA&pli=1. Accessed 14 Dec 2010 [Article access reconfirmed http://www.law.nyu.edu/sites/default/files/upload_documents/tumpelpaper.pdf 12/10/2014].

Chapter 2
History of Tax

"In this world nothing can be said to be certain, except death and taxes" (Franklin, Benjamin Letter to Jean-Baptiste Le Roy, 13 November 1789. Available at http://www.notable-quotes.com/f/franklin_benjamin.html [Accessed 01/12/14]) – Benjamin Franklin (1706–90) (Franklin, Benjamin (1706–90), *"American statesman, inventor and scientist. A wealthy printer and publisher, he was one of the signatories to the peace between the USA and Great Britain after the American War of Independence"*. [***Oxford English Reference Dictionary* (Second Edition) (1996) ("*Oxford English Reference Dictionary*"). Oxford University Press. p550**]).

Abstract Is tax a means of extracting money from the people by the government, or is it a fee we pay for the privilege of living in an organised society? The trite point at issue is that taxes represent a payment imposed by governments to raise funds. Tax evasion is a form of resistance to mandatory taxation.

Tax is a cultural phenomenon. While British income tax represents the vanguard of modern tax, the first known records of tax date back to Ancient Egypt in the reign of King Scorpion I. A tax is rarely rescinded, however, there are historical records of such practices.

VAT is a modern tax but sales tax and customs duties date back to the Roman Empire. VAT, first devised in post WWI Germany to replace 'cascading' turnover tax, has evolved into a multi-stage VAT system. In the 1960s less than ten countries had adopted VAT. Today technology and globalisation have precipitated the dissemination of VAT to more than 130 countries.

The technological revolution has compelled a re-examination and 'reconceptualisation' of traditional principles of taxation and application, and has engendered the challenge of implementing and enforcing an international taxing regime subject to the authority of international organisations, for example, the OECD.

A.M. Bardopoulos, *eCommerce and the Effects of Technology on Taxation*,
Law, Governance and Technology Series 22, DOI 10.1007/978-3-319-15449-7_2

2.1 Introduction

Regardless of the reasons or motivation for the imposition of tax, taxation has been *"implemented by different empires in different places and time; perhaps like temple and monument construction, taxation is a common phenomenon of human society"*.[1]

A review of the history of taxation and a synopsis of its development in ancient economies provides a foundation for the study and understanding of the reasons for the development of VAT. In turn, an understanding of the motivation for the implementation of a new taxing system in the twentieth century is essential to the argument for VAT as an effective taxing system. Furthermore, a review of the history of tax through to the development of international tax promotes the understanding of the necessity for taxation and international tax co-ordination.

2.2 History of Taxation, Globalisation and International Trade

It is trite that taxes represent a payment, a financial charge, imposed by governments to raise funds for direct and indirect benefits. Otherwise referred to as 'direct taxes' and 'indirect taxes', the former is generally imposed for the provisioning for, maintenance and administration of the public sector, and the latter is associated with the *"benefit [which the taxpayers] gain from their link with that country"*.[2]

Throughout the history of taxation, the collection of taxes has been a method by means of which a government may exact money from the citizens of that country. And while some may define taxation as a *"compulsory levy made by public authorities for which nothing is received directly in return"*,[3] a more apt definition may be *"the dues that we pay for the privileges of membership in an organised society"*.[4]

Due to poor historical records, coupled with the diverse social and cultural structures of ancient civilizations, it is uncertain when the first system of taxation was actually implemented.[5] The oldest taxation records were unearthed with the discovery of King Scorpion the I's tomb. The discovery of these tax records was not only significant for the history of taxation, but also for written language. Indeed, the unearthed records have the *"oldest use of writing with symbols*

[1]Lymer, Andrew & Hasseldine, John *The International Taxation System* (2002) (*"International Tax System – 2002"*), USA, p22.

[2]ibid p2.

[3]supra.

[4]Roosevelt, Franklin D. Available at http://thinkexist.com/search/searchquotation.asp?search=tax&page3 [Accessed 8 May 2008].

[5]op cit, Lymer & Hasseldine p21.

representing constancies and forming syllables – hieroglyphics".[6] Gunter Dreyer, the archaeologist who unearthed the tomb of King Scorpion I, observed that "*writing emerged as an innovation because of economic necessity rather than from creative expressions of mankind*".[7] 'Economic necessity' may here be defined as an exigent need for efficient tax collection and as such was a major component in the development of writing![8]

Resistance to mandatory taxation has always taken the form of tax evasion. Indeed, the phenomenon of cockney slang allegedly derives from the rigorous implementation of income taxation in Britain by the British government. It has been reported that cockney slang was devised by barrow sellers in an attempt to confound tax collectors and evade taxation.[9] Thus it may be contended that the development of writing and the inception of a distinguishing class of dialects derive directly from the evolution and promulgation of taxation.

The Ancient Egyptian concept of taxation was espoused by Ancient Greece. Hence "*ideas about taxes, developed in a particular time and place, were transported to and adopted in other times and in other places*".[10]

The espousal of the concept of tax was significant in that it distinguished levels of civilisation in the ancient world. "*In the ancient civilisations, taxation arose independently such that taxes, like writing, characterised civilised society. Yet, it is the uncivilised acts of war that often seems to be the impetus for developing or adopting a new form of tax*".[11] The Ancient Greeks imposed various forms of taxation, including a special tax during times of war. Furthermore, the Ancient Greeks were one of the first and few "*societies that were able to rescind the tax . . . [after] the emergency . . . [or war] was over*".[12]

British income tax represents the vanguard of modern tax. Analogous to Ancient Greece, Britain formulated an income tax to finance her engagement in the Napoleonic wars. With the resolution of the wars against Napoleon after the Battle of Waterloo in 1816, Britain rescinded the income tax. Opponents to the tax attempted to destroy all records of the income tax, including the repealing thereof, as it was contended that the sole purpose for such a tax was to finance war. However, complete destruction of the records was prevented as "*copies were retained in the basement of the tax court*".[13,14]

---

[6] supra.

[7] supra.

[8] supra.

[9] Goldswain, George Kenneth *Remission of Penalties in Income Tax Matters*. Available at http://etd.unisa.ac.za/ETD-db/theses/available/etd-08242004-114134/unrestricted/02dissertation.PDF [Accessed 18 November 2006].

[10] idem, p22.

[11] supra.

[12] Tax World '*Tax World . . . A History of Taxation*'. Available at http://www.taxworld.org/History/TaxHistory.htm [Accessed 30 June 2010].

[13] supra.

[14] supra.

Furthermore, during the Second War of Independence in 1812[15] the USA (brandishing the watchword of the American Revolution, "*[t]axation without representation is tyranny*"[16]) considered implementing an income tax based on the British Tax Act of 1798. Thus in addition to archival preservation of the British War tax records, other countries had already studied the British model, therefore making it impossible to strike the model from record. However, implementation of such income tax in the USA was postponed due to the Treaty of Ghent in 1815 which ended hostilities and, therefore, the urgent necessity for such a tax. The postponement of imposing such an income tax in the USA was temporary as finance was required for the Civil War. The USA Tax Act of 1861 proposed that "*there shall be [tax] levied, collected, and paid, upon annual income of every person residing in the U.S. whether derived from any kind of property, or from any professional trade, employment, or vocation carried on in the United States or elsewhere, or from any source whatever*".[17,18]

2.3 The Rise of VAT

The twentieth century generated mounting revenue requirements which could not be met by traditional indirect taxes and income tax systems. The concept of VAT was first devised in Germany post World War I. Prior to the introduction of VAT, a "*cascading turnover tax was imposed every time . . . goods were transferred in the process of production and distribution to the consumer*".[19] Other forms of indirect taxes included sales taxes and customs duties.

While VAT is a modern tax, sales taxes and customs duties date back to the Roman Empire. *Portorium*, customs duty and tax imposed on imports and exports, was one of the earliest taxes to be implemented in the Roman era. The concept of indirect taxes was defined with the imposition of sales tax during the reign of Julius

---

[15]Kelly, Martin About.com Guide to American History. About.com: American History. Available at http://americanhistory.about.com/od/warsanddiplomacy/u/warsandevents.htm [Accessed 12 September 2010].

Kelly summarises the War of 1812 as follows:

> *The war of 1812 has sometimes been called the Second War of Independence and was fought between the United States and Great Britain. During the war, Washington D.C. was taken over, and president Madison was forced to flee. The war ended in 1815 essentially restoring the status quo between the two countries.*

[16]*The Penguin Dictionary of Quotations* (1970). Hazell Watson & Viney Ltd., Great Britain ("*Penguin Dictionary of Quotations*"). p276.2.

[17]idem Refer to footnote 15 of this paper [p24].

[18]supra.

[19]op cit Schenk, Alan and Oldman, Olivier *Value Added Tax, A Comparative Approach* (2007), USA, p3.

Caesar. By the reign of Caesar Augustus "*the sales tax was 4 [four] per cent for slaves and 1 [one] per cent for everything else.*"[20]

In Germany Dr. Wilhelm von Siemens,[21] upon recognising the problems with the existing turnover taxes, devised a new tax system which is commonly referred to today as VAT. It was deemed that a major flaw with the turnover taxes was that they were "cascading". Simply stated, "*cascading taxes cannot be reclaimed by the purchaser, so that the tax component of the price of goods becomes larger and larger the more stages there are between producer and consumer – with obvious distortionary effects as between highly integrated enterprises and other enterprises*".[22] France extended this 'new taxing system' in 1954. The 'new extended' version of the 'new taxing system' was fondly labelled "value-added tax".[23]

Following Dr, Wilhelm von Siemens of Germany, Thomas Adams[24] discussed the concept of value added type taxation in the USA in 1921 based on "*[t]he principle..[of] reduc[ing] the tax on sales by the tax already paid on business inputs in order to avoid the tax-on-a-tax effect and to remove the incentive to vertically*

---

[20]op cit, Tax World '*Tax World... A History of Taxation*'. Available at http://www.taxworld.org/History/TaxHistory.htm [Accessed 30 June 2010].

[21]Wilhelm von Siemens, a German businessman, invented VAT after World War I. "*The main problem [Wilhelm von Siemens] was concerned with was cascading – taxes being levied on taxes – which was a common problem with manufacturers' excise taxes. The VAT solved this problem by giving producers and distributors a credit for taxes previously paid so double taxation was eliminated.*". **[Bartlett, Bruce. *VAT Time? A Money Machine that Conservatives Shouldn't Oppose* (5 June** 2009**). Forbes.com. Available at** http://www.forbes.com/2009/06/04/value-added-tax-opinions-columnists-bartlett.html **[Accessed 19 September 2010]**].

[22]op cit, Schenk, Alan and Oldman, Olivier, p3.

[23]Keen, Michael, *IMF Working Paper, VAT Attacks!* (2007) Introduction, p3. Available at http://www.imf.org/external/pubs/ft/wp/2007/wp07142.pdf [Accessed 12/08/2008].

[24]Thomas S. Adams (1873–1933), an American economist, "*is credited with much of the taxation policy of the World War I and post-war period*". The Wisconsin Historical Society provide the following bibliography of Thomas Sewall Adams:

> *economist, professor, b. Baltimore, Md. He graduated from Johns Hopkins Univ. (A.B., 1896; Ph.D., 1899). Except for a year spent teaching at Washington Univ., St. Louis (1910–1911), he was professor of economics at the Univ. of Wisconsin from 1901 to 1916. As a member of the Wisconsin Tax Commission (1911–1915), he helped draft the state income tax law of 1911. He was a professor at Yale Univ. from 1916 until his death. As an economic adviser to the U. S. Treasury (1917–1933), he is credited with much of the taxation policy of the World War I and post-war period. He was president of the National Tax Association (1922–1923), American Economic Association (1927), and member of the fiscal committee, League of Nations (1929–1933). Adams was the author of several books on economics and taxation. M. Curti and V. Carstensen, Univ. of Wis. (2 vols., Madison, 1949); Who's Who in Amer., 17 (1932); [G. A. Boissard, comp.], In Appreciation of T. S. Adams [Madison, 1933]; Madison Wis. State Journal, Feb. 9, 1933; Madison Capital Times, Feb. 9, 1933.*

Available at http://www.wisconsinhistory.org/dictionary/index.asp?action=view&term_id=3075&term_type_id=1&term_type_text=people&letter=A [Accessed 7 February 2012].

integrate a business".[25] VAT has developed since its inception and is now commonly a multi-stage VAT. However, prior to the widespread use of the multistage VAT system, a single stage consumption tax was imposed by several countries and it is this single stage consumption tax that is still utilised at the retail level "*by almost all states in the United States and by several provinces in Canada*".[26] The single stage consumption tax is often referred to as sales tax.

It should be noted that the USA remains one of the few industrialised countries that has not adopted VAT. Another country without a central VAT system is India. The USA and India are the most populous countries without a central VAT system. It has been contended that "*it is unlikely to be a coincidence . . . that both are federal countries with a strong presence of the states in the levying of general consumption taxes . . .* ".[27] Other countries which have not implemented VAT are primarily small countries with small economies and, therefore, the possible VAT gain over a broad-based tariff is relatively too diminutive to necessitate the implementation of VAT.[28]

While this paper is aimed at examining the effectiveness of VAT as the eTax solution, a synopsis of the current retail tax system practised by most of the states in the USA is essential, because the USA is a huge commercial hub and a key player and participant in eCommerce. The USA indirect tax system is essentially a "*patchwork of [retail] sales tax utilization and sales tax rates*"[29] and will be discussed further.[30]

The expansion of VAT accelerated in the late 1960s and the "*pace of VAT implementation . . . [has been described as remaining] rapid until the late 1970s, at which point it slackened for a decade before picking up again in the latter part of the 1980s and well into the 1990s*".[31] The 'rapid rise' of VAT since its inception has been described as "*the most dramatic – and probably most important – development in taxation in the latter part of the twentieth century, and it still continues*".[32] This 'rapid rise' flourished especially between the years 1987 to 1997, with many eastern

[25]op cit, Schenk, Alan and Oldman, Olivier, p4.

[26]supra.

[27]op cit, Ebrill, Liam, Keen, Michael, Bodin, Jean-Paul & Summers Victoria, *The Modern VAT*, USA, p7.

[28]supra.

[29]Duncan, Harley T *State and Local Retail Sales Taxes, Federation of Tax Administrators April (2005)*, p1. Available at http://www.taxadmin.org/fta/rate/taxreformpanel.pdf [Accessed 27/03/2010].

[30]Refer to Chap. 20 – United States of America, Part V of this paper [p240–253].

[31]op cit, Ebrill & Keen et al. p5.

[32]Ebrill, Liam *Finance and Development*, quoted in Wendy H. Mason et al. *Value-Added Tax – The VAT Assessment Process, History of Value-Added Tax*. Available at http://www.referenceforbusiness.com/management/Tr-Z/Value-Added-Tax.htm [Accessed 12/08/2008].

European and Asian countries and the former Soviet Republic introducing VAT into their taxing systems.[33]

Reasons and motivation for adopting VAT vary, but the following are indicative reasons:

> *In Western Europe, adoption of the VAT was intimately associated with the drive for greater economic integration among the member states of the European Communities: the VAT is particularly well suited to avoiding the trade distortions associated with the cascading indirect taxes that it replaced. In South America, the VAT was seen as a more efficient revenue-raising tax that would be consistent with the increasingly outward orientation of economic policies. The rapid adoption of the VAT in the transition economies reflected the need to replace the traditional sources of revenues... that were declining as a result of economic transformation with a tax regime geared to the emerging market economy; in some cases it may also have reflected the status of the VAT as a precondition for joining the European Union. In many developing countries, adoption of the VAT has been given additional impetus by the long-run revenue implications of trade reform – the economic efficiency arguments favouring the VAT have been bolstered as trade tax revenues have come under pressure with deepening trade liberalization commitments.*[34]

To date, more than 130 countries worldwide have introduced VAT into their national taxing systems compared to the late 1960s when less than ten countries had adopted the VAT system.[35] While diverse reasons for implementing an incontrovertible VAT system can be debated *ad nauseum,* perhaps the compelling allure of VAT is simply her 'irresistible' nature:

> *...the VAT may be thought of as the Mata Hari of the tax world – many are tempted, many succumb, some tremble on the brink, while others leave only to return, eventually the attraction appears irresistible.*[36]

The European VAT system influenced the adoption of VAT by NZ in 1985. However, NZ implemented VAT with a much broader taxing base. It may be said that NZ, in effect, adopted the European VAT system and then removed all recognised imperfections. South Africa adopted the NZ VAT system effective as of 30 September 1991. CAN implemented her VAT system in the same year as the RSA; however, CAN's VAT system had to be adjusted to accommodate the taxing system implemented in her Native American reserves.[37] Japan implemented VAT in

---

[33]Mason, Wendy H et al. *Value-Added Tax – The VAT Assessment Process, History of Value-Added Tax.* Available at http://www.referenceforbusiness.com/management/Tr-Z/Value-Added-Tax.html [Accessed 12/08/2008].

[34]op cit, Ebrill & Keen et al. p6.

[35]OECD *Consumption Tax Trends, VAT / GST and Excise Rates, Trends and Administration Issues* OECD Publishers (2006) p18 & 20.

[36]Tait, Alan *Value Added Tax: International Practice and Problems* International Monetary Fund (1988). Also, New York School of Law, *Value Added Taxation of Electronic Supply of Services, Tait, Alan.* Available at http://www.jeanmonnetprogram.org/papers/01/013301-02.html [Accessed 9 August 2008].

[37]A 'reserve' is land over which a First Nation (Indian band) land (Canadian Native Nations) exercises governmental control, and taxable supplies made on such land to an Indian will not be subject to the Canadian type VAT, i.e. Goods and Services Tax. It may be of interest to note that

1989. Japan's VAT system is in effect different from other VAT systems[38] and will thus be discussed[39] separately in this work.

"[W]riting emerged as an innovation because of economic necessity rather than from creative expressions of mankind",[40] the economic necessity being the exigency of effective imposition and collection of taxation. Just as the development of writing was impelled by the exigencies of taxation, so the stringent necessities of taxation are impelling a shift in our perception of the virtual world and our concept of and principles pertaining to 'presence'. Principles of taxation and application are being continuously re-examined and 'reconceptualised' apropos of greater flexibility in the face of the technological revolution. New taxes have been introduced and the introduction of further taxes to combat this new phenomenon are urgent points at issue, the resolution of which will secure exponential growth in tax revenue; however, failure will result in unfathomable loss to government coffers.

Given the present challenge of economic commerce, it behoves to note that various economic exigencies over a long period have promoted taxation's ability to adapt. Tax has evolved progressively over thousands of years in a non-electronic world. However, the impact of technology has compelled an exponential evolution of tax in the last 100 years. Technology and globalisation have precipitated the dissemination of VAT to 130 countries globally in less than half a century – an inconceivable phenomenon prior to the industrial revolution. Technology has, furthermore, facilitated easier, quicker and more effective cross-border transactions, further promoting globalisation. Indeed, technology has precipitated a more rapid evolution of globalisation than was realised during the aeons since its conception. It is therefore necessary to comment, albeit briefly, upon the development of modern forms of globalisation.

2.4 Globalisation – Its Impact

While globalisation may have first been defined by Roland Robertson of the University of Pittsburgh as "*the compression of the world and the intensification of the consciousness of the world as a whole*",[41] it may be contended that the vision of globalisation was first conceived by Alexander the Great in his vision of a coalition of states. Alexander the Great's philosophy of war was to establish a confederation

---

"*several band councils or other governing bodies of a First Nation adopted the First Nation GST (FNGST) [Goods and Services Tax]. The FNGST is comparable to the Canadian GST... Where enacted, the FNGST, not the Canadian GST, applies to taxable supplies on First Nation lands*". Ibid, Schenk & Oldman 19.

[38]idem, p18.

[39]Refer to 18.3.2. Japan, Part V of this paper [p215].

[40]supra.

[41]Mainelli, Michael, Professor, of the Gresham College. Available at http://www.gresham.ac.uk/printtranscript.asp?EventId=514 [Accessed 17 June 2008].

facilitating secure and stable trade. His vision was to forge an economic union in the known ancient world. Alexander the Great's vision of a global economy was precluded by his inauspicious death at the age of 33.

Actual implementation of globalisation was recorded during the Mongolian Empire 1206–1368.[42] However, nineteenth century liberalisation is often referred to as the "*first era of globalisation*".[43] The "*first era of globalisation*" collapsed after the Great War, followed by the "Gold Standard Crisis".[44] Despite set-backs globalisation could not be halted, and since World War II globalisation "*... has been driven importantly by advances in technology. By lowering the costs of gathering information and conducting transactions, new technologies have reduced market frictions and provided significant impetus to the process of broadening world markets*".[45] In effect globalisation may be "*viewed as a centuries long process, tracking the expansion of human population and the growth of civilisation, that has accelerated dramatically in the past 50 years*".[46]

Globalisation has resulted in critical international policy changes with regard to taxation as the "*pressure for tax rate convergence gravitating towards lower rates*"[47] mounts, otherwise referred to as 'tax competition'. 'Tax competition' has resulted in the reduction of domestic "*governments' ability to raise [national] revenue through taxes*".[48] The primary reason for this reduction is due to the increased labour and capital mobility which has made it easier to destroy the tax base of governments around the world.[49]

It has been asserted that economic superpowers of the past thrived, grew and existed as a consequence of their extensive and well established international trading. International trading has evolved into one of the aspects of modern day 'globalisation'. A further sub-category of modern 'globalisation' is the Internet and eCommerce.

Prior to examining whether VAT is indeed the solution for eCommerce, an assessment of international tax viewed with the interest of the international economic tide is necessary. This involves an examination of the causes which gave rise to the institution of international tax and the development of international tax systems

---

[42] *Timeline of the Mongolian Empire, The Mongolian Empire: A Historical Website*. Available at http://www.geocities.com/Athens/Forum/2532 [Accessed 5 January 2009].

[43] Lindsey, Brink, *The Decline and Fall of the First Global Economy, how nationalism, protectionism, and collectivism spawned a century of dictatorship and war* (December 2001) Reason.com. Available at http://www.reason.com/news/show/28241.html [Accessed 17 June 2008].

[44] supra.

[45] Greenspan, Alan, *Testimony of Chairman Alan Greenspan, Trade Policy Before the Committee on Finance, U.S. Senate. April 4, 2001*. Available at http://www.federalreserve.gov/boarddocs/testimony/2001/200104042/default.htm [Accessed 17 June 2008].

[46] *The Financial Express*. Available at http://www.financialexpress.com/news/No-boundaries/245732/ [Accessed 17 June 2008].

[47] Nattrass, Nicoli, *Macroeconomics Theory and Policy in South Africa* (2003) p309.

[48] supra.

[49] supra.

and guidelines. The booming of international trade within eCommerce and the Internet provokes questions regarding 'taxing rights', definitions to be applied, etc. International taxation is concisely the *"international aspects of domestic laws"*.[50] Briefly stated, 'international tax' is a subject of study that deals with international tax treaties and international aspects of domestic tax laws. No international tax laws, *per se*, actually exist. However, when countries enter into double tax treaties or other multi-national agreements, such treaties and agreements approximate international law. The reason why such treaties and agreements only 'come close' to international law, and are not in fact international law, is because only the 'Contracting States' are obliged to follow these treaties or agreements.[51] Thus, to understand international taxation one must understand the interaction between the two/multiple 'Contracting States' tax systems.[52]

An important aspect of international tax is that it deals with the 'domestic income tax laws' of different countries and, as such, implementation and enforcement of an international taxing regime is a challenge as different jurisdictional authorities are involved. Intrinsic to the effective implementation of international tax guidelines, principles and rules is the establishment and common recognition of an international body which oversees, and is recognised as the authority of, such international tax laws. The OECD is such an international body. The OECD, within the context of this paper, is significant in respect of international tax and global regulation of tax. An outline of the history and development of the OECD as such an authority is essential to the understanding of the necessity for OECD-like institutions as a means of developing forms of global governance in the era of globalisation.

Bibliography

Secondary Sources

Bartlett, Bruce. 2009, June 5. *VAT time? A aoney machine that conservatives shouldn't oppose.* Forbes.com. Available at http://www.forbes.com/2009/06/04/value-added-tax-opinions-columnists-bartlett.html. Accessed 19 Sept 2010.

Duncan, Harley T. *State and local retail sales taxes, federation of tax administrators April (2005).* Available at http://www.taxadmin.org/fta/rate/taxreformpanel.pdf. Accessed 27 Mar 2010.

Ebrill, Liam, Michael Keen, Jean-Paul Bodin, and Victoria Summers. 2001. *The modern VAT.* Washington: International Monetary Fund.

Ebrill, Liam. *Finance and development*, quoted in Mason, Wendy H, et al. *Value-Added Tax – The VAT Assessment Process, History of Value-Added Tax.* Was available at http://www.referenceforbusiness.com/management/Tr-Z/Value-Added-Tax.htm. Accessed 12 Aug 2008.

---

[50]Olivier, Lynette and Honiball, Michael, *International Tax, A South African Perspective* (2008) p1.

[51]Olivier, Lynette and Honiball, Michael, *International Tax, A South African Perspective* (2005), p1.

[52]Supra.

Franklin, Benjamin. 1789, November 13. *Letter to Jean-Baptiste Le Roy*. Available at http://www.notable-quotes.com/f/franklin_benjamin.html. Accessed 1 Dec 2014.

Franklin, Benjamin (1706–1790). 1996. *Oxford English reference dictionary*, 2nd ed. New York: Oxford University Press.

Goldswain, George Kenneth. *Remission of penalties in income tax matters*. Available at http://etd.unisa.ac.za/ETD-db/theses/available/etd-08242004-114134/unrestricted/02dissertation.PDF. Accessed 18 Nov 2006.

Greenspan, Alan. *Testimony of Chairman Alan Greenspan, trade policy before the committee on finance, U.S. Senate. April 4, 2001*. Available at http://www.federalreserve.gov/boarddocs/testimony/2001/200104042/default.htm. Accessed 17 June 2008.

Keen, Michael. 2007. *IMF working paper, VAT attacks!* Washington, DC: International Monetary Fund. Available at http://www.imf.org/external/pubs/ft/wp/2007/wp07142.pdf. Accessed 12 Aug 2008.

Kelly, Martin. About.com Guide to American History. About.com: American History. Available at http://americanhistory.about.com/od/warsanddiplomacy/u/warsandevents.htm. Accessed 12 Sept 2010.

Lindsey, Brink. 2001, December. *The decline and fall of the first global economy, how nationalism, protectionism, and collectivism spawned a century of dictatorship and war*. Reason.com. Available at http://www.reason.com/news/show/28241.html. Accessed 17 June 2008.

Lymer, Andrew and John Hasseldine. 2002. *The International Taxation System*. New Jersey: Kluwer Academic Publishers.

Mainelli, Michael, Professor of the Gresham College. Available at http://www.gresham.ac.uk/printtranscript.asp?EventId=514. Accessed 17 June 2008.

Mason, Wendy H., et al. *Value-added tax – The VAT assessment process, history of value-added tax*. Available at http://www.referenceforbusiness.com/management/Tr-Z/Value-Added-Tax.html. Accessed 12 Aug 2008.

Nattrass, Nicoli, Jeremy Wakeford, and Samson Muradzikwa. 2003. *Macroeconomics Theory and Policy in South Africa* 3ed Revised (2003) South Africa

OECD. 2006. *Consumption tax trends, VAT/GST and excise rates, trends and administration issues*. Paris: OECD Publishers.

Olivier, Lynette, and Michael Honiball. 2005. *International tax, a South African perspective*, 3rd ed. Cape Town: Siber Ink CC.

Olivier, Lynette, and Michael Honiball. 2008. *International tax, a South African perspective 2008*, 4th ed. Cape Town: Siber Ink CC.

Roosevelt, Franklin D. Available at http://thinkexist.com/search/searchquotation.asp?search=tax&page3. Accessed 8 May 2008.

Schenk, Alan, and Oliver Oldman. 2007. *Value added tax, a comparative approach*. New York: Cambridge University Press.

Tait, Alan. 1988. *Value added tax: International practice and problems*. Washington: International Monetary Fund.

Tait, Alan, New York School of Law. *Value added taxation of electronic supply of services, Tait, Alan*. Available at http://www.jeanmonnetprogram.org/papers/01/013301-02.html. Accessed 9 Aug 2008

Tax World. *Tax world... a history of taxation*. Available at http://www.taxworld.org/History/TaxHistory.htm. Accessed 30 June 2010.

The *Financial Express*. Available at http://www.financialexpress.com/news/No-boundaries/245732/. Accessed 17 June 2008.

The Penguin Dictionary of Quotations. 1970. Hazell Watson & Viney Ltd., Great Britain.

The Wisconsin Historical Society. *Bibliography of Thomas Sewall Adams*. Available at http://www.wisconsinhistory.org/dictionary/index.asp?action=view&term_id=3075&term_type_id=1&term_type_text=people&letter=A. Accessed 7 Feb 2012.

Timeline of the Mongolian Empire, The Mongolian Empire: A Historical Website. Available at http://www.geocities.com/Athens/Forum/2532. Accessed 5 Jan 2009.

Chapter 3
The OECD and the EU

Abstract Ravaged by centuries of wars and decimated by WWI and II, the E.U. was created in 1957 for the express purpose of establishing a peaceful and unified European Union. The establishment of the OECD in 1967 was crucial to global harmonization with regard to international taxation. Furthermore, the OECD is internationally recognised as a forerunner in the issuing of commentary pertinent to eCommerce and the taxing implications of eCommerce.

Analogous to the OECD, the E.U.'s taxation policies and commentary on the next generation of commercial transactions, that is, eCommerce, implicate salient points at issue, especially in respect of VAT. Indeed, the EU VAT Directive addresses services supplied electronically and may be compared to a multinational treaty agreement between EU Member States.

3.1 OECD and Its Development

The twentieth century has witnessed the establishment of diverse organisations in an attempt to deal with 'globalisation'. Model tax Conventions are usually used when entering into and establishing a DTA between two or more States. Various organisations have independently issued Model Tax Conventions, of which the three most commonly known and used are the UN, the OECD and the USA Draft Model Income Tax Conventions. These models, however, relate primarily to direct tax. For indirect tax purposes the EU has issued a European VAT Directive which is applied by all EU Member States.

The USA has independently published a Model Convention which is used to negotiate USA treaties. While the USA Model Convention is based on the OECD Model Convention, it includes specific USA policy concerns. By publishing and utilising an exclusive Model Convention the USA differs from most countries which, as a rule, do not have exclusive Model Conventions. The purpose of the Model Convention is to ensure improved global unification with regard to negotiating international taxation, as treaties are based on the UN or OECD Model Conventions.[1]

[1] Vogel, Klaus, Professor Dr; University of Munich and Co-authors, *Klaus Vogel on Double Tax Conventions, 2nd Ed* (1991), Netherlands, p10.

A.M. Bardopoulos, *eCommerce and the Effects of Technology on Taxation*,
Law, Governance and Technology Series 22, DOI 10.1007/978-3-319-15449-7_3

The UN Model Tax Convention is aimed at serving the interest of developing countries. While the UN Model Tax Convention structure corresponds to that of the OECD Model Tax Convention, the content of the UN Model Tax Convention is biased in that in negotiations between developed and developing countries it benefits developing countries.[2] The OECD, on the other hand, is "*looking ahead to a post-industrial age in which it aims to tightly weave OECD economies into a yet more prosperous and increasingly knowledge-based world economy*".[3] As such, the OECD, rather than the UN, will be the predominant reference throughout this paper.

It may be submitted that the establishment of the OEEC and then the OECD was crucial to globalisation. The OEEC was initially devised to expedite the administration of Canadian and USA post World War II aid for the reconstruction of Europe. The OEEC encouraged free trade between the Member States in a growing 'globalising' world. The OECD replaced the OEEC in 1961. The OECD offers a platform to Member States upon which they can work together and, furthermore, address issues such as "*economic, social and governance challenges of globalisation*".[4] The OECD promotes opportunities for negotiating taxation, indeed, it has "*paved the way for bilateral [and now even multilateral] treaties around the world*",[5] and is internationally recognised as a forerunner in the issuing of commentary pertinent to eCommerce and the taxing implications of eCommerce.[6] The OECD, created and developed as a prerequisite to effectual 'globalisation', effectively promotes international co-operation in taxation between Member States.

3.2 The European Union

Ravaged by wars for centuries, decimated by World War I and II in the twentieth century, the six founding Members of the EU, Belgium, France, Italy, Luxemburg, West Germany and the Netherlands, created the EU in 1957 for the express purpose of establishing a peaceful, unified European Community. Since its inception the EU has grown in both size and objectives. The Treaty of Rome, 1957, created the

[2] supra.

[3] OECD *Overview of the OECD: What is it? History? Who does what? Structure of the organisation?* Available at http://www.oecd.org/document/18/0,3343,en_2649_201185_2068050_1_1_1_1,00.html [Accessed 5 January 2009].

[4] OECD *Overview of the OECD: What is it? History? Who does what? Structure of the organisation?* Available at http://www.oecd.org/document/18/0,3343,en_2649_201185_2068050_1_1_1_1,00.html [Accessed 5 January 2009].

[5] supra.

[6] The OECD has issued several commentaries and a taxation framework pertinent to the subject, *inter alia "Taxation and Electronic Commerce: Implementing the Ottawa Taxation Framework Conditions", "OECD Tax Policy Studies, E-commerce: Transfer Pricing and Business Profits Taxation*", etc.

European Economic Community which is otherwise referred to as the 'Common Market'.[7] Within the context of this paper, 'Common Market' taxation, specifically appertaining to VAT policies, is of prime importance, while other achievements, policies and objectives are ancillary.

Various policies and common systems were devised with the establishment of a 'Common Market'. One such common system is the EU VAT Directive. Similar to DTAs, the VAT Directive may be compared to a multinational VAT treaty agreement between EU Member States. The VAT Directive, a common system of VAT, may be described as follows:

> *This Directive codifies the provisions implementing the common system of VAT, which applies to the production and distribution of goods and services bought and sold for consumption within the European Union (EU). To ensure that the tax is neutral in impact, irrespective of the number of transactions, taxable persons of VAT may deduct from their VAT account the amount of tax which they have paid to other taxable persons. VAT is finally borne by the final consumer in the form of a percentage to the final price of the goods or services.*[8]

A comprehensive analysis of the EU VAT Directive, including policies and notes which have been issued in pursuance of determining effective eCommerce tax policies, is essential to this paper. The EU VAT Directive addresses 'services supplied electronically', the significance of which appertains directly to a prevalent point at issue of this paper. The EU has expanded from its initial six founding members to a 27 member community with numerous further countries aspiring to join the ranks of EU membership. The establishment of the 'Common Market' engendered by the advent of the EU in a desire for peace and unity, distinguishes itself as a model example of globalisation and the slow integration of legislation and a common VAT policy across jurisdictional borders. Like the OECD, the EU's policies and commentary on the next generation of commercial transactions, that is, eCommerce, are salient.

When the European Community VAT was introduced by way of the First VAT Directive in 1967, eCommerce and, therefore, digital supplies were not on the agenda of transactions covered by the Directive. However, amendments have since been made to ensure the inclusion of electronically supplied services, including strategy to include suppliers established outside the EU.[9] The objective of the EU's special arrangements, applicable to services supplied electronically, "*is to create a level playing field for European Union (EU) businesses with regard to the indirect taxation of electronic commerce. The Directive also aims to make compliance for*

[7]Europa – *The EU at a glance – The History of the European Union*. Available at http://europa.eu/abc/history/index_en.htm [Accessed 2 July 2010].

[8]Europa – Summaries of EU Legislation – Taxation. *Common system of value added tax (VAT) ('the VAT Directive')*. Available at http://www.europa.eu/legislation_summaries/taxation/131057_en.htm [Accessed 2 July 2010].

[9]Rendahl, Pernilla, *Cross-Border Consumption Taxation of Digital Supplies*, p17.

non-EU businesses as easy and straightforward as possible. The changes modernise the existing VAT place-of-supply rules for services by including the electronic commerce sector".[10]

Bibliography

Secondary Sources

Europa – Summaries of EU Legislation – Taxation. *Common system of value added tax (VAT). ('the VAT Directive')*. Was available at http://www.europa.eu/legislation_summaries/taxation/131057_en.htm. Accessed 2 July 2010.

Europa – Summaries of EU Legislation – Taxation. *VAT: Special arrangements applicable to services supplied electronically*. Was available at http://www.europa.eu/legislation_summaries/taxation/131044_en.htm. Accessed 2 July 2010.

Europa – *The EU at a glance – The history of the European Union*. Available at http://europa.eu/abc/history/index_en.htm. Accessed 2 July 2010.

OECD. *Overview of the OECD: What is it? History? Who does what? Structure of the organisation?* Available at http://www.oecd.org/document/18/0,3343,en_2649_201185_2068050_1_1_1_1,00.html. Accessed 5 Jan 2009.

Rendahl, Pernilla. 2009. *Cross-border consumption taxation of digital supplies*. Amsterdam: IBFD.

Vogel, Professor Dr Klaus, University of Munich, and Co-Authors. 1991. *Klaus Vogel on double tax conventions*, 2nd ed. Deventer: Kluwer Law and Taxation Publishers.

[10]Europa – Summaries of EU Legislation – Taxation. *VAT: Special arrangements applicable to services supplied electronically*. Available at http://www.europa.eu/legislation_summaries/taxation/131044_en.htm [Accessed 2 July 2010].

Part II
Internet, Ecommerce, Servers and ISPS

Chapter 4
ARPANET

> *"Death and taxes and childbirth! There's never any convenient time for any of them"* – Margaret Mitchell, Gone With the Wind. (Margaret Mitchell in Gone With the Wind 1939, Warner Bros. Production, 1939)

Abstract Inspired by hostility between superpowers, the Internet is an ingenious invention. ARPANet was designed and implemented for governmental and military purposes. With its evolution into the modern Internet it has become globally accessible to hundreds of millions of users. The critical point at issue is a global society's escalating use of the Internet and its 'on-line tools' to execute eCommerce transactions, which are impacting upon trade and taxation, and which have broached a new-age war between government-coffers and consumers.

4.1 Introduction

In order to examine the practicality of an effective taxing system within the eCommerce environment a core understanding of eCommerce components, operation and laws governing such an environment is essential. Technology has created a 'virtual world' and a lack of understanding or acknowledgement of such an environment may effect imposition of ineffective taxing systems on eCommerce. Thus it is important to understand how eCommerce functions and, therefore, a capsulization of the laws governing this environment is of interest. Therefore, a considered survey of the 'internet' and its development is significant. To date the OECD has attempted to address eCommerce taxing issues by introducing guidelines for defining and determining "source" within this environment. However, as technology is continuously advancing and extending the maximising potential of the internet, such guidelines have become increasingly obsolete within a short period of time. The Doctrine of Moore's Law *"that the number of transistors on a chip would double every 24 months"*[1] should be taken into account when considering possible methods of imposition and implementation of tax within eCommerce.

[1] *"The 'law' was adopted after Intel co-founder Gordon Moore [stated] in a 1965 article that the number of transistors on a chip would double every 24 months."* BBC News, Moore's Law

A.M. Bardopoulos, *eCommerce and the Effects of Technology on Taxation*,
Law, Governance and Technology Series 22, DOI 10.1007/978-3-319-15449-7_4

It is imperative that a brief study of the Internet, its components and how the internet and computers operate, is conducted in this paper to serve as a foundation for an understanding of the various taxing issues intrinsic to the 'virtual world'. Indeed, it is submitted that the imposition of an effective and adaptable taxing system upon the 'virtual world' may only be possible if the 'virtual world', its components and *modus operandi* are understood.

4.2 History of the Internet

The internet was conceived by the USA in retaliation to the Soviet Union's launching of the space satellite, Sputnik I, in 1957: an ingenious creation inspired by hostility between super powers.[2]

ARPA was created and established in the USA's attempt to regain the technological lead in the 'arm's race'. ARPA gleaned computer scientists nationally to research 'networks'.[3] As scientists from various institutes increasingly joined the research team there was an escalating demand for additional 'computers'. In order to limit the number of computers requested, ARPA argued that scientists could "*share a smaller number of computers if these computers were connected together by means of a data network*"[4]; and thus the first form of the Internet, known as ARPANet, came into being.[5]

---

on chips marks 40th (18 April 2005). Available at http://news.bbc.co.uk/2/hi/technology/4446285.stm [Accessed 21/07/2009].

2 "*The Space Age spawned two outstanding space programs as a result of the hot competition between the United States and the Soviet Union. Both countries gave primary emphasis in their space efforts to a combination of national security and foreign policy objectives, turning space into an area of active competition for political and military advantage ….*

The bumpy U.S.-U.S.S.R. relationship in the years between 1957 and 1991 often was characterized by periods of mistrust and overt hostility … ".

Sagdeev, Roald, United States-Soviet Space Cooperation during the Cold War University of Maryland, and Eisenhower, Susan, The Eisenhower Institute. Available at http://www.nasa.gov/50th/50th_magazine/coldWarCoOp.html [Accessed 04/10/2011].

3 "*…employed, at one time or another, some of the finest engineers and scientists of the late 20th century… It wasn't until 1962…that ARPA began investigating the idea of networked computers…* ".

Elon University School of Communications *Imagining the Internet's Quick Look at the Early History of the Internet.* Available at http://www.elon.edu/e-web/predictions/early90s/internethistory.xhtml [Accessed 04/10/2011].

4 Kleinrock, Leonard, *Personal History/Biography: The Birth of the Internet* The University of California. Available at http://www.lk.cs.ucla.edu/LK/Inet/birth.html [Accessed 20/06/2008] or http://www.lk.cs.ucla.edu/personal_hsitroy.html [Accessed 21/01/2012].

5 *Internet History – One Page Summary.* Available at http://www.livinginternet.com/i/ii_summary.htm [Accessed 20/06/2008].

In essence the internet is "*a worldwide system of computer networks – a network of networks in which users at any one computer can, if they have permission, get information from any other computer (and sometimes talk directly to users at other computers)*".[6] In 1995 the term "Internet" was defined by the Federal Networking Council as follows:

> *'Internet' refers to the global information system that – (i) is logically linked together by a globally unique address space based on the Internet Protocol (IP) or its subsequent extensions / follow-ons; (ii) is able to support communications using the Transmission Control Protocol / Internet Protocol (TCP/IP) suite or its subsequent extensions / follow-ons, and / or other IP-compatible protocols; and (iii) provides, uses or makes accessible, either publicly or privately, high level services layered on the communications and related infrastructure described herein.*[7]

A side benefit of ARPANet's original design was that, "*because messages could be routed or rerouted in more than one direction, the network could continue to function even if parts of it were destroyed in the event of a military attack or other disaster*".[8] This aspect of ARPANet's design may still be found in contemporary Internet. Although ARPANet was designed and implemented for governmental and military purposes, modern Internet has become a "*public, cooperative, and self-sustaining facility accessible to hundreds of millions of people worldwide*".[9]

Communications and the computer have been revolutionised as a result of the Internet and its ever-expanding capabilities. The Internet Society has appropriately described the Internet as "*at once a world-wide broadcasting capability, a mechanism for information dissemination, and a medium for collaboration and interaction between individuals and their computers without regard for geographic location*".[10] The Internet is currently a widespread information matrix impacting information acquisition, as well as community operations, as a result of a global society's escalating use of the Internet and its 'on-line tools' to execute eCommerce transactions.[11]

The Internet continues to flourish and develop in consequence of expanding global use, which in turn has resulted in expansion of electronic commerce. The Internet has evolved to meet current users' needs, and will continue to evolve as

---

[6] TechTarget. Available at http://searchwindevelopment.techtarget.com/sDefinition/0,,sid8_gci212370,00,html [Accessed 17 June 2008].

[7] Internet Society (ISOC) All About The Internet: History of the Internet. Available at http://www.isoc.org/internet/history/brief.shtm [Accessed 2 July 2010].

[8] Whatis.com. *Internet Definition*. Available at http://searchwindevelopment.techtarget.com/sDefinition/0,,sid8_gci212370,00.html [Accessed 17/06/2008].

[9] op cit, TechTarget. Available at http://searchwindevelopment.techtarget.com/sDefinition/0,,sid8_gci212370,00,html [Accessed 17 June 2008].

[10] op cit, Internet Society (ISOC) All About The Internet: History of the Internet. Available at http://www.isoc.org/internet/history/brief.shtm [Accessed 2 July 2010].

[11] supra.

users' needs multiply. The emergence of the World Wide Web has created a global community of users far exceeding the Internet's initial capabilities.[12]

The unbridled amelioration of internet technology in a borderless world has had a dynamic impact upon trade and taxation, and has stimulated urgent further evaluation and adaptation of taxation in a new-age war between government's coffers and consumers.

Bibliography

Secondary Sources

BBC News. 2005, April 18. *Moore's Law on chips marks 40th*. Available at http://news.bbc.co.uk/2/hi/technology/4446285.stm. Accessed 21 July 2009.

Elon University School of Communications. *Imagining the Internet's Quick Look at the Early History of the Internet*. Available at http://www.elon.edu/e-web/predictions/early90s/internethistory.xhtml. Accessed 4 Oct 2011.

Internet History – One Page Summary. Available at http://www.livinginternet.com/i/ii_summary.htm. Accessed 20 June 2008.

Internet Society (ISOC). *All about the internet: History of the internet*. Available at http://www.isoc.org/internet/history/brief.shtm. Accessed 2 July 2010.

Kleinrock, Leonard. *Personal history/biography: The birth of the internet*. The University of California. Available at http://www.lk.cs.ucla.edu/personal_hsitroy.html. Accessed 21 Jan 2012.

Margaret Mitchell in Gone With the Wind. 1939. Warner Bros. Production, 1939.

Sagdeev, Roald. *United States-Soviet Space Cooperation during the Cold War University of Maryland, and Susan Eisenhower*. The Eisenhower Institute. *Available at*http://www.nasa.gov/50th/50th_magazine/coldWarCoOp.html. Accessed 4 Oct 2011.

TechTarget. Available at http://searchwindevelopment.techtarget.com/sDefinition/0,,sid8_gci212370,00,html. Accessed 17 June 2008.

Whatis.com. Internet Definition. Available at http://searchwindevelopment.techtarget.com/sDefinition/0,,sid8_gci212370,00.html. Accessed 17 June 2008.

[12]supra.

Chapter 5
Development of Technology

Abstract The Web has had a greater adverse impact on taxation than the radio, television or mobile phone!

A Web site is "*somewhere in cyberspace*", located somewhere in a 'virtual world' that is the WWW. The portal to this 'virtual world' is the ISP.

The point at issue in respect of taxation policy is that technological amelioration may separate the ISP from its fixed geographical location. ISPs utilise overseas failover sites to control 'web-traffic' with 'load-balancing'.

Perceptive Method, Fastest Response Time Method, Round Robin DNS and Network Load Balancing are diverse methods used to achieve 'load balancing'. Clustering technology requires no dedicated hardware and is essentially an algorithm which provides 'load-balancing' and enhances TCP/IP-based services which allow computers to interconnect, always assuming the semblance of a single server running the Web application!

5.1 Websites, Servers, IPSs & Technological Solutions

The creation of the Web may be directly attributed to a technology which has promoted an exponential quantity of eCommerce transactions, and, therefore, a technology which is one of the primary technologies to have had an adverse impact on taxation. Other technologies to have had an adverse impact on taxation are the radio, television and mobile phone, but none so much as that achieved by the Web, "*to reach 50 million users, it took 38 years for the radio, 13 years for the television and 4 years for the Internet*"[1]!

A Web site may affect diverse forms, including 'Web presence', 'Web site', 'Internet presence'.[2] A 'Web site' is not 'the Web'/WWW. Essentially a Web site

[1]Nellen, Annette *Overview to E-Commerce Taxation – Guide to Understanding the Current Discussions and Debates (July 2003)* p8. Available at www.cob.sjsu.edu/facstaff/NELLEN_A/ECOMM.pdf [Accessed 24 December 2008].

[2]Different terminologies found at http://searchsoa.techtarget.com/sDefinition/0,,sid26_gci213352,00.html and http://www.webopedia.com/TERM/P/presence.html [Accessed both 20/06/2008].

A.M. Bardopoulos, *eCommerce and the Effects of Technology on Taxation*, Law, Governance and Technology Series 22, DOI 10.1007/978-3-319-15449-7_5

is a collection of Web pages.[3] A Web site "*is a related collection of WWW files that includes a beginning file called a home page*".[4] The 'home page' is used as the address by means of which an individual user can access a Web site. A user may obtain access to all the other Web pages on a Web site from the 'home page'. Large Web sites, which could consist of several Web pages, can be spread over a number of 'servers' that are located in different geographical locations.[5]

The term 'site' contained within a Web site is often confused with a 'Web server' due to the fact that 'site' implies a geographic location. However, "*a server is a computer that holds the files for one or more 'sites'*".[6] Furthermore, a Web site cannot be confined to one geographic location, as a Web site is "*somewhere in cyberspace*"[7] – located somewhere in a 'virtual world' that is the WWW.

The ISP is a portal to the 'virtual world'. That is, "*an ISP has the equipment and the telecommunication line access required to have a 'point-of-presence' on the Internet for the geographic area served*".[8] The geographic location of an ISP is currently determinable as the ISP is dependent upon physical tangible equipment. However, technological amelioration may possibly separate the ISP from its fixed geographical location. Therefore, when considering possible taxing policies, the possibility of an unattached ISP should be of significant account.

In the year 2010 it is not uncommon for ISPs to utilise overseas failover sites. That is, one ISP's tangible equipment may be located in two, or even more, different geographical locations – should one ISP fail to connect to the Internet, the connection is routed to another ISP reducing the possibility of total connection failure.[9] Indeed, requisite for the proliferation of 'web traffic', 'load balancing' was developed as a technological solution to inordinately prolonged Internet response time. A simplified explanation of 'web traffic' is to imagine a single water distribution point and the ensuing road traffic congestion:

> *…the infrastructure of the Internet, and the World Wide Web built on top of it, is inherently inefficient. Underneath the breathtaking technology and capabilities of the Internet lies a distribution model that is still fairly unsophisticated. Typically, every time someone views online content it has been obtained directly from the server where the source information is stored.*
>
> *To appreciate the problems inherent in this system, imagine if water was delivered to the public in the same way the Internet delivers information to users. Currently, water is stored in local reservoirs and piped directly into homes and businesses. Imagine instead if*

---

[3]TechTerms.com. Available at http://www.techterms.com/definition/website [Accessed 20/06/2008].

[4]op cit, TechTarget.

[5]supra.

[6]supra.

[7]supra.

[8]TechTarget. Definition of ISP. Available at http://searchwindevelopment.techtarget.com/sDefinition/0,,sid8_gci214028,00.html [Accessed 20 June 2008].

[9]Tyson, Jeff. *How Network Address Translation Works, Multi-Homing*. Available at http://computer.howstuffworks.com/nat6.htm [Accessed 23/06/2008].

there were only a single distribution point – say a well in Ohio. Anytime someone needed water, anywhere in the country he or she would have to drive to Ohio, fill up some water tanks at the well, and drive home. Now if you imagine the traffic jams that would occur for miles around the well, you begin to understand why users can experience such slow and frustrating response times from the Internet.[10]

In other words, as Internet usage has intensified, the use of one ISP has proved to be ineffective in managing increased 'Web traffic'. Too many users attempting to access one Web site, all Web pages inclusive, hosted on one ISP causes a bottleneck resulting in access to the desired web site becoming 'jammed' and inaccessible.

5.2 Technical & Illustrative Examination of Load Balancing

Theoretically, 'load balancing' is technology which enhances server performance which *"leads to their optimal utilisation and ensures that no single server is overwhelmed.... The process... is straightforward. A webpage request is sent to the load balancer, which forwards the request to one of the servers. That server responds back to the load balancer, which in turn sends the request on to the end user."*[11]

Diverse methods may be utilised to achieve 'load balancing', such as the Perceptive Method, the Fastest Response Time Method, Round Robin DNS and Network Load Balancing. Briefly, the Perceptive Method utilises historical and current data to predict the server and the Fastest Response Time Method is self explanatory.[12] Round Robin DNS simply *"works by assigning multiple IP addresses to the fully qualified domain name... of a resource. The IP addresses are rotated so that one server IP address is handed out first, then the next request is given the next IP in the list."*[13] Round Robin DNS is viewed as the simplest approach to 'load balancing'.[14]

NBL, on the other hand, is a Microsoft clustering technology which *"enhances the scalability and availability of mission-critical, TCP/IP-based services, such as Web, Terminal Services, virtual private networking, and streaming media servers."*[15] This clustering technology requires no dedicated hardware and is essentially an

---

[10]3Com Corporation. *White Paper, Web Caching: Optimizing for Internet and Web Traffic.* (2002) p2. Available at http://www.3com.com/other/pdfs/infra/corpinfo/en_US/503093.pdf [Accessed 13/06/2008].

[11]www.wisegeek.com *What is Load Balancing?* Available at http://www.wisegeek.com/what-is-load-balancing.htm [Accessed 2 July 2010].

[12]supra.

[13]Petri, Daniel *Load Balancing Exchange Front-End Servers* (2009). Available at http://petri.co.il/load_balancing_exchange_front_end_servers.htm [Accessed 7 July 2010].

[14]supra.

[15]Microsoft Technet *Network Load Balancing Technical Overview* p1. Available at http://technet.microsoft.com/en-us/library/bb742455.aspx [Accessed 2 July 2010].

algorithm which provides 'load balancing'. TCP/IP is simply computer 'language' which allows computers "*to find and connect with each other*".[16]

Regardless of the method utilised, 'load balancing' resolves 'web traffic' congestions by distributing the 'web traffic' between several servers in order to 'balance the usage load'. 'Load balancing' has been defined as "*the fine tuning of a computer system, network or disk subsystem in order to more evenly distribute the data and/or processing across available resources. For example, in clustering, load balancing might distribute the incoming transactions evenly to all servers, or it might redirect them to the next available server*".[17] In other words, 'load balancing' is in effect several servers running a Web application concurrently. Furthermore, 'load balancing' operates in such a way that it appears as if a single server is running the Web application.[18]

A hypothetical example explains the *modus operandi* of 'load-balancing'[19]:

Illustrative Example Alpha
Purchasing a Movie from Amazon.com*

Pre-Load Balancing

Kosta, an Internet user, wishes to purchase a movie from Amazon.com. Kosta enters the address www.amazon.com and is taken to the Amazon Web site Home Page hosted on an ISP in California, USA. Prior to 'load balancing', the entire Web site, inclusive of all Web pages, would have been hosted on this one ISP in California.

Post-Load Balancing

With the introduction of 'load balancing', the technological solution to 'web traffic' congestion, multiple ISPs located in several geographical locations may be used by Amazon.com to facilitate the acquisition of a single DVD. Thus, Kosta's single DVD electronic purchase transaction may possibly be routed as follows:

1. Kosta, who resides in Cape Town, South Africa enters the Web site address www.amazon.com in search of movies. Kosta is taken to the 'Amazon Home Page' which may be hosted on an ISP in California, USA.

(continued)

[16]About.com *TCP/IP – Transmission Control Protocol/Internet Protocol*. Available at http://compnetworking.about.com/od/tcpip/TCPIP_Transmission_Control_Protocol_Internet_Protocol.htm [Accessed 24 May 2010].

[17]Answers.com. Available at http://www.answers.com/topic.load-balancing-computing?cat=technology [Accessed 13/06/2008].

[18]Viswanathan, Vivek. *Load Balancing Web Applications* (2001). Available at http://www.onjava.com.pub.a/onjava/2001/09/26/load.html [Accessed 13/06/2008].

[19]Bardopoulos, A. 'International Taxation & Domestic Taxation: Determining 'Source' within and out of an E-Commerce Environment' (Dissertation 1 of 2), Chapter 2, p14. UCT, 2009.

2. Kosta selects 'movies' and is taken to another Web page that lists all the available 'movies'. This Web page may be hosted on an ISP in Berlin, Germany.
3. Next, Kosta selects the 'movie' he wishes to purchase, and is taken to a third Web page containing details for the chosen 'movie'. This Web page may be hosted on an ISP in New York, USA.
4. Next, Kosta will select "PAY NOW", and this takes Kosta to yet another Web page requesting the user's credit card details. This Web page may be hosted on an ISP in London, United Kingdom.

   [Note: If Amazon uses PayPal for the payment transaction, this will add a third party to the transaction which may entail the use of additional ISPs.]
5. After Kosta's credit card details have been entered, Kosta selects "PROCEED" for the payment to be authorised and finalised. This payment confirmation occurs as follows:

   (i) Amazon connects to its bank in Switzerland, where the Swiss bank proceeds with the payment confirmation and finalisation. The Swiss bank uses an ISP hosted in Switzerland.
   (ii) In order to authorise payment, the Swiss bank connects to Kosta's local bank, e.g. Investec. Investec in turn will confirm that the customer has sufficient funds and, in doing so, Investec's ISP will be used which is hosted in Johannesburg, South Africa.
   (iii) Once authorisation has been granted, Investec will connect back to the Swiss bank relaying the relevant information, and the Swiss bank will in turn relay back to the Amazon Web page, hosted in New York, USA, which will then allow Amazon to proceed to the final Web page of the transaction – the 'movie' downloading Web page.

6. The 'movie' downloading Web page may be hosted on an ISP located in Hong Kong. Once Kosta selects "DOWNLOAD", the "DOWNLOADING" application is then shifted over to Kosta's ISPs, which are located in Cape Town, South Africa and Paris, France. At the commencement of the transaction it cannot be predicted which ISP of Kosta's will be utilised.

Furthermore, the route used in the example above will not necessarily be the route used each time a user wishes to purchase a 'movie' from Amazon. For example, if Michèle, who, for argument's sake, also resides in Cape Town, South Africa, logs onto Amazon.com and acquires the exact same movie as Kosta at the exact same time, Michèle may be re-routed to the 'available movies' page hosted on an ISP in Dublin, Ireland if the 'Web traffic' is too great for the ISP in Berlin, Germany.

(continued)

Throughout the entire transaction, both Kosta and Michèle may have been under the impression that they had each accessed Amazon.com located in America and that they had each been connected to a single ISP located in the USA. Whereas, in actual fact, each single transaction may have been routed through multiple ISPs situated in several diverse countries.

(It may be argued that the quantity of ISPs utilized within this example is excessive, however this 'excessive' quantity has been used to illustrate that such a network connection and structure can exist.)

The above hypothetical example, provided here to elucidate the practise of 'load balancing', may be referred to later within this paper to illustrate potential 'source' and 'residence' determination problems for income tax purposes.

Bibliography

3Com Corporation. 2002. *White paper, web caching: Optimizing for internet and web traffic*, p2. Available at http://www.3com.com/other/pdfs/infra/corpinfo/en_US/503093.pdf. Accessed 13 June 2008.

About.com. *TCP/IP – Transmission Control Protocol/Internet Protocol*. Available at http://compnetworking.about.com/od/tcpip/TCPIP_Transmission_Control_Protocol_Internet_Protocol.htm. Accessed 24 May 2010.

Answers.com. Available at http://www.answers.com/topic.load-balancing-computing?cat=technology. Accessed 13 June 2008.

Bardopoulos, Anne. 2007. *International taxation & domestic taxation: Tax avoidance and double tax agreements*. University of Cape Town Postgraduate Diploma in Taxation Dissertation.

Definition of 'Presence' and 'web presence'. Available at http://www.webopedia.com/TERM/P/presence.html. Accessed both 20 June 2008.

Microsoft Technet. *Network load balancing technical overview*, p1. Available at http://technet.microsoft.com/en-us/library/bb742455.aspx. Accessed 2 July 2010.

Nellen, Annette. *Overview to e-Commerce taxation – Guide to understanding the current discussions and debates (July 2003)*. Available at www.cob.sjsu.edu/facstaff/NELLEN_A/ECOMM.pdf. Accessed 24 Dec 2008.

Petri, Daniel. 2009, January 18. *Load balancing exchange front-end servers*. Petri IT Knowledgebase. Available at http://petri.co.il/load_balancing_exchange_front_end_servers.htm. Accessed 7 July 2010.

TechTerms.com. Available at http://www.techterms.com/definition/website. Accessed 20 June 2008.

TechTarget. *Definition of ISP*. Available at http://searchwindevelopment.techtarget.com/sDefinition/0,,sid8_gci214028,00.html. Accessed 20 June 2008.

TechTarget. *What is a Website*. At http://searchsoa.techtarget.com/sDefinition/0,,sid26_gci213352,00.html. Accessed both 20 June 2008.

Tyson, Jeff. *How network address translation works, multi-homing*. Available at http://computer.howstuffworks.com/nat6.htm. Accessed 23 June 2008.

Viswanathan, Vivek. 2001. *Load balancing web applications*. Available at http://www.onjava.com.pub.a/onjava/2001/09/26/load.html. Accessed 13 June 2008.

Wisegeek.com. *What is load balancing?* Available at http://www.wisegeek.com/what-is-load-balancing.htm. Accessed 2 July 2010.

Chapter 6
Mega Cyber Corporations

Abstract The internet has fathered the 'virtual world'. Amazon.com is a founding father of the 'virtual marketplace'.

The urgent point at issue is the monumental impact eCommerce has had on traditional tax, as well as upon the methods of collecting tax. The USA has initiated a revision of its Sales Tax system in respect of eTransactions and the non-collection of Retail Sales Tax where the retailer does not have a 'physical presence' in the consumers' State. The imposition of the 'Internet Sales Tax', coined the 'Amazon Tax', is a direct consequence of this issue.

A further perturbing implication of eCommerce is the issue of Internet privacy in that consumer anonymity is not possible in the virtual marketplace. Herculean corporations operate within the virtual world:

- Microsoft – a predominant purveyor of technological information
- Google – a multibillion-dollar, multinational corporation
- eBay – a virtual marketplace role model
- PayPal – the virtual world's banking and financial storage facilitator, boasting an excess of 100 million accounts globally.
- iTunes – enables music and media to be downloaded from the virtual world

Second Life, a three-dimensional world, is a virtual community and a burgeoning virtual commercial hub and has facilitated a Virtual World Conference for the IBM Academy of Technology.

Second Life customers include multi-national corporations, *inter alia*, the World Bank, US Army, Walt Disney, Accenture, Nokia, Intel, Xerox and IBM.

Second Life is a significant point at issue in respect of technology and taxation and the argument for VAT as the eTax solution.

6.1 Amazon.com

Several eCommerce tools and eRetailers exist, such as eBay, PayPal, Microsoft, Google, iTunes and Amzaon.com, all of which contribute to the exponential growth of eCommerce transactions. While these companies are only a few of the eRetailers and/or eCommerce tools available within the 'virtual world', the above listed

A.M. Bardopoulos, *eCommerce and the Effects of Technology on Taxation*,
Law, Governance and Technology Series 22, DOI 10.1007/978-3-319-15449-7_6

eRetailers are internationally recognised as the largest and most commonly recognised. A synopsis of eBay, PayPal, Microsoft and iTunes, specifically pertaining to services provided by these eRetailers and the consequent promotion of eCommerce transactions, will allow for greater cognizance of some of the activities occurring in the virtual world.

Amazon.com and Second Life,[1] however, will be given precedence. Amazon.com, one of the world's largest eRetailer companies, has had a monumental impact on traditional tax, as well as upon the methods of collecting tax as a direct result of eCommerce transactions. The USA's sales tax system differs from VAT systems implemented in other countries. The concept of the USA's Sales Tax system will be examined later.[2] For purposes of quantifying the impact of technology on taxation, it is notable that the USA has initiated a revision of its Sales Tax system as a requisite for eTransactions which have resulted in Sales Tax not being duly collected or paid over to revenue authorities. Amazon.com has been discerned as one of the predominant perpetrators of this problem. It is, therefore, most important to not only examine and understand what Amazon.com is and how it works, but also how Amazon.com has contributed to first the campaigning for, and then the subsequent implementation of an 'Internet Sales Tax', otherwise coined as the 'Amazon Tax', in New York State and the subsequent introduction of this tax in other states.[3]

While Amazon.com has contributed to change in the way business is conducted, Second Life may be attributed to the fundamental and progressive changes in business procedures. Second Life, a virtual world, provides an environment for socialising, education, meetings and living. Not only is it a growing economy, but it is a virtual economy which facilitates, among many other activities, trading and earning money all of which occur within the virtual world of Second Life.

Amazon.com and Second Life will be discussed with reference to VAT application in the virtual world. The implications of Amazon.com and Second Life are significant points at issue in the argument for VAT as the eTax solution.

6.1.1 Microsoft

Microsoft, the leading producer of computer software internationally, was founded by Bill Gates and Paul Allen in 1976. Prior to Microsoft, Bill Gates and Paul Allen initially approached Micro Instrumentation and Telemetry Systems to write the software programme required for the introduction of home-based computers; however, this was a short lived relationship. In 1981 Microsoft equipped IBM with

[1] Refer to 6.1.6. Second Life, Part II of this paper [p54].

[2] Refer to Chap. 20 – United States of America, Part V of this paper [p240].

[3] Refer to Footnotes 27–30 of this paper [p56–58].

the necessary operating system for the new IBM personal computer and since then Microsoft has flourished to become "*one of the most formidable and influential providers of information technology*"[4] in the world.[5]

6.1.2 Google

Google has swelled into a multibillion-dollar, Multinational Corporation from its humble beginnings as a two-man Ph.D project. Larry Page and Sergey Brin, then students at Standford University, undertook a project to develop an efficient search engine for the Internet. While Google currently offers various services, including email, storage facilities, mobile phone operating systems, etc., an efficient and effective search engine remains Google's core activity. Googol, a mathematical term for a one (1) followed by 100 zeros, is said to be the root of the name Google.[6]

6.1.3 eBay

eBay, one of the few companies to survive the dot com era, was founded in 1995 and still operates today primarily out of its initial geographical location, San Jose, California, USA. However, the company's physical location is irrelevant to the eBay business structure as there is no physical eBay store as the entire service exists on-line within the 'virtual world'. eBay may be equated to, or defined as, a 'virtual marketplace' allowing eMerchants, located anywhere in the world, who have registered with eBay to trade within this 'virtual world'. eBay now operates from several cities across the world. eBay's virtual business structure allows "*all aspects of business other than the delivery of bought and sold items themselves*"[7] to be handled through the eBay website. This operating system is upheld in eBay's

[4]TechTarget.com *What is Microsoft? – Definition from Whatis.com*. Available at http://searchwinit.techtarget.com/sDefinition/0,,sid1_gci799450,00.html [Accessed 7 July 2010].

[5]supra.

[6]How Stuff Works *How Google Works*. Available at http://computer.howstuffworks.com/internet/basics/google.htm [Accessed 7 July 2010].

[7]Hsiao, Aron *What is eBay? An Introduction to the World's Online Marketplace*. About.com. Available at http://ebay.about.com/od/gettingstarted/a/gs_whatisebay.htm [Accessed 7 July 2010].

mission statement whereby "*eBay's mission is to provide a global trading platform where practically anyone can trade practically anything*".[8, 9]

By the year 2010, only 15 years after eBay's inception, eBay had become one of the world's largest Internet success stories and may be vaunted as the 'virtual world's' role model, demonstrating the capabilities, autonomy and self-governance of the virtual world with regard to eCommerce transactions.

eBay, akin to a company operating within a physical world, has successfully colluded with third party companies in providing a successful and effective virtual marketplace. One such example is PayPal, which is essentially a payment service providing potential buyers within the virtual marketplace the convenience, confidence and security when buying from on-line eMerchants. Through PayPal the buyer can purchase goods without the concern of providing credit card details to an unknown, unseen eMerchant.

6.1.4 PayPal

PayPal ensures the safety and protection of eConsumer information within the virtual world. PayPal may perhaps be described as the virtual world's banking and financial information storage facilitator. An eConsumer wishing to acquire goods or services within the virtual marketplace will pay the on-line eMerchant through PayPal. Essentially this means that an eConsumer never provides the eMerchant with personal account information. Instead, the eConsumer instructs PayPal to pay the eMerchant with regard to the eTransaction. PayPal effects payment to the relevant eMerchant. This facilitates secure, private online purchasing.[10]

PayPal has proved to be such an effective payment system within the virtual marketplace that "*PayPal now boasts more than 100 million accounts worldwide*".[11] In addition to PayPal providing a secure and reliable payment service in the virtual world, PayPal also offers a variety of other financial services.

---

[8] Supra.

[9] op cit Hsiao. Available at http://ebay.about.com/od/gettingstarted/a/gs_whatisebay.htm [Accessed 7 July 2010]. Also, Wisegeek *What is eBay?* Available at http://wisegeek.com/what-is-ebay.htm [Accessed 7 July 2010].

[10] Wisegeek *What is PayPal?* Available at http://www.wisegeek.com/what-is-paypal.htm [Accessed 7 July 2010].

[11] Grabianowski, Ed *How PayPal Works*. Howstuffworks. Available at http://money.howstuffworks.com/paypal.htm/printable [Accessed 7 July 2010].

6.1.5 iTunes

As a reaction to the copyright debacle following the widespread use of file-sharing programs such as Napster,[12] *Apple's music program has allowed the legal and safe distribution of media over the Internet.*[13]

Music, movie programs and software in the virtual world can be freely 'downloaded' by users. The question as to whether such free 'downloading' is legal has excited much legal debate concerning primarily copyright infringement. However, websites perpetrating copyright infringement is a study on its own and is outside the ambit of this paper. The primary focus of this paper will be transactions occurring within the virtual world which result in or give rise to eCommerce as in "*the plain, plump fact*"[14] of iTunes.

---

[12]Napster technology works on peer-2-peer ("P2P") technology which basically operates anonymously in the sense that if the user does not disclose his identity then the only identification available is the user's computer ISP number. The A & M Records, Inc, et al. V. Napster, Inc No. C99-05183 MHP (N.D. Cal. 2000) case ("Napster case") was the first real case dealing with P2P technology copyright infringements. Napster's defence, albeit a failed attempt, relied on the precedence established in the Sony Corp. of Amer. V. Universal City Studios, Inc., 464 U.S. 417 (1984) ("Sony Betamax case") in terms of which Napster argued that it could not be held accountable for the conduct of a user utilising its technology for infringing activities. However, the fundamental difference between the Sony Betamax case and the Napster case was that Napster was perpetrating infringing activities which allowed users to download non-authorised copyright material.

Martin Samson summarises Napster's activities and the Napster case as follows:

Napster transmits "... MP3 files by and among the various users of its system ... Napster informs the user's computer of the location of a computer on which MP3 files the user seeks are stored, and its willingness to permit the user to download such files, all files transfer directly from the computer of one Napster user through the Internet to the computer of the requesting user ... "

[Samson, Martin. Internet Library of Law and Court Decisions. Available at http://www.internetlibrary.com/topics/copyright.cfm **[Accessed 10 August 2009]]**

...Napster makes available for free on its web site its MusicShare software. A user who wishes to use Napster's service downloads this software onto his/her personal computer. The user may then seek to access the Napster system. Once the user logs on, the MusicShare software reads a list of MP3 files the user has elected to make available to other users then on Napster's system, and communicates that list to Napster's servers. These servers, in turn, add this list to a transient directory of MP3 files that users currently logged on to the Napster system are willing to share. Once the user logs off, the list of files he/she is willing to share is deleted from this directory...

[Samson, Martin. Internet Library of Law and Court Decisions. Available at http://www.internetlibrary.com/cases/lib_case42.cfm **[Accessed 12 September 2010]]**.

[13]Wisegeek *What is iTunes?* Available at http://www.wisegeek.com/what-is-itunes.htm [Accessed 7 July 2010].

[14]Browning, Robert (1812–1889) English poet, Oxford English Reference Dictionary, Sec. Ed (1996), p186.

iTunes is a media computer application which enables music and media, that is, music files, to be both played and/or 'downloaded' from the virtual world. Since its introduction to the virtual marketplace iTunes has evolved to a stage where a user is able to connect directly to the iTunes 'store' from the iTunes application. Here a user is able to 'download' free, legal, media files or purchase desired media files. iTunes has been described as being "*as groundbreaking as the invention of video tapes or CDs*".[15,16]

6.1.6 Second Life

Second Life, created and developed by Linden Labs, was founded in 1999 and employed more than 300 employees across the USA, Europe and Asia as of 2009.[17]

"*Second Life is a pioneer and industry leader in the growing virtual world and virtual goods markets.*"[18] Second Life, a three-dimensional world, is a virtual community where participants, otherwise referred to as 'residents', may reside, interact, socialise with one another, work and participate in numerous other activities. [19] Sec-

[15]Op cit Wisegeek, http://www.wisegeek.com/what_is_itunes.

[16]supra.

[17]Linden Lab. *Case Study: How Meeting in Second Life Transformed IBM's Technology Elite Into Virtual World Believers* (2009), p8. Available at http://secondlifegrid.net.s3.amazonaws.com/docs/Second_Life_Case_IBM_EN.pdf [Accessed 5 September 2010].

[18]Second Life. *Second Life Develop – Why Develop in Second Life?* Available at http://develop.secondlife.com/whysl/ [Accessed 5 September 2010].

[19]Second Life, is described by Wisegeek.com as, "*a three-dimensional virtual community created by its membership. Members assume an identity and take up residence in Second Life, creating a customized avatar or personage to represent themselves... Residents buy property, start businesses, game with other residents, create objects, join clubs, attend classes, or just hang out....*

As of fall 2006, over 3,000 residents reportedly make an excess of 20 thousand US Dollars (USD) per year running businesses in Second Life. Most of them sell objects they've created that other residents want. One Second Life resident landed a Business Week cover story for earning a three-figure income – that's real world dollars – selling virtual real estate.

Property purchased in Second Life is owned by the buyer using a scheme referred to as Internet Protocol (IP) Copyright. Some owners reward members for staying at their property with Linden Dollars, Second Life's currency. Linden Dollars can also be purchased with real dollars using a credit card. Part of the exchange rate goes to Linden Inc., with Second Life purportedly generating over 64 million USD a year.

Real world corporations are also taking interest in the virtual world. In September 2006, Popular Science reported that Wells Fargo Bank bought an island on Second Life, where they may one day offer real world banking. Wal-Mart and Intel are just two of the mega-giants considering corporate training classes in Second Life – a business model that could save corporations, big and small, millions of dollars in travel and lodging fees. Future possibilities include virtual universities that replicate their real-life counterparts with classrooms and professors teaching interactive classes in real time, virtual interactive congressional sessions, and three-dimensional customer and tech support.

ond Life facilitates directors' meetings whereby diverse directors located in diverse jurisdictions can meet together in a virtual meeting-place. 'Residents' navigate this world with the aid of an Avatar which represents the 'real world' individual. Commercially, 'residents' are able to shop, sell commodities, set-up businesses and even acquire virtual world property. Second Life is a burgeoning virtual commercial hub.

The IBM Academy of Technology has hosted a Virtual World Conference and an Annual Meeting in Second Life. IBM designed a special conference space to host a conference and meeting in the virtual world which assured a secure environment.[20] "*The meeting in Second Life was everything that you could do at a traditional conference – and more – at one fifth the cost and without a single case of jet lag.*"[21]

An increasing number of multi-national corporations are Second Life customers, including inter alia the World Bank, US Army, Walt Disney, Accenture, Nokia, Intel, Xerox and IBM. Second Life is an ideal case study for the impact of technology on taxation.

6.1.7 Amazon.com

Amazon.com, founded in 1994 by former D.E. Shaw & Company hedge fund financial analyst, Jeffrey P. Bezos, has thrived with the expansion of the virtual marketplace and has burgeoned into the world's largest eRetailer. It has been referred to as "*one of the iconic companies of the Internet era*".[22,23] While the Internet may be referred to as the father of the virtual world, Amazon.com may be referred to as one of the founding fathers of the virtual marketplace.

Initially, Amazon.com was an on-line bookstore, but over the past two decades it has expanded its business to encompass practically all spheres of marketable products from furniture to groceries!

Amzaon.com has provoked much controversial debate regarding not only the imposition of indirect tax within the virtual marketplace, but more importantly, the

---

Second Life is the brainchild of Phillip Rosedale, the former Real Networks guru credited with spearheading the development of online streaming technologies . . . Anyone over 13 years of age can open a free account at Second Life, though members between 13 and 18 participate in Teen Second Life, a separate virtual community. Within the adult version of Second Life, there are PG areas and adult areas where different modes of behaviour are acceptable. According to the terms of service contract, harassment of any kind in Second Life results in permanent expulsion.... ".

www.wisegeek.com *What is Second Life?* Available at http://www.wisegeek.com/what-is-second-life.htm [Accessed 11 July 2010].

[20]Op cit Footnote 17 of this paper [p54].

[21]op cit Footnote 17 of this paper [p54]- Joanne Martin, President, IBM Academy of Technology.

[22]Ells, Scott *Amazon.com Inc. News*. The New York Times. Available at http://topics.nytimes.com/top/news/business/companies/amazon_inc/index.html [Accessed 7 July 2010].

[23]supra.

effective collection of indirect tax. As will be further discussed,[24] *"[i]n the United States, [that is, in all] forty-five states and the District of Columbia ... retail sales taxes [are imposed] at the state and typically at the local level as well*".[25] Similarly in the EU, while there is a common VAT Directive to which each EU Member is required to adhere, the collection of VAT in each individual EU Member State is for that State's account and coffers. In the USA, for a retailer to be obligated to collect Sales Tax on behalf of, say, New York State, that retailer must have a physical presence in New York. In the EU the collection of VAT is dependent upon the specific VAT registration requirements of each respective VAT legislative EU Member State. For the purpose of examining the importance of Amazon.com's impact on taxation in the virtual world, the USA's defining of 'physical presence' within the virtual world is significant.

The non-collection of retail Sales Tax, as a result of the retailer not having a 'physical presence' within the consumer's state, has resulted in millions of dollars of uncollected retail Sales Tax. New York legislators viewed this as a 'loophole' in the system which not only resulted in consumers not paying the necessary retail Sales Tax but also resulted "*in an unfair competitive advantage*" for "*out-of-state online retailers*".[26] New York legislators, therefore, in effect deemed out-of-state retailers to have a 'physical presence' within New York because sales to New York consumers were occurring in New York. Opponents to the imposition of the newly coined "*Amazon tax*"[27] have argued a 1992 USA Supreme Court ruling, Quill Corp. v. North Dakota[28] (Quill), to prevent the implementation of the Amazon

---

[24]Refer to Chap. 20 – United States of America, Part V of this paper [p240].

[25]Schenk, Alan & Oldman, Olivier, *Value Added Tax, A Comparative Approach* (2007), USA, p451.

[26]loc cit, Ells, http://topics.nytimes.com/top/news/business/companies/amazon_inc/index.html.

[27]Refer to 6.1. Amazon.com, Part II of this paper [p49].

[28]USA Supreme Court Quill Corp v North Dakota (91–0194), 504 U.S. 298 (1992).

The Legal Information Institute of Cornell University Law School provides the following summary of the Quill Corp. v. North Dakota, 504 U.S. 298 (1992) ("Quill case") as prepared by Christopher Trovato in 2002:

> Summary
>
> *Quill Corporation ("Quill") is a mail-order house incorporated in Delaware that sells office furniture, equipment, and other supplies. Quill catered to the national market and solicited its business through catalogs, flyers, periodical advertisements, and telephone calls. Quill maintained no offices or warehouses in North Dakota. None of its employees worked or resided in North Dakota. However, Quill's North Dakota customer base numbered approximately 3,000 patrons and accounted for nearly $1,000,000 in annual sales. The company filled these orders via mail or common carrier from out-of-state distribution centers.*
>
> *North Dakota law imposes a use tax on all property purchased for storage, use, or consumption within the state that requires every "retailer" to collect the tax from its customers and remit it to the state. See N. D. Cent. Code § 57–40.2-07 (Supp. 1991). The statute defines a "retailer" as any person who "engages in regular or systematic solicitation" of a consumer market in the state. § 57–40.2-01(6).*

tax. In terms of Quill, "*the Court determined that out-of-state retailers cannot be required to collect sales tax on purchases sent to states where they did not have a*

North Dakota brought an action in a North Dakota state court to compel Quill to collect and pay the use tax for goods sold within the state. The trial court held that the mail-order house was not required to pay the use tax as Quill lacked sufficient nexus with the state to be subject to the tax. The Supreme Court of North Dakota reversed on appeal holding that neither the Due Process clause nor the Commerce Clause required a "physical presence" nexus to validate the imposition of a state use tax upon a defendant with established State contacts. The United States Supreme Court granted certiorari.

Issue & Deposition

Issue(s)

1. *Whether a vendor whose only connection with a state is through common carrier or the mail system is free from paying a state-imposed use tax because the vendor lacks a proper nexus with the taxing state as required by the Due Process Clause of the U.S. Constitution.*
2. *Whether a vendor whose only connection with a state is through a common carrier or U.S. mail is exempt from a state-imposed use tax because the vendor lacks proper nexus with the taxing state as required by the Commerce Clause of the U.S. Constitution.*

Deposition

1. *No. The Due Process Clause speaks to notions of fair play and substantial justice; thus, so long as the commercial actor's activity is purposefully directed towards residents of the taxing state and the tax is related to the benefits received from the state, the actor's physical presence is not necessary to establish the nexus sufficient to impose the tax.*
2. *Yes. The Commerce Clause speaks to concerns about a state's regulatory effect upon the flow of the national economy; thus, a state whose only connection with the vendor is through mail or common carrier lacks the nexus required by the Commerce Clause to impose the tax. However, because Congress has plenary power to regulate interstate commerce, it retains ultimate authority to decide which taxes unduly burden interstate commerce."*

[Available at http://www.law.cornell.edu/background/internet/Quill.htm **[Accessed 12 September 2010]]**

The Quill case has had a significant impact on the imposition of retail sales tax in several states of the USA. As an example, the State of Connecticut Department of Revenue Service issued the following statement on its website after the Quill case:

> **ENFORCEMENT OF 1989 CONN. PUB. ACTS 41:** Given the fact that the North Dakota statute struck down in Quill Corp. v. North Dakota and 1989 Conn. Pub. Acts 41, §§1 and 2 are virtually identical and that the Connecticut statute, like its North Dakota counterpart, would require mail order companies to collect Connecticut use tax when the companies have no physical presence within Connecticut, the Department will not enforce 1989 Conn. Pub. Acts 41, §§1 and 2 by requiring out-of-state retailers that have merely an "economic presence" in Connecticut to collect Connecticut use tax. If Congress does enact legislation that would allow States to require out-of-state retailers with no physical presence within a State to collect and remit use tax without violating the Commerce Clause, the Department will begin to enforce 1989 Conn. Pub. Acts 41, §§1 and 2, to the extent its provisions are consistent with legislation enacted by Congress.

[Available at http://www.ct.gov/drs/cwp/view.asp?A=1514&Q=268516 **[Accessed 12 September 2010]]**.

physical presence … [The Court held] that compelling merchants to adhere to the complexities of the state and local tax codes would place unreasonable burden on interstate commerce".[29]

While retail sales tax may differ from VAT it is, nevertheless, the indirect tax and 'physical presence' in the virtual world as defined by the Amazon tax that is of the utmost significance. Whether the Amazon tax[30] results in the collection of Sales Tax or VAT is irrelevant, but it is relevant that Amazon is deemed to hold "*physical presence in the state because it derives sales through its affiliates who live there*".[31]

Implementation of the Amazon tax has whipped up a fury of outrage and contention concerning not least of all the issue of internet privacy. It is contended that to comply with the Amazon tax requirements, Amazon will be forced to release customers' details and customers' "*private content choices*"[32] to the revenue authorities should the latter wish to conduct, for example, an audit to measure Amazon's compliance.

Amazon filed a complaint in Seattle's Federal Court arguing that an audit constituted a violation against the privacy rights of the consumer, the First Amendment and Amazon itself.[33]

Revenue authorities argue that there will be no violation of internet privacy as such detailed information is not necessary for the assessment of Amazon's

---

[29]loc cit, Ells, http://topics.nytimes.com/top/news/business/companies/amazon_inc/index.html.

[30]The attractive lure of the 'Amazon tax', which was introduced by the State of New York, has begun to spread to other states within the USA. Following the footsteps of the State of New York, the State of Connecticut has introduced the 'Amazon tax' – the success of which is still to be determined.

The State of California has also been described as "*one of the most recent battlegrounds in the fight over Internet sales tax collection. [The State of California] engaged a law that tried to boost tax collections by expanding the definition of 'physical presence' in the state to include marketing affiliates, who steer online customers to the retail site, and to sister companies … [Amazon, in response,] initially called the law illegal and spent more than $5 million to gather signatures for a 2012 ballot referendum to repeal the law. But a compromise was later reached between state lawmakers and Amazon … [which] delayed the expanded online tax collections until at least September 2012 …* ".

The State of Tennessee is following close on the heels of the States of New York, California and Connecticut and has reached an agreement with Amazon whereby Amazon has "*agreed to begin collecting sales taxes in [the State of Tennessee] in 2014*".

And the State of South Carolina, following in close pursuit, has enacted new legislation whereby "*Amazon will be required to begin collecting sales taxes in January 2016 …* ".

The Wall Street Journal *Conn. Gets Tough with Amazon, Pushing on with Tax* (October 9, 2011). Available at http://online.wsj.com/article/AP417635c7832e49a9b628ba6d9c8a4778.html#printMode [Accessed 6 November 2011].

[31]loc cit, Ells, http://topics.nytimes.com/top/news/business/companies/amazon_inc/index.html.

[32]Cohen, Noam *In a State's Search for Sales Tax, Amazon Raises Privacy Concerns* (2 May 2010). p1. The New York Times. Available at http://www.nytimes.com/2010/05/03/business/media/03link.html?ref=sales_tax&pagewanted=print [Accessed 7 July 2010].

[33]loc cit, Cohen, http://www.nytimes.com/2010/05/03/business/media/03link.html?ref=sales_tax&pagewanted=print.

compliance in the collection of sales tax. Revenue authorities argue that they "*... have too much data. The last thing [they] need is data [they] don't need*".[34]

Amazon's lawyers argue that Amazon as a company is protected by the Constitution just so Amazon "*may sell – and customers may read, hear or view – a broad range of popular and unpopular expressive materials with the customers' private content choices protected from unnecessary government scrutiny.*"[35]

Amazon has collected a treasure trove of data detailing "*who is reading what*".[36] If Amazon released to the government data detailing customers' reading choices such data could be embarrassing and injurious to the customer. Consider "*what the government could do with 'Converting to Islam for Dummies' or 'Plant Your Own Marijuana Field'*".[37]

In the real world it is possible for a consumer to maintain anonymity when making a cash purchase, however, consumer anonymity is not possible in the virtual marketplace as the eConsumer's personal information, including a detailed description of the item purchased is necessary to effect a sale.

It is a sobering thought that "*detailed information [is] held by companies like Amazon and Google, which [may] have a strong business incentive to fight off government. Yet even as they go to court to protect the information they have collected, that information still represents a 'honey pot for the government'*".[38]

While the privacy issue is a study on its own, it is inexorably linked to possible eTax solutions, such as the Amazon tax, purely because of the quantity of data collected and stored with an eTransaction compared to traditional cash transactions. Such issues will be briefly discussed later under Electronic Transactions Law,[39] as such points at issue are of interest when considering methods of enforcing tax compliance within the virtual world.

Bibliography

Primary Sources

Cases

United States of America Cases

USA Supreme Court Quill Corp. v. North Dakota (91-0194), 504 U.S. 298. 1992. [USA]. Available at http://www.law.cornell.edu/background/internet/Quill.htm. Accessed 12 Sept 2010. Available at http://www.ct.gov/drs/cwp/view.asp?A=1514&Q=268516. Accessed 12 Sept 2010.

---

[34] supra.

[35] supra.

[36] supra.

[37] supra.

[38] loc cit , Cohen, http://www.nytimes.com/20...=print

[39] Refer to 7.3. Electronic Transactions Law, Part II of this paper [p65]

Secondary Sources

Browning, Robert (1812–1889) English Poet. 1996. *The Oxford English reference dictionary*, 2nd ed. New York: Oxford University Press.

Cohen, Noam. 2010. *In a State's search for sales tax, Amazon raises privacy concerns*. The New York Times. Available at http://www.nytimes.com/2010/05/03/business/media/03link.html?ref=sales_tax&pagewanted=print. Accessed 7 July 2010.

Ells, Scott. *Amazon.com Inc. news*. The New York Times. Available at http://topics.nytimes.com/top/news/business/companies/amazon_inc/index.html. Accessed 7 July 2010.

Grabianowski, Ed. *How PayPal works*. Howstuffworks "How PayPal Works". Available at http://money.howstuffworks.com/paypal.htm/printable. Accessed 7 July 2010.

How Stuff Works. *How Google works*. Available at http://computer.howstuffworks.com/internet/basics/google.htm. Accessed 7 July 2010.

Hsiao, Aron. *What is eBay? An introduction to the world's online marketplace*. About.com. Available at http://ebay.about.com/od/gettingstarted/a/gs_whatisebay.htm. Accessed 7 July 2010.

Linden Lab. 2009. *Case study: How meeting in second life transformed IBM's technology elite into virtual world believers*, p.8. Available at http://secondlifegrid.net.s3.amazonaws.com/docs/Second_Life_Case_IBM_EN.pdf. Accessed 5 Sept 2010.

Samson, Martin. *Internet library of law and court decisions*. Available at http://www.internetlibrary.com/topics/copyright.cfm. Accessed 10 Aug 2009.

Samson, Martin. *Internet library of law and court decisions*. Available at http://www.internetlibrary.com/cases/lib_case42.cfm. Accessed 12 Sept 2010.

Schenk, Alan, and Oliver Oldman. 2007. *Value added tax, a comparative approach*. New York: Cambridge University Press.

Second Life. *Second life develop – Why develop in second life?* Available at http://develop.secondlife.com/whysl/. Accessed 5 Sept 2010.

State of Connecticut Department of Revenue Service. SN 92(19), Effect of *Quill Corp. v. North Dakota* on the collection of use tax by retailers who engage in business in Connecticut only by selling items through mail order catalogs with delivery by common carriers. Available at http://www.ct.gov/drs/cwp/view.asp?A=1514&Q=268516. Accessed 12 Sept 2010.

TechTarget.com. *What is microsoft? – Definition from Whatis.com*. Available at http://searchwinit.techtarget.com/sDefinition/0,,sid1_gci799450,00.html. Accessed 7 July 2010.

Wall Street Journal. 2011, October 9. The *Conn. Gets tough with Amazon, pushing on with tax*. Available at http://online.wsj.com/article/AP417635c7832e49a9b628ba6d9c8a4778.html#printMode. Accessed 6 Nov 2011.

Wisegeek.com. *What is eBay?* Available at http://wisegeek.com/what-is-ebay.htm. Accessed 7 July 2010.

Wisegeek.com. *What is iTunes?* Available at http://www.wisegeek.com/what-is-itunes.htm. Accessed 7 July 2010.

Wisegeek.com. *What is PayPal?* Available at http://www.wisegeek.com/what-is-paypal.htm. Accessed 7 July 2010.

Wisegeek.com. *What is second life?* Available at http://www.wisegeek.com/what-is-second-life.htm. Accessed 11 July 2010.

Chapter 7
Unbounded Technology

Abstract The inevitability of an interplanetary gateway as a next generation ISP is imminent. It is foreseeable that such technology will be universally accessible. Therefore, taxing solutions should not be rigidly confined to current technology, but should be flexible so as to make allowance for currently unimaginable technological amelioration. To date policies purposely issued to resolve potential eTax issues have been rendered obsolete.

A narrow definition of eCommerce may prove most amenable to flexibility when dealing with technical amelioration. The Australian Taxation Office has defined eCommerce narrowly and simply as "*the buying and selling of goods and services on the Internet*" (Pinto, Dale *E-Commerce & Source-Based Income Taxation* (2003), Netherlands, p2). The point at issue is the conducting of transactions, via the Internet, between three parties, the trader, the ISP and the customer.

The UNCITRAL Model Law Functional Equivalence approach is that traditional tax laws and requirements should be applied to eCommerce. However, the point at issue is that the Internet will challenge the adequate and effective application of current OECD rules and guidelines, double tax agreements and domestic laws to eCommerce tax issues.

Threat of infringement of privacy in the virtual world is an explosive issue. Opponents to the 'Amazon Tax' (Refer to discussion and explanation of the 'Amazon tax', which is not specific law in itself but rather a tax 'coined' as the 'Amazon tax', in 6.1.7., Chap. 6, Part II, pages 55–59 of this paper.) contended that compliance checks pertaining to Internet Sales Tax could allow governments unrestricted access to eConsumers' purchases and personal information. The essence of the problem is the means of successful imposition and implementation of an eTax while yet respecting the axiom of privacy protection.

A.M. Bardopoulos, *eCommerce and the Effects of Technology on Taxation*,
Law, Governance and Technology Series 22, DOI 10.1007/978-3-319-15449-7_7

7.1 Future Technological Advancements

Recent broadband connection to the Internet is already obsolete. NASA is already working on a 'travelling wave tube amplifier' to receive data from the Moon.[1] The Lunar Reconnaissance Orbiter, equipped with a K-band transmitter operates by using electrodes in a vacuum tube in order to amplify microwave signals to a high data power rate.[2]

The Inter Planetary Network (IPN), a sub-department of the Jet Propulsion Laboratory which provides NASA with the capacity to perform such data communication, presides over the project of providing Space with the Internet. The 'gateway' to interplanetary Internet is satellites which will in fact constitute and operate as a network. "*The concept of the gateways can be understood as being the local . . . ISP, who enables us to access Internet through phone or the digital subscriber line etc. The location of the interplanetary gateway as a processing centre could be either on an earth-based station, on a planet's surface or on a spacecraft present in the orbit.*"[3]

It has been conjectured that *"[t]he push to have ISPs in outer space will not be driven by our earth-based needs, but rather by our foreseeable interplanetary colonisation*",[4] and the inevitability of the interplanetary 'gateway' as a next generation ISP is imminent. Furthermore, it is foreseeable that such technology will be universally accessible. Current concerns that load balancing travelling several jurisdictions either as an ISP providing access to the Internet or in the multi-routed processing of one simple transaction will be exacerbated when load balancing outstrips earthly jurisdictions.

Intrinsic to the intellectual basis of this paper is the contention that taxing solutions should not be rigidly confined to current technology operations and systems when contending with the impact of technology on taxation, but should be flexible so as to make allowance for the impact of unforeseen, currently unimaginable technological amelioration.

Typically, existing eTax policies have a predilection determined by the geographical location of an ISP's tangible equipment and do not make allowance for the possibility of outer space locations.

Within the internet's short life-span there has been such an unstoppable burgeoning of technology that policies purposely issued to resolve potential eTax issues have

[1]Farrell, Nick *NASA puts ISPs to shame, Luna broadband pretty good* (2009). The Inquirer. Available at http://www.theinquirer.net/inquirer/news/1529741/nasa-isps-shame [Accessed 6 July 2010].

[2]supra.

[3]Hassam *Possibility of Internet Service In The Outer Space*. Available at http://www.hubpages.com/hub/Possibility-Internet-Service-In-The-Outer-Space [Accessed 6 July 2010].

[4]Kontos, Kosta BSc (CompSci) (UCT), MBA (UCT). Managing Director (MD) of Kontos Technologies. (1st July 2010). The intellectual basis of Kosta Kontos's MBA thesis deals with the "Core *Issues Influencing the Adoption of Software as a Service*", published by UCT in 2011.

already become obsolete. Within the context of this paper this matter is a significant point at issue and is discussed further.[5] Relative to this problem is the OECD's Commentary Note on eCommerce which defines a server as meeting the 'physical presence' test for purposes of determining a person's 'permanent establishment' for income tax purposes.[6]

7.2 eCommerce

In addressing the issue of eCommerce it is important to understand that "*[t]here is not one homogeneous definition of e-commerce. It may cover different technical solutions of conducting business via electronic media such as the Internet or mobile telephone or have a more delimited scope.*"[7] To understand the concept of eCommerce and the various forms eCommerce may assume is essential when examining the impact of this technology on taxation. After all, "*the Internet is an important cultural phenomenon ....[however, it fails] to comply with basic economic laws ... [because] it was devised by a bunch of hippie anarchists*".[8]

The UNCITRAL Model Law on Electronic Commerce with Guide to Enactment of 1996 (UNCITRAL Model Law) refers to eCommerce but does not provide a specific definition of eCommerce:

> *While a definition of 'electronic data interchange (EDI)[9]' is provided ... the Model Law does not specify the meaning of 'electronic commerce'. In preparing the Model Law, the Commission decided that, in addressing the subject matter before it, it would have in mind a broad notion of EDI, covering a variety of trade-related uses of EDI that might be referred to broadly under the rubric of 'electronic commerce'.*[10]

---

[5]Refer to 8.2. Conclusion, Part II of this paper [p82]; Discussion of 'Residence' in 10.1. – Applying Virtual World Attributes to the Traditional 'Residence Definition, Part III of this paper [p97]; 10.2. – 'Residence' within the Virtual World, Part III of this paper [p102]; 13 – *Defining 'Source' within an eCommerce Context*, Part IV of this paper [p131].

[6]"*... if the enterprise owns (or leases) and operates the server ... the place where the server is located could constitute a permanent establishment of the enterprise if the other requirements of the Article are met*". [**OECD *OECD Model Tax Convention on Income and on Capital, Condensed Version – July 2005*** (2005), **France, p104**].

Refer also to 13 – *Defining 'Source; within an eCommerce Context,* Part IV on of this paper [p131].

[7]op cit, Rendahl, Pernilla, *Cross-Border Consumption Taxation of Digital Supplies,* Netherlands, p19.

[8]Nolle, Thomas. Available at www.quotegarden.com.internet.html [Accessed 8 May 2008].

[9]EDI is defined in Article I of Chapter I of the UNCITRAL Model Law as "*the electronic transfer from computer to computer of information using an agreed standard to structure the information*". UNCITRAL Model Law on Electronic Commerce (1996), United Nations Publication, New York.

[10]Paragraph 7 of Part B (Scope) of the Guide to Enactment of the UNCITRAL Model Law on Electronic Commerce (1996). Available at http://www.uncitral.org/pdf/english/texts/electcom/05-89450_Ebook.pdf [Accessed 21/01/2012].

The Green Paper on Electronic Commerce for South Africa has defined eCommerce more broadly as:

> *The use of electronic networks to exchange information, products, services and payments for commercial and communication purposes between individuals (consumers) and businesses, between businesses themselves, between individuals themselves, within government or between the public and government and, last, between business and government.*
>
> *This definition encompasses the many kinds of business activities that are being conducted electronically, and conveys the notion that electronic commerce* is *much more comprehensive than simply purchasing of goods and services electronically.*[11]

Conversely the Australian Taxation Office has defined eCommerce narrowly and simply as "*the buying and selling of goods and services on the Internet*".[12] Paradoxically a narrow definition of eCommerce may be more amenable to flexibility when dealing with technological amelioration, whereas a broader definition may prove inadequate when pertaining to ameliorating technology making redefinition for the purpose of adaptation mandatory.

Although within the more comprehensive definition of eCommerce the various categories or forms of eCommerce are highlighted, it is the transactions between businesses (B2B), businesses and consumers (B2C), and consumers and businesses that will be the primary focus of this paper. In the matter of these transaction categories, the eCommerce activities are further categorised into direct and indirect eCommerce. Defined briefly, indirect eCommerce is the 'electronic ordering of tangible goods',[13] and direct eCommerce is the electronic ordering of intangible goods.[14] With regard to the former, indirect eCommerce, the Internet is utilised for "*the purposes of providing information, ordering products and perhaps payment*",[15] but the delivery of goods or services occurs through the traditional channels (i.e. outside of the virtual world). Direct eCommerce, however, "*utilises the virtual marketplace to [the] full extent, not only as a means of transferring information*",[16] ordering and payment, but also for the delivery of 'services'.

---

[11]Introduction to the Green Paper on Electronic Commerce for South Africa, Co-ordinated and complied by the Department of Communications Republic of South Africa (November 2000).

[12]Pinto, Dale *E-Commerce and Source-Based Income Taxation* (2003), Netherlands, p2.

[13]Hargitai, Cecilia *Classification of E-Commerce Transactions of Chapter III, Value Added Taxation of Electronic Supply of Services within the European Community* ("VAT within European Community") (2001). Available at http://www.jeanmonnetprogram.org/papers/01/013301-03.html [Accessed 9 April 2008].

Also, The Jean Monnet Center for International & Regional Economic Law & Justice, The NYU Institutes on the Park *Chapter III: Shortcomings of the Present European VAT System with Respect to Electronic Supplies, Classification of E-Commerce Transactions ["Shortcomings of the Present European VAT System"]*. Available at http://centers.law.nyu.edu/jeanmonnet/papers/01/013301-03.html [Accessed 05/10/2011].

[14]loc cit Jean Monnet Center, *Shortcomings of the Present European VAT System,* http://centers.law.nyu.edu/jeanmonnet/papers/01/013301-03.html.

[15]supra.

[16]supra.

B2B eCommerce transactions make use of the Internet "*to integrate the value-added chain that can extend from the supplier of raw materials to the final consumer*".[17] B2B ecommerce transactions represent the bulk of eCommerce. However, it is B2C eCommerce transactions, the retailing segment of eCommerce,[18] that attracts disproportionately significant attention.

The impact of technology on taxation is of primary importance within the context of this paper the prime focus of which is the conducting of transactions "*through the Internet [by means] of three parties, namely the ISP, the trader and the customer*",[19] which is "*a way of doing real-time business transactions via telecommunications networks, when the customer and the merchant are in different geographical places . . . Electronic commerce operates on a bona fide basis, without prior arrangements between customers and merchants.*"[20]

7.3 Electronic Transactions Law

There are differing opinions regarding the regulation of the Internet. One such view is that the Internet should be allowed to regulate itself. Opponents to unregulated internet, which was "*devised by a bunch of hippie anarchists*",[21] contend that a virtual world without rules invites anarchy. However, eBay as an eMerchant has effectively implemented self-regulation. eBay is not governed by any country, and apart from the odd lawsuit, eBay has generally been very successful in implementing self-regulation. Notwithstanding eBay's self-regulating success, it is questionable whether eBay's trade ethics would have legal substance if taken to court.

The Internet has had a profound impact upon the manner in which we conduct business, the imposition of tax and methods of tax collection and has facilitated flagrant tax evasion. The abuse and corruption facilitated by the Internet and eCommerce is exposed in the eLegend or eMythical tale of the sale of a Lamborghini over the Internet. A Lamborghini was bought via the Internet at a super-car market related price. It transpired that the Lamborghini, delivered by post, was a model car of a Lamborghini. As a model car it matched the description and picture displayed on the Internet. The eSeller neither informed the ePurchaser that the Lamborghini tendered on the internet was a model of a Lamborghini, nor that its purpose was not for transport on public roads!

Laws are created and implemented as a consequence of social and economic issues. "*Several policy issues arise as a result of the proliferation of e-commerce.*

---

[17]op cit Pinto, p4.

[18]supra.

[19]supra.

[20]Telecom Glossary 2K, *e-commerce* (2002). Available at http://www.its.bldroc.gov/projects/devglossary/_e-commerce.html [Accessed 26 June 2008].

[21]Idem Nolle, www.quotegarden.com.internet.html.

These include development and access to the ICTs; taxation; security and privacy; protection of intellectual property; content development and regulation; electronic payment systems; standards and interoperability".[22] Papers pertaining to such issues were published in the year 2000 when governments were compelled to recognise the impact of eCommerce, the Internet and the amelioration of technology on society. The implementation and enforcement of laws in a seamless virtual world is a challenge of unprecedented dimensions.

There are diverse legal issues pertaining to the Internet, including contracts, jurisdictional rights and authority, data privacy, communication privacy, crime, ISP liability, etc. The overall impact technology has had on the law is a study in itself. However, "*one of the main concerns generated by e-commerce is the priority that must be accorded to issues such as privacy of personal information to safeguard public interest*".[23] For purposes of examining the implementation of an effective eTax within the virtual world, the privacy issues raised by several jurisdictions are of relevance as has already been noted[24] with the promulgation of the Amazon tax[25] in New York, USA. As such, a synopsis of the privacy issues will be examined later.[26]

7.3.1 Functional Equivalence Approach

> *Legislation governing... trade that is technology neutral is required. The use of an electronic medium should not affect the laws that would ordinarily govern the transaction.*[27]

The above principle is pertinent to the various codes of law which have been proposed to govern the virtual world, including methods of taxation.

It is important to note that law governing electronic transactions may vary from jurisdiction to jurisdiction subject to local legislation or prevailing case law. It is not the aim of this paper to examine electronic transaction law legislation in each country or in respect of specific countries, but rather to provide a general overview of the international model laws/conventions which have been introduced to address electronic transactions, specifically in respect of the Doctrine of Functional Equivalence and the importance in respect of taxation. The Doctrine of

[22]op cit, Introduction to the Green Paper on Electronic Commerce for South Africa (November 2000).

[23]op cit, Introduction to the Green Paper on Electronic Commerce for South Africa (November 2000).

[24]Refer to 6.1.7. *Amazon.com,* Part II of this paper [p55].

[25]Refer to discussion and explanation of the 'Amazon tax', which is not specific law in itself but rather a tax 'coined' as the 'Amazon tax', in 6.1.7., Chap. 6, Part II, pages 55–59 of this paper.

[26]Refer to 7.3.2. Electronic Transactions Law, Privacy, Part II of this paper [p68].

[27]op cit Contracting and Trade Laws, Green Paper on Electronic Commerce for South Africa (November 2000).

Functional Equivalence is ensconced in diverse local legislations, as is illustrated by the above principle quoted from the South African Green Paper on Electronic Commerce for South Africa.

Extracts from the New Zealand Electronic Transactions Act[28] highlight the "purpose" of promulgating such legislation:

> *"The purpose of this Act is to facilitate the use of electronic technology by –*
>
> (a) *Reducing uncertainty regarding*
>
> (i) *The legal effect of information that is in electronic form or that is communicated by electronic means; and*
> (ii) *The time and place of dispatch and receipt of electronic communications; and*
>
> (b) *Providing that certain paper-based legal requirements may be met by using electronic technology that is **functionally equivalent** to those legal requirements."*[29] [Emphasis added]

The New Zealand Act explicitly refers to functional equivalence, analogous to the functional equivalence theory set out in UNCITRAL Model Law and addressed by the OECD. This sub-chapter accentuates the potential of the Doctrine of Functional Equivalence as a crucial principle of electronic transactions law in respect of its applicability to eCommerce.

The UNCITRAL Model Law relies on the new Functional Equivalence approach for eCommerce and is "*based on the recognition that legal requirements prescribing the use of traditional paper-based documentation constitute the main obstacle to the development of modern means of communication*".[30] The UNCITRAL Model Law is extensively used as a standard for validating electronic transactions by countries implementing equivalent legislation. The Functional Equivalence Approach may be described as "*an analysis of the purposes and functions of the traditional paper-based requirement with a view to determining how those purposes or functions could be fulfilled through electronic-commerce techniques*".[31]

The Functional Equivalence approach in principle recognises "*that legal requirements prescribing the use of traditional paper-based documentation constitute the main obstacle to the development of modern means of communication*"[32] and, therefore, the development and progression of eCommerce. That is, in terms of the Doctrine of Functional Equivalence, laws pertaining to the paper-based world (i.e. the physical world) are first examined and then evaluated as to whether such laws can be implemented within the electronic world (i.e. the virtual world) and

---

[28]New Zealand Electronic and Transactions Act, No. 35 of 2002 (as amended).

[29]Section 3 of the New Zealand Electronic Transactions Act, No. 35 of 2002 (as amended).

[30]UNCITRAL Part E ("Functional Equivalent" Approach) of the *UNCITRAL Model Law on Electronic Commerce with Guide to Enactment 1996, with additional Article 5 bis as adopted in 1998* (1996) p20. Available at http://www.uncitral.org/pdf/english/texts/electcom/05-89450_Ebook.pdf [Accessed 5/10/2011].

[31]supra.

[32]supra.

consequently can be deemed valid in the electronic world.[33] The Doctrine of Functional Equivalence has been extended to the imposition of tax on electronic commerce, as is evident in the tax principles pertaining to eCommerce as presented to the OECD by the Committee on Fiscal Affairs:

> *The taxation principles that guide governments in relation to conventional commerce should also guide them in relation to electronic commerce....*[34]

The OECD has adopted the view that, for purposes of determining whether a transaction is subject to tax and, furthermore, which jurisdiction has taxing rights, current domestic laws and DTAs must first be applied to resolve any tax issues within eCommerce.[35] However, where it is not possible to resolve the tax issue with the aid of current laws, then the OECD Rules and Guidelines may be referred to for assistance and application. In other words, like the UNCITRAL Model Law Functional Equivalence approach, traditional tax laws and requirements are applied to eCommerce. However, "*the reality is . . . that the Internet will make the challenge [of adequately and effectively applying current domestic laws, double tax agreements and OECD rules and guidelines to an eCommerce tax issue] much more complicated and difficult.*"[36]

This 'challenge' is undoubtedly temporary as it is in the nature of tax to be infinitely adaptable. Taxation is an integral part of human history, past and present, and the virtual world is commerce's future. At the moment the internet and ameliorating technology facilitate much tax evasion, but when "*the best things in life are free . . . sooner or later the government will find a way to tax them*".[37]

7.3.2 *Privacy*

Privacy and information protection rules and regulations differ in diverse jurisdictions. However, with the Internet, there is an increasing need for standardised regulations relating to privacy because the virtual world is borderless and, in effect, jurisdictionless.

The EU has a very strict policy regarding privacy and information protection, whereas other countries, such as the USA, have adopted the self-regulatory approach towards privacy and information protection. That being said, if a country wishes to

---

[33]op cit UNCITRAL Model Law, http://www.uncitral.org/pdf/english/texts/electcom/05-89450_Ebook.pdf, p21.

[34]OECD *Tax Administration Aspects of Electronic Commerce: Responding to the Challenges and Opportunities* (2001), 4. Available at http://www.oecd.org/dataoecd/46/44/1923272.pdf [Accessed 30 May 2008].

[35]supra.

[36]op cit Lymer, Andrew & Hasseldine, John, *The International Taxation System,* USA, p72.

[37]Anonymous. Available at http://www.quotegarden.com/taxes.html [Accessed 8 May 2008].

transact commercially with an EU Member State, that country must comply with the EU's privacy laws and regulations. A latterly focus of interest is the protection of data within the virtual world. Protection of an individual's personal information is necessary as the "*processing [of] personal info[rmation] threatens [an] individual in [two] ways: [1] compilation and distribution of personal information creates a direct threat to the individual's right to be left alone without interference; [2] the acquisition and disclosure of false or misleading information may lead to an infringement of identity*".[38]

Several countries view privacy as a constitutional right which must be protected. Furthermore, privacy and protection of 'identity' should not be restricted to individuals alone. Companies, as juristic persons, also have privacy concerns. However, certain courts have recognised that this 'constitutional right' to privacy is not an absolute right and there can be exceptions.

Regardless of the controls utilised by diverse countries for privacy protection, that is, self-regulatory or by implementation of strict rules, privacy protection has become an increasing concern with the advent of the Internet era. As discussed earlier,[39] opponents to the Amazon tax[40] attempted to prevent the promulgation of the Amazon tax act alleging that it threatened privacy. Opponents contended that possible compliance checks pertaining to the collection of Internet sales tax could entail disclosure of sales records, giving government unrestricted access to detailed descriptions of eConsumers' purchases and personal information.

Threat of infringement of privacy within the domain of the virtual world is an explosive issue. If, for example, Microsoft, registered in Ireland, provided USA revenue authorities with all relevant records pertaining to USA on-line sales, such compliance to an audit would provoke furious debate in respect of Microsoft's failure to protect USA customers' personal data from a USA perspective, and Microsoft's alleged contravention of the strict privacy regulations of the EU. The Internet's borderless environment has made it increasingly imperative to adopt standardised definitions and regulations in all spheres of the law. Within the context of this paper, informed scrutiny of diverse perspectives of privacy laws is advocated as being essential to the successful imposition of taxing systems within the virtual world. The essence of the problem is not the tax itself but the means of successful imposition and implementation of the tax while yet respecting the axiom of privacy protection.

---

[38]Hofman, Julien eLaw 1, Topic 10: Data Privacy [Lecture slides] (2005) Department of Commercial Law, University of Cape Town.

[39]Refer to 6.1.7. Amazon.com, Part II of this paper [p55].

[40]Refer to discussion and explanation of the 'Amazon tax', which is not specific law in itself but rather a tax 'coined' as the 'Amazon tax', in 6.1.7., Chap. 6, Part II, pages 55–59 of this paper.

Bibliography

Primary Sources

Statutes

Green Paper on Electronic Commerce for South Africa, Coordinated and Compiled by the Department of Communications Republic of South Africa (November 2000).

New Zealand Electronic Transactions Act, No. 35 of 2002 (as amended).

OECD. 2005. *OECD model tax convention on income and on capital, condensed version – July 2005*. Paris: OECD Publishers.

UNCITRAL. 1999. *Model law on electronic commerce with guide to enactment of 1996*. New York: United Nations Publication. Available at http://www.uncitral.org/pdf/english/texts/electcom/05-89450_Ebook.pdf. Accessed 5 Oct 2011.

Secondary Sources

Anonymous. Available at http://www.quotegarden.com/taxes.html. Accessed 8 May 2008.

Farrell, Nick. 2009. *NASA puts ISPs to shame, Luna broadband pretty good*. The Inquirer. Available at http://www.theinquirer.net/inquirer/news/1529741/nasa-isps-shame. Accessed 6 July 2010.

Hargitai, Cecilia. 2001. *Classification of e-Commerce transactions of chapter III, value added taxation of electronic supply of services within the European Community*. Joint venture of the Jean Monnet Centre at NYU School of Law and the Academy of European Law at the European University Institute. Available at http://www.jeanmonnetprogram.org/papers/01/013301-03.html. Accessed 9 April 2008.

Hassam. *Possibility of internet service in the outer space*. Available at http://www.hubpages.com/hub/Possibility-Internet-Service-In-The-Outer-Space. Accessed 6 July 2010.

Hofman, Julien. 2005. *eLaw 1, Topic 10: Data privacy* [Lecture slides]. Department of Commercial Law, University of Cape Town.

Jean Monnet Center for International & Regional Economic Law & Justice, The, The NYU Institutes on the Park *Chapter III: Shortcomings of the present European VAT system with respect to electronic supplies, classification of e-Commerce transactions*. Available at http://centers.law.nyu.edu/jeanmonnet/papers/01/013301-03.html. Accessed 5 Oct 2011.

Kontos, Kosta BSc (CompSci) (UCT), MBA (UCT). Managing Director (MD) of Kontos Technologies.

Lymer, Andrew, and John Hasseldine. 2002. *The international taxation system*. New Jersey: Kluwer Academic Publishers.

Nolle, Thomas. Available at www.quotegarden.com.internet.html. Accessed 8 May 2008.

OECD. 2001. *Tax administration aspects of electronic commerce: Responding to the challenges and opportunities*. Available at http://www.oecd.org/dataoecd/46/44/1923272.pdf. Accessed 30 May 2008.

Pinto, Dale. 2003. *E-Commerce and source-based income taxation*. Amsterdam: IBFD Publications.

Rendahl, Pernilla. 2009. *Cross-border consumption taxation of digital supplies*. Amsterdam: IBFD.

Telecom Glossary 2K. 2002. *E-Commerce*. Available at http://www.its.bldroc.gov/projects/devglossary/_e-commerce.html. Accessed 26 June 2008.

Chapter 8
Is the Virtual World Real?

Abstract *"[To] get others to come into our way of thinking, we must go over to theirs"* (Hazlitt, William (1778–1830). "*English essayist and critic. From about 1812 he wrote many articles on diverse subjects for several periodicals, including the Edinburgh Review and the Morning Chronicle; his essays were collected in Table Talk (1821–2) and The Plain Speaker (1826)"*. **[op cit *The Oxford English Reference Dictionary, The (Second Edition) (1996, USA,* p647]**) (Hazlitt).

'Physical presence' within the virtual world is a primary point at issue specifically with regard to effective imposition and implementation of eTax on eCommerce. To 'be' in the Internet or to transact business in the virtual marketplace has made the virtual world commensurate with the real world. A common perception is that a person cannot be 'physically present' within the virtual world or in another jurisdiction per the Internet.

The Amazon Tax (Refer to discussion and explanation of the 'Amazon tax', which is not specific law in itself but rather a tax 'coined' as the 'Amazon tax', in 6.1.7., Chap. 6, Part II, pages 55–59 of this paper) states that "*a retailer such as Amazon holds a physical presence in the state because it derives sales through its affiliates who live there*" (Corbin, Kenneth *'Amazon Tax' Lands in New York*. InternetNews.com (April 10, 2008) Available at http://www.internetnews.com/ec-news/print.php/3740056 [Accessed 24/09/2014]). By qualifying 'physical presence', the Amazon Tax justifies imposition and collection of consumption taxes in eCommerce. The point at issue is that tax legislation apropos eCommerce should be cognizant of the credibility of 'physical presence' 'here' and 'there' being synchronically possible within the context of the virtual world of the Internet.

Technical terminology such as 'Telepresence' refers to the human perception of being present in a location other than that of one's physical body by means of teleoperating systems. Recognition of 'physical presence' in the Internet would constitute a predominant factor in determining tax liability of eRetailers such as Amazon, regardless of 'customer base' or the "*use of in-state affiliate to promote sales*" (Literature on the matter is limited as the 'Amazon Tax' is a fairly new tax law. As reported in The New York Times, 7th May 2010: "*. . . New York has taken matters into its own hands. The Legislature passed a smart law in 2008, requiring online retailers to collect sales taxes from New York customers. Amazon challenged the law in court, lost and appealed. The appeals court is expected to rule soon. If successful, the New York law could serve as a model for other*

A.M. Bardopoulos, *eCommerce and the Effects of Technology on Taxation*,
Law, Governance and Technology Series 22, DOI 10.1007/978-3-319-15449-7_8

states . . . " **[Editorial, Amazon and Sales Tax (May 7, 2009). The New York Times. Available at** http://www.nytimes.com/2010/05/07/opinion/07fri3.html?_r=1&ref=amazon_inc&pagewanted=print **[Accessed 7 July 2010]]**). By adopting a common broad view of 'physical presence' in the virtual world, a more flexible application of real world laws in the virtual world would be possible especially in the case of the prevalent Functional Equivalence Approach.

8.1 The Virtual World Versus The Physical World

The proposition in question is whether rules applying to the 'physical world' can be effectively applied to and imposed upon the 'virtual world'. A comparative analysis should be made of how 'physical world' rules applying to the physical world differ when applied to eCommerce transactions on account of the basic principles and concepts intrinsic to the 'virtual world'. For example, for an individual in the 'physical world' to 'physically render' a service to a client in a foreign country, the individual would have to physically travel to that foreign country, whereas within the 'virtual world' the internet spans time and space globally and an individual is capable of travelling to a client's computer electronically. In effect, while an individual is physically sitting in, say, Australia, he is capable of 'physically' working on another's network, and even computer in, say Denmark, as if he were in fact sitting in front of that client's computer in that other country. Can it be said that the individual is actually 'physically rendering' services in that other country with the aid of 'virtual transportation'?

Scrutiny and debate of the above comparative analysis is a prerequisite for a discussion on effective imposition and implementation of tax, especially VAT in a 'virtual world' and, furthermore, precipitates the deliberation of the issue in question, specifically, whether VAT principles are sufficiently flexible that they may be effectively applied to the virtual world despite the differences between the physical and virtual worlds. Essential to this issue in question is whether 'physical presence' can exist within the virtual world. Indefatigable technological amelioration has escalated the problem as to whether 'physical world' laws can be applied within the 'virtual world'. As such, 'physical presence' within the 'virtual world' is a primary focus of this paper as this issue is specifically essential to the broader issue in question which is the effective imposition and implementation of eTax on eCommerce. Furthermore, as this paper is primarily concerned with applying taxing laws to the 'virtual world', the analysis below will concentrate essentially on application of tax within the virtual marketplace.

The "*fundamental nature of*. . . **reality and existence**"[1] [emphasis added] is especially pertinent to the 'virtual world' and its impact on society, law, governance

[1] 'Philosophy' as defined in the Oxford Dictionary of English, Third Edition (2010) Oxford University Press, UK.

and tax. The 'virtual world' has become actuality and this Chapter discusses the meaning of "*reality and existence*" in respect of the Internet because of its pertinence to law, governance and tax. It may be argued that this Chapter is too 'philosophical' in nature in respect of VAT and eCommerce and that all discussion devolves into the mere 'theoretical', which is "*concerned with or involving the theory of a subject or area of study rather than its practical application*".[2] However, the significance of the issue of the 'virtual world' is supported by other published papers and is, furthermore, powered by a universally evolving attitude by Internet users, especially in respect of the younger generations, towards the 'virtual world'. This point at issue is addressed by Jennifer Z. Gong[3] in her paper 'Defining and Addressing Virtual Property in International Treaties', "*[t]he boundary lines of physical and online worlds blur as children growing up with new technologies no longer, if they ever did, distinguish between virtual property and 'real property*'".[4] The Y-Generation, and subsequent generations, can relate to Gong's comment regarding the "blurred" lines in respect of the physical and virtual world. The concept of 'blurred' lines is a point at issue which has legal ramifications. The focus of this Chapter is not a study of 'reality and existence' as an academic discipline. The point in question is, on the contrary, the issues of 'reality and existence', practicality and effective applicability in respect of the Internet, law, governance and tax within the virtual world, rather than "*the study of the theoretical basis of a particular branch of knowledge or experience*".[5]

The virtual world has not only changed the manner in which business is conducted but has had a profound impact upon the traditional conception of real as is implied by the real world. To 'be in the Internet', or to transact business in the virtual marketplace has made the virtual world commensurate with the real world. Within the recent past we have witnessed the birth of a virtual community and way of life called 'Second Life'.[6] In 'Second Life' a person can assume an identity, have a job and buy a house. 'Second Life' has its own currency and has established exchange rates with 'real world' currencies. Technological amelioration has blurred distinction between 'real' and 'virtual'.

Defining 'physical presence' is a principal issue in the debate as to whether consumption tax should be imposed on eCommerce, and if imposed should it be the obligation of the merchant to collect consumption tax (either Sales Tax or

---

[2]Op cit 'Philosophy' as defined in the Oxford Dictionary of English, Third Edition (2010), p1335.

[3]Per the description provided in Jennifer Z. Gong's paper, Defining and Addressing Virtual Property in International Treaties: "J.*D., Boston University School of Law,* 2011*; A.B. cum laude Human Evolutionary Biology and Archaeology, Harvard University, 2007*". Available at https://www.bu.edu/law/central/jd/organizations/journals/scitech/volume171/documents/Gong_Web.pdf [Accessed 13/10/2014].

[4]Supra, Gong, *Defining and Addressing Virtual Property in International Treaties*, https://www.bu.edu/law/central/jd/organizations/journals/scitech/volume171/documents/Gong_Web.pdf.

[5]Op cit Oxford Dictionary of English, 3rd Edition, 1335.

[6]Refer to *6.1.6. Amazon.com, 'Second Life'*, Part II of this paper [p54].

VAT) on behalf of revenue authorities? A common perception is that a person cannot be 'physically present' within the virtual world or in another jurisdiction per the Internet. The Amazon Tax[7] states that "*a retailer such as Amazon holds a physical presence in the state because it derives sales through its affiliates who live there*".[8] By qualifying 'physical presence', the Amazon Tax justifies imposition and collection of consumption taxes in eCommerce, and this rule of the Amazon Tax law may very well be adopted by other jurisdictions in order to prevent the loss of consumption taxes.[9]

A significant issue pertaining to imposition and implementation of eTax is that if an eMerchant is not obligated to impose and collect consumption tax, then theoretically the eConsumer is obligated to pay the consumption tax over to the revenue authorities. However, not only is it doubtful whether an 18 year old downloading David Guetta's latest song from iTunes for $3.00 will visit the local revenue authority office to pay, say, the 16 % consumption tax, but it is equally unlikely that the average revenue authority would know how to deal with such a situation! Realistically, the cost of enforcing collection of consumption taxes directly from the eConsumer may not be worth the revenue raised. However, if revenue authorities were able to enforce collection of consumption tax by eMerchants, implementation would be feasible from a cost perspective.

'Physical presence' is commonly perceived to mean a geographical location. In terms of this perception it is not possible to be 'physically present' within the virtual world. However, careful scrutiny of the words 'physical', 'virtual' and 'location' with regard to connotation and pertinency makes the restriction of 'physical presence' to 'geographical location' debatable.

The Oxford Dictionary,[10] defines 'physical' as "*of or pertaining to material nature; pertaining to or connected with matter*",[11] 'virtual' as "*that is so in essence or effect although not formally or actually*"[12]; and 'presence' as "*the fact or condition of being present; the state of being before, in front of, or in the same place with a person or thing; being there*".[13]

The conventional perception is that 'presence here' and 'presence there' at the same time is not possible. Zhao postulates that 'being there' is "*a metaphor, referring to presence in an environment other than where one's body is. In the literal sense of the word, therefore, 'being there' is impossible because nobody can be here*

[7]Refer to discussion and explanation of the 'Amazon tax', which is not specific law in itself but rather a tax 'coined' as the 'Amazon tax', in 6.1.7., Chap. 6, Part II, pages 55–59 of this paper.

[8]Corbin, http://www.internetnews.com/ec-news/print.php/3740056

[9]Subsequent to the completion of this paper Amazon Tax has been adopted by other jurisdictions – Footnotes 27–30 of this paper [p56–58].

[10]The Shorter Oxford English Dictionary on Historical Principles (1986). ("Oxford Dictionary on Historical Principles") University Printing House, Oxford. Great Britain.

[11]idem p1575.

[12]idem p2480.

[13]idem p1659.

and there at the same time. To get there from here, one needs to relocate one's body in space and time through locomotion, yet as soon as one gets there, what was once here will become there. Thus, at any given point in time, a person can only be 'here' ... ".[14] Zhao argues that 'presence' is subject to time and space which are absolute. Minkowski,[15] however, argues that space and time are relative, "*henceforth space by itself, and time by itself, are doomed to fade away into mere shadows, and only a kind of union between the two will preserve an independent reality*".[16] The relativity of time and space is emphasized by Geroch's[17] hypothesis that "*the space – time interval ... determines whether or not a pair of events can be causally connected, that is, whether a signal not exceeding the speed of light can be sent from the (space-time) location of one event to another – an 'invariant' fact independent of ones' state of motion*".[18] 'Presence here' and 'presence there' has been made possible by way of the Internet and the unprecedented phenomenon of cyber space. Within the virtual world one has never to reach 'there' in order for 'there' to become 'here', one can be 'here' and 'there' at the same time without the need "*to relocate one's body in space and time through locomotion*".[19] Through the medium of the virtual world we have a "*kind of union between*" time and space making 'presence here' and 'presence there' synchronically possible. The point at issue is that 'physical presence here' and 'physical presence there' within the context of the virtual world is synchronically possible. Therefore, tax legislation with regard to eCommerce should be cognizant of the credibility of 'physical presence' in the virtual world of the internet.

The issue of 'physical presence' has been vigorously debated consequent to technological amelioration which has enabled one to transact as a physical presence 'there' while being physically present 'here'. Loomis (1992) offers an interesting analysis of this phenomenon:

> *The perceptual world created by our senses and the nervous system is so functional a representation of the physical world that most people live out their lives without ever suspecting that contact with the physical world is mediated; moreover, the functionality*

---

[14]Zhao, Shanyang *"Being there" and the Role Presence Technology*. Available at http://www.neurovr.org/emerging/book4/4_09SYZHAO.pdf [Accessed 10 July 2010].

[15]*The Oxford Companion to Philosophy* ("*Oxford Companion to Philosophy*"). (1995). Oxford University Press, New York, USA. p843.

[16]supra.

[17]supra.

[18]supra.

[19]Op cit Zhao, *"Being there" and the Role Presence Technology*, http://www.neurovr.org/emerging/book4/4_09SYZHAO.pdf.

of perception impedes many reflective individuals from appreciate[ing] the insights about perception that derive from philosophical inquiry. Oddly enough, the newly developing technology of teleoperator and virtual displays is having the unexpected effect of promoting such insight, for the impression of being in a remote or simulated environment experienced by the user of such systems can be so compelling as to force a user to question the assumption that the physical and perceptual world are one and the same.[20]

Defining 'presence', and more importantly 'physical presence', has become increasingly significant with the rapid amending of technology and the creation of virtual environments. Diverse terminology is used to refer to presence in the Internet, such as *inter alia*, telepresence and virtual presence. Telepresence, a term coined in 1980 by Marvin Minsky,[21] refers to the human perception of being present in a location other than that of one's physical body by means of teleoperating systems. While Telepresence, conceptually similar to virtual presence, was conceived as a result of the teleoperating systems, 'virtual presence' was coined

[20]Loomis, J.M. *Distal attribution and presence. Presence*, (1992), cited in Biocca, Fran *The Cyborg's Dilemma: Progressive Embodiment in Virtual Environments* (1997). Available at http://jcmc.indiana.edu/vol3/issue2/biocca2.html [Accessed 10 July 2010].

[21]Referenced in Lee, Kwan Min *Presence, Explicated* (2004). Available at http://www.fineminddesign.com/site/media/Readings/Week10/Lee(2004)_PresenceExplicated_CT.pdf [Accessed 10 July 2010].

The Massachusetts Institute of Technology ("MIT") provides the following biography on Marvin Minsky:

Marvin Minsky has made many contributions to AI, cognitive psychology, mathematics, computational linguistics, robotics, and optics. In recent years he has worked chiefly on imparting to machines the human capacity for commonsense reasoning. His conception of human intellectual structure and function is presented in two books: The Emotion Machine and The Society of Mind (which is also the title of the course he teaches at MIT).

He received the BA and PhD in mathematics at Harvard (1950) and Princeton (1954). In 1951 he built the SNARC, the first neural network simulator. His other inventions include mechanical arms, hands and other robotic devices, the Confocal Scanning Microscope, the "Muse" synthesizer for musical variations (with E. Fredkin), and one of the first LOGO "turtles&quot". A member of the NAS, NAE and Argentine NAS, he has received the ACM Turing Award, the MIT Killian Award, the Japan Prize, the IJCAI Research Excellence Award, the Rank Prize and the Robert Wood Prize for Optoelectronics, and the Benjamin Franklin Medal.

[Available at http://web.media.mit.edu/~minsky/ [Accessed 18 September 2010].

in 1992 by Sheridan[22] to differentiate between the two technologies (i.e. telephones and computers).[23]

In "Presence Explicated" Kwan Min Lee[24] ("Lee") examines the diverse definitions of 'presence' analysed by various scholars. Lee has formulated a proposed common definition:

> *There have been various attempts to explicate the concept of presence. For example, Steuer (1992) defined it as 'the extent to which one feels present in the mediated environment, rather than in the immediate physical environment' (p. 76). Similarly, Witmer and Singer (1998) referred to it as 'the subjective experience of being in one place or environment, even when one is physically situated in another' (p. 225). Based on the Heideggerian/Gibsonian view of the ontology of being, Zahorik and Jenison (1998) proposed that 'presence is tantamount to successfully supported action in the environment'.... Biocca (1997) traced the origin of the term and concluded that presence has been generalised to the illusion of 'being there' whether or not 'there' exists in physical space. He proposed that this sense of presence oscillates around physical..., virtual..., or imaginal... environments.*
>
> *...Lombard...defined presence as 'the perceptual illusion of nonmediation' (Lombard & Ditton, 1997...p.77). The term 'perceptual' means that the feelings of presence 'involves*

---

[22]Referenced in *Lee*, http://web.mit.edu/slava/space/interview/interview-sheridan.htm.

MIT, in relation to an interview conducted by Slava Gerovitch (9 April 2003), provides the following brief biography of Thomas B. Sheridan:

> *Thomas B. Sheridan received his B.S. in Mechanical Engineering in 1951 from Purdue University, M.S. in Engineering in 1954 from the University of California at Los Angeles, and Sc.D. in 1959 from MIT. He joined MIT faculty in 1959. Since 1984, he has been Professor of Engineering and Applied Psychology; since 1993, Professor of Aeronautics and Astronautics. Dr. Sheridan is Former president, IEEE Systems, Man and Cybernetics Society; Former president, Human Factors Society; Former chair, Human Factors Committee, National Research Council; Former chair, IVHS Safety and Human Factors Committee; Senior Editor, Presence (MIT Press journal). He has served on a variety of government and non-government advisory committees. He is the author of over 200 published papers and several books, including Man-machine Systems: Information, Control, and Decision Models of Human Performance, MIT Press, 1974 (with William R. Ferrell); Monitoring Behavior and Supervisory Control, Plenum Press, 1976 (edited, with Gunnar Johannsen); Telerobotics, Automation, and Human Supervisory Control (MIT Press, 1992); Perspectives on the Human Controller, Erlbaum, 1997 (edited, with Anton VanLunteren); and Humans and Automation: System Design and Research Issues (J. Wiley, 2002). His research interests include human factors in automation with respect to aviation, highway and rail systems, telerobotics, process control, health care, humanitarian demining, computer-interaction, virtual environments.*

[23]Idem, p29. Available at http://www.fineminddesign.com/site/media/Readings/Week10/Lee(2004)_PresenceExplicated_CT.pdf [Accessed 10 July 2010].

[24]*"Kwan Min Lee (PhD, Stanford University) is an [assistant] professor in the Annenberg School for Communication, University of Southern California. An earlier version of... [the paper, 'Presence, Explicated'] was presented at the annual conference of the International Communication Association (ICA) in May, 2003. This work was supported in part by a grant from KISDI (Korea Information Strategy Development Institute)."*

From the note on the author, http://www.fineminddesign.com/site/media/Readings/Week10/Lee(2004)_PresenceExplicated_CT.pdf, p48.

continuous (real time) responses of the human sensory, cognitive, and affective processing systems to objects and entities in a person's environment' ... By illusion of nonmediation, they refer to a phenomenon in which 'a person fails to perceive or acknowledge the existence of a medium in his or her communication environment and responds as he or she would if the medium were not there' ...

... presence can be further defined as 'a psychological state in which virtual (... artificial) objects are experienced as actual objects in either sensory or nonsensory ways.'[25] [Emphasis added]

However, for the purposes of this paper, the point at issue is the integral import of 'physical presence'. Lee's paper highlights the definitions relating to 'physical presence' as follows:

Biocca (1997) identified three types of presence: physical, social, and self presence. Physical presence refers to the sense of being physically located in a virtual environment. He proposed that at any given moment of technology use, users feel being present in any one of the following environments – physical environment, virtual environment, or in the imaginal environment. By defining physical presence as a subjective feeling of being in a virtual environment, Biocca emphasized the feeling of transportation into a virtual environment from the real physical environment as an integral part of physical presence ...

... Following Biocca (1997), ... [Lombard and Ditton (1997)] define physical presence as the sense of being physically located in a virtual world... Schloerb (1995) [on the other hand] emphasized the objective validity of experience itself by differentiating two types of telepresence: subjective vs. objective. Subjective ... is defined as users' feeling of presence in a remote environment...he operationally defined subjective presence as the probability of users' responding that they are physically located in a virtual environment when they are actually not. Objective ... refers to the ability ... to successfully manipulate a remote environment, which can be objectively confirmed by actual changes in the remote environment.[26] [Emphasis added]

Lee examines diverse scholastic definitions of 'physical presence'. Although definitions may vary they hold the common postulation that 'physical presence' is possible in the virtual world. Lee confers with scholastic opinion that 'physical presence' can be achieved and can exist within the virtual world. Lee postulates the following definition of 'physical presence':

Physical presence is defined as 'a psychological state in which virtual (para-authentic or artificial) physical objects are experienced as actual physical objects in either sensory or non-sensory ways". In other words, physical presence occurs when technology users do not notice either the para-authentic nature of mediated objects (or environments) or the artificial nature of simulated objects (or environments). Unlike the definition of telepresence, the current definition does not require the feeling of self-existence inside a virtual world (or the feeling of remote location) as a necessary condition. Therefore, no sense of transportation is required for physical presence to occur.[27] [Emphasis added]

[25]op cit, *Lee,* http://www.fineminddesign.com/site/media/Readings/Week10/Lee(2004)_PresenceExplicated_CT.pdf, p30–32 & 37.

[26]idem, p42–43.

[27]idem, p45.

In Lee's interpretation of 'physical presence' Lee distinguishes between 'objective physical presence' and 'subjective physical presence'.

'Objective' is defined philosophically as "*possessing the character of a real object existing independently of the knowing mind in contrast to 'subjective'*".[28] 'Objective presence' is the "*object or perception of thought, as distinct from the perceiving or thinking subject; hence, that is, or is regarded as, a 'thing' external to the mind; real*".[29] Distinct from 'objective', 'subjective' relates to "*the thinking subject; proceeding from or taking place within the subject; having its source in the mind; (in the widest sense) belonging to the conscious life*".[30] 'Objective' is also defined as "*pertaining or considered in relation to its object; constituting, or belonging to, an object of action, thought or feeling, 'material', as opposed to 'subjective'...; of or pertaining to the object or end as the cause or action*".[31]

It may be argued, therefore, that in the promulgation of the Amazon Tax, elements of both 'objective' and 'subjective' 'physical presence' have been taken into account. However, the literature on 'physical presence' in the internet and per the internet with regard to the Amazon Tax law is limited.[32] Therefore, whether the Amazon Tax act took subjective and/or objective 'physical presence' in the internet into account, or whether the Amazon Tax relied essentially on the indisputable fact of a "*customer base*" and/or the "*use of in-state affiliates to promote sales*"[33] is a

---

[28]Dictionary of Philosophy (1976) Littlefield, Adams & Co., USA. p217.

[29]Op cit, Oxford Dictionary on Historical Principles, 1986, p1426.

[30]idem p2167.

[31]idem p1426.

[32]Literature on the matter is limited as the 'Amazon Tax' is a fairly new tax law. As reported in The New York Times, 7th May 2010: "*...New York has taken matters into its own hands. The Legislature passed a smart law in 2008, requiring online retailers to collect sales taxes from New York customers. Amazon challenged the law in court, lost and appealed. The appeals court is expected to rule soon. If successful, the New York law could serve as a model for other states...*".

[Editorial, Amazon and Sales Tax (May 7, 2009). The New York Times. Available at http://www.nytimes.com/2010/05/07/opinion/07fri3.html?_r=1&ref=amazon_inc&pagewanted=print **[Accessed 7 July 2010]]**.

[33]Editorial. Yes, You Owe That Tax (November 27, 2009). The New York Times:

> *New York's Legislature made the right decision in 2008 when it passed a law requiring Amazon.com and other Internet retailers to collect taxes on sales to New York customers. Amazon challenged the law in a lower court, and lost in January. A New York appeals court is expected to rule soon...*
>
> *... The deciding factor is whether the retailer has a physical presence in the state where the customer is located. If so, the retailer is obligated to collect the tax. If not, not.*
>
> *...Amazon and others collect the tax only in states where they have headquarters or some other physical presence.... It turns out that Amazon and other retailers make wide use of in-state affiliates to promote sales. These are generally local businesses and nonprofit organisations that place links on their Web sites to the retailers' sites and receive a commission when someone clicks through. New York, citing Supreme Court cases from 1960 and 1987, holds that the affiliate relationship is on a par with a physical presence in the state, obligating the retailer to collect the sales taxes.*

disputed point. However, recognition of 'physical presence' in the internet would constitute a predominant factor in determining tax liability of eRetailers such as Amazon, regardless of "*customer base*" or the "*use of in-state affiliates to promote sales*".[34] Therefore, it may be argued that while 'subjective' physical *presence exists in the Internet as "proceeding from . . . the subject",*[35] *'objective'* physical presence exists in the Internet as "*constituting . . . an object of action . . . pertaining to the object or end as the cause or action*".[36] 'Objective physical presence' exists in the virtual world in respect of virtual market place trading, as *"cause or action*", the effects of which can be materially measured in the real world.

The point at issue is understanding the concept of 'physical' presence in a 'virtual world' and redefining the concept of 'virtual' and 'physical' within the realm of technology. The legal ramifications of this issue are significant and should be neither ignored nor neglected. While Gong's paper primarily addresses 'virtual property in international treaties' it, nevertheless, provides useful insight into legal aspects of 'virtual presence', the 'virtual world' and our concept of 'physical presence'. Gong argues that *"[t]he online world has matured beyond proxy into reality, and the laws under which it operates must recognize the intangible, but valid interests that have emerged*".[37] This issue is further addressed in Jessica M. Natale's paper, *Exploring Virtual Legal Presence: The Present and the Promise*, wherein she holds that "*the crux in the presence issue lies in the public's opinion about virtual presence and its acceptability in being tantamount to physical presence at meetings*".[38] Gong contends that:

> *[C]loud computing and increasing ease of connectivity mean that property is no longer tethered to a physical location. Because an acre of land in Second Life . . . can be accessed whether the user is in Mozambique or Monaco, the monetary, social and criminal exchanges that occur in [Second Life] are judged as part of the 'international' sphere of exchanges of the Internet. Current international treaties tether floating concepts like virtual property and Internet crime to the nations in which the servers reside, even though the authors, perpetrators, and victims are not the same nationality as the administrators.*[39]

Available at http://www.nytimes.com/2009/11/27/opinion/27fri1.html?ref=sales_tax&pagewanted=print [Accessed 7 July 2010].

[34]Loc cit footnote 32 of this paper [p79].

[35]op cit, Oxford Dictionary on Historical Principles, 1986, p2167.

[36]idem p1426.

[37]op cit, Gong, *Defining and Addressing Virtual Property in International Treaties,* https://www.bu.edu/law/central/jd/organizations/journals/scitech/volume171/documents/Gong_Web.pdf

[38]Natale, Jessica M *Exploring Virtual Presence: The Present and the Promise* Journal of High Technology Law, Suffolk University, Law School, Volume I Number 1 (2002), p158. Available at https://www.suffolk.edu/documents/jhtl_publications/JNATALEV1N1N.pdf [Accessed 13/10/2014]

[39]op cit, Gong, *Defining and Addressing Virtual Property in International Treaties,* https://www.bu.edu/law/central/jd/organizations/journals/scitech/volume171/documents/Gong_Web.pdf

The need to acknowledge the actuality of the virtual world and its impact on society and law should be recognised by all legal academics. ‘Virtual presence’ has impacted law by reconceptualising the manner in which ‘virtual presence’, or ‘physical presence’ within a virtual world, may be defined and applied. Gong’s paper refers to legal issues emanating from this point at issue. This same point at issue has impacted effective application of taxation in respect of virtual world transactions. It is an issue which is difficult to address from a legal perspective due to the open, borderless nature of the virtual world and the reluctance of jurisdictions to relinquish jurisdictional and sovereign rights in the application of local laws,[40] despite the ineffectuality of such ‘local’ laws within the realm of the ‘virtual world’.

There does not appear to be any concise legal definition for ‘virtual presence’, and to date there is no clearly stated legal definition of ‘virtual presence’ in legal dictionaries such as the Oxford Law Dictionary and the Canadian Law Dictionary.[41] Within the tax community, the ordinary meaning of such words, how such words and terms are interpreted by society and how they may have been interpreted in courts of law may be applied for legal purposes. However, the definition and application of ‘virtual presence’ or ‘physical presence’ within a virtual world may differ from country to country, because there are no concise global legal definitions of these terms. Similarly, the concept of “being there” is also a crucial point at issue in respect of legal definition and application, as has been emphasized by Natale in her conclusion:

> *Most states are addressing the issue of virtual presence . . . The future will reveal a better idea of ‘presence’ albeit be virtual or physical. Indeed someday ‘being there’ could be established by virtue of someone’s computer being turned on. When it comes to virtual presence, it should be thought of as an enhancement rather than a replacement of physical presence. The possibilities of what virtual presence could bring society are endless, as long as society has the courage to be virtually present for the future.*[42]

It may be argued that the obstacle to effective application of tax laws and effective application of general legal concepts, treaties and laws emanates from the dilemma of interpreting ‘virtual presence’ and ‘physical presence in a virtual world’. “Existence” within the virtual world has become, albeit not, as of yet, acknowledged by all, an actuality. The point at issue is that for effective application of general law principles, concepts, terms and provisions in respect of a limitless borderless world, acknowledgment of virtual presence and the dissolution of independent sovereign application of laws pertaining to virtual presence are essential.

---

[40]Supra Gong, *Defining and Addressing Virtual Property in International Treaties,* https://www.bu.edu/law/central/jd/organizations/journals/scitech/volume171/documents/Gong_Web.pdf, regarding the sovereignty of nations.

[41]Not ever published legal dictionary has been researched in respect of ‘virtual presence’, therefore conclusive comment cannot be made as to whether or not ‘virtual presence’ has been formally legally defined.

[42]op cit, *Exploring Virtual Presence: The Present and the Promise,* https://www.suffolk.edu/documents/jhtl_publications/JNATALEV1N1N.pdf, p178.

8.2 Conclusion

Within the context of eCommerce, to impute a *parti pris* definition to 'physical presence' would prejudice the issue of 'physical presence' in the Internet for the purposes of determining taxing rights, imposition of consumption tax as well as enforcing obligation to collect consumption taxes on behalf of revenue authorities. A narrow conception of 'physical presence' within the virtual world will induce an inflexible taxing system. It is essential that any taxing system adopted to be imposed within the virtual world should have the flexibility to be adapted to unpredictable taxing issues precipitated by technological amelioration. Therefore, educated cognizance of technology terms, definitions and concepts is essential. Attempting to enforce a narrow view of tax principles on technology is proving to be increasingly difficult, especially as traditional taxing precepts have fallen victim to the proverbial generation gap and as such are not synchronous with contemporary technological concepts of the Y-Generation, particularly with regard to the concept of 'physical presence' in the internet.

New York State legislators have set a precedent which may be adopted internationally whereby a broad view of the definition of 'physical presence' is encouraged and applied. Implementation of the Amazon Tax does have unresolved controversial ramifications, such as the issues of privacy. However, the significance of the Amazon Tax is that it adopts a broader view of 'physical presence' than that previously applied against the "*metaphorical anticipation of*" and in "*preparation for*"[43]the challenge of eCommerce and technological amelioration. States which include a 'place of supply' rule with regard to the imposition of consumption tax, or require an eMerchant to be 'physically present' within that jurisdiction in order to be obligated to collect consumption taxes, do not clarify whether the 'physical presence' is subjective or objective. It is not that the legislation does not adopt a broad view of 'physical presence', but that it does not define the type of 'physical presence' recognised by legislation. As such, the definition of 'physical presence' could be interpreted as either 'subjective' or 'objective' depending upon the circumstances of each case.

However, it would appear that some states do not currently have occasion to adopt a broad view of 'physical presence' deeming that provisions have been promulgated to overcome legislative complications preceding from eCommerce. For example, the NZ GST Act[44] includes provisions such as "*telecommunications services are treated as being supplied in New Zealand if the supplier is a non-resident, physically in New Zealand, initiates the supply from a telecommunications supplier, whether or not the person initiates the supply on behalf of another person*",[45] and "*if a telecommunications supplier cannot apply section 8(6) [that is, the first quoted NZ*

[43]op cit, *Oxford English Reference Dictionary*, 1996, p23.

[44]NZ Goods and Services Tax Act 1985 (as amended) (NZ GST Act).

[45]Section 8(6) of the NZ GST Act 1985 (as amended).

GST Act section] because it is impractical for the supplier to determine the physical location of a person due to the type of service or to the class of customer to which the person belongs, the supplier must treat a supply of telecommunications services as being supplied in New Zealand if the person's address for receiving invoices from the supplier is in New Zealand".[46]

However, just as it has become increasingly important to standardise the definition of 'presence' within the communications industry, it is also important to recognise a common interpretation of 'physical presence' within the virtual marketplace for tax purposes. The virtual marketplace has resulted in an exponential increase in international trade and, to all intents and purposes, has become a jurisdiction in its own right – a separate and independent jurisdiction upon which all participating 'geographical' jurisdictions wish to impose taxes and, more importantly, effectively collect taxes. Thus, a unified and flexible taxing system would not only prevent double, and even possibly multiple, taxation of eConsumers and eMerchants, but also prevent the substantial loss of taxes belonging to each rightful jurisdiction.

By adopting a common broad view of 'physical presence' in the virtual world, a more flexible application of real world laws in the virtual world will be possible, especially in the case of the prevalent Functional Equivalence Approach. Furthermore, such a stance may enable the Functional Equivalence Approach to maintain ascendancy over possible future technological advances such as space ISPs.

Tax authorities targeting the virtual tax mine of wealth may gratify their predilection by espousing the Y-Generations' philosophy of technology and their concept of being 'physically present' in the Internet, which is, furthermore, supported by technology academics as discussed earlier.[47] Tax authorities should seize the advantage of conceding to Hazlitts'[48] axiom that *"[t]o get others to come into our way of thinking, we must go over to theirs; and it is necessary to follow, in order to lead*". [49]

[46]Section 8A(1) of the NZ GST Act 1985 (as amended).

[47]Refer to 8.1. The Virtual World versus The Physical World, Part II of this paper [p72].

[48]Hazlitt, William (1778–1830). "*English essayist and critic. From about 1812 he wrote many articles on diverse subjects for several periodicals, including the Edinburgh Review and the Morning Chronicle; his essays were collected in Table Talk (1821–2) and The Plain Speaker (1826)*". **[op cit *The Oxford English Reference Dictionary*, 1996, p647]**

[49]Shanahan, John M. (Ed). *The Most Brilliant Thoughts of All Times*; Hazlitt, William (1778–1830); Harper Collins, Inc.; New York, USA (1999). p275

Bibliography

Primary Sources

Statutes

New Zealand Goods and Services Tax Act, No. 141 of 1985 (as amended).

Secondary Sources

Corbin, Kenneth. 2008 April 10. *'Amazon Tax' lands in New York.* InternetNews.com. Available at http://www.internetnews.com/ec-news/print.php/3740056. Accessed 24 Sept 2014.

Dictionary of Philosophy. 1976. Littlefield, Adams & Co., USA.

Editorial. 2009 May 7. *Amazon and sales tax.* The New York Times. Available at http://www.nytimes.com/2010/05/07/opinion/07fri3.html?_r=1&ref=amazon_inc&pagewanted=print. Accessed 7 July 2010.

Editorial. 2009 November 27. *Yes, you owe that tax.* The New York Times. Available at http://www.nytimes.com/2009/11/27/opinion/27fri1.html?ref=sales_tax&pagewanted=print. Accessed 7 July 2010.

Gong, Jennifer Z. 2011, Winter. Defining and addressing virtual property in international treaties. *Boston University Journal of Science & Technology Law* 17(1): 101. Available at https://www.bu.edu/law/central/jd/organizations/journals/scitech/volume171/documents/Gong_Web.pdf. Accessed 13 Oct 2014.

Hazlitt, William (1778–1830). 1996. *The Oxford English reference dictionary*, 2nd ed. New York: Oxford University Press.

Lee, Kwan Min. 2004. *Presence, explicated.* Washington, DC: International Communication Association. Available at http://www.fineminddesign.com/site/media/Readings/Week10/Lee(2004)_PresenceExplicated_CT.pdf. Accessed 10 July 2010.

Loomis, J.M. 1997. *Distal attribution and presence. Presence.* (1992) from the paper prepared by Biocca, Fran *The Cyborg's Dilemma: Progressive embodiment in virtual environments*. Media Interface and Network Design (M.I.N.D.) Lab, Michigan State University. Available at http://jcmc.indiana.edu/vol3/issue2/biocca2.html. Accessed 10 July 2010.

Natale, Jessica M. 2002. Exploring virtual presence: The present and the promise. *Journal of High Technology Law, Suffolk University, Law School* I(1): 158. Available at https://www.suffolk.edu/documents/jhtl_publications/JNATALEV1N1N.pdf. Accessed 13 Oct 2014.

Oxford Dictionary of English, 3rd ed. 2010. Oxford University Press, UK.

Shanahan, John M. (ed). 1999. *The most brilliant thoughts of all times*, Hazlitt, William (1778–1830). New York: Harper Collins, Inc.

The Massachusetts Institute of Technology. 2003 April 9. *An interview conducted by Slava Gerovitch.* Available at http://web.mit.edu/slava/space/interview/interview-sheridan.htm. Accessed 18 Sept 2010.

The Massachusetts Institute of Technology. *Biography on Marvin Minsky.* Available at http://web.media.mit.edu/~minsky/. Accessed 18 Sept 2010.

The Oxford Companion to Philosophy. 1995. Oxford University Press, New York, USA.

The Oxford English Reference Dictionary, 2nd ed. 1996. New York: Oxford University Press.

The Shorter Oxford English Dictionary on Historical Principles. 1986. University Printing House, Oxford, Great Britain.

Zhao, Shanyang. 2003. *"Being there" and the role presence technology*, Chapter 9 of *Being there: Concepts, effects and measurement of user presence in synthetic environments*, G. Riva, F. Davide, W.A. IJsselsteijn, eds., Amsterdam: Ios Press. Available at http://www.neurovr.org/emerging/book4/4_09SYZHAO.pdf. Accessed 10 July 2010.

Part III
Defining 'Residence' for Taxation Purposes

Chapter 9
What Does 'Residence' Mean?

> *"To tax and to please, no more than to love and to be wise, is not given to men"* – Edmund Burke – On American Taxation. (Burke, Edmand (1729–97) *"Burke was a prolific writer on the issues of political emancipation and moderation . . . protesting against the harsh handling of the American colonies".*
> **[op cit *Oxford English Reference Dictionary* [Sec. Ed.], 1996, p195]**)

Abstract Traditional income tax is founded upon theoretical principles which directly obstruct adaptability and flexibility of income tax provisions in a 'virtual world', especially regarding 'residence', 'source' and 'permanent establishment'. The OECD solution was to determine the location of 'permanent establishment'. However, when 'load balancing' was introduced the OECD's recommendation became immediately redundant. Various domestic laws apply diverse methods to determine residence of an individual, inter alia, the 'physical presence test' and the 'ordinary resident' test. Where a DTA dual residence occurs a 'tie-breaker clause' is applied to resolve the issue.

Various 'tests' for, and definitions of, residence of a company exist internationally, inter alia, 'place of management', 'place of effective management', place of incorporation, place of residence of management. The USA applies place of incorporation as the residency test for corporations. However, 'place of effective management' is the preferred test implemented by the OECD within its Model Convention. The leading UK DeBeers (De Beers consolidated Mines Ltd v Howe (Surveyor of Taxes) (1906) AC455 [UK]) case established a precedent by applying the ruling that 'central management and control' "*ordinarily coincides with the place where the directors of the company exercise their power and authority*". (op cit OECD Taxation & eCommerce, France, p146) The Northern Australia Pastoral case (Northern Australia Pastoral Co Ltd v FCT (1946) 71 CLR 623 [Australia]), however, held that the residence of a company is located where actual business operations are carried on. The OECD MC Commentary has defined 'place of effective management' as "*the place where the key management and commercial decisions . . . are in substance made*" (op cit OECD MC (2005), France, p82). According to Vogel the place of management of an enterprise "*is where*

A.M. Bardopoulos, *eCommerce and the Effects of Technology on Taxation*,
Law, Governance and Technology Series 22, DOI 10.1007/978-3-319-15449-7_9

the managements' important policies are actually made"(op cit Vogel, Professor Dr Klaus, University of Munich, and Co-Authors Klaus *Vogel on Double Tax Conventions,* Netherlands, p183).

9.1 Introduction

One of the crucial considerations to be taken into account with regard to the imposition of income tax principles upon eCommerce, is the assessment as to whether income tax principles are flexible enough to be effectively imposed on eCommerce Transactions. Because traditional income tax is founded on theoretical principles, there may be too many criteria which directly obstruct adaptability and flexibility of income tax provisions in a 'virtual world' due to continuously ameliorating technology. As this paper is concerned primarily with the analysis and evaluation of VAT as the eTax solution, it is, therefore, imperative to examine certain inefficiencies of traditional income tax provisions within the eCommerce environment pertaining principally to 'residence' and 'source' provisions and principles within the income tax analysis.

Within the compass of the application of traditional tax laws in an international context, examination of double tax agreements and commentaries is a prerequisite. Technology poses various issues in regard to traditional tax concepts, for example, is it possible to be 'resident' in a 'virtual world' where the normal laws of physics do not exist? And if we attempt to apply 'source' rules as an alternative solution, the question begs as to whether such taxing principles are practicable. For example, one jurisdiction, in which contracting to a DTA exists, may not tax the business profits of an enterprise deemed to be a resident of another contracting jurisdiction unless the enterprise is conducting business through a 'permanent establishment' within the first contracting jurisdiction. However, determining the location of 'permanent establishment' is becoming increasingly difficult in an environment conducting business primarily through the means of technology. A board of directors dispersed across several jurisdictions, conducting board meetings via video conferencing and having no set or fixed physical location, constitutes a portion of impediments encountered when attempting to fit an eBusiness into the definition of 'permanent establishment' to determine a jurisdiction's taxing rights.

The OECD published a solution to such a problem whereby the physical location of the business' 'server' may be used to determine the location of the 'permanent establishment'. However, the OECD's recommendation of utilising the geographical location of a server to determine the location of 'permanent establishment' failed to presuppose possible technological advancements and the implications thereof. When 'load balancing' was introduced to the internet, for purposes of increasing internet speed and effectiveness, the OECD's recommendation, it may be argued, became immediately redundant and ineffective as the principle of 'load-balancing' utilises several servers, often located in several geographical locations for one transaction. While the OECD recognises the possibility of several servers being used by one ISP, it only addresses circumstances where one of the several servers is utilised for any given transaction and does not provide a solution for circumstances where several servers are utilised for any one transaction.

Thus, prior to examining the effectiveness or ineffectiveness of VAT within eCommerce, basic income tax principles should be examined in terms of 'residence', including 'permanent establishment', and 'source' principles as the core of income tax.

Jurisdictions generally impose income taxation in terms of conventional principles which are either 'residence', 'source', or a combination of both. Defining 'residence', and even 'source', within a growing virtual world commerce, based on existing concepts and laws may become increasingly difficult consequent to the possible inflexibility of such concepts preventing adaptive application congruent with technological advancements, that is, 'residence' and 'source' concepts and laws may be too rule based for a constantly changing environment. The possibility of developing income tax laws which may be effectively applied within the virtual world may in all probability require significant changes to the various existing domestic laws and, furthermore, the establishment of cohesive common international laws.

9.2 Traditional Definition and Approach to 'Residence'

Several definitions and tests are used internationally to determine 'residency'. 'Residence' in its ordinary meaning, and as defined by the Oxford Dictionary, means "*to have one's usual dwelling-place or abode; to reside; to establish oneself; to settle; the circumstances or fact of having one's permanent or usual abode in or at a certain place*".[1] However, the application of 'residence' for tax purposes may differ between jurisdictions; so much so that it is possible for two jurisdictions to classify one individual (or corporation) as being resident in each State. Under such circumstances, and assuming that a DTA exists between the two States, the DTA (as will be discussed later[2]) may be able to resolve which of the two States is the resident State.

Regardless of how the term 'residence' is applied in the various States which have adopted a 'residence basis' tax system, the principle behind adopting such a tax system appears to be the same. An RSA Commission report summarises the principle of the residence basis tax system as follows:

> *[R]esidents enjoy the protection of the State [in which they reside], and should therefore contribute to the cost of the government of the country in which they reside, even with tax on income earned [i.e. sourced] outside that State.*[3]

[1] op cit, *Shorter Oxford English Dictionary on Historical Principles,* p1806.

[2] Refer to 9.2.1. Traditional Definition and Approach to 'Residence', Individuals, Part III of this paper [p90]; 9.2.2. Traditional Definition and Approach to 'Residence', Persons other than a Natural Person, Part III of this paper [p92].

[3] Republic of South Africa, Fifth Interim Report of the Commission of Inquiry into certain Aspects of the Tax Structure of South Africa *Basing the South African Income Tax System on the Source*

Alternatively, the residence basis tax system may be "*viewed as a sacrifice owed to a country due to the higher moral value of community purposes over individual aims*".[4] This theory was referred to by Klaus Vogel[5] (Vogel) as the 'sacrifice theory'.

For the purpose of this paper various definitions of 'residence' as applied by different jurisdictions and international treaties will be examined. The USA Model Tax Convention, UN Model Tax Convention and OECD Model Tax Conventions define 'residence' respectively as follows[6]:

> USA MC – "*'resident of a Contracting State' means any person who, under the laws of that State, is liable to tax therein by reason of his domicile, residence, citizenship, place of management, place of incorporation, or any other criterion of a similar nature....*"
>
> UN MC – "*'resident of a Contracting State' means any person who, under the laws of that State, is liable to tax therein by reason of his domicile, residence, place of management or any other criterion of a similar nature.*"
>
> OECD MC – "*'resident of a Contracting State' means any person who, under the laws of that State, is liable to tax therein by reason of his domicile, residence, place of management or any other criterion of a similar nature. But this term does not include any person who is liable to tax in that State in respect only of income from sources in that State or capital situated therein.*" [Emphasis added]

The application of 'residence' in relation to an individual differs from that of a company and, as such, 'residence' in respect of individuals and companies will be examined separately.

9.2.1 Individuals

Various domestic laws apply diverse methods to determine residence of an individual. For example, the RSA applies two different methods referred to as the 'physical presence test' and the 'ordinarily resident' test. In terms of the former

---

or Residence Principle – Options and Recommendations (1997) p4. Also referred to as the KATZ Commission.

Available at http://www.polity.org.za/polity/govdocs/commissions/katz-5.html [Accessed 13 May 2008].

[4]op cit, Pinto, Dale *E-Commerce and Source-Based Income Taxation* (2003), Netherlands, p17,18.

[5]Klaus Vogel, per the Foundation for International Tax's bibliographic synopsis on its former Honorary President, "*was professor emeritus at the University of Munich. Prior to that date, he had been a professor at Erlangen-Nurembourg University (1964–66), Heidelberg (1966–77) and Munich (from 1977), where he retired as professor of public law and head of the Research Centre for German and International Tax Law. He was a member of the permanent scientific committee of the International Fiscal Association from 1974–1990 and a visiting professor at Harvard, Berkeley, Perugia and Vienna universities. Over the years, he ha[s] written about 15 books and 240 articles on constitutional, administrative and tax law. He was the principal author of the renowned book on* ***"Double Taxation Conventions".*** *Professor Vogel passed away in December 2007 in Germany*".

Foundation for International Taxation. Available at http://www.fitindia.org/chairmen_speakers.htm [Accessed 12 September 2010].

[6]'Resident' is defined in Article 4 of each respective OECD Model Tax Convention.

an individual will be classified as a resident of the RSA should his stay in the RSA exceed the number of days required to satisfy the 'physical presence test'; that is, the person is a resident because he is physically present in the RSA long enough to be classified as a resident. Alternatively, an individual may be 'resident' in the RSA in terms of the ordinarily residence test. Interpretation as to the meaning of 'ordinarily resident' varies internationally. Generally, the facts and circumstances of each case are examined to determine whether an individual is 'ordinarily resident'. 'Ordinarily resident' was defined by the RSA Courts in Cohen v CIR[7] as follows:

> *the country to which he would naturally as a matter of fact return from his wanderings, as contrasted with other lands it might be called his usual or principal residence and would be described more aptly than other countries as his real home.*

The Canadian Court case Thompson v Minister of National Revenue[8] defined 'ordinarily resident' as the place "*where in the settled routine of his life he regularly normally and customarily lives*" or "*at which he in mind and in fact settles into or maintains or centralises his ordinary mode of living with its accessories in social relations, interest and conveniences*".[9] 'Ordinarily resident' was defined in the English Court case Shah v Barnet London Borough Council and Other Appeals in 1983[10] as "*a person [who] must be habitually and normally resident [in a specific country], apart from temporary or occasional absences of long or short duration*".[11] The definition of 'ordinarily resident' was readdressed in the English Court case, Shepherd v Revenue and Customs Commissioners in 2006[12] in which several circumstances and points at issue were identified which must be considered when determining whether an individual satisfies being 'ordinarily resident' in a particular State: Points at issue and circumstances are summarised as follows:

- *The concepts of residence and ordinary residence ... [if not] defined in the legislation....should therefore be given their natural and ordinary meanings;*
- *The words 'residence' and 'to reside' mean 'to dwell permanently or for a considerable time, to have one's settled or usual abode, to live in or at a particular place';*
- *The concept of 'ordinary residence' requires more than mere residence; it connotes residence in a place with some degree of continuity; 'ordinary' means normal and part of everyday life or a regular, habitual mode of life in a particular place which has persisted despite temporary absences and which is voluntary and has a degree of settled purpose;*
- *The question whether a person is or is not resident in ... [a State] is a question of fact;*
- *....The duration of an individual's presence in ... [a State] and the regularity and the frequency of visits are facts to be taken into account; also birth; family and business ties; the nature and the connections with ... [a] country may all be relevant;*

---

[7]Cohen v CIR 13 SATC 362 (1946) [RSA] at 371. Alternatively, Olivier, Lynette and Honiball, Michael *International Tax, SA Perspective – 2008,* South Africa, p61.

[8]Thompson v Minister of Naitonal Revenue (1946) 2 DTC 812 (SCC) [Canada].

[9]op cit Olivier and Honiball, p61.

[10]Shah v Barnet Borough Councils (1983) 1 All ER 226 (HL) 234b-c [UK].

[11]idem Olivier and Honiball, p61.

[12]Shepherd v Revenue and Customs Commissioners [2006] STC 1821 [UK].

- *The reduced presence in . . . [a State] of a person whose absences are caused by his employment and so are temporary absences does not necessarily mean that the person is not residing in . . . [that State];*
- *The fact that an individual has a home elsewhere is of no consequence; a person may reside in two places....;*
- *A difference exists between the case where . . . [a State] subject has established a residence in . . . [that State] and then absences from it and the case where a person has never had a residence in . . . [that State] at all;*
- *If there is evidence that a move abroad is a distinct break, this could be a relevant factor in treating an individual as non-resident; . . .* [13] [Emphasis Added]

While the above Court cases evince a general affinity in the determination of 'ordinarily resident', the application of the facts and circumstances of each case may, nevertheless, result in an individual being classified as 'ordinarily resident' in, say, both Canada and the United Kingdom. The circumstances of the case may satisfy the definition of 'ordinarily resident' in both countries because it is the application of the facts that determines 'ordinarily resident' and not a common precise test. Where dual residence occurs and a DTA between the two States in question exists, a 'tie-breaker clause' is applied to determine in which State the individual is regarded as resident and such determination will be for purposes of the treaty only. Two such points at issue are the State in which the individual has a permanent home and the State in which the individual's 'centre of vital interests' is located. Where an individual has a permanent home in both States, his 'centre of vital interests' is examined especially in terms of the individual's personal and economic relations.[14] This test is fact based.

9.2.2 Persons Other Than a Natural Person

Various 'tests' for and definitions of residence of a company exist internationally. The more common 'tests' include, *inter alia*, 'place of management', 'place of effective management', place of incorporation, place of residence of management (i.e. directors). Place of residence of shareholders may also be examined in an attempt to determine the residence of a corporation.

Similar to the USA's citizenship test to determine residency of an individual, the USA applies place of incorporation as the residency test for corporations. However, it should be noted that this is not a method preferred or applied by the OECD. Place of incorporation was rejected as an OECD tie-breaker clause in circumstances where a corporation is viewed as a resident in two States as *"[i]t would not be [an] adequate solution to attach importance to a purely formal criterion like registration . . . "*.[15] However,

[13] idem Olivier and Honiball, p62–63.

[14] idem Olivier and Honiball, p70.

[15] op cit *OECD Taxation & eCommerce* (2001) p152.

'place of incorporation' may be considered relevant and applied for the purpose of applying the 'place of effective management' test to determine residence.

If *"a person other than an individual is a resident of both Contracting States, then [the Company liable to taxation] shall be deemed to be a resident of the State in which its place of effective management is situated"*.[16] 'Place of effective management' is the preferred test implemented by the OECD within its Model Convention. 'Central management and control' and 'place of management' are the two points at issue generally considered for the purpose of defining 'place of effective management'. 'Central management and control' *"ordinarily coincides with the place where the directors of the company exercise their power and authority (which will generally be where they meet)"*.[17] De Beers Consolidated Gold Mines Ltd case (De Beers case),[18] a leading UK case, established a precedent by applying the aforementioned ruling which has subsequently been applied by several courts of other jurisdictions. Briefly, De Beers' head office, an RSA registered diamond mining company, was located in the RSA and, furthermore, all general meetings of shareholders occurred in the RSA. However, Directors' meetings were held in both the RSA and the UK. In determining the country of residence, the Lord Chancellor found that *"the Directors' meetings held in the United Kingdom ... [was] where real control of the company was exercised"*.[19, 20]

Various Canadian cases have relied on the De Beers case in determining the location of 'central management and control' and the factors examined and considered are, *inter alia*, the following:

- *Place of incorporation;*
- *Place of residence of shareholders and directors;*
- *Where the business operations take place;*
- *Where financial dealings of the company occurred; and*
- *Where the seal and minute books of the company were kept.*[21]

The Australian case, Northern Australia Pastoral Co Ltd v FCT,[22] however, did not follow the De Beers case judgement and held that the residence of a company is located where actual business operations are carried on and occur despite Directors' meetings being held in a different location. That being said, Malayan Shipping Co Ltd v FC of T,[23] another Australian court case, in the same year as the Northern Australia Pastoral Co Ltd case, held that the company's residence was Australia

[16] Article 4 of the OECD MC (2005).

[17] op cit OECD Taxation & eCommerce (2001) p146.

[18] De Beers Consolidated Mines Ltd v Howe (Surveyor of Taxes) (1906) AC 455 [UK].

[19] supra.

[20] supra.

[21] supra.

[22] Northern Australia Pastoral Co Ltd v FCT (1946) 71 CLR 623 [Australia].

[23] Ibid (1946) 71 CLR 156.

because the managing director exercised 'management and control' of the company in Australia. The Malayan Shipping Co Ltd case opposed the Northern Australia Pastoral Co Ltd case ruling and, furthermore, upheld the De Beers case ruling.[24]

According to Vogel, and similar to the German domestic law, the place of management of an enterprise *"is where the management's important policies are actually made"*.[25] In other words, *"[w]hat is decisive is not the place where the management directives take effect but rather the place where they are given"*.[26] The OECD MC Commentary has defined the 'place of effective management' as:

> *the place where the key management and commercial decisions that are necessary for the conduct of the entity's business are in substance made. The place of effective management will ordinarily be the place where the most senior person or group of persons (for example a board of directors) makes its decisions, the place where the actions to be taken by the entity as a whole are determined; however, no definitive rule can be given and all relevant facts and circumstances must be examined to determine the place of effective management. An entity may have more than one place of management, but it can have only one place of effective management at any one time.*[27]

Bibliography

Primary Sources

Cases

Australian Cases

Northern Australia Pastoral Co Ltd v FCT. 1946. 71 CLR 623. Available at http://law.ato.gov.au/atolaw/view.htm?dbwidetocone=05%3ALRP%3AHigh%20Court%3A1946%3ANorth%20Australian%20Pastoral%20Co%20Ltd%20v.%20Federal%20Commissioner%20of%20Taxation%3A%2302%23Judgment%20by%20Dixon%20J%3B. Accessed 22 Jan 2012.

Canadian Cases

Thompson v Minister of National Revenue 2 DTC 812 (SCC). Available at http://scc.lexum.org/en/1946/1946scr0-209/1946scr0-209.html. Accessed 22 Jan 2012.

Republic of South African Cases

Cohen v CIR *13 SATC 362 (1946).*

United Kingdom Cases

De Beers Consolidated Mines Ltd v Howe (Surveyor of Taxes). 1906. AC 455. Available at http://www.uniset.ca/other/cs5/19052KB612.html. Accessed 22 Jan 2012.

Shah v Barnet London Borough Council and Other Appeals 1983 1 All ER 226 (HL) 234b-c. Available at http://uniset.ca/microstates/barnet.html. Accessed 22 Jan 2012.

Like the De Beers case, the actual operations and trading activities of the company occurred in another jurisdiction, however, as the managing director made decisions and, therefore, 'managed and controlled' the company from Australia, Australia was found to be the country of residency.

[24] op cit, OECD Taxation & eCommerce (2001) p147.

[25] op cit Vogel, Univ. of Munich and Others, p183.

[26] supra.

[27] Op cit, *OECD MC* (2005) p82.

Shepherd v Revenue and Customs Commissioners [2006] STC 1821. Available at http://newsgroups.derkeiler.com/Archive/Misc/misc.taxes/2007-07/msg00221.html. Accessed 22 Jan 2012.

Statutes

OECD. 2005. *OECD model tax convention on income and on capital, condensed version – July 2005*. Paris: OECD Publishers.

Secondary Sources

Burke, Edmund (1729–1797). 1996. *The Oxford English reference dictionary*, 2nd ed. New York: Oxford University Press.

Foundation for International Taxation. *Bibliographic synopsis of Professor Klaus Vogel*. Available at http://www.fitindia.org/chairmen_speakers.htm. Accessed 12 Sept 2010.

OECD. 2001. *Taxation and electronic commerce, implementing the Ottawa taxation framework conditions*. Paris: OECD Publications.

Olivier, Lynette, and Michael Honiball. 2008. *International tax, a South African perspective 2008*, 4th ed. Cape Town: Siber Ink CC.

Pinto, Dale. 2003. *E-Commerce and source-based income taxation*. Amsterdam: IBFD Publications.

Republic of South Africa, Fifth Interim Report of the Commission of Inquiry into certain Aspects of the Tax Structure of South Africa. 1997. *Basing the South African Income Tax System on the Source or Residence Principle – Options and Recommendations*, p4. Also referred to as the KATZ Commission. Available at http://www.polity.org.za/polity/govdocs/commissions/katz-5.html [Accessed 13 May 2008].

The Shorter Oxford English Dictionary on Historical Principles. 1986. University Printing House, Oxford. Great Britain.

Vogel, Professor Dr Klaus. 1997. *Klaus Vogel on Double Tax Conventions*, 3rd ed. The Hague : Kluwer Law International.

Vogel, Professor Dr Klaus, University of Munich, and Co-Authors. 1991. *Klaus Vogel on Double Tax Conventions*, 2nd ed. Deventer: Kluwer Law and Taxation Publishers.

Chapter 10
Is 'Residence' in the Virtual World Possible?

Abstract In the virtual world meeting venue the 'effective management' of a company may be in diverse geographical locations and jurisdictions synchronically.

If the virtual world were to be recognised as an autonomous jurisdiction then "*the place of effective management... shall be deemed to be in the contracting State in which the home [ISP] of the [virtual world] is situated, or, if there is no such home [ISP], in the contracting State of which the operator of the [virtual world] is resident*" (Adaptation of Paragraph 3 of Article 8 of the OECD MC (2005)).

If a business 'incorporates' itself within the Second Life virtual property market then 'place of incorporation' as a solution for resolving place of residence for the tie-breaker purposes will exacerbate the problem of determining which State may claim 'residency' of the virtual real estate agency.

A separate but significant issue is the impact of technology on the definition of 'residence' in reference to the individual. Within Second Life a person lives vicariously through an Avatar 'residing' in the virtual world and meeting all the requirements of residence tests applied within the 'physical world'.

The question at issue is which, if any, sovereignty is entitled to impose and implement effective taxation within a virtual world that is without jurisdictional borders. It may be contended that rather than attempting to adapt traditional 'residence' tests to the virtual world for income tax purposes, it may be more expedient to devise provisions more apposite to the virtual world business model.

10.1 Applying Virtual World Attributes to the Traditional 'Residence' Definition

Technology has created a new managerial environment for corporations whereby Directors are no longer required to travel to diverse specific locations for meetings. The development of the telephone and conference calling facilities contributed towards new management abilities, however, the development and increasingly widespread use of the 'virtual world' has created unprecedented issues and problems in determining the place of effective management. The virtual world, effectively and efficiently, enables diverse directors residing in diverse jurisdictions to conduct directors' meetings and take decisions via, for example, video conferencing. Indeed, it is possible for directors' meetings to occur exclusively within the virtual world.

A.M. Bardopoulos, *eCommerce and the Effects of Technology on Taxation*,
Law, Governance and Technology Series 22, DOI 10.1007/978-3-319-15449-7_10

Technology has enabled directors to be present at directors' meetings precluding the necessity of travelling to specific locations. The concept of 'effective management' being able to operate successfully in multiple separate jurisdictions was already recognised in the 'traditional' (non-technologically advanced) business world in the 1960 Bullock v The Unit Construction Co Ltd[1] case, where Lord Radcliffe held that:

> *...individual cases have not always so arranged themselves as to make it possible to identify any one country as the seat of central management and control at all. Though such instances must be rare, the management and control may be divided or even, at any rate in theory, peripatetic.*[2]

Technological amelioration has wrought drastic changes upon the business environment since the Bullock case, making effective management of a company operating in multiple separate jurisdictions increasingly common. Indeed, one of the objectives of Second Life[3] is to provide a virtual environment for business meetings, such as directors' meetings, which occur entirely on-line within the virtual world in order to reduce travelling costs for corporations. The impact of the virtual world meeting-venue is not only made manifest by 'effective management' of a company in diverse geographical locations and jurisdictions, but, it may be argued, that the virtual meeting-venue itself constitutes yet a further jurisdiction, albeit virtual, to be considered as the 'place of effective management' of a company.

According to Dr Michael Dirkis,[4] the Australian Review of International Taxation Arrangements Consultation Paper *"acknowledges that more uncertainty arises in a technological age...as the ascertainment of the residence under both non-incorporation tests is broadly based upon geographical ties determined as a question of fact"*.[5] Dr Dirkis concludes that *"[t]he central management and control test remains a problem child... To ensure that the central management and control test does operate more effectively, it is clear that legislative reform is the only option"*.[6]

The OECD recognises concerns and issues arising as a consequence of effective management operating in multiple jurisdictions. Furthermore, to the *"extent that the place of effective management test fails to provide a clear allocation of residence to*

[1]Bullock v The Unit Construction Co. Ltd (1959) 38 TC 712, 739 at page 739 per *OECD Taxation & eCommerce* p150 & Dirkis, Michael *Still a Problem Child: Central Management and Control After RITA* (2005), p138. Available at http://www.austlii.edu.au/au/journals/RevenueLJ/2005/7.pdf [Accessed 14 July 2010].

[2]supra.

[3]Refer to 6.1.6. Amazon.com, Second Life, Part II of this paper [p54]; Footnote 19 of this paper [p54].

[4]Dr Dirkis is a Senior Tax Counsel, Taxation Institute of Australia.

[5]Dirkis, http://www.austlii.edu.au/au/journals/RevenueLJ/2005/7.pdf, p139.

[6]supra.

one country ... it may be seen to be an ineffective rule".[7] Thus, to overcome such a problem the OECD has suggested the consideration of the following options:

(A) ***Replace the place of effective management concept ...***

(i) *Place of incorporation or, in the case of an unincorporated association, place where corporate law applies to the enterprise*

While the place of incorporation test has the advantage of being easily understood, has minimal administration and compliance costs in many cases, there are nevertheless arguments against its adoption as a tie-breaker test.

In today's environment the act of incorporating an enterprise or establishing an incorporated association is relatively simple....[8] [Emphasis Added]

While the 'place of incorporation' may be a plausible solution to the escalating problem of determining residency as a result of increased technological applications within the business environment, 'place of incorporation' is encumbered with its own host of issues. For example, it is possible for a company to be 'incorporated' in two jurisdictions depending on the jurisdictions and domestic company law, thus, in such circumstances determining the country of residence has not been resolved. Furthermore, and a potentially significant argument against the 'place of incorporation' test to determine residence, such a test may result in greater tax avoidance as companies migrate to the few remaining tax havens.

The OECD has proposed diverse tests which may be applied to determine 'place of effective management':

(i) *Place where the directors/shareholders reside*

... a test relying solely on where the directors/senior managers or shareholders reside will not always give a clear result ... "

(ii) *Where the economic nexus is strongest*

The economic connection to a State may be characterised by the extent that land, labour, capital and enterprise (the factors of production) are used by the company in deriving its profits ...

While on the surface it may appear that such an option is more aligned to source taxation rationale, it also may have some links to the underlying rationale for residence taxation ...[9]

Examining the 'economic nexus' as a possible solution to the problem once again fails to take into account the volatile impact technology will have on the manner in which business is conducted. Application of the 'economic nexus' test

---

[7]op cit, OECD Taxation & eCommerce (2001) p151.

[8]idem p152.

[9]idem OECD Taxation and eCommerce (2001), p153.

may be an effective solution for determining place of management of certain companies where the 'effective management' occurs in multiple jurisdictions, but it fails to take into account business models which are conducting more and more activities within the virtual world and, furthermore, generating income within the virtual world from customers and clients located worldwide. Furthermore, increased cross-border transactions consequent to technological amelioration have increased the consumption base of some companies which, in turn, has necessitated the establishment of offices in multiple jurisdictions in order to conduct business as in the case of Google. While it may be possible to currently determine jurisdiction in terms of strongest 'economic nexus', cognizance should be taken of the possibility of an annually vacillating 'economic nexus' by reason of globalisation of business operations.

However, the OECD, in relation to the 'economic nexus' proposal, states that *"the concept of economic nexus could still be used as a tie-breaker even if it is not used as a basis for residence taxation. It should be noted that such a concept being used in a residence tie-breaker is not unprecedented. For example, the individual tie-breaker uses 'centre of vital interests' as a determining factor in deeming residence"*.[10] While this is a valid statement, difficulties may proceed from the application of such a 'tie-breaker clause' if the 'centre of vital interests' were to vacillate annually. In other words, assuming the argument holds that Google's strongest 'economic nexus' may not be located consistently in one jurisdiction, the 'centre of vital interests' test as a tie-breaker clause would have to be applied on an annual basis. Furthermore, if the argument holds that it is possible for a person, including a corporation, to be 'physically present' within the virtual world, then it may be postulated that a company's 'centre of vital interests' can be located within the virtual world.

(B) ***Refine the place of effective management test***

In refining the existing place of effective management test, two options have been suggested. Either, making a determination on the basis of predominant factor(s) or giving a weighting to various factors . . .

However, where analysis of these predominant factors does not produce a single place of effective management, it may be necessary to consider other additional factors, as is suggested in paragraph 24 of the Commentary where it states that 'however, no definitive rule can be given and all the relevant facts and circumstances must be examined to determine the place of effective management'. Other facts which may be considered in association with the dominant factors could include:

- *Location of and functions performed at the headquarters;*
- *Information on where central management and control of the company is to be located contained within company formation documents (articles of association etc.);*
- *Place of incorporation or registration;*

[10] supra.

- *Relative importance of the functions performed within the two States; and*
- *Where the majority of directors reside ...* [11] [Emphasis Added]

The refined 'place of effective management test' does not appear to deviate from the previous 'place of effective management tests'. Instead the 'refined' test examines all of the previous tests and determines the predominant factors.[12] However, application of a 'refined' test does not resolve the issues initiated and expanded by technology. A company could be incorporated in a tax haven, and establish its 'headquarters' within that tax haven. All company functions may occur over the Internet; that is, communication, decisions, effecting decisions, orders, etc. As an internet based company, the company may have several directors, each holding equal voting rights, and each residing in a different jurisdiction. Furthermore, meetings, decisions and management will not be restricted to a specific time or place, but will occur independently from time and place by means of videoconference calls, emails, and general Internet usage.

The OECD recommends provisions similar to paragraph 3 of Article 8 as a possible solution to the problem of the mobility of effective management. Paragraph 3 of Article 8 states that "*[i]f the place of effective management ... is aboard a ship or boat, then it shall be deemed to be situated in the Contracting State in which the home harbour of the ship or boat is situated, or, if there is no such home harbour, in the Contracting State of which the operator of the ship or boat is a resident.*"[13]

The OECD recommendation states that "*[i]n effect, the provision recognises that a place of effective management which is located on board a ship will be mobile, and to overcome this problem, operates to deem the place of effective management to be in the jurisdiction with which the shipping enterprise has its closest links.*" While the OECD postulates that a like provision may be a solution to mobility of 'effective management' it declines to address the problem of 'effective management' existing simultaneously in multiple jurisdictions, "*[i]t will not however address situations where a place of effective management could be said to exist simultaneously in multiple jurisdictions.*"[14] It may be argued that paragraph 3 of Article 8 proposes a solution to the problem that if the virtual world were to be recognised as a jurisdiction in its own right, and if the ship analogy were to be applied to the virtual world, then the "*the place of effective management ... shall be deemed to be situated in the Contracting State in which the home [ISP] of the [virtual world] is situated, or, if there is no such home [ISP], in the Contracting State of which the operator of the [virtual world] is a resident.*"[15]

---

[11] idem OECD Taxation and eCommerce (2001) p154.

[12] idem p154.

[13] idem OECD Taxation and eCommerce (2001), p155/Refer to Footnote 17, p114. OECD Taxation and eCommerce (2001) p154–155.

[14] supra.

[15] Adaptation of Paragraph 3 of Article 8 of the OECD MC (2005).

However, while the above may appear to be a plausible solution to the problem of determining 'place of effective management', technological amelioration has rendered such a solution obsolete. Consideration of the above solution as an example in conjunction with 'load balancing' and the use of multiple ISPs for one transaction, emphasizes the possible improbability of determining a 'home ISP', or a virtual world operator's 'residence'.

(C) ***Establish a hierarchy of tests, as in the individual***

Article 4 paragraph 2 of the Model Convention establishes a hierarchical approach for the individual residency tie-breaker. A similar approach may provide assistance in applying the corporate tie-breaker...
...A possible structure for such a hierarchy may be:

- *Place of effective management;*
- *Place of incorporation;*
- *Economic nexus; and*
- *Mutual agreement...*
- ***A combination of options B and C***[16] [Emphasis Added]

While 'place of incorporation' would appear to be ineffective for determining residence, it would, nevertheless, appear to be the currently preferred solution of those previously discussed for determining residence in a technology driven environment. However, as a premise 'place of incorporation' is inherently flawed and, therefore, the question begs as to whether it is not already redundant before even being applied.

10.2 'Residence' Within the Virtual World

While Second Life[17] is a virtual environment for transacting business and in which directors can meet and conduct business, it has created an environment for business transactions which are unique to Second Life. Second Life has established a virtual property market. Second Life real estate is not 'real' property with geographical co-ordinates, but virtual property, the sale of which has become an increasingly profitable enterprise within the virtual world. It may be anticipated that if it has not as yet transpired that a business has 'incorporated' itself within Second Life, such an eventuality is imminent. A business 'incorporated' within Second Life will be a business that exists and operates solely within Second Life. Thus, if 'place of incorporation' is used as a solution for resolving place of residence for tie-breaker purposes, it will exacerbate the problem of determining which State may claim 'residency' of the virtual real estate agency.

The impact of technology on the definition of 'residence' in terms of the corporation has been extensively discussed by OECD Taxation and Electronic

[16]idem p154–155.

[17]Refer to 6.1.6. Amazon.com, 'Second Life', Part II of this paper [p54].

essentially within the compass of Ottawa Taxation Framework Conditions. It is possible that the problem of determining residence between diverse States with regard to the virtual world may best be resolved by making the virtual world a jurisdiction in its own right. A separate but significant issue is the impact of technology on the definition of 'residence' in reference to the individual. Within Second Life a person lives vicariously through an Avatar. The Avatar 'resides' in the virtual world and meets all the requirements of residence tests applied within the 'physical world', excepting that the Avatar does not reside in the physical world, and such a stipulation is not a legislative requirement. A person, Kosta, resides in say, the UK. Kosta is a real estate agent. Kosta's Avatar, through whom he lives vicariously in Second Life, is a financially successful real estate speculator in Second Life. Kosta's Avatar 'dwells permanently' within Second Life, and meets the following requirements for permanent residency as set out in the Shepherd v RCC[18] case:

- *...' to dwell permanently or for a considerable time, to have one's settled or usual abode, to live in or at a particular place;*
- *...a place with some degree of continuity;... normal and part of everyday life or a regular, habitual mode of life in a particular place which has persisted despite temporary absences and which...has a degree of settled purpose...*

The question that is posed is whether Kosta is liable for transaction in the UK if his Avatar, who 'dwells permanently' in the virtual world makes financial gain. While it may not be currently possible for the UK 'residence' test to be completely broken, therefore allowing the UK to uphold residence within the UK, it is possible that technological amelioration may very well result in a full break from 'residence' in the foreseeable future.

10.3 Conclusion

If the argument holds that it is possible to be 'physically present' in the virtual world, then it may be further argued that current 'residency' tests can be satisfied within the virtual world. However, the point at issue is which, if any, sovereignty is entitled to impose and implement effective taxation within a virtual world that is without jurisdictional borders and is, furthermore, an environment which has redefined the concept of physics held by society when common income tax laws were promulgated. Indeed, the 'true contention' is not whether but how physical world laws can best be applied to the virtual world. *Perhaps it may be more accurately said that the true contention, which requires analytical assessment, is [that] once physical world concepts can be applied within the virtual world, how can they be applied fairly and to the benefit of different jurisdictions and government coffers?* If an individual and a corporation satisfy the requirements for permanent residency in the virtual world then both that individual and corporation exit the realm of society

[18]Shepherd v Revenue and Customs Commissioners [2006] STC 1821 [UK].

as we know it and both enter a self-governing borderless environment in which governments are scrambling to claim jurisdictional rights.

However, and regardless of whether the criteria for 'residency' can or cannot be satisfied in the virtual world, traditional income tax provisions dismally lack the flexibility to be effectively applied to the virtual world – the theoretical principles upon which traditional income tax is founded are all too often couched in concepts which directly obstruct the necessary adaptability and flexibility of income tax provisions in respect of ameliorating technological society. The problem of inflexible tax laws is especially pertinent in a society which is still adapting to the concept of being 'physically present' within a virtual world. The concept of being 'physically present' and having 'residency' in the virtual world is to many "*a riddle wrapped in a mystery inside an enigma*".[19] The acknowledgement of 'physical presence' in the virtual world with the aim of determining jurisdiction of residency generates the predicament of electing how to apply provisions for determining residency, a prerequisite of which is geographical location.

Dr Dirkis' contends that "*…it is clear that legislative reform is the only option*".[20] Indeed, it may be argued that legislative reform for determining 'residency' in the virtual world for income tax purposes should presuppose provisions especially structured to accommodate flexibility of application. In the traditional business world, the 'effective management' test is principle based in that an examination of the facts and circumstances of each case is a requisite for determining jurisdiction of residency of a company. However, determining place of 'effective management' within the virtual world has proved to be more rule based than principle driven. Thus, it may be contended that rather than attempting to adapt traditional 'residence' tests to the virtual world for income tax purposes, it may be more expedient to devise provisions more apposite to the virtual world business model.

Bibliography

Primary Sources

Cases

United Kingdom Cases

Shepherd v Revenue and Customs Commissioners [2006] STC 1821. Available at http://newsgroups.derkeiler.com/Archive/Misc/misc.taxes/2007-07/msg00221.html. Accessed 22 Jan 2012.

[19]Churchill, Sir Winston (Leonard Spencer) (1874–1965). *"British conservative statesman, Prime Minister 1940-5… [R]eplaced Neville Chamberlain as Prime Minister in May 1940. Serving as war leader of a coalition government until 1945, Churchill demonstrated rare qualities of leadership and outstanding gifts as an orator"*. **[op cit *Oxford English Reference Dictionary*, p262]**.

[20]op cit, Dirkis, http://www.austlii.edu.au/au/journals/RevenueLJ/2005/7.pdf p139.

Statutes

OECD. 2005. *OECD model tax convention on income and on capital, condensed version – July 2005*. Paris: OECD Publishers.

Secondary Sources

Churchill, Sir Winston (Leonard Spencer) (1874–1965). 1996. *Oxford English Reference Dictionary*, 2nd ed. New York: Oxford University Press.

Dirkis, Micahel. 2005. *Still a problem child: Central management and control after RITA*. Available at http://www.austlii.edu.au/au/journals/RevenueLJ/2005/7.pdf. Accessed 14 July 2010.

OECD. 2001. *Taxation and electronic commerce, implementing the Ottawa taxation framework conditions*. Paris: OECD Publications.

Part IV
Defining 'Source' for Taxation Purposes

Chapter 11
The Meaning of 'Source'

Abstract A critical issue pertaining to source is the practicability of taxing principles. With regard to businesses, several jurisdictions will tax the business profits of an enterprise which is resident of another State if that enterprise is conducting business through a 'permanent establishment', thereby satisfying a fundamental 'source' requirement.

'Permanent establishment' has become a topical subject pertinent to 'source-based' taxation systems applied within the eCommerce context.

It is not advocated that income tax principles such as 'source-based' tax systems be totally abandoned, but the governments affected by the advent of the Internet should recognise that it may be several years before problematic income taxing provisions are effectively resolved. *Income* tax principles have possibly been stretched to their finite point of elasticity, and the virtual world may be more amenable to the application of VAT than to the application of 'source-based', or other income tax, principles.

While a policy may be perfect in theory, the true test of a policy is in the worth of its practical effectuality.

11.1 Introduction

As noted earlier[1] it is imperative to examine certain inefficiencies of traditional income tax provisions within the eCommerce environment preparatory to analysing and evaluating the efficiency of VAT as the eTax solution. Part III was a discussion of provisions for and principles of 'Residence'. In Part IV provisions for and principles of 'Source' will be discussed. For the purpose of expediency active income derived from businesses or enterprises will be primarily examined in relation to source, that is, business profits as opposed to passive income such as royalties, interest, etc.

A critical issue pertaining to source is the practicability of taxing principles. With regard to businesses, several jurisdictions will tax the business profits of an enterprise which is resident of another State if that enterprise is conducting business through a 'permanent establishment', thereby satisfying a fundamental 'source'

[1]Refer to 9.1. Introduction, Part III of this paper [p88].

A.M. Bardopoulos, *eCommerce and the Effects of Technology on Taxation*,
Law, Governance and Technology Series 22, DOI 10.1007/978-3-319-15449-7_11

requirement. 'Permanent establishment' has become a topical subject pertinent to 'source-based' taxation systems applied within an eCommerce context.

The focus of this paper is to highlight the current efficiencies of VAT and consumption taxes in contradistinction to the inefficiencies of income tax principles which have possibly been stretched to their finite point of elasticity. This paper is not concerned with an in-depth discussion of the various issues relating to the application of source within an eCommerce environment, and the measures which have to be taken in order to effectively apply a 'source-based' taxing system within the virtual world. Dr Dale Pinto[2] ("Pinto") discusses these issues in great detail within his doctoral thesis, *E-Commerce and Source-Based Income Taxation*, and he asserts the need for 'source-based' taxation to be "*reconceptualised*" rather than abandoned in its entirety:

> *...the issue of whether source-based taxation should continue to apply to electronic commerce transactions [has been approached] from an incorrect perspective. This is because many of the reasons advanced for the abandonment of source-based taxation in an electronic commerce environment are principally based on practical and administrative considerations and are therefore based on expedience, rather than being founded on theoretical grounds. That is, the basis of arguments calling for the abandonment of source-based taxation have hitherto generally been that, since source-based taxation of electronic commerce transactions will be difficult, it may therefore no longer be relevant. Against this, however, ... [Pinto's] thesis has taken the position that how something can be done (which involves practical or administrative considerations) should be a secondary consideration to whether it can be theoretically justified and therefore should be done in the first place ...*[3]

The intention of this paper is not to advocate the total abandonment of income tax principles such as 'source-based' tax systems. However, it is crucial for all governments affected by the advent of the Internet to recognise that it may be several years before problematic income taxing provisions are effectively resolved. Indeed, the virtual world, engulfed in its own complications and perplexities, may be more amenable to the application of VAT than to the application of 'source-based', or other income tax, principles. Similar to Pinto's thesis, the theoretical application of VAT within the virtual world will be examined in this paper and then the practicality of applying such a system will be examined. However, the theoretical examination will not be so extreme as to become unrealistic, thus rendering the practicality of application impossible.

Through the ages theoretically perfect economic policies have been propounded. However, those that have been implemented have proved to be effectually imperfect. The utopian ideal of a consummate social and political system can only prevail in

[2]Dr Dale Pinto submitted his thesis, *E-Commerce and Source-Based Income Taxation*, in total fulfilment of the requirements of the degree of Doctor of Philosophy in March 2002 through the Faculty of Law at the University of Melbourne. Dr Pinto, an Associate Professor and Head of the Taxation Department at Curtin University in Perth, Western Australia, has published extensively and presented papers at several conferences in relation to Taxation.

[3]op cit, Pinto, Dale *E-Commerce and Source-Based Income Taxation* (2003), Netherlands, p233.

the abstract. Utopian ideology habitually lambastes "*social inequality, economic exploitation*"[4] and "*other possible forms of domination*".[5]

Plato's[6] Republic describes "*an imagined perfect place of things*",[7] and was not the first of a genre of literature that has percolated through the ages. The word 'utopia' was first used by Sir Thomas More[8] in his book Utopia (1516) in which he describes an imaginary island, Utopia, which is "*governed on a perfect political and social system*".[9] The genre is manifest in Tommaso Campanello's[10] City of the Sun (1612–23), Francis Bacon's[11] New Atlantis (1626) and the social utopianism of Fourier,[12] Saint-Simon[13] and Owen.[14] The prime focus of Utopian ideology is creative imaginings of the quintessential society.

---

[4]Henderich, T. (ed). *Oxford Philosophy,* USA p893.

[5]supra.

[6]Plato (c429 – c347) "*Greek philosopher. He was a disciple of Socrates and the teacher of Aristotle, and he founded the Academy of Athens ... Plato's political theories appear in the Republic, in which he explored the nature and structure of a just society*". **[op cit Oxford English Reference Dictionary, 1996, p1111]**.

[7]op cit, *Oxford English Reference Dictionary*, 1995, p1591.

[8]More, Sir Thomas (1478–1535) "*English scholar and statesman ... Regarded as one of leading humanists of the Renaissance, he owed his reputation largely to his Utopia (1516), describing an ideal city state*". **[Op cit, Oxford English Reference Dictionary, 1996, p939]**.

[9]op cit, *Oxford English Reference Dictionary*, 1995, p15.

[10]Campanella, Tommese (2568–2639) "*... a political philosopher. In his City of the Sun he conceived a Utopia built on Platonic lines*". **[*Op cit* Dictionary of Philosophy, 1976, p441]**.

[11]Bacon, Francis (1561–1626). "*Inspired by the Renaissance, and ... proposed an inductive method of discovering truth founded upon empirical observation ... [t]he impediments to the use of ... [which] are ... grouped ... under four headings, or Idols*" **[Op cit Dictionary of Philosophy, 1976, p34]/[Op cit Oxford English Reference Dictionary, 1996, p75]**.

The "*four kinds of intellectual idol [Hypothetico–deductive method] ... perceptual illusions ('idols of the tribe'), personal biases ('idols of the cave'), linguistic confusions ('idols of the market-place'), and dogmatic philosophical systems ('idols of the market-place')*". **[Oxford University Press., New York 1995, pg75]**.

The New Atlantis describes an Utopian society on an imaginary island called Bensalem in the Pacific and an "*ideal college called Solomon's House, dedicated to natural philosophy*". **[Cambridge Guide to English Literature, Press Syndicate of the University of Cambridge, New York 1983, pg. 633]**

[12]Fourier, Charles (1772–1837) "*French social theorist who advocated a reconstruction of society based on communal association of producers known as phalange ... His system came to be known as Fourierism ... [and] foreshadowed the ideas of Karl Marx. Co-operative settlements based on Fouriers' ideas were started in France and especially the US, among which [one of] the best known ... [is] the short-lived Brook Farm in Massachusetts (1841–1846)*". [Britannica, Macropaedia Ready Reference, Encyclopaedia Britannica, New York, 1991, Volume 4, pg 906.

[13]Saint-Simon, Claude-Henri de Rouvroy (1760–1825) "*French social reformer and philosopher*". **[Op cit Oxford English Reference Dictionary, 1996, p1275]**.

[14]Owen, Robert (1771–1858) "*Welsh social reformer and industrialist. A pioneer socialist thinker, he believed that character is a product of the socialist environment*". **[Op cit, Oxford English Reference Dictionary, 1996, p1040]**.

The word 'utopia' is derived from the Greek words 'ou' and 'topos' meaning 'not place'. Germane to utopianism is unrealistic, fanciful hypotheses.

Marx[15] and Engels[16] supported utopianism's relativizing social equality, but they criticized its inability to succeed politically because of its failure to fully understand and analyse the prevailing social state of affairs. Thus, Marxism[17] rejected utopianism for its "*theoretical unconnectedness with the social status-quo*"[18] and not for its inherent equivalent imaginative reasoning. However, Marxism, although reputed to be a theoretically unflawed economic system, itself proved to be effectually impracticable, because it failed to take into account human nature and essential human inequalities, the historically irrefutable consequence of which is dystopia as is vividly illustrated in George Orwell's[19] *Animal Farm (1945)*. In the latter the euphoric vision of an animal 'Utopia' disintegrates into a frightening 'dystopia' where "*all animals are equal, but some animals are more equal than others*",[20] and the inevitable social divide between exploiter and exploited is re-established.

Thus, while a policy may be perfect in theory, the true test of a policy is in the worth of its practical effectuality.

Part IV is a brief discussion of the concept of 'source' and current issues regarding current 'source' principle methods. Traditional application of 'source' and the application of 'source' within the compass of an electronic environment will be considered. Furthermore, as international trading activities are pertinent to this paper, both traditional and electronic interaction with the OECD MC will be discussed.

---

[15]Marx, Karl Heinrich (1818–83) "*German political philosopher and economist... The founder of modern communism with Engels, he collaborated with him in the writing of the Communist Manifesto (1848)*". **[op cit Oxford English Reference Dictionary, 1996, p886]**.

[16]Engels, Friedrich (1820–95) "*German socialist and political philosopher... The founder of modern communism with Karl Marx.*" **[op cit Oxford English Reference Dictionary, 1996, p466]**.

[17]Marxism "the political and economic theories based on the writings of Karl Marx and Friedrich Engels, and later developed by their followers with dialectical materialism to form the basis for the theory and practice of communism". **[op cit Oxford English Reference Dictionary, 1996, p886]**.

[18]idem footnote 4 of this paper [p111].

[19]Orwell, George (1903–50) "*British essayist and novelist... His most famous works are Animal Farm (1945), a satire of communism as it developed under Stalin, and Nineteen Eighty-Four (1949), a dystopian account of a future state in which every aspect of state is controlled by Big Brother*". **[op cit Oxford English Reference Dictionary, 1996, p1027]**.

[20]George Orwell – *Animal Farm* – Chapter X. Available at http://ww.goerge-orwell.org/Animal_Farm/9.html [Accessed 29/07/2010].

Bibliography

Secondary Sources

Bacon, Francis (1561–1626). 1983. *Cambridge guide to English literature*. New York: Press Syndicate of the University of Cambridge.

Campanella, Tommase (1568–1639). 1976. *Dictionary of philosophy*. Totowa: Littlefield, Adams & Co.

Fourier, Charles (1772–1837). 1991. *Britannica, Macropaedia ready reference, Encyclopaedia Britannica*, Vol. 4, New York.

Henderich, T (ed.). 1996. *The Oxford English reference dictionary*, 2nd ed. New York: Oxford University Press.

Marx, Karl Heinrich (1818–1883). 1996. *The Oxford English reference dictionary*, 2nd ed. New York: Oxford University Press.

More, Sir Thomas (1478–1535). 1996. *The Oxford English reference dictionary*, 2nd ed. New York: Oxford University Press.

Orwell, George – Animal Farm – Chapter II. Available at http://www.george-orwell.org/Animal_Farm/1.html. Accessed 29 July 2010.

Orwell, George (1903–1950). 1996. *The Oxford English reference dictionary*, 2nd ed. New York: Oxford University Press.

Orwell, George – Animal Farm – Chapter X. Available at http://ww.goerge-orwell.org/Animal_Farm/9.html. Accessed 29 July 2010.

Owen, Robert (1771–1858). 1996. *The Oxford English reference dictionary*, 2nd ed. New York: Oxford University Press.

Pinto, Dale. 2003. *E-Commerce and source-based income taxation*. Amsterdam: IBFD Publications.

Plato (c429–c347). 1996. *The Oxford English reference dictionary*, 2nd ed. New York: Oxford University Press.

Plato 429BC-347BC. Available at http://www.quotesandpoem.com/quotes/listquotes/subject/taxes. Accessed 22 Jan 2007.

Saint-Simon, Claude-Henri de Rouvroy (1760–1825). 1996. *The Oxford English reference dictionary*, 2nd ed. New York: Oxford University Press.

Chapter 12
The Traditional Concept of 'Source'

Abstract The implications of 'source' have been diversely interpreted by both academics and judges. It is possible to have a state of affairs where there are multiple sources and two 'dominant' causes for generating income.

Vogel's 'benefit theory' argues that the country that furnished the majority of benefits pertinent to the generating of income carries the costs of such benefits and should be entitled to exclusive taxation rights as compensation.

The 'entitlement theory' is based on the source State being entitled to tax income generated within its geographical borders. The 'economic allegiance' theory attributed to the introduction of the 'permanent establishment' concept, which is utilised to attribute profits of a business to the 'source' country. 'Permanent establishment' is a topical issue apropos the virtual world. Contentious points at issue are 'place of business', 'fixed' and 'carried out'.

Implicit to the 'geographical location' test is that the 'specific location' need not be a specific 'fixed point' and a 'geographical area' will suffice. The 'duration' test requires that an activity is regularly repeated during a certain period of time but there may be interruption in business operations. 'Permanent establishment' has been extended to embrace the concept of 'agent'.

Vogel deems 'source' to be the "*state that in some way or other is connected to the production of the income in question, to the state where value is added to a good*" (Pinto refers to Klaus Vogel, "*Worldwide vs Source Taxation of Income – A Review and evaluation of Arguments (Part I)*" (1998) 8–9 Intertax, pp. 216, 223 **[op cit Pinto, Dale *E-Commerce and Source-Based Income Taxation* (2003), Netherlands, p48]**).

12.1 Traditional Definition of 'Source'

Pinto suggests that the idea of 'source' is "*an obvious concept about which not much disagreement is possible. However, conclusions that may be drawn from the body of international tax law, including case law dealing with disputes regarding the source of income, suggest that the meaning of source is far from unambiguous.*"[1]

[1]op cit Pinto, p48.

A.M. Bardopoulos, *eCommerce and the Effects of Technology on Taxation*, Law, Governance and Technology Series 22, DOI 10.1007/978-3-319-15449-7_12

Most jurisdictions have not proclaimed a clear definition of 'source' within domestic law the determination of which devolves upon the courts. However, the USA is one of the few jurisdictions which has proclaimed source rules within legislation.[2] The implications of 'source' have been diversely interpreted by both academics and judges. Vogel deems 'source' to be the "*state that in some way or other is connected to the production of the income in question, to the state where value is added to a good*".[3] Within the Rhodesia Metals Ltd case,[4] the Rhodesian[5] judge presiding over the ruling defined 'source' to mean "*not a legal concept but rather something which a practical man would regard as the real source of income.*"[6] Further definitions include "*the country in which the business conducts its trade and earns its income is usually referred to as the 'source country*'",[7] and the "*place of income generating activity*".[8] The RSA Lever Brothers and Unilever tax case[9] also held that "*the source of income is not the quarter from which it comes but rather the originating cause of its receipt*".[10]

---

[2]op cit Olivier, Lynette and Honiball, Michael, *International Tax, A South African Perspective 2008*, Fourth Edition (2008), South Africa p52.

[3]Pinto refers to Klaus Vogel, "*Worldwide vs. Source Taxation of Income - A Review and evaluation of Arguments (Part I)*" (1988) 8–9 *Intertax*, pp. 216, 223 **[op cit Pinto, p48]**.

[4]Rhodesia Metals Ltd (In Liquidation) v Commissioner of Tax 11 SATC 244 (1938).

[5]**Rhodesia** is the "*former name of a large territory in central-southern Africa, divided into Northern Rhodesia (now Zambia) and Southern Rhodesia (now Zimbabwe). The region was developed by and named after Cecil Rhodes, through the British South Africa Company, which administered it until Southern Rhodesia became a self-governing British colony in 1923 and Northern Rhodesia a British protectorate in 1924. From 1953 to 1963 Northern and Southern Rhodesia were united with Nyasaland (now Malawi) to form the federation of Rhodesia and Nyasaland*".

As per Encyclopedia.com et al. **A Dictionary of World History** (2000). **Available at** http://www.encyclopedia.com/doc/1O48-Rhodesia.html **[Accessed 5 January 2009]**.

[6]Ibid, Rhodesia Metals Ltd (In Liquidation) v Commissioner of Tax 11 SATC 244 (1938). Also, op cit Olivier and Honiball, p53.

[7]op cit, Pinto, p48.

[8]idem. Pinto references definition to Richard and Peggy Musgrave, p48.

[9]Lever Brothers & Unilever, CIR v 1946 AD 441, 14 SATC 441 [RSA] ("Lever Brothers case").

[10]supra.

The Lever Brothers and Unilever case[11] established a two part test to determine source. The test requires the determination of the originating cause followed by the location of the determined originating cause.[12] However, in the RSA CIR v Black tax case[13] it was acknowledged that it is possible for there to be more than one 'originating cause' and, therefore, it was held that the "*main, the real, the dominant, the substantial source of the amounts accrued was the use of the taxpayer's capital in ... [the disputed 'source' country, UK], and the entering into and carrying out of the ... [relevant income producing] transactions [was] in ... [the disputed 'source' country, UK]*".[14] Thus, even in circumstances where it may be said that two or more contingent events relate to the income earning activity, the 'dominant source' will indicate the 'source location'. Furthermore, determining the 'dominant' source or cause, where two or more causes may be attributed to the generating of income, was upheld in the Botswana case, Transvaal Associated Hide and Skin Merchants

[11]Ibid, Lever Brothers case (1946) [RSA].

The Lever Brothers case laid down authority in South African tax case law that "source" means the "originating cause". Briefly, the facts and judgement of the Lever Brothers Case were as follows: A Dutch company held shares in companies carrying on business in different parts of the world along with debts owed by certain Dutch companies. A South African company acquired the Dutch company, and as such took over the debt liability. The South African Commissioner sought to tax the interest paid by the South African company to its creditors based on the contention that the source of the interest paid on the loan was the debt which was located where the debtor, now a South African company, resides. However, none of the agreements relating to the debt were entered into in South Africa. The court held that the sale, which gave rise to the debt, occurred in England and not in South Africa. "*In determining the source of income it must first be determined what the source is from which the income is derived and when this has been determined, the place where that source is located must be ascertained. The source of income is not the quarter from which it comes but rather the originating cause of its receipt*". It was thus held that the source of the interest received was not derived from a South African source. - **[ibid, Emslie, Trevor; Davis, Dennis; Hutton, SJ; & Olivier, Lynette Income *Tax Cases & Materials* 3rd Ed** (2001), **South Africa, p105-110]**.

[12]op cit, Olivier and Honiball, p52.

[13]CIR v Black 957 (3) SA 536 (A), 21 SATC 226, 1957 Taxpayer 172 at 542 [RSA]. Also, Emslie *et al. Income Tax Cases & Materials* 3rd Ed (2001), p130:

In the Black case the taxpayer was a stockbroker on the Johannesburg Stock Exchange. The taxpayer opened what is referred to as a 'Speculation Account' in London, England, where 'speculative dealings in shares' were carried out. These 'speculative dealings in shares' gave rise to debit and credits occurring on the taxpayer's 'Speculation Account'. Furthermore, the taxpayer authorised the London brokers to deal on his behalf without reference to him. While such authorisation had been granted it should be noted that in practice reference was in fact made to the taxpayer in almost all cases. The taxpayer made a profit from those London share dealings and SARS sought to include this profit in the taxpayer's taxable income in RSA. It was determined, upon this matter proceeding to court, that a "*reasonable conclusion was that the main, the real, the dominant, the substantial source of the amount accrued was the use of the taxpayer's capital in London*". Thus, the profit could be said to have a dominant source in London and, therefore, was not taxable in South Africa.

[14]supra.

v CIT,[15] where it was held that a distinction must be made between the 'dominant' cause and the 'incidental' cause when there are more than two 'originating causes' relating to the generation of income.[16]

In W. Dunn & Co.,[17] a Rhodesian case, it was found that "*in the case of an ordinary business based upon capital it has been held that in determining the source of the income, regard must be had to the place where the capital was employed which produced the profits*".[18] Millin v CIR,[19] an RSA tax case, supports application of the location where the 'capital was employed' to determine the dominant cause where multiple 'sources' of income exist. Millin, an author, wrote her novels in the RSA but had her works published in the UK. While income was generated from the publishing and marketing of the books, it was the employment of her capital, that is her authorship, which may be identified as the dominant cause generating income.

It is possible to have a state of affairs where there are multiple sources and two 'dominant' causes for the generation of income. While perhaps jurisdictionally limited, support for apportioning income earned between capital and revenue may be found in the application of the *quid pro quo* test. This would require an examination of the work performed by the taxpayer to earn the receipt of money received.[20]

Vogel's 'benefit theory', that is 'source based' taxation, proposes that "*a jurisdiction's right to tax rests on the totality of benefits and state services provided*

[15]Transvaal Associated Hide and Skin Merchants v Collector Tax Botswana, *29 SATC 97* 1967 (BCA) [Botswana] ("Transvaal Hide case").

The taxpayer's business activities, washing, curing and selling of hides, were located in RSA and Botswana. However, the washing and curing of the hides, which occurred in Botswana was viewed as the 'dominant' cause as the curing process was an '*essential feature of the business'*. Thus, while the "*selling [of] the cured hides was necessary and a causa sine qua non of the accrual of the income*", the location of the causa sine qua non cannot be the decisive factor in determining source as there may be multiple causae sine qua non. **[op cit, Emslie et al., p124]**.

[16]Ibid, Transvaal Hide case (1967) [Botswana].

[17]Commissioner of Taxes v. W. Dunn & Co. Ltd (1918, AD, 614) [Rhodesia].

[18]supra.

[19]Millin v CIR *3 SATC 170* 1928 AD207 [RSA].

[20]Support for the apportioning of income earned where more than one dominant cause exists may be found in the RSA tax case, Tuck v CIR *49 SATC 28* 1988 (3) SA 819 (A) ("Tuck v CIR"), which set a precedent in the RSA allowing apportionment of an amount between capital and revenue. It is, however, uncertain whether such a case would apply in other jurisdictions or whether it may even be applied successfully as support for the application of quid pro quo apportionment within an international tax, cross-border, context.

In terms of the Tuck v CIR case, an employee received shares in 10 annual instalments upon retirement. The delivery of such shares was subject to the restraint of trade clause imposed upon the employee. However, the employee reflected the receipt of the instalments as relating half to the restraint of trade and the other half as the receipt of a lump sum received for compensation for the termination of services. Within RSA tax legislation, the receipt of the lump sum at the time of the Tuck v CIR case met the definition of revenue and was taxable, and the amount received for the restraint of trade clause met the definition of capital and was not taxable. The RSA Commissioner, dissatisfied that a portion of the amount was not taxable, disallowed the employee's assessment and

to taxpayers that interact with a country".[21] Vogel's supporting argument to the benefit theory is that the "*country of source that...provided most or all of the benefits relevant for the production of income and therefore incurred costs in providing ... [such] benefits*"[22] should be entitled to exclusive taxation rights with regard to such income as 'compensation to the government' for bearing the costs incurred.

'Source-based' taxation is further rationalised in regard to the 'entitlement theory' proposed by Peggy Musgrave.[23] The concept of 'entitlement' is based on the source State being entitled to tax income generated within its geographical borders.[24] The reason for the 'entitlement theory', as emphasized by Pinto, is that "*it is the source country as the 'place of income-generating activity' rather than the country where the income-producer resides ... that economically contributes to the production of income ...*".[25] Furthermore, an essential aspect of 'source' basis taxation is that the State in whose geographical borders the income is generated has first claim to tax such income. Thus, practicably it may prove difficult to prevent States from taxing income generated within their borders.[26]

Pinto references the historical development of defining source in order to ascertain the "*type of connection that is needed to establish source*".[27] According to Pinto the historical development of the definition of source evolves from a "*preference for relying on the concept of 'economic allegiance' to establish [the*

---

assessed the employee for tax based on the entire amount received. Tuck, the employee, appealed to the Supreme Court of Appeal based on two main arguments, namely:

(i) *That the causally relevant factor which resulted in the receipt of the shares was the taxpayer's compliance with the restraint agreement; and*
(ii) *Alternatively, that the receipt of the shares was attributable at least in part to the taxpayer's compliance with the restraint agreement and hence an apportionment of the receipt as between income and capital should take place.* **[op cit, Emslie et al., p282]**

Tuck's contentions referred to the judge's dictum as held in the Lever Bros case; that is "*that the source of receipts, received as income, is not the quarter whence they come, but the originating cause of their being received as income, and that this originating cause is the work which the taxpayer does to earn them, the quid pro quo which he gives in return for which he received them*". **[op cit, Emslie et al., p283]**.

[21]op cit, Pinto, p17.

[22]idem p19.

[23]As cited by Pinto: Richard Musgrave and Peggy Musgrave, "Inter-Nation Equity" in *Modern Fiscal Issues: Essays in Honor of Car S. Shoup* (1972), p71, cited in Richard Doernberg and Luc Hinnekens, *Electronic Commerce and International Taxation* (1999), p306 (note 641). **[op cit Pinto, p36]**.

[24]op cit, Pinto, p36/Refer to Footnote 28, p120, Pinto, p49.

[25]supra.

[26]idem p41.

[27]idem p49.

type of connection that is needed to establish source] and thereby determine the source of income."[28] Pinto postulates that "*the concept of 'economic allegiance' is central to the way in which source is currently defined*"[29] and he upholds the theory of 'economic allegiance' as devised by Georg von Schanz[30]:

> *Economic allegiance to a State can be based on mere consumption or it can be based on business activities, including investment activities. To the extent economic allegiance is founded on consumption, residence would constitute a suitable criterion, but it could not be the only controlling principle.* ***Where a person is economically bound*** *not only to the state of his or her residence, but also* ***to another state through business activities or by way of income arising in the other state****, Schanz deems the allegiance to this other state, the source state, to be more important than that to the state of emphasis.*"[31] [Emphasis as added by Pinto]

The theory of 'economic allegiance' was applied by the League of Nations[32] when formulating the 1927 Draft Convention as a solution to double taxation proceeding from an international frame of reference, whereby determination of the 'origin', that is the 'source', of income earned through application of "*human and material resources*"[33] would be a decisive factor. Pinto attributes Schanz's 'economic allegiance' theory to the introduction of the 'permanent establishment' concept.[34] 'Permanent establishment' is a familiar concept utilised by several jurisdictions' domestic law and the OECD Model Convention as a method of attributing profits of a business/enterprise to the 'source' country. Application of the 'permanent establishment' concept is a topical subject of prime import within the compass of the virtual world frame of reference and will be discussed later.[35] Generally the 'permanent establishment' concept may be applied to determine

---

[28]supra.

[29]op cit, Pinto, p36/Refer to Footnote 28, p120, Pinto, p49.

[30]Georg von Schanz, accredited as the "*inventor of the accrual concept of income taxation*" was the founder of "*Finanzarchiv [which] is the world's oldest public finance journal. ... Finanzarchiv, which switched from German to English in 1999, is now one of the official journals of the International Institute of Public Finance.*" **[Sinn, Hans Werner, Please Bring me the New York Times on the European Roots of Richard Abel Musgrave, (July 2007) p8. CESifo Working Paper No. 2050, Category I: Public Finance. Available at** http://www.econstor.eu/bitstream/10419/26095/1/538342781.PDF **[Accessed 19 September 2010]]**.

[31]supra.

[32]Predecessor of the United Nations, the League of Nations was founded and established post World War I with the signing of the Treaty of Versailles, in an effort to avoid another war with devastating consequences, as experienced with World War I, from occurring again. The League of Nations also dealt with other matters relating to international affairs, laws and economics. With the advent of World War II, the League of Nations had clearly failed to achieve its goals and objectives. Post World War II, the League of Nations was replaced by the United Nations.

[33]op cit, Pinto, p52.

[34]supra.

[35]Refer to 13 Defining 'Source' within an eCommerce Context, Part IV of this paper [p131].

'origin' and, therefore, it may be considered as a 'source' rule. The OECD has referred to the permanent establishment concept as follows:

> *The permanent establishment concept also acts as a source rule to the extent that, as a general rule, the only business profits of a non-resident that may be taxed by a country are those that are attributable to a permanent establishment.*[36]

12.2 Permanent Establishment

"[A] fixed place of business through which the business of an enterprise is wholly or partly carried on"[37] constitutes a permanent establishment as defined in Article 5 of the OECD MC. The OECD MC Commentary proceeds to state that "*[t]he main use of the concept of a permanent establishment is to determine the right of a Contracting State to tax the profits of an enterprise of the other Contracting State*".[38] The 'permanent establishment concept' has been referred to as "*nothing more than the provision of a legal framework for the circumstances in which the source country will have the right to tax a non-resident enterprise on sourced income"*[39] the justification of which *"can be found in the belief that until the enterprise sets up a permanent establishment, the infrastructure of the source country is not relied upon to earn income*".[40]

'Permanent establishment', as analysed by Vogel, is a "*rule [that] is designed to ensure that business activities will not be taxed by a State unless and until they have created significant economic bonds between the enterprise and that State*".[41] Vogel suggests that:

> *[T]he permanent establishment concept employed in international tax law is narrower [than that employed in domestic legislation]. Taxation by the State of source is to some extent restricted in favour of taxation by the State of residence. This serves to simplify taxation and is thus in line with trends to encourage liberalisation of international trade. In fact, growing economic interdependence on an international scale resulted in treaty practice narrowing more and more the definitions of the term 'permanent establishment', particularly among industrialised countries... The general trend to restrict the 'permanent establishment' concept in the interest of trade appears to have reached its peak, and probably also to have come to a temporary halt, when OECD MC was finalised.*[42] [Emphasis Added]

[36]OECD Tax Policy Studies *E-Commerce: Transfer Pricing and Business Profits Taxation* (2005) ("OECD E-Commerce Transfer Pricing") p77.

[37]op cit, *OECD MC (2005)*, p26.

[38]idem, p85.

[39]op cit, Olivier and Honiball, p93.

[40]supra.

[41]op cit, Vogel, Professor Dr Klaus, University of Munich, and Co-Authors Klaus *Vogel on Double Tax Conventions* (2nd Edition) (1991), Netherlands, p200.

[42]Supra Vogel, Univ. of Munich and Co-authors, p200.

The OECD MC Commentary to Article 5 stipulates that to qualify for 'permanent establishment' the following conditions must be met:

- *The existence of a 'place of business', i.e. a facility such as premises or, in certain instances, machinery or equipment;*
- *This place of business must be 'fixed', i.e. it must be established at a distinct place with a certain degree of permanence;*
- *The carrying on of the business of the enterprise through this fixed place of business. This means usually that persons who, in one way or another, are dependent on the enterprise (personnel) conduct the business of the enterprise in the State in which the fixed place is situated.*[43]

Therefore, to satisfy 'permanent establishment' an enterprise must have a 'place of business' which is fixed and through which business is 'carried out'. However, that which constitutes a 'place of business', 'fixed' and 'carried on' is vigorously debated.

In a discussion on the diverse interpretations of 'place of business', 'fixed' and 'carried on', a significant reference is the evolution of the interpretation of the concept of 'permanent establishment' in an attempt to "*overcome double taxation in intermunicipal relations in Prussia by specifying the need for a stehendes Gewerbe*"[44] in order to determine the source jurisdiction and, therefore, apply 'source-basis' taxation. A *stehendes Gewerbe* essentially is "*a trade with a fixed place of business*".[45] The requirement for "*a trade with a fixed place of business*" expanded so as to encompass the two further requirements of "*a fixed physical location*", referred to as a *Bestriebsstatte*, and a "*visible business activity*".[46]

The concept of 'permanent establishment' was adopted and included in several double tax conventions before being included in the OEEC MC and, later, in the OECD MC. Since its inception, the concept of 'permanent establishment' has been expanded to embrace the possibility of 'permanent establishment' through the service of an agent. The concept of 'permanent establishment' through the use of an agent will be further discussed[47] within this subchapter. The OECD MC's insistence upon 'physical presence' within a State for the purpose of determining 'permanent establishment' is significant to this paper.[48]

Defining 'physical presence' especially with reference to the virtual world and striding technological amelioration is a topical issue. 'Physical presence' has been challenged academically by Arvid Skaar[49] ("Skaar") and Vogel. Skaar's contention, as summarised by Pinto, is "*that even if a business does not have a physical presence*

---

[43]op cit, *OECD MC (2005)*, p85.

[44]op cit, Pinto, p76.

[45]supra.

[46]supra.

[47]Refer to 12.2. Permanent Establishment, Part IV of this paper [p121]; 13. Defining 'Source' within an eCommerce Context, Part IV of this paper [p131].

[48]op cit, Olivier and Honiball, p95.

[49]The OECD provides the following brief biography of Arvid Aage Skaar:

in a source country it benefits substantially from its infrastructure and therefore should make a contribution to the source country, consistent with the benefit theory of taxation".[50] This is supported by Vogel's contention that "*states have [a claim] to tax income received from sales to their residents, reasoning that this income would not have been earned without the market [that the respective state] provide[d]*".[51]

However, despite academic contentions, a customer base was not held to satisfy physical presence in the USA case, Piedras Negras.[52] Furthermore, the court's reasoning in this case was reinforced by the repetitive 'geographic location' test requirement which relates to the further condition that the enterprise be conducted through a 'fixed' place of business.

The Amazon tax,[53] while an indirect tax based on consumption, relies on the customer base to justify Amazon's presence in the State of New York. The issue of the Piedras Negras case was determining source of income for tax purposes,

---

> *[A] partner in the law firm Wiersholm (Oslo) and an adjunct professor of tax law at the Norwegian School of Management (Handelshøyskolen BI). He received his doctorate from the University of Oslo in 1991. His main publications are 'Permanent Establishment – Erosion of a Tax Treaty Concept' (1991); 'Taxation Issues relating to Captive Insurance Companies' (1998); editor of 'Norsk skatteavtalerett' (Norwegian Tax Treaty Law) (2005). He has published a number of articles and books, and has been teaching international tax law in Norway and abroad. He has been active in the International Fiscal Association (IFA) for many years.*

Available at http://www.oecd.org/speaker/0,3438,en_21571361_40047302_40414394_1_1_1_1_1,00.html [Accessed 26 July 2010].

[50]op cit, Pinto, p92.

[51]supra.

[52]Piedras Negras Broadcasting Co v. Commissioner of Internal Revenue (1941) BTA 297, aff'd 127 F 2d 260 (5th Circuit 1942) [USA] - as cited in Pinto, p92.

Brief description of the Piedras Negras case, as cited in Goldberg, Sandford, *Internet Sales Pose International Tax Challenges* ("Goldberg – Internet Sales") (1 June 1996). Available at http://www.robertsandholland.com/article.ihtml?id=86 [Accessed 30 July 2010]:

> "*[A] foreign corporation which executed contracts abroad relating to broadcasts designed to be heard by listeners in the U.S. was held not subject to U.S. income tax on the income from those contracts. The circuit court's opinion in the case rested solely on the ground that the taxpayer's source of income was outside the U.S., but the lower court also found that the foreign corporation was not engaged in a U.S. trade or business in the U.S. The lower court's opinion was based on the in personam jurisdiction cases which had held that mere solicitation of business, where goods were shipped from outside the jurisdiction, was not sufficient to constitute 'doing business' for nexus purposes. In Piedras Negras, the Court held that the foreign broadcasting corporation cannot be said to be doing business in the U.S. solely due to its broadcasting. The Court reasoned that if a sale of merchandise, a solicitation of a sale or a distribution of a magazine by a foreign publisher, cannot constitute transacting business in a state, neither could mere broadcasting*". In other words, the customer base, as a sole examination, will not cause the supplier to be present in that state.

[53]Refer to discussion and explanation of the 'Amazon tax', which is not specific law in itself but rather a tax 'coined' as the 'Amazon tax', in 6.1.7., Chap. 6, Part II, pages 55–59 of this paper.

however, the rationale of the Amazon tax law ostensibly contradicts the Piedras Negras ruling that a customer base does not constitute 'physical presence'. The North Dakota case, Quill,[54] also supported the concept that a customer base will not effectuate the 'physical presence' of the supplier in that state. However, subsequent cases to Piedras Negras, such as International Shoe Co. v. Washington,[55] adopted differing approaches and opinions on the matter. In response to contradictory rulings on this issue the USA Congress passed legislation whereby "*no State shall have the power to tax the net income derived within such State by a non-resident through interstate commerce if the non-resident's only business activity within such State during the taxable year is the solicitation of orders for sales of tangible personal property where approval and filling of the order occurs outside such State*".[56]

Implicit to the 'geographic location' test "*the key requirement is that the business should commercially and geographically consist of a coherent whole. An important factor in this regard is whether the enterprise regularly returns to a specific location*".[57] Thus the 'specific location' need not be a specific 'fixed point', and a 'geographical area' will suffice provided there is sufficient connection or link between the 'place of business' and the geographical area[58]:

> *a relationship or connection to a geographical area – instead of a fixed point – suffices to create a permanent establishment if the activity is regularly repeated over a long period of time in the same location, if the work is being performed for the same principal as parts of one project, or if particularly large or complex equipment is used, such as drilling rigs.*[59]

The 'geographic location' test is one of two tests applied to determine whether a place of business is 'fixed'. The second test is the 'duration' test, the requirement of which is that an activity is regularly repeated. The 'duration' test requires a certain degree of performance at the 'location' of the 'place of business'. Lynette Olivier ("Olivier")[60] and Michael Honiball ("Honiball"),[61] propose that 'duration' denotes "*that it is not so much the activities that need to be exercised with the necessary*

[54]idem USA Supreme Court Quill Corp v North Dakota (91-0194), 504 U.S. 298 (1992) [USA]. Refer to footnote 28 of this paper [p56].

[55]International Shoe Co. v Washington 326 U.S. 310 (1945) [USA]. Cited in Goldberg, Sandford, *Internet Sales Pose International Tax Challenges* (1 June 1996). Available at http://www.robertsandholland.com/article.ihtml?id=86 [Accessed 30 July 2010].

[56]op cit, Goldberg, http://www.robertsandholland.com/article.ihtml?id=86.

[57]op cit, Olivier and Honiball, p97.

[58]op cit, Vogel, Univ. of Munich and Co-authors *l*, p205.

[59]op cit, Vogel, Univ. of Munich and Co-authors, p280 as cited in Pinto, p109.

[60]Lynette Olivier "*is a Professor of Law at Pretoria University, a former tax Consultant with Pricewaterhouse Coopers, and now the CEO of the SARS Service Monitoring Office. She is the author and co-author of several tax publications*". **[op cit, Olivier and Honiball, 2005]**.

[61]Michael Honiball "*is a Tax Director at KMPG (Pty) Ltd, where he is countrywide head of International Tax and Transfer Pricing Services. He lectures at both the University of the Witwatersrand and at RAU, and he has published extensively on tax matters*". **[op cit Olivier and Honiball, 2005]**.

degree of performance but rather that the place of business needs to be set up with a certain degree of performance".[62] Vogel endorses this point at issue by declaring that *"the place of business must have been designed to serve the enterprise with a certain degree of permanence rather than merely temporarily . . . If the enterprise carries on its operations on a regular basis and in its place of business, a permanent establishment must be taken to exist..."*.[63]

Implicit to the concept of 'fixed' is *"a certain length of time . . . "*.[64] The OECD MC defines 'fixed' as having a minimum-period rule of 12 months. However, this minimum-period rule relates specifically to building construction sites only and, therefore, does not apply to non-building business activities.[65] Pinto cites the case Henriksen v. Grafton Hotel Ltd[66] in which *"the court decided that permanent was a relative term that was not synonymous with everlasting"*.[67] Philip Baker[68] ("Baker") declares that *"permanence does not mean that the right to use the place of business must be perpetual"*.[69] 'Fixed' should not be interpreted to mean that there may be no interruption in business operations, but rather that business operations should be conducted on a regular basis in order to satisfy the 'duration' test.[70] The Transvaal Hide case[71] argued application of 'fixed' to determine 'permanent establishment'.[72]

---

[62]op cit, Olivier and Honiball, p99.

[63]op cit, Vogel, Univ. of Munich and Co-authors, p206.

[64]supra.

[65]*"The . . . twelve-month test applies only to building sites or construction or assembly projects and must not be interpreted to imply that a place of business should generally be deemed to be a 'permanent' one only if it had existed for a minimum of twelve months"* **[op cit, Vogel, Univ. of Munich and Co-authors, p207]**.

Per Article 5(3) of the OECD MC, *"A building site or construction or installation project constitutes a permanent establishment only if it lasts more than twelve months"*. **[op cit, *OECD MC (2005)*, p27]**.

[66]Henriksen (Inspector of Taxes) v. Grafton Hotel Ltd [1942] 2 KB 184, 196 [Northern Territory of Australia].

[67]op cit, Pinto, p110.

[68]The OECD provides the following brief biography of Philip Baker:

> *Philip Baker is a barrister and QC practising from Grays Inn Tax Chambers. He was called to the bar in 1979, began practising in 1987 and took silk in 2002. He specialises in international tax issues, with a particular emphasis on double tax conventions, and on European Union law and taxation. He has a particular interest in the European Convention on Human Rights and taxation.*
>
> *. . . He is the author of Double Taxation Conventions and International Tax Law and the editor of the International Tax Law Reports.*

Available at http://www.oecd.org/speaker/0,3438,en_21571361_42209831_42839670_1_1_1_1,00.html [Accessed 30 July 2010].

[69]ibid Pinto, p110.

[70]ibid Olivier and Honiball p99.

[71]loc cit Transvaal Hide case (1976) [Botswana].

[72]Refer to 12.1. Traditional Definition of 'Source', Part IV of this paper [p115].

Business operations were conducted at a 'fixed' location in Botswana which occasioned tax liability at that location of permanence despite the fact that Transvaal Hide and Skin Merchants was a RSA company.

As previously discussed the concept of 'permanent establishment' expanded since its inception so as to incorporate the utilisation of an 'agent'. The term 'agent' is defined in the Oxford Dictionary as "*a person whose job is to act for, or manage the affairs of, other people in business* . . . ".[73] Otherwise defined as "*one authorised to carry on business or affairs for another*".[74] An 'agent' may either be 'dependent' or 'independent' and this distinction is established in the OECD MC and analysed by Vogel. Article 5 of the OECD MC specifically states that "*where a person – other than an agent of an independent status . . . – is acting on behalf of an enterprise and has, and habitually exercises, in a Contracting State an authority to conclude contracts in the name of the enterprise, that enterprise shall be deemed to have a permanent establishment in that State in respect of any activities which that person undertakes for the enterprise* . . . ".[75] Thus utilisation of a 'dependent agent' will generally fall within the ambit of the 'permanent establishment' definition. Vogel submits that "*it is only a person who is both bound to follow the instructions of, and is also personally dependant on, the enterprise he represents who can be a dependent agent for the purposes of Article 5 (5) of the OECD MC*".[76]

An 'independent agent' will generally not satisfy 'permanent establishment' requirements, however, this is subject to the provision that the 'independent agent' "*continues to be independent of the enterprise both legally and economically and, when exercising activities on behalf of the enterprise, acts in the ordinary course of his business*".[77] Vogel submits that a person should generally be regarded as an 'independent agent' where the person is not an employee of the enterprise. However, this is subject to the provision that the non-employee person "*is not subject to an obligation to make his services as comprehensively available as he would have to under a contract of employment and as long as he acts as an independent entrepreneur*".[78]

Guidelines which may be applied to determine the dependency or independency status of an agent, whether an individual or juristic person, include an examination of the following factors:

---

[73]'Agent' as defined by the on-line Oxford Advanced Learner's Dictionary. Oxford University Press, 2010. Available at http://www.oxfordadvancedlearnersdictionary.com/dictionary/agent [Accessed 27/07/2010].

[74]Collins Dictionary Thesaurus., Bookman, Franklin Electronic Publishers, 1995.

[75]Article 5(5) of the OECD MC. op cit, *OECD MC (2005)*, p27.

[76]op cit, Vogel, Univ. of Munich and Co-authors, p257.

[77]Supra Vogel, Univ. of Munich and Co-authors, p135.

[78]op cit, Vogel, Univ. of Munich and Co-authors, p135.

(i) *The amount of freedom he . . . has to enter into contracts on behalf of the enterprise, for example, operating under detailed instructions and control indicate a dependent status; and*
(ii) *Entrepreneurial risk: if the risk is borne by the agent, he . . . acts independently.*[79]

As emphasized in the above guidelines and Article 5(5) of the OECD MC the 'dependent' agent must have the ability and authority to conclude contracts on behalf of the enterprise and must, furthermore, 'habitually exercise' such authority in order to satisfy the definition and criteria of a 'dependent agent'. Thus, in order to qualify as a 'dependent agent' *"the person making use of the authority must do so repeatedly and not merely in isolated cases"*.[80]

Vogel observes that the OECD and US MCs' provisions regarding 'dependent agent' are effectually comparable, while the OECD, US and UN MCs' provisions regarding 'independent agent' are generally in agreement. However, the UN MC's provisions regarding 'dependent agent', and in essence 'independent agent', vary. While all three MCs generally conform in respect of 'independent agent' rules, the UN MC introduces an additional provision regarding dependency whereby *"an agent whose activities are exercised wholly or almost wholly on behalf of an enterprise can no longer be considered to be 'independent' in the sense that term has under the rule"*.[81] Also, the UN MC introduces a provision regarding 'dependent agent', not included in the USA and OECD MCs' rules, relating to insurances. Furthermore, the UN MC *"fails to exempt stocks of goods maintained for delivery from constituting a permanent establishment"*[82] and, moreover, specifically stipulates *"that an agent who maintains stocks of goods for delivery shall constitute a permanent establishment even if he has no authority to conclude contracts"*.[83]

An agent of an independent nature, therefore, will not necessarily satisfy permanent establishment requirements. This may be illustrated in the RSA SIR v Downing[84] case, where an independent stockbroker located in the RSA, who managed a portfolio of shares for a client, a resident of Switzerland, was not deemed a permanent establishment in the RSA for the Swiss resident.[85]

---

[79]op cit, Olivier and Honiball, p105.

[80]supra.

[81]ibid Vogel, Univ. of Munich and Co-authors, p257.

[82]ibid, Vogel, Univ. of Munich and Co-authors, p248.

[83]ibid, Vogel, Univ. of Munich and Co-authors, p248.

[84]Secretary for Inland Revenue v Downing (1975) 4 SA 518 (A) [RSA].

[85]op cit, Olivier and Honiball, p104.

Bibliography

Primary Sources

Cases

Republic of South African Cases

CIR v Black 957 (3) SA 536 (A), 21 SATC 226.

CIR v Lever Brothers & Unilever 1946 AD 441, *14 SATC 441.*

Millin v CIR *3 SATC 170* 1928 AD207.

Secretary for Inland Revenue v Downing 1975 4 SA 518 (A).

Tuck v CIR *49 SATC 28* 1988 (3) SA 819 (A).

United States of America Cases

International Shoe Co. v. Washington 326 U.S. 310. 1945. [USA]. Available at http://caselaw.lp.findlaw.com/cgi-bin/getcase.pl?court=US&vol=326&invol=310. Accessed 22 Jan 2012.

Piedras Negras Broadcasting Co v. Commissioner of Internal Revenue. 1941. BTA 297, aff'd 127 F 2d 260 (5th Circuit 1942). Available at http://www.google.co.za/url?sa=t&rct=j&q=piedras%20negras%20broadcasting%20co.%20v%20commissioner&source=web&cd=1&ved=0CB4QFjAA&url=http%3A%2&F%2Flawcourses.haifa.ac.il%2FTaxation_and_tax_treaties%2Findex%2Fmain%2Fsyllabus%2Fcourse_materials%255CPiedras_Negras.doc&ei=6u8bT76wD8TDmQXBiO2vCg&usg=AFQjCNFJfaQeMUXrCusiRocJEOC-Kji4Gw. Accessed 22 Jan 2012.

USA Supreme Court Quill Corp. v. North Dakota (91-0194), 504 U.S. 298. 1992. [USA]. Available at http://www.law.cornell.edu/background/internet/Quill.htm. Accessed 12 Sept 2010. Available at http://www.ct.gov/drs/cwp/view.asp?A=1514&Q=268516. Accessed 12 Sept 2010.

Other Cases

Citation Henriksen (Inspector of Taxes) v. Grafton Hotel Ltd [1942] 2 KB 184, 196 [Calcutta High Court, India]. Available at http://indiankanoon.org/doc/11048/. Accessed 22 Jan 2012.

Commissioner of Taxes v. W. Dunn & Co. Ltd (1918, AD, 614) [Rhodesia, presently Zimbabwe].

Rhodesia Metals Ltd (In Liquidation) v Commissioner of Tax 11 SATC 244. 1938. [Rhodesia, presently Zimbabwe].

Transvaal Associated Hide and Skin Merchants v Collector of Income Tax, Botswana 29 SATC 97 1967 (BCA) [Botswana].

Statutes

OECD. 2005. *OECD model tax convention on income and on capital, condensed version – July 2005*. Paris: OECD Publishers.

Secondary Sources

Collins Dictionary Thesaurus., Bookman, Franklin Electronic Publishers, 1995.

Emslie, Trevor, Dennis Davis, S.J. Hutton, and Lynette Olivier. 2001. *Income tax cases & materials*, 3rd ed. Cape Town: The Taxpayer.

Goldberg, Sandford, Howard Levine, and Peter Glicklich. 1996 June 1. Internet sales pose international tax challenges. *Journal of Taxation*. New York/Washington DC: Publications *Roberts & Holland LLP*. Available at http://www.robertsandholland.com/article.ihtml?id=86. Accessed 30 July 2010.

OECD. *Biography of Arvid Aage Skaar.* Available at http://www.oecd.org/speaker/0,3438,en_21571361_40047302_40414394_1_1_1_1_1,00.html. Accessed 26 July 2010.

OECD. *Biography on Philip Baker*. http://www.oecd.org/speaker/0,3438,en_21571361_42209831_42839670_1_1_1_1,00.html. Accessed 30 July 2010.

OECD Tax policy studies. 2005. *E-Commerce: Transfer pricing and business profits taxation* No. 10. Paris: OECD.

Olivier, Lynette, and Michael Honiball. 2008. *International tax, a South African perspective 2008*, 4th ed. Cape Town: Siber Ink CC.

Pinto, Dale. 2003. *E-Commerce and source-based income taxation*. Amsterdam: IBFD Publications.

Rhodesia – Encyclopedia.com. 2000. *A dictionary of world history*. Available at http://www.encyclopedia.com/doc/1O48-Rhodesia.html. Accessed 5 Jan 2009.

Sinn, Hans Werner. 2007, July. *Please bring me the New York times on the European roots of Richard Abel Musgrave*. CESifo working paper no. 2050, Category I: Public Finance. Available at http://www.econstor.eu/bitstream/10419/26095/1/538342781.PDF. Accessed 19 Sept 2010.

The On-line Oxford Advanced Learner's Dictionary. 2010. Oxford University Press. Available at http://www.oxfordadvancedlearnersdictionary.com/dictionary/agent. Accessed 27 July 2010.

Vogel, Professor Dr Klaus, University of Munich, and Co-Authors. 1991. *Klaus Vogel on double tax conventions*, 2nd ed. Deventer: Kluwer Law and Taxation Publishers.

Vogel, Professor Dr Klaus. 1997. *Klaus Vogel on double tax conventions*, 3rd ed. Deventer: Kluwer Law International.

Chapter 13
Defining 'Source' Within an eCommerce Context

Abstract Traditional criteria relevant to 'presence', 'fixed' and 'agent' cannot be effectively applied in an eCommerce environment.

The Australian Tax Offices' 'Tax and the Internet' report in 1997, which allowed for greater flexibility in the application of 'source' principles to eCommerce is a compelling example of attempts to adapt direct taxation principles to technology. Since its inception the alternative approach has become increasingly superannuated as an effective taxing tool for determining 'permanent establishment' in an eCommerce environment.

The point at issue is whether an ISP in outer space constitutes 'permanent establishment'. A satellite cannot constitute 'permanent establishment' because its location cannot be considered *"part of the territory of a contracting State under the applicable rules of international laws . . . "*, (OECD. Commentary 5.5. of Article 5. *The 2010 Update to the Model Tax Convention* (22 July 2010). P15. Available at http://www.oecd.org/dataoecd/23/43/45689328.pdf [Accessed 12 September 2010]) therefore, neither can an ISP in space.

The primary point at issue is that the application of traditional concepts and rules defining 'permanent establishment' for the purpose of determining 'source' in eCommerce, which is continuously evolving, is becoming increasingly obsolescent and ineffectual.

As 'source' is normatively defined by 'presence', Pinto has identified the following factors as possibly constituting 'presence' for the purpose of defining 'source' within an electronic commercial environment:

(a) *The foreign customer base . . . which generates business profits;*
(b) *The delivery of . . . [digitised services to customers];*
(c) *The place where a contract is concluded between [the enterprise] and its customers;*
(d) *The use of local access numbers by customers that enables them to connect to [the enterprise's] web site from overseas;*
(e) *The use by [the enterprise] of telecommunications infrastructure in foreign countries in which it operates;*
(f) *[The enterprise's] web site that is available to customers worldwide;*
(g) *The presence of a computer server in foreign countries; or*

A.M. Bardopoulos, *eCommerce and the Effects of Technology on Taxation*, Law, Governance and Technology Series 22, DOI 10.1007/978-3-319-15449-7_13

(h) *Representative presences of [the enterprise] – both personal agents (e.g. ISPs) and mechanical or software agents (e.g. bots).*[1]

The OECD has, on the other hand, published the following views with the resolve of clarifying "*how current treaty rules for the taxation of business profits apply in the context of electronic commerce and [the examination of] proposals for alternative rules*"[2]:

(i) *"A web site cannot, in itself, constitute a permanent establishment;*
(ii) *A web site hosting arrangement typically does not result in a permanent establishment for the enterprise that carries on business through that web site; and*
(iii) *An ISP will not, except in very unusual circumstances, constitute a dependent agent of another enterprise so as to constitute a permanent establishment of that enterprise . . . ;*
(iv) *[Furthermore, having examined] . . . the issue, the conclusion has been reached that human intervention is not a requirement for the existence of a permanent establishment . . . "*[3]

Within the compass of the above rules pertaining to 'permanent establishment', as well as the OECD's Commentary on what will not constitute 'permanent establishment', it is manifest that traditional criteria relevant to 'presence', 'fixed' and 'agent' cannot be effectively applied in an eCommerce environment.

While the OECD MC Commentary acknowledges the commonality of ISPs providing web site hosting services for other enterprises on their own servers, an ISP will, nevertheless, "*not constitute an agent of the enterprise to which the web site belongs, because they will not regularly conclude such contracts or because they will constitute independent agents acting in the ordinary course of their business . . . [and, therefore,] cannot apply to deem a permanent establishment to exist by virtue of the web site being an agent of the enterprise . . .*"[4]

It has been submitted that the innovation of eCommerce has made it possible for businesses to conduct business operations within a country without having to have a 'fixed place of business' situated within that country.[5] Therefore, deliberation of 'fixed', a concept pertinent to traditional criteria for determining 'source', may no longer be apposite to an eCommerce environment. The OECD Commentary submits that the 'server' hosting the web site is physical equipment situated at a geographical location. Thus, it may be possible for such a location to constitute the enterprise's 'fixed place of business'. It is not uncommon for enterprises to

---

[1]op cit, Pinto, Dale *E-Commerce and Source-Based Income Taxation* (2003), Netherlands, p91.

[2]OECD Committee on Fiscal Affairs *Clarification on the Application of the Permanent Establishment Definition in E-Commerce: Changes to the Commentary on the Model Tax Convention on Article 5* (2000) p3.

[3]idem p3.

[4]op cit, OECD *OECD Model Tax Convention on Income and on Capital, Condensed Version – July 2005 (*2005*) OECD Publishers, Paris, France*, p106.

[5]op cit, Olivier, Lynette and Honiball, Michael International Tax, *A South African Perspective 2008*, Fourth Edition (2008), South Africa, p98.

utilise hosting services provided by another, however, as discussed above,[6] an ISP will not constitute an agent. Furthermore, the web site itself does not constitute a fixed place of business because, as submitted by the OECD, "*an Internet web site, which is a combination of software and electronic data, does not in itself constitute tangible property. It therefore does not have a location that can constitute a 'place of business' as there is no 'facility such as premises or, in certain instances, machinery or equipment' ... as far as the software and data constituting that web site is concerned*".[7,8]

The Australian Tax Office submitted an alternative approach within the '*Tax and the Internet*'[9] Report published in 1997. This alternative approach requires the examination of the functions performed at the place where the business occurs, "*irrespective of whether that 'place' occupies physical space ..., or electronic space*".[10] In other words, "*[a] web site located on a server, that is fixed in time and location, and through which business is carried on may constitute a [permanent establishment]*".[11] However, this approach contradicts the OECD opinion regarding web sites not constituting 'permanent establishment'. However, the ATO 1997 Report may be considered more forward thinking than the OECD's Commentary, allowing for a greater flexibility in the application of 'source' principles to eCommerce.

However, the applicability of the ATO '*Tax and the Internet*' Report of 1997 has been pre-empted by technological amelioration with 'load balancing' and 'failover'. The average website in the year 2010 is no longer "*located on* a *server that is fixed in time and location*". 'Load balancing' and 'failover' technology has made it possible for a website to be located on several servers simultaneously. While each of the several 'servers' may be 'fixed in time and location', it is possible for the 'locations' to extend across several jurisdictions. Determining 'source' in such circumstances may be attempted by application of the 'dominant cause' test, however, as a single transaction can occur over several diverse servers located in several diverse jurisdictions,[12] all of which may not be the same each time the website is accessed, determining the server which constitutes 'dominant cause' becomes an increasingly difficult challenge, if not impossible.

"*[W]ith the advent of open source software and the subsequent commoditisation of enterprise-level software – functionality such as load-balancing and failover have become more affordable and thus more common amongst less mission-critical*

[6]Refer to preceding paragraph of this Chapter [p132].

[7]OECD Commentary on Article 5, paragraph 42.2, op cit, *OECD Model Tax Convention on Income and on Capital, Condensed Version (*2005*)*, p103.

[8]supra.

[9]As cited in Pinto, p103 – "*Australian Taxation Office, Electronic Commerce Project Team, Tax and the Internet – Volume 1 (1997)*".

[10]op cit, Pinto, p103.

[11]ibid Pinto, p103.

[12]Refer to the *Illustrative Example Alpha*, Chap. 5, Part II of this paper [p46–48].

technology systems".[13] The concept of 'load balancing' and 'failover' servers would have existed in 1997 when the ATO issued their report, however, it may be presumed that the advantage of such technology was confined primarily to banks, credit card companies, intelligence agencies, et al. and was not extended to the average business.[14] Indeed, it is most probable that in the 1990s multiple servers were utilised by companies as 'mission-critical systems', but it is highly improbable that such servers were located in multiple jurisdictions, excepting possibly for intelligence agencies such as the CIA and Interpol.[15]

In 1997 when the ATO suggested the alternative approach allowance was not made for the possibility of multiple servers being utilised by the average web site. The ATO's '*Tax and the Internet*' report serves as a compelling example of attempts to adapt direct taxation principles to technology, prompted by technological amelioration since its inception only 13 years ago, the alternative approach has become increasingly superannuated as an effective taxing tool for determining 'permanent establishment' in an eCommerce environment.

As discussed previously,[16] while future technological ameliorations cannot be predicted with absolute precision, the 'next generation ISP' in space is imminent. The recently amended OECD MC Commentary[17] has incorporated the following with regard to satellites in geostationary orbit:

> *5.5. Clearly, a permanent establishment may only be considered to be situated in a Contracting State if the relevant place of business is situated in the territory of that State. The question of whether a satellite in geostationary orbit could constitute a permanent establishment for the satellite operator relates in part to how far the territory of a State extends into space. No member country would agree that the location of these satellites can be part of the territory of a Contracting State under the applicable rules of international law and could therefore be considered to be a permanent establishment situated therein. Also, the particular area over which a satellite's signals may be received (the satellite's "footprint") cannot be considered to be at the disposal of the operator of the satellite so as to make that area a place of business of the satellite's operator.*[18]

The point at issue is not whether an ISP in outer space constitutes 'permanent establishment' 'should technology extend to space', but preferably 'once technology has extended fully to space'. OECD commentary, previously issued and not deleted in the OECD 2010 Update to the Model Tax Convention, states that an ISP may constitute 'permanent establishment'. However, according to the inclusion of

---

[13]Kontos, Kosta (22 July 2010), BSc (CompSci) (UCT), MBA (UCT). Managing Director (MD) of Kontos Technologies. Also, *idem* Kontos, Kosta, refer to footnote 4 of this paper [p62].

[14]supra.

[15]supra.

[16]Refer to 7.1. Future Technological Advancements, Part II of this paper [p62].

[17]As per the 2010 update to the Model Tax Convention, 22 July 2010.

[18]OECD. Commentary 5.5 of Article 5. The 2010 Update to the Model Tax Convention (22 July 2010). p15. Available at http://www.oecd.org/dataoecd/23/43/45689328.pdf [Accessed 12 September 2010].

additional commentary regarding satellites, quoted above, it should follow that ***if*** a satellite cannot constitute a 'permanent establishment' because the location is not considered "*part of the territory of a Contracting State under the applicable rules of international law . . .*",[19] neither can an ISP in space. This surely demonstrates, yet again, the inflexibility of traditional rules and principles when applied to the defining of 'source' in a technologically evolving world. Therefore, it may be argued that the application of traditional concepts and rules defining 'permanent establishment' for the purpose of determining ' source' in eCommerce, which is continuously evolving, is becoming increasingly obsolescent and ineffectual.

Bibliography

Primary Sources

Statutes

OECD. 2005. *OECD model tax convention on income and on capital, Condensed Version – July 2005*. Paris: OECD Publishers.

Secondary Sources

Kontos, Kosta BSc (CompSci) (UCT), MBA (UCT). Managing Director (MD) of Kontos Technologies.

OECD. 2010, July 22. *The 2010 update to the model tax convention*. Available at http://www.oecd.org/dataoecd/23/43/45689328.pdf. Accessed 12 Sept 2010.

OECD Committee on Fiscal Affairs. 2000. *Clarification on the application of the permanent establishment definition in e-Commerce: Changes to the commentary on the model tax convention on article 5*. Paris: OECD Publications.

Olivier, Lynette, and Michael Honiball. 2008. *International tax, a South African perspective 2008*, 4th ed. Cape Town: Siber Ink CC.

Pinto, Dale. 2003. *E-Commerce and source-based income taxation*. Amsterdam: IBFD Publications.

[19]supra.

Chapter 14
Conclusion

Abstract A discussion of the application of 'source' within the context of eCommerce prescribes a perspicacious examination of the interaction of 'permanent establishment' prerequisites within the virtual world. This presupposes, *inter alia*, reassessing concepts such as 'physical presence', 'fixed', and location of 'place of business', as well as utilisation of an agent and that which constitutes an agent.

Extensive taxation literature refutes argument for 'physical presence' in a virtual world or effected by a virtual world. The Amazon Tax is a manifestation of the closest proximity of interpretation of 'physical presence' in the virtual world by taxation authorities and technology and communication masters. However, implicit to the Amazon Tax (Refer to discussion and explanation of the 'Amazon tax', which is not specific law in itself but rather a tax 'coined' as the 'Amazon tax', in 6.1.7., Chap. 6, Part II, pages 55–59 of this paper) the 'physical presence' of Amazon in the State of New York is deduced by the evidence of an Amazon 'consumer base' in the State of New York, and not because 'physical presence' of Amazon is either in the Internet or effected by the Internet.

The point at issue is that tax should adjust its principles and perceptions to those of the technology and communication industries and not demand the reverse.

It is submitted that the current flexibility of the indirect tax principles of consumption tax, primarily VAT, may be effectively applied to eCommerce without resorting to the problematic mission of the 'reconceptualisation' of consumption tax principles.

A discussion of the application of 'source' within the context of eCommerce prescribes a perspicacious examination of the interaction of 'permanent establishment' requisites within the virtual world. This presupposes, *inter alia*, reassessing concepts such as 'physical presence', 'fixed', and location of 'place of business', as well as utilisation of an agent and that which constitutes an agent.

Pinto submits that the requisites of application and determination of 'physical presence' is reduced within the compass of eCommerce:

> *Arguably, the most significant characteristic of electronic commerce which impacts on the way in which source is defined is the 'irrelevance of geographical consideration' and borderless nature of the medium:*

A.M. Bardopoulos, *eCommerce and the Effects of Technology on Taxation*,
Law, Governance and Technology Series 22, DOI 10.1007/978-3-319-15449-7_14

'All tax laws stand on the twin pillars of territoriality and enforceability, and tax laws cannot exist outside this framework... How does one mark territory in a seamless, digital world? How does one map nations and taxing jurisdictions in a world that is not based on geography?'[1]

As discussed earlier,[2] philosophical postulation of 'physical presence' in the virtual world and in diverse geographical locations effected by virtual transportation is proffered primarily by the technology and communications profession. Extensive taxation literature refutes argument for 'physical presence' in a virtual world or effected by a virtual world.[3] The Amazon tax[4] is a manifestation of the closest proximity of interpretation of 'physical presence' in the virtual world by taxation authorities and technology and communication masters. However, implicit to the Amazon tax the 'physical presence' of Amazon in the State of New York is deduced by the evidence of an Amazon 'consumer base' in the State of New York, and not because 'physical presence' of Amazon is either in the internet or effected by the internet.

Pinto summarises the impact of technology on 'physical presence' and, therefore, source as follows:

> *[I]f businesses choose to operate without physical or representative presences in source countries, then despite the theoretical arguments that were advanced... which suggested that source-based taxation of electronic commerce transactions* is *theoretically justifiable and therefore should occur, it is likely that the way source is currently defined under the permanent establishment threshold may not allow for the source-based taxation of business profits which arise from electronic commerce transactions. This suggests that the way in which source is defined for active income may need to be reconceptualised and the detailed analysis to support this proposition in the case of the permanent establishment threshold [has been extensively examined]... [I]t is recognised that despite the possibilities that electronic commerce offers for such commerce to be conducted in source countries without a physical or human presence, the reality is that it is still in an embryonic stage of its development... [T]he point being made here is that electronic commerce allows for the possibility that business may be conducted without a physical or representative presence in source countries and this possibility arguably suggests that a reconsideration of the way in which source is defined may be necessary to determine the source of active business profits which arise from electronic commerce transactions.*[5] [Emphasis added by Pinto]

---

[1]op cit, Pinto, Dale *E-Commerce and Source-Based Income Taxation* (2003), Netherlands, p58. Within this citation Dr Dale Pinto cites the following two works respectively:

Doernberg et al., Electronic Commerce and Multijurisdictional Taxation (2001), p6; and an address by Ajay Thakkar at the International Fiscal Association Asia Regional Conference on E-Commerce and International Taxation, Mumbai, India, November 2000.

[2]Refer to 8.1. *The Virtual World versus the Physical World*, Part II of this paper [p72].

[3]For example, Pinto, p58. Pinto advocates a reduced need for 'physical presence'; op cit, Olivier, Lynette and Honiball, Michael *International Tax, A South African Perspective 2008*, Fourth Edition (2008), South Africa, p98, submit that determining 'fixed' place of business in pursuance of determining permanent establishment is 'outdated'.

[4]Refer to discussion and explanation of the 'Amazon tax', which is not specific law in itself but rather a tax 'coined' as the 'Amazon tax', in 6.1.7., Chap. 6, Part II, pages 55–59 of this paper.

[5]op cit, Pinto, p63.

It should be possible for tax principles to be applied in a manner compatible with the technology and communication industry's perception of 'presence'. The Internet has had a drastic impact on society and, moreover, the economy. It is imperative that we recognise that "*the Internet [is] an important cultural phenomenon ... [which has, however,] failed to comply with basic economic laws ... [probably because] it was devised by a bunch of hippie anarchists*".[6] The point at issue is taxation, either direct or indirect, in an eCommerce environment, which is subject to technology and technological concepts, and, as such, it may be proposed that tax should adjust its principles and perceptions to those of the technology and communication industry and not demand the reverse. The question begs as to whether the continuing attempt to impose 'basic economic laws' on an environment which defies such laws is not in itself a futile exercise.

While the concept of 'physical presence' has promoted much academic debate and is a most significant and challenging issue in the argument for "reconceptualising"[7] 'source' principles to effectively effectuate the imposition of direct taxation in an eCommerce environment, the issue, however, falls outside the ambit of this paper. The intention of this paper is to assess the current flexibility of the indirect tax principles of consumption tax, primarily VAT, and to submit that indirect tax principles may be effectively applied to eCommerce without resorting to the problematic mission of the 'reconceptualisation' of consumption tax principles.

However, although the primary interest of this paper is not the manner in which 'physical presence' is perceived, 'physical presence' is, nevertheless, a significant issue, the impact of which on sales in, for example, Second Life, and the relevance of which in regard to imposition of VAT in Second Life cannot be disregarded and, therefore, this issue will be further discussed in Parts V (5) and VI (6).

Bibliography

Secondary Sources

Nolle, Thomas. Available at www.quotegarden.com.internet.html. Accessed 8 May 2008.

Olivier, Lynette, and Michael Honiball. 2008. *International tax, a South African perspective 2008*, 4th ed. Cape Town: Siber Ink CC.

Pinto, Dale. 2003. *E-Commerce and source-based income taxation.* Amsterdam: IBFD Publications.

---

[6]Nolle, Thomas. Available at www.quotegarden.com.internet.html [Accessed 8 May 2008].

[7]"Reconceptualisation" of 'source-based' principles is addressed extensively in Dr Dale Pinto's doctorial thesis – op cit Pinto.

Part V
Value Added Taxation

Chapter 15
Introduction

> The art of taxation consists in so plucking the goose as to get the most feathers with the least hissing" – Ascribed to Jean Baptist Colbert ("*French statesman, chief minister to Louis XIV (1665–83). A vigorous reformer, he put order back into the country's finances, boosted industry and commerce, and established the French navy as one of the most formidable in Europe. His reforms, however, could not keep pace with the demands of Louis' war policies and extensive royal building programme, and by the end of Louis' reign the French economy was again experiencing severe problems.*" **[op cit, *Oxford English Reference Dictionary*, (*Second Edition*), (*1996*), *USA*. p282]**) (1619–83)

Abstract The fundamental principle of VAT remains invariable – VAT is an indirect taxing system which is based on consumption. VAT is levied on goods and services consumed by the taxpayer whereby the end user bears the brunt of the tax as it is a 'consumption tax'.

The European VAT system provides an excellent example of harmonization. Several Southern Hemisphere countries have adopted a variation of the New Zealand VAT legislation. Canada imposed both retail sales tax and VAT systems, and in some provinces a harmonized VAT system which is effectively both retail sales tax and VAT imposed together. The Japanese consumption tax has departed from the EU VAT system. The above specified VAT systems represent the basis of all implemented VAT systems.

A point at issue is that a small variation in legislation may cause diverse implications and application of VAT legislation in respect of the virtual world.

The investigation of VAT as a possible eCommerce taxing solution should of necessity probe the effectiveness of eTransaction VAT collection and the effectiveness of the monitoring of VAT in eCommerce, and the application of VAT in the virtual world.

Prior to assessing the effectiveness of VAT within the "virtual world", VAT itself, as a taxing system, should be analysed and understood. Therefore, the history and

A.M. Bardopoulos, *eCommerce and the Effects of Technology on Taxation*, Law, Governance and Technology Series 22, DOI 10.1007/978-3-319-15449-7_15

development of VAT will be examined, pursued by a review of the various VAT liability calculating methods.[1]

Regardless of the varied VAT systems utilised in diverse countries, the fundamental principle of VAT remains invariable – VAT is an indirect taxing system which is based on consumption. In other words, VAT, as an indirect tax, is levied on goods and services consumed by the taxpayer whereby the end user bears the brunt of the tax as it is a 'consumption tax'. That being said, varied 'indirect tax' legislations and systems have been implemented in diverse countries. Thus, prior to examining whether VAT is the eTax solution, the varied systems should be examined and understood.

The European VAT system provides an excellent example of harmonization. The EU VAT system has been aptly described as being 'harmonised', *"[t]he most prevalent form of VAT is the harmonized VAT in the EU member states. The EU model has the most extensive case law on VAT issues. More recent entrants to the VAT family have expanded the VAT base and made other significant changes."*[2] Following the EU VAT system is the New Zealand VAT system[3] which *"...departed from the EU model in a number of significant ways, including the expansion of the tax base...by limiting exemptions and zero rating and by taxing many government services"*.[4] It is important to note that several Southern hemisphere countries which have implemented VAT, have adopted a variation of the New Zealand VAT legislation. Canada, unlike the USA (discussed below), has implemented a harmonized VAT system which will also be examined. Lastly, the Japanese consumption tax system will also be examined as, like New Zealand, Japan has also departed from the EU VAT system. It is important to note that *"[u]nder the Japanese Consumption Tax (CT), taxable firms are not required to issue VAT invoices that represent a central feature of other VAT regimes."*[5] While further variations in VAT systems may be cited for the import of interpretations, judgements and comparative studies (for example, the South African VAT legislation), the above specified VAT systems represent the basis of all VAT systems.

Of course a vital aspect of examining VAT as the eTax solution is to take into account countries which have not implemented an indirect taxing system such

[1]A practical review of the VAT history, development and various VAT liability calculating methods was covered in my M.Phil in Commercial Law, Part II Dissertation – material derived from the aforementioned dissertation will be used to introduce and promote the understanding of VAT, and will be expanded where necessary.

Bardopoulos, A. *UCT M.Phil in Commercial Law Dissertation: VAT Implications in E-Commerce from a South African Perspective* (2009).

[2]op cit Schenk, Alan & Oldman, Oliver *Value Added Tax, A Comparative Approach* (2007), USA, P58.

[3]New Zealand's indirect legislation, the New Zealand Goods and Services Tax Act, No. 141 of 1985 (as amended), otherwise referred to as the GST Act, is the New Zealand VAT equivalent legislation.

[4]op cit Schenk & Oldman, p58.

[5]op cit Schenk & Oldman, p58.

as VAT. Thus, while this paper will examine whether VAT is the eTax solution with specific reference to countries which have a VAT system, it is, nevertheless, important to examine the various problems which may arise as a result of countries not yet following VAT. *In other words, what is the possible impact on countries not following VAT with regard to eTransactions?*

Examining the efficiency of VAT as a taxing system when trading between the USA and another VAT jurisdiction presupposes the effectiveness of indirect tax to date. A relevant example of cross-border (albeit primarily between various USA States rather than on an international level, but nevertheless a form of cross-border) eTransactions may be Amazon.com the *raison d'étre* of which has been under USA scrutiny for several years. In fact, in 2009 New York State imposed a new tax law dubbed the "Amazon tax"[6] requiring Amazon to collect sales tax even if Amazon did not have a physical presence in New York.[7]

It is vital to examine the indirect taxing system in the USA because the USA is a huge commercial hub. The USA consists of a "*patchwork of [retail] sales tax utilization and sales tax rates*",[8] apart from a few states that have adopted some form of VAT. The intricate sales tax system of the USA is a study in its own right and, while this paper will not focus in depth on the USA sales tax regime, it should, nevertheless, be examined, even if only sample states are briefly examined. As the USA indirect taxing system is still evolving, it may be assumed that the USA does not have a harmonized indirect taxing system administered at national level. However, with the development of technology and the prevailing 'Amazon Problem' several states have entered into a 'Streamlined Sales and Use Tax Agreement' in an effort to "*regularize Internet sales taxation ... [which] may lead ... Congress*[9] *to*

---

[6]Refer to discussion and explanation of the 'Amazon tax', which is not specific law in itself but rather a tax 'coined' as the 'Amazon tax', in 6.1.7., Chap. 6, Part II, pages 55–59 of this paper.

[7]Chang, Jacqui, *Sales Tax Holiday May be Over for Amazon, Other E-Tailers* (13/01/2009). Available at http://arstechnica.com/tech-policy/news/2009/01/sales-tax-holiday-may-be-over-for-amazon-other-e-tailers.ars [Accessed 22/03/2010].

[8]Harley T. Duncan *State and Local Retail Sales Taxes, Federation of Tax Administrators April 2005*, p1. Available at http://www.taxadmin.org/fta/rate/taxreformpanel.pdf [Accessed 27/03/2010].

[9]The United States House of Representatives website provides the following description of 'Congress':

> *'All Legislative Powers herein granted shall be vested in a Congress of the United States, which shall consist of a Senate and House of Representatives.'*
>
> *(Article I, Section 1, of the United States Constitution)*
>
> *The chief function of Congress is the making of laws. The legislative process comprises a number of steps, and much information is available from this page concerning the legislation introduced and considered in the 111th Congress. To help you understand the information and how it interrelates, a very brief overview of the legislative process within the House of Representatives is presented below. There are many aspects and variations of the process which are not addressed here ... The work of Congress is initiated by the introduction of a proposal in one of four principal forms: the bill, the joint resolution, the concurrent resolution, and the simple resolution.*

loosen rules against inter-state sales taxation".[10] The Streamlined Sales Tax Project and most specifically New York State and the implementation of the 'Amazon Tax' will be examined.

Furthermore, the impact of differing VAT legislations within the eCommerce environment contributing to possible conflict of application and collection of taxes will be examined. For example, New Zealand VAT legislation has incorporated a 'place of supply' rule which South African legislation failed to include when adopting New Zealand legislation. The lack of a 'place of supply' rule creates uncertainty, in certain circumstances, as to where the supply occurs and, therefore, where such supply should be taxed. For example, in terms of New Zealand VAT legislation "*... services ... shall be deemed to be supplied outside of New Zealand if the supplier is not resident in New Zealand: provided that ... services shall be deemed to be supplied in New Zealand if the supplier is not resident in New Zealand and ... the services are physically performed in New Zealand by any person who is in New Zealand at the time the services are performed...*".[11] However, as a comparative example, South African VAT legislation allows "*services [which] are physically rendered elsewhere than in the Republic ...*"[12] to be zero-rated[13] for VAT purposes. Within the context of the "virtual world" such a small variation may give rise to diverse implications and application of VAT legislation in determining where the supply occurs. One aspect which will be examined with regard to the "virtual world" is the ability for an individual to travel, via electronic means, to a computer across the world while all the time remaining physically within one country. In terms of New Zealand legislation the physical location of the individual must be determined, whereas in South African legislation determination must be made as to where the services are physically rendered.

The investigation of VAT as a possible eCommerce taxing solution should of necessity probe the effectiveness of eTransaction VAT collection and the effectiveness of the monitoring of VAT in eCommerce, and the application of VAT in the virtual world.

United States House of Representatives. *Tying It All Together: Learn about the Legislative Process*. Available at http://www.house.gov/house/Tying_it_all.shtml [Accessed 13/12/2010].

[10]United States Sales Tax Site: Sales on the Internet. Available at http://www.usa-sales-use-tax-e-commerce.com/sales_on_internet.asp [Accessed 2/12/2010].

[11]Imposition of goods and services tax on supply in terms of Section 8 of New Zealand Goods and Services Tax Act 1985 141.

[12]Section 11(2)(k) of the South African VAT Act, No. 89 of 1991 (as amended).

[13]Some VAT systems offer a multi-tier rate system. Zero-rated supplies are still taxable supplies but merely subject to VAT at 0 %.

Bibliography

Primary Sources

Statutes

New Zealand Goods and Services Tax Act, No. 141 of 1985 (as amended).
South Africa Value-Added Tax Act, No. 89 of 1991 (as amended).

Secondary Sources

Bardopoulos, Anne. 2009. *VAT implications in e-Commerce from a South African perspective.* University of Cape Town Masters of Philosophy in Commercial Law Dissertation.

Chang, Jacqui. *Sales tax holiday may be over for Amazon, other e-Tailers* (13/01/2009). Available at http://arstechnica.com/tech-policy/news/2009/01/sales-tax-holiday-may-be-over-for-amazon-other-e-tailers.ars. Accessed 22 Mar 2010.

Duncan, Harley T. *State and local retail sales taxes, federation of tax administrators April (2005).* Available at http://www.taxadmin.org/fta/rate/taxreformpanel.pdf. Accessed 27 Mar 2010.

Schenk, Alan, and Oliver Oldman. 2007. *Value added tax, a comparative approach.* New York: Cambridge University Press.

The Oxford English Reference Dictionary, 2nd ed. 1996. New York: Oxford University Press.

United States House of Representatives. *Tying it all together: Learn about the legislative process.* Available at http://www.house.gov/house/Tying_it_all.shtml. Accessed 13 Dec 2010.

United States Sales Tax Site: *Sales on the Internet.* Available at http://www.usa-sales-use-tax-e-commerce.com/sales_on_internet.asp. Accessed 2 Dec 2010.

Chapter 16
Development of VAT and Adoption of VAT in Various Countries & Multistage Tax Methods

Abstract VAT is a consumption tax imposed at each step of the manufacturing process enabling revenue authorities to collect the tax in stages. There are various multistage methods. In terms of the 'destination principle' VAT is imposed on the consumer in the country where the goods or services are consumed. Conversely the 'origin principle' is effectively the inverse of the 'destination principle'. 'Output tax' refers to the tax imposed and collected by a seller on a taxable sale. 'Input tax' is a "*credit that a taxpayer may take against output tax for the VAT that was paid on the purchases that qualify for credit*" (Schenk, Alan & Oldman, Olivier, Value Added Tax, *A Comparative Approach* (2007) Cambridge University Press, New York, USA, p21).

In the 'addition method' VAT is determined by the company's 'economic factors' appertaining to production for a period and multiplying it by the tax rate. The 'sales-subtraction' method is a 'period tax'. VAT liability is determined based on the 'cumulative data' (*idem* p42).

The credit-subtraction method does not rely on VAT invoices. The indirect tax VAT method adopted by Japan is a variation of the credit-subtraction method.

The credit-invoice method is presently the dominant VAT system implemented in a variety of jurisdictions.

A crucial 'shared basic principle' supported by the OECD is based on the 'destination principle'. However, there are currently no commonly held principles prescribing how VAT should be imposed on international trade in services and intangibles. The 'multi-tier' VAT rate system has been identified by the OECD as an area which may give rise to increased compliance and enforcement costs and which, furthermore, creates legal uncertainty and effectuates increased fraud occurrences.

16.1 Development of VAT and Adoption of VAT in Various Countries

As previously discussed under Part I sales taxes and customs date back to the Roman Empire. VAT, however, is a modern tax devised by Dr Wilhelm von Siemens in the 1920s to replace the existing turnover taxes because of problems inherent to the latter. In the early 1960s VAT proliferated. Prior to this VAT experienced a slow

A.M. Bardopoulos, *eCommerce and the Effects of Technology on Taxation*,
Law, Governance and Technology Series 22, DOI 10.1007/978-3-319-15449-7_16

adoption period. The first VAT system introduced into France was in 1948 and the former French colonies Cote d'Ivoire and Senegal followed suit in 1960 and the 1960s respectively.[1]

The adoption of VAT in Western Europe has been described as "*intimately associated with the drive for greater economic integration among the member states of the European Communities: the VAT is particularly well suited to avoiding the trade distortions associated with the cascading indirect taxes that it replaced.*"[2] South America on the other hand viewed VAT "*as a more efficient revenue-raising tax that would be consistent with the increasingly outward orientation of economic policies.*"[3]

Taxes customarily fall into two different categories of either "direct taxes" or "indirect taxes". Alan Schenk[4] provided the following comparative explanation of the two types of tax categories:

> *A direct tax is one that is assessed upon the property, business or income of the individual who is to pay the tax. Conversely indirect taxes are taxes that are levied upon commodities before they reach the consumer who ultimately pay[s] the taxes as part of the market price of the commodity.*[5]

VAT, an indirect tax, may be very broadly defined as "*a broad-based tax levied on commodity sales up to and including, at least, the manufacturing stage, with systematic offsetting of tax charged on commodities purchased as inputs – except perhaps on capital goods – against that due on outputs*".[6]

The indirect tax is levied at each stage "value is added" to the product. Thus, VAT is imposed at each step of the production and distribution process. As VAT is a tax borne by the end user the liability is effectively passed from the manufacturer to the distributor and then onto the consumer as the end user. Dr Pernilla Rendahl[7]

[1]Ebrill, Liam; Keen, Michael; Bodin, Jean-Paul & Summers Victoria, *The Modern VAT* (2001). International Monetary Fund, Washington, USA, p4–5.

[2]*ibid*, p6.

[3]supra.

[4]Per the biographical précis of Alan Schenk which may be found on the back of his book, Schenk & Oldman, *Value Added Tax, A Comparative Approach*:

> *Alan Schenk teaches VAT at Wayne State University [USA] and has taught VAT at other universities such as Harvard University [USA], University of Michigan [USA], and the University of San Diego [USA]. For the past eight years, Professor Schenk has served as Technical Advisor for the International Monetary Fund, drafting and reviewing legislative proposals for sales and value added tax for several countries in Africa and for emerging economies of Eastern Europe. He is the author of four books and has published many articles on VAT including several involving the taxation of financial services.*

[5]op cit, Schenk & Oldman, p5: Alan Schenk's definition may be found in *The Guide to American Law, vol. 10:25 (1984).*

[6]*op cit*, Ebrill et al., p2.

[7]Dr Pernilla Rendahl submitted her thesis, Cross-Border Consumption Taxation of Digital Supplies, in total fulfilment of the requirements of the degree of Doctor of Laws in November 2008

described the objective of an indirect tax based on consumption as "*to tax expenditures made by persons for their private purposes*".[8] This process, as a rough example, results in the manufacturer incurring VAT on purchases of raw materials, which is then passed onto the distributor by including this VAT in the selling price. The manufacturer in turn claims the VAT expense incurred on the acquisition of raw materials back from the revenue authorities. This process repeats itself until the product reaches the end consumer. The end consumer is unable to claim the VAT paid and, therefore, bears the tax burden.[9]

While VAT is a consumption tax, which is borne by the end consumer, it is, nevertheless, imposed at each step of the manufacturing process through to the distribution process enabling the revenue authorities to collect the tax in stages rather than all at once at the end of the process when the consumer makes his purchase. This type of indirect tax, interchangeably referred to above as VAT, is otherwise referred to as a 'multistage tax'. "*The indirect tax on consumption may[, however,] take the form of a single-stage tax like the retail sales tax or a multistage tax like value-added tax*".[10] In terms of the 'single-stage tax' method the indirect tax is imposed and collected at a single stage which is the final point of distribution to the consumer. The single-stage tax includes the 'retail sales tax' similar to the indirect taxes imposed by several USA states and even some provinces in Canada.[11]

---

through the Jonkoping International Business School of Sweden. Dr Pernilla Rendahl's thesis aims include:

> *To evaluate if cross-border consumption tax of digital supplies is rational from an international coordination perspective. The aim specifically covers a comparative study of double tax and unintentional non-tax in B2C [business to consumer] e-commerce",* as well as, "*to examine how the place of supply is decided for digital supplies and what consequences do these rules have for cross-border B2C supplies*". Dr Pernilla Rendahl's study examines "*whether consumption taxation upholds the internationally agreed upon principles, which are part of the Ottawa Taxation Framework Conditions (the Framework Conditions). The evaluation of rationality is carried out through the use of an evaluation model, for which the Framework Conditions provide a basis. The principles which are part of the Framework Conditions are: neutrality efficiency certainty and simplicity effectiveness and fairness and flexibility.*

[8]op cit, Rendahl, Pernilla *Cross-Border Consumption Taxation of Digital Supplies* (2009) IBFD, Netherlands, p21.

[9]Mason, Wendy H., *Value-Added Tax – The VAT Assessment Process, History of Value-Added Tax*. Available at http://www.referenceforbusiness.com/management/Tr-Z/Value-Added-Tax.html [Accessed 12/-8/2008].

[10]op cit, Schenk & Oldman, p30.

[11]idem p33.

16.2 Multistage Tax Methods

There are various multistage tax methods which may be applied, of which the commonly known methods include the "addition method", "sales-subtraction method" and two different types of "credit-subtraction methods".[12]

An examination of the different multistage tax methods and the various VAT systems implemented internationally presupposes a fundamental comprehension of the 'destination principle', the 'origin principle' and the meaning of an 'input credit' and 'output tax'.

16.2.1 Basic Principles and Definitions

In terms of the 'destination principle' VAT is imposed on the consumer in the country where the goods or services are consumed. By definition this implies that imported goods or services should be subject to VAT and exported goods or services should be free of VAT. Practically, however, "*[m]ost nations with destination principle . . . tax only some imported services and zero rate only some exported services*".[13] Conversely the 'origin principle' is effectively the inverse of the 'destination principle' in that VAT is imposed in the jurisdiction "*where the goods are produced and services rendered*".[14] By definition this implies that imported goods or services will be free of VAT and exported goods or services will be subject to VAT.[15]

'Output tax' refers to the tax imposed and collected by a seller on a taxable sale. This tax is effectively imposed and collected by the seller on behalf of the relevant revenue authority. 'Input credit', otherwise referred to as 'input VAT' or 'input tax', is essentially "*a credit that the taxpayer may take against output tax for the VAT that was paid (or deemed to have been paid) on the purchases that qualify for credit...*".[16] The qualifying credits may vary in jurisdictions, but generally a registered supplier is entitled to an input credit in respect of "*VAT paid on purchases of capital goods, inventory, and intermediate goods and services used in his taxable activities*".[17]

---

[12]idem p 34.

[13]idem p21.

[14]idem p22.

[15]idem p21–22.

[16]op cit, Schenk & Oldman, p21.

[17]supra.

16.2.2 Addition Method

In this method VAT is determined by the company's 'economic factors' appertaining to production for a period and multiplying it by the tax rate. Thus, in determining VAT a taxable firm is required to "*calculate tax liability for each tax period by adding the firm's economic factors of production for the period (wages, rent and interest expense, and profit for VAT purposes) and [then multiplying] the total by the tax rate*".[18]

Israel employs the Addition Method to tax financial institutions and insurance companies. However, this VAT method has not, to date, been implemented as a national tax in any other jurisdiction.[19]

16.2.3 Sales-Subtraction Method

In terms of the sales-subtraction method "*the taxpayer pays tax at the applicable VAT rate on the difference between taxable sales and allowable (generally previously taxed) purchases, both inclusive of tax*".[20] The sales-subtraction method is not an indirect tax imposed on individual transactions, but rather a 'period tax'. In determining the 'period tax' 'cumulative data' is compiled based on sales for the period. The VAT liability is determined based on the 'cumulative data'.[21]

16.2.4 Credit-Subtraction Method That Does Not Rely on VAT Invoices

The indirect tax VAT method adopted by Japan in 1989 is determined in the same manner as the credit-subtraction method with invoices, except businesses are not required to issue tax invoices and VAT registered businesses are entitled to claim VAT on taxable supplies acquired from non-registered businesses. This method allows registered businesses to claim VAT credits on purchases from both registered businesses and exempt small businesses. As no invoices are required the tax liability is determined by the "*total taxable sales for the period (exclusive of tax), multiplied*

[18]idem p42.

[19]idem p43.

[20]idem p22.

[21]idem p42.

by the tax rate",[22] and VAT credits are determined based on "*the tax-inclusive costs recorded in purchase records*".[23,24]

16.2.5 Credit-Invoice Method

The credit-invoice method, the inaugural adoption of which was by Western European countries post-World War II, is presently omnipresent and appears to be the dominant VAT system implemented in a variety of jurisdictions. The credit-invoice method, otherwise referred to as the EU-style VAT is applied in "*international transactions under the destination principle, [imposition of] tax on a consumption base, and typically calculates output tax on tax-exclusive prices*".[25] In terms of the credit-invoice method VAT is imposed on transactions and "*relies on tax invoices to verify tax reported on taxable sales by sellers and input credit claimed by purchasers on allowable taxable purchases*".[26]

16.2.6 'Shared Basic Principles'

Basic principles and definitions such as the 'destination principle', the 'origin principle', 'output tax' and 'input tax credit' were previously briefly examined. As noted the 'destination principle' and the 'origin principle' were effectively opposites. Furthermore, it was noted that qualifying 'input tax credits' may vary from jurisdiction to jurisdiction. While there may be different multistage tax methods available which may be adopted in connection with imposing VAT it is, nevertheless, essential that 'shared basic principles' exist between the different jurisdictions applying the multistage tax system. Globalisation and international trade, impelled by eCommerce, presuppose and compel greater 'shared basic principles' between the various jurisdictions in order to "*prevent double taxation, involuntary non-taxation, tax evasion and distortion of competition*".[27]

---

[22] op cit, Schenk & Oldman, p41.

[23] supra.

[24] supra.

[25] Idem p39.

[26] idem p20.

[27] op cit OECD *Consumption Tax Trends, VAT/GST and Excise Rates, Trends and Administration Issues* OECD Publishers (2006), p24.

The Ottawa Framework Conditions stipulate that taxation principles[28] applied in eCommerce should not differ from those applied in conventional commerce[29] and has summarised said principles as follows:

- ***Neutrality****: Taxation should seek to be neutral and equitable between forms of commerce. Business decisions should be motivated by economic rather than tax considerations. Taxpayers in similar situations carrying out similar transactions should be subject to similar levels of taxation.*
- ***Efficiency****: Compliance costs for taxpayers and administrative costs for the tax authorities should be minimized as far as possible.*
- ***Certainty and simplicity****: The tax rules should be clear and simple to understand so that taxpayers can anticipate the tax consequences of a transaction, including knowing when, where and how the tax is to be accounted.*
- ***Effectiveness and fairness****: Taxation should produce the right amount of tax at the right time. The potential for tax evasion and avoidance should be minimized while keeping counter-acting measures proportionate to risks involved.*
- ***Flexibility****: The systems for taxation should be flexible and dynamic to ensure that they keep pace with technological and commercial developments.*[30]

The OECD has published common core criteria to be applied by the various jurisdictions which have adopted value added taxes which may be described as follows:

- *Value added taxes are taxes on consumption, paid, ultimately, by final consumers.*
- *The tax is levied on a broad base (as opposed to e.g. excise duties that cover specific products).*
- *In principle, business[es] should not bear the burden of the tax itself since there are mechanisms in place that allow for a refund of the tax levied on intermediate transactions between firms.*
- *The system is based on tax collection in a staged process, with successive taxpayers entitled to deduct input tax on purchases and account for output tax on sales. Each business in the supply chain takes part in the process of controlling and collecting the tax, remitting the proportion of tax corresponding to its margin i.e. on the difference between the VAT paid out to suppliers and the VAT charged to customers. In general, OECD countries with value-added taxes impose the tax at all stages and normally allow immediate deduction of taxes on purchases by all but the final customer.*[31]

A crucial 'shared basic principle' supported by the OECD is that *"[f]or the international trade in goods there is a commonly held principle that exports should be exempted and imports should be taxed"*.[32] This is based on the 'destination

---

[28]Dr Rendahl has analysed and examined "*whether consumption taxation upholds the internationally agreed upon principles, which are part of the Ottawa Taxation Framework Conditions*" within her doctoral thesis 'Cross-Border Consumption Taxation of Digital Supplies'.

[29]This concept was examined in 7.3.1. Functional Equivalence Approach, Part II of this paper [p66].

[30]op cit OECD *Consumption Tax Trends, VAT/GST and Excise Rates, Trends and Administration Issues,* p95.

[31]op cit OECD *Consumption Tax Trends, VAT/GST and Excise Rates, Trends and Administration Issues,* p94.

[32]idem p95.

principle' that the goods should be taxed where consumed. In other words, the *"[r]ules for the consumption taxation of cross-border trade should result in taxation in the jurisdiction where consumption takes place"*.[33] However, the OECD statement goes on to say that *"international consensus should be sought on circumstances under which supplies are held to be consumed in a jurisdiction"*.[34] Thus, while the OECD establishes certain 'shared basic principles', there are still certain 'shared basic principles' which need to be determined, defined and established. International trade in services and intangibles is a further example of a 'shared basic principle' not yet established.

There are currently no commonly held principles prescribing how VAT should be imposed on international trade in services and intangibles. The OECD does, however, provide the following comments regarding services and intangibles:

> *The... general principles can be adapted to the cross-border trade in services and intangibles as follows, for both business to business and business to consumer transactions:*
>
> - *For consumption tax purposes internationally traded services and intangibles should be taxed according to the rules of the jurisdiction of consumption.*
> - *The burden of value added taxes themselves should not lie on taxable businesses except where explicitly provided for in legislation.*[35] [Emphasis Added]

The OECD comments regarding services and intangibles are challenging in that they do not provide, *per se*, a 'shared basic principle' pertaining to the imposition of VAT on services and intangibles in cross-border transactions. While the common principle that consumption tax should be imposed according to the rules of the jurisdiction of consumption is promoted, such rules may vary from jurisdiction to jurisdiction. The application of diverse rules is problematical in the bid to *"prevent double taxation, involuntary non-taxation, tax evasion and distortion of competition"*,[36] especially with the proliferation of eCommerce which has instigated a burgeoning of cross-border supply of services and intangibles.

16.2.7 VAT Rates

A jurisdiction implementing any one of the four VAT methods may utilise either a 'single-tier' VAT rate or a 'multiple-tier' VAT rate. 'Single-tier' VAT rate is simply the imposition of one tax rate, the standard rate. Jurisdictions utilising a 'multiple-tier' VAT rate impose different VAT rates on different categories of goods and services within the market. Usually the imposition of 'multiple-tier' VAT rates

---

[33] idem p96.

[34] Supra.

[35] op cit OECD *Consumption Tax Trends, VAT/GST and Excise Rates, Trends and Administration Issues*, p96.

[36] idem p24.

consists of the standard rate and reduced rates whereby there may be only one reduced rate or several reduced rates.

South Africa ('SA') is an example of the multiple-tier VAT rate whereby the standard rate is 14 % and the reduced rate is zero per cent. Various categories of goods or services may fall within the zero rating provisions, for example, basic foodstuffs such as rice, but the reduced VAT rate of zero per cent may only be applied if the goods or services fall within the zero rating provisions. Sweden on the other hand applies a standard rate of 25 % on goods and services, a reduced rate of 12 % on a variety of goods and services including foodstuffs and letting of rooms in hotels, and a further reduced rate of 6 % on a further variety of goods and services including travelling expenses and books.[37]

The OECD has provided the following explanation for the varying VAT rates which may be imposed in the various VAT jurisdictions:

> *One of the reasons for the introduction of a differentiated rates structure is the promotion of equity (ensuring a fairer distribution of aggregate income). It is considered desirable to alleviate the tax on goods and services that form a larger share of expenditure of the poorest households (e.g. basic foods, clothes).*[38]

However, the effectiveness of achieving such desirable alleviation has also been questioned by the OECD for the following reasons:

> *The wealthier members of the population also benefit from these reduced rates and in terms of expenditure on non-essential goods the wealthier are anyway likely to pay more tax in absolute terms. Using VAT/GST rates to meet social objectives may not always be the most efficient way of ensuring that those who need assistance actually receive it.*[39]

---

[37] *Skatterverket SKV 552B Edition 9: The VAT Brochure*. Available at http://www.skatteverket.se/download/18.2132aba31199fa6713e800013050/552B09.pdf [Accessed 7/01/2009]. Rates confirmed for the 2010 year via the TMF Group website, available at http://www.tmf-vat.com/vat/eu-vat-rates.html [Accessed 9/12/2010].

The TMF Group is a multi-national company offering a variety of services including administration and advisory. The TMF Group website offers the following description of the company and its services (extract only provided herewith):

> *Working... in 67 countries, TMF Group is the world's leading independent provider of accounting and corporate secretarial services. The group's activities are divided up into nine services lines...*
>
> *TMF Group's international client base is diversified and includes fortune 500 companies and other listed multinational companies, insurance and real estate companies, financial institutions, pension funds, reputable private companies and high net worth individuals.*
>
> *[TMF Group] service all industries, and have formed specialized teams with the necessary sector experience and expertise...*

TMF Group *About Us* Available at http://www.tmf-group.com/en/Algemeen/about-us.html [Accessed 4 February 2011].

[38] op cit OECD *Consumption Tax Trends, VAT/GST and Excise Rates, Trends and Administration Issues*, p39.

[39] Supra.

The 'multiple-tier' VAT rate system has also been identified by the OECD as an area which may give rise to increased compliance and enforcement costs and which, furthermore, creates legal uncertainty and effectuates increased fraud occurrences. With the proliferation of eCommerce such points at issue have become increasingly significant areas of concern. The OECD has published desirable factors which are requisite for greater efficiency in the management and collection of consumption tax by the various tax authorities in different VAT jurisdictions:

(i) *A broad base at the standard rate;*
(ii) *Minimal exemptions and reduced rates;*
(iii) *A registration threshold that allows tax administration to concentrate on core significant taxpayers.*[40]

Of course with the proliferation of eCommerce a 'multiple-tier' VAT system may be a useful tool for cross-border transactions. For example, within the South African VAT system, the reduced VAT rate of zero per cent may also be applied to the exportation of goods, subject to provisions, and even to the rendering of services to a non-resident who is not present in South Africa at the time the services are rendered.[41]

Bibliography

Primary Sources

Statutes
South Africa Value-Added Tax Act, No. 89 of 1991 (as amended).

[40]op cit OECD *Consumption Tax Trends, VAT/GST and Excise Rates, Trends and Administration Issues,* p24.

[41]Section 11(2)(l) of the South African VAT Act, No. 89 of 1991 (as amended):

> *11. Zero rating. – (2) Where, but for this section, a supply of services would be charged with tax at the rate referred to in section 7(1) [i.e. the standard rate of 14 per cent], such supply of services shall, subject to compliance with subsection (3) of this section, be charged with tax at the rate of zero per cent where –*
> *(l) the services are supplied to a person who is not a resident of the Republic, not being services which are supplied directly – …*
> *(iii) to the said person or any other person, …, if the said person or such other person is in the Republic at the time the services are rendered…*

Secondary Sources

Ebrill, Liam, Michael Keen, Jean-Paul Bodin, and Victoria Summers. 2001. *The modern VAT*. Washington, DC: International Monetary Fund.

Mason, Wendy H. *Value-added tax – The VAT assessment process, history of value-added tax*. Available at http://www.referenceforbusiness.com/management/Tr-Z/Value-Added-Tax.html. Accessed 12 Aug 2008.

OECD. 2006. *Consumption tax trends, VAT/GST and excise rates, trends and administration issues*. Paris: OECD Publishers.

Rendahl, Pernilla. 2009. *Cross-border consumption taxation of digital supplies*. Amsterdam: IBFD.

Schenk, Alan, and Oliver Oldman. 2007. *Value added tax, a comparative approach*. New York: Cambridge University Press.

Skatterverket SKV 552B Edition 9: The VAT Brochure. Available at http://www.skatteverket.se/download/18.2132aba31199fa6713e800013050/552B09.pdf [Accessed 7/01/2009]. Rates confirmed for the 2010 year via the TMF Group website, available at http://www.tmf-vat.com/vat/eu-vat-rates.html. Accessed 9 Dec 2010.

TMF Group. *About us*. Available at http://www.tmf-group.com/en/Algemeen/about-us.html. Accessed 4 Feb 2011.

Chapter 17
eCommerce Transactions: OECD Commentary

Abstract The EU has implemented a 'VAT Directive' allowing member states to apply common 'shared principles' for purposes of defining the 'place of consumption', and the USA has introduced a Streamlined Sales Tax Agreement in an attempt to prevent double taxation in cross-state border transactions.

The OECD guidelines address the difficulties in determining the place of consumption of products which are electronically supplied or digitally downloaded via the Internet (op cit OECD *Taxation and Electronic Commerce, Implementing the Ottawa Taxation Framework Conditions* (2001), OECD Publications, Paris, France, p24).

The OECD advocates the 'destination based principle' for determining the 'place of supply' of services and intangible property, and endorses the 'place of consumption principle'.

The point at issue is the identification of a 'virtual customer's' jurisdiction of residence. Furthermore, collection of VAT by customs officials is plausible in terms of tangible goods but is not an option in terms of intangible property and services provided via the Internet.

The OECD has considered a new collection system which would require the enlisting of third parties to collect consumption taxes in respect of electronically supplied services. However, it was deemed that such a system would be initially costly to implement and would substantially alter the character of most consumption tax systems. However, such a system may become practicable in respect of virtual market places such as Second Life.

It is submitted that the indirect tax model, VAT, is a more flexible system than income tax models and would be more easily adaptable to such substantial changes.

Prior to a review of various jurisdictions' VAT systems, especially in respect of eCommerce, an initial review of the commentary published by the OECD in respect of eCommerce transactions is expedient.

'Place of consumption', which is a contentious topic in the matter of determining which jurisdiction has taxing rights in respect to the supply of goods or services, has been defined by the OECD in published guidelines. The OECD guidelines encompass the manner in which VAT should be imposed in regard to eCommerce

A.M. Bardopoulos, *eCommerce and the Effects of Technology on Taxation*, Law, Governance and Technology Series 22, DOI 10.1007/978-3-319-15449-7_17

transactions. The success of VAT as a taxing solution to technology is inhibited by the lack of international double tax agreements with regard to VAT.

The EU has successfully implemented a 'VAT Directive' allowing member states to apply common 'shared principles' for purposes of defining the 'place of consumption', and the USA has recently introduced a Streamlined Sales Tax Agreement with which numerous USA states are in accord in an attempt to prevent double taxation in cross-state border transactions. However, there is a general lack of double tax agreements relative to VAT as VAT generally does not fall within the ambit of Double Tax Agreements. In this regard adherence to OECD commentaries may form a crucial base for determining the 'place of consumption' for cross-border supply of services or intangible property due to global recognition of the OECD by both Member States and non-Member States. For example, despite not being an OECD member, South Africa follows OECD Commentaries pertaining to Double Tax Agreements, and application of OECD Commentaries for interpreting tax treaties has been upheld as acceptable in court.[1]

The purpose of the guidelines is to address difficulties which have arisen with regard to determining the place of consumption of products which are electronically supplied or digitally downloaded via the Internet.[2] If a product is delivered electronically the purchaser generally does not provide the supplier with a physical delivery address as is the case with conventional delivery.[3] The intention of the OECD guidelines (the drafting of which is a direct result of eCommerce) defining 'place of consumption' is that they are to be applied to international cross-border supply of services and intangible property. However, such application is subject to the proviso that the suppliers are not resident and, furthermore, are neither registered nor required to be registered as VAT vendors within the jurisdiction of consumption, as defined by the OECD guidelines.[4]

---

[1]Secretary for Inland Revenue v Downing (1975) (4) S.A. 518 (A), 37 SATC 249 is the South African court case which upheld the application of the OECD Commentaries for interpreting tax treaties. A brief summary of the Downing case is as follows:

> Downing lived in South Africa, after which he emigrated to, and became a resident of, Switzerland. Due to South African Exchange Control regulations Downing was not allowed to remove all his money and, as a result, left a large portfolio of shares in South Africa. Downing appointed Smith to look after and deal with his shares and to manage his portfolio. The South African Revenues Services (hereinafter "SARS") stated that there was a permanent establishment in South Africa, due to the use of an 'agent' (Smith), and as such taxed the profits arising from the portfolio. However, if Downing could prove that there was no permanent establishment then SARS would not have been able to tax him as only his resident country would have such a right in terms of the Double Tax Agreement between South Africa and Switzerland. This case laid down authority for courts to use the OECD Commentary as guidelines.

[2]op cit OECD *Taxation and Electronic Commerce, Implementing the Ottawa Taxation Framework Conditions* (2001), p24.

[3]supra.

[4]idem p98.

The OECD Ottawa Taxation Framework Conditions[5] delineated the following guidelines for the purpose of effective imposition of VAT:

(i) *Rules for the consumption taxation of cross-border trade should result in taxation in the jurisdiction where consumption takes place and an international consensus should be sought on the circumstances under which supplies are held to be consumed in a jurisdiction.*
(ii) *For the purpose of consumption taxes, the supply of digitised products should not be treated as a supply of goods.*
(iii) *Where business and other organisations within a country acquire services and intangible property from suppliers outside the country, countries should examine the use of the reverse charge, self-assessment or other equivalent mechanisms where this would give immediate protection of their revenue base and of the competitiveness of domestic suppliers.*
(iv) *Countries should ensure that appropriate systems are developed in co-operation with the WCO and in consultation with carriers and other interested parties to collect tax on the importation of physical goods, and that such systems do not unduly impede revenue collection and the efficient delivery of products to consumers.*[6] [Emphasis Added]

The OECD advocates that the supply of digitised products should be treated as the supply of services. It should be noted that there is an opposing school of thought to the Ottawa Taxation Framework regarding computer software,[7] questioning whether such software constitutes 'goods' or 'services'. Supported by case law from some jurisdictions, such software is considered to constitute 'goods' rather than 'services'.[8] Limited research[9] pertaining to the opposing school of thought was effected, as case laws cited[10] pre-date the Ottawa Taxation Framework.

[5]The OECD Ottawa Framework Conditions were published, and endorsed by Ministers in October 1998, due to *"[t]he development of e-commerce in the late 1990s [which] led governments to adopt several principles in the field of consumption taxes. Although they were designed in the context of e-commerce taxation, they remain valid for the more global interaction of consumption tax systems and broadly reflect the philosophy of the existing tax rules in most countries. In addition, the Ottawa Framework Conditions specify that the taxation principles that guide governments in relation to conventional commerce should not be different than those applicable to electronic commerce."*

[op cit OECD *Taxation and Electronic Commerce, Implementing the Ottawa Taxation Framework Conditions* (2001)**, p95]**.

[6]idem p231.

[7]Computer software such as 'Shrink-wrapped computer software packages'.

[8]McKenzie, Alastair. *GST – A Practical Guide* (Edition 8) (August, 2008), New Zealand, p117.

[9]Limited research was effected with regard to case law cited in support of the differing school of thought because the case law pre-dated the Ottawa Taxation Framework.

[10]Case law cited, per McKenzie, p117, includes:

- Toby Constructions Products (Pty) Ltd v Computa Bar (Sales) (Pty) Ltd [1983] 2 NSWLR 48 [Australia]
- Advent Systems Ltd v Unisys Corporation 925F 2d 670 (3rd Circ, 1991) [United States of America Court of Appeals]

The OECD advocates the 'destination based principle' rather than the 'origin based principle' for purposes of determining the 'place of supply' of services and intangible property and, therefore, the jurisdiction entitled to impose VAT. The OECD endorses the 'place of consumption' principle as it "*will serve to create a level playing field and is thus more neutral within and amongst conventional and electronic forms of commerce*".[11]

The OECD guidelines with regard to the 'place of consumption' pertaining to "*cross-border [B2B] supplies of services and intangible property that are capable of delivery from a remote location made to a non-resident business recipient should be the jurisdiction in which the recipient has located its business presence*".[12] According to the OECD "*the 'business presence' is, in principle, the establishment (for example, headquarters, registered office, or a branch of the business) of the recipient to which the supply is made*".[13] The OECD provided different guidelines in regard to cross-border B2C supplies of services and intangible property.

With regard to B2C transactions "*[t]he place of consumption for cross-border supplies of services and intangible property that are capable of delivery from a remote location made to a non-resident private recipient should be the jurisdiction in which the recipient has their usual residence*".[14]

Various verification methods were analyzed by the OECD for purposes of determining the customer's location in B2C transactions. While the current recommended guideline requires taxation at the recipient's 'usual residence' concerns were, nevertheless, expressed regarding the capacity to identify a 'virtual' customer's jurisdiction of residence. The concern expressed was that, "*with exception of digital certificates, technology is likely to be able to determine a consumer's location only in the long term*".[15] While technology may develop the capacity to determine the customer's location, technological horizons are limitless. Therefore, technology may also develop ensuring increased customer privacy and security thus preventing suppliers from verifying customers' locations.

Various verification methods explored included digital certificates, credit card information and tracing the Internet Provider's number. However, credit card information has not proved to be a reliable method for determining location or

– South Central Bell Telephone Company v Barthelemy 643 So 2nd 1240 (La 1994) [United States of America, Louisiana Supreme Court]

[11] op cit OECD *Taxation and Electronic Commerce, Implementing the Ottawa Taxation Framework Conditions* (2001), p24.

[12] Idem p44.

[13] supra.

[14] op cit OECD *Taxation and Electronic Commerce, Implementing the Ottawa Taxation Framework Conditions* (2001), p45.

[15] idem p27.

residence of the customer. Likewise, tracing the Internet Provider's number is also unreliable as it may be easily manipulated.[16]

Once the 'place of consumption' has been determined, different collection mechanisms may be implemented for purposes of collecting VAT on cross-border supplies. The OECD has recognised five different types of collection mechanisms, of which three are typically used. The five different collection mechanisms are 'self-assessment' or the reverse charge mechanism, registration of non-resident suppliers, collection by trusted third parties (for example, collection of the VAT from the customs officials), tax at source and the source revenue authority transfers the VAT collected to the 'place of consumption' jurisdiction, and technology based solutions.[17] The first three are the common collection mechanisms. Collection of VAT from customs officials is, however, plausible in terms of tangible goods but is not an option in terms of intangible property and services provided via the internet.

The self-assessment or reverse charge mechanism, which is currently implemented in several jurisdictions' cross-border transactions, and predominantly B2B cross-border transactions. In terms of the reverse charge mechanism the recipient of the supply is required to determine the VAT liability on the purchase and declare same to their local revenue authority. The reverse charge mechanism has proved to be effective in regard to B2B transactions, but does not offer a viable solution with regard to B2C transactions.[18]

In terms of the registration system, the non-resident supplier would be obligated to register for VAT in the relevant jurisdiction of consumption. While this solution would resolve the problem of non-collection of VAT primarily on B2C transactions, it may result in increased administrative costs for the non-resident suppliers, especially if the non-resident supplier supplies customers in diverse jurisdictions. However, this could, to a certain extent, be overcome with the use of a VAT registration threshold. In terms of a VAT registration threshold, the supplier will not be obligated to register for VAT unless the taxable supplies within that jurisdiction exceed a certain threshold. While concerns were expressed in the matter of the threshold model, it is, nevertheless, a well established and applied model internationally and, therefore, the OECD has recommended the use of the VAT registration threshold model.[19]

The tax at source and transfer mechanism would, effectively, require the supplier to charge and collect the VAT from the recipient and then declare and remit the amount collected to the supplier's local revenue authorities. The supplier's revenue authority would then transfer the amount to the jurisdiction of consumption. Reservations were expressed in regard to this method because of the increased administrative costs and need for international treaties in order to ensure an effective

---

[16]idem p28.

[17]idem p30.

[18]op cit OECD *Taxation and Electronic Commerce, Implementing the Ottawa Taxation Framework Conditions* (2001), p30.

[19]idem p31.

collect and transfer system. However, the collect and transfer mechanism was also supported as a feasible solution "*arguing that technology could be creatively harnessed to facilitate such an approach and address its perceived shortcomings. Administrative costs, for example, could be minimised through the use of 'intelligent networks', which could route payments through to the appropriate revenue authorities*".[20] A collect and transfer type mechanism has, to a certain extent, been implemented in the EU as will be examined later with regard to the 'one-stop-scheme'.[21]

The OECD also considered a completely new collection system which would require the enlisting of third parties to collect consumption taxes in respect of electronically supplied services. The third party would be responsible for both collecting the consumption tax and then remitting the consumption tax to the respective tax authorities. However, while such a system was recognised as having the potential of being effective, it was considered that such a system "*would involve significant start-up costs and fundamentally change the operation of most consumption tax systems*"[22] and, therefore, was considered to be not currently expedient.[23]

However, it is not implausible that such a system may become practicable as the concrete of rapidly evolving business methods spurred by unbridled proliferation of technology, especially in the realm of virtual marketplaces such as Second Life. Such a system may "*fundamentally change the operation of most consumption tax systems*",[24] while commerce has already been fundamentally changed with the inception of the virtual world. The significance, however, is that the indirect tax model, VAT, is perhaps a more flexible system than income tax models and, therefore, would be able to adapt to such "*fundamental changes*" more easily. Essentially, 'fundamental changes' would encompass payment, collection and, generally, administrative aspects. 'Basic principles' governing VAT are relatively common amongst countries utilising a VAT system. There are, nevertheless, still conflicting methods of determining, for example, place of consumption, but any changes with regard to such principles will merely result in a heightened harmonised VAT system.

Technology based and facilitated options were also reviewed by the OECD, and while such solutions are feasible and possible,the general opinion was that they are

---

[20]op cit OECD *Taxation and Electronic Commerce, Implementing the Ottawa Taxation Framework Conditions* (2001), p32.

[21]Discussed further in 18.1.1. European Union VAT Law, Part V of this paper [p171].

[22]op cit OECD *Taxation and Electronic Commerce, Implementing the Ottawa Taxation Framework Conditions* (2001), p32.

[23]supra.

[24]supra.

long term solutions and, as such, are not feasible as short term solutions. The OECD expresses the following as an interim solution:

> *While endorsing self-assessment/reverse charge as a coherent option for B2B transactions on an ongoing basis, in the short term, and without prejudice to the pursuit of longer-term technology-based solutions, the business members of the Consumption Tax TAG*[25] *felt that, for B2C transactions, only the registration option was practicable, although its long-term viability was questionable.*[26]

Bibliography

Primary Sources

Cases

Republic of South African Cases

Secretary for Inland Revenue v Downing (1975) (4) SA 518 (A), 37 SATC 249.

Secondary Sources

McKenzie, Alastair. 2008, August. *GST – A practical guide* (Edition 8). Auckland: CCH New Zealand Limited, A Wolters Kluwer Business.

OECD. 2006. *Consumption tax trends, VAT/GST and excise rates, trends and administration issues*. Paris: OECD Publications.

OECD. 2001. *Taxation and electronic commerce, implementing the Ottawa taxation framework conditions*. Paris: OECD Publications.

---

[25]Technical Advisory Groups were established, consisting of both government and business participants from OECD Member and Non-Member countries, relative to the deliberations which occurred in formulating the recommended guidelines. The TAGs included a 'Treaty Characterisation TAG', 'Business Profits TAG', 'Consumption Tax TAG', 'Technology TAG', and 'Professional DATA Assessment TAG'.

[26]op cit OECD *Taxation and Electronic Commerce, Implementing the Ottawa Taxation Framework Conditions* (2001), p34.

Chapter 18
Jurisdictional Analysis

Abstract The EU VAT Law will be examined with specific reference to the interaction and co-ordination of VAT systems between Member States, specifically with regard to eCommerce supplies. The USA does not have a nationally imposed VAT system, but each state applies a retail sales tax system. As the USA is a major commercial hub it is obligatory to examine its retail sales tax system specifically regarding electronic commerce.

The OECD upholds the place of consumption to be where the consumer 'usually resides' (op cit Rendahl, Pernilla *Cross-Border Consumption Taxation of Digital Supplies* (2009), IBFD, Netherlands, p256). Certain eRetailers are already using a customer's IP address to determine the customer's downloading location. Amazon.com may be able to detect whether the location of the 'downloading' computer and the billing address are inconsistent.

'Electronic services' are defined and electronically supplied services are detailed in Annex L of the Sixth Directive of the EU VAT Directive. However, electronically supplied services detailed in Annex II to the VAT Directive is not an exhaustive list and software which may not be included may still meet the definition of 'electronically supplied services'. However, amendments to the VAT Directive see a shift away from such an exhaustive list which may allow for a more flexible application.

The 'one-stop-scheme' allows the non-EU established supplier to register in one EU jurisdiction of his choice in regard to taxable supplies throughout the EU, but he will be required to levy VAT on electronically supplied services at the VAT rate applicable in the 'destination jurisdiction' (idem, p257).

The EU 'one-stop-scheme' would not only reduce administrative burden but would probably increase VAT compliance internationally. Such a scheme could, potentially, be administered by an international organisation such as the OECD.

For the purpose of analysing the impact of differing VAT legislations on cross-border transactions, specifically within an eCommerce environment, sample countries which have adopted a VAT system will be examined. The analysis will be divided into regions, namely Europe, the Southern Hemisphere, Asia, and Canada.

Appendix 1

A.M. Bardopoulos, *eCommerce and the Effects of Technology on Taxation*,
Law, Governance and Technology Series 22, DOI 10.1007/978-3-319-15449-7_18

The USA will be dealt with separately as the USA does not have a nationally imposed VAT system but conversely each state applies a retail sales tax system. However, as the USA is a major commercial hub it is obligatory to examine the retail sales tax system currently ensconced in the USA.[1] For the purpose of examining VAT/GST in the various jurisdictions, either a brief overview of the VAT system imposed including basic facts will be provided, or relevant legislation will be examined, or guidelines and publications issued by the relevant revenue authority regarding electronic commerce will be cited.[2]

A detailed study will be made of the legislation of selected jurisdictions and not all the jurisdictions included in Chap. 18, Part V of this paper. Selected legislative extracts are provided where relevant or necessary in respect of specific analyses or practical examples. Relevant extracts from the European Union VAT Directive 2006/112/EC have been cited. In theory there should be harmonization of concepts and principle between EU countries applying or adhering to the EU VAT Directive. The EU VAT Directive in respect of the jurisdictions of members of the EU, rather than specific EU jurisdictions, is of significant relevance to the focus of this paper. Relevant information in respect of practical application is cited from the revenue authority publication of respective jurisdictions, especially in respect of European jurisdictions.

18.1 Europe

Within the European Union the sample countries include the United Kingdom, Sweden, Austria, and Ireland, the former two being reviewed in greater detail than the latter two. For the purpose of examining the interaction between EU countries and non-EU countries, Russia and Switzerland will also be briefly reviewed.

The European Community ('EC')[3] VAT Law will also be examined with specific reference to the interaction and co-ordination of VAT systems between Member

[1] It should be noted that the information of particular countries in respect of jurisdictional analysis was obtained primarily from the respective countries official revenue authority website. Furthermore, the information obtained is restricted to the applicable revenue websites information as from April 2010 through December 2010.

[2] Where current VAT/GST legislation has been obtained, an analysis of the various definitions, etc will be provided. However, where research was limited, an overview of the basic VAT/GST facts have been provided for purposes of illustrating either differences or similarities between jurisdictions applying a VAT model. Furthermore, the electronic commerce publications and/or guidelines issued by different revenue authorities may be the only source of information referring to relevant enacted legislation or the manner in which the relevant jurisdiction deals with electronic commerce transactions. Certain VAT/GST legislated sections regarding various definitions, 'place of supply rules', etc may also be provided in full in the footnotes only.

[3] The European Community and, therefore, the abbreviation EC, has been replaced by the name European Union and, therefore, the abbreviation EU in terms of the Treaty of Lisbon. However, the name European Community, and abbreviation EC, is still, nevertheless, found in several

States, specifically with regard to eCommerce supplies. The EC Sixth VAT Directive (77/388/EC), amended by the EC VAT Directive (2006/112/EEC)[4] ("the EC VAT Directive") is of specific importance as it harmonises the VAT systems of EC Member States. The EC VAT Law will, nevertheless, be examined after review of the European sample States. A basic overview and understanding of the VAT systems applied in the different EC states will provide a useful foundation to the analysis of the EC VAT Law.

18.1.1 European Union VAT Law

The EU VAT system, created in 1967, encompasses a common VAT framework the objectives of which are:

(i) *ensur[ing] against distortions of competition;*
(ii) *Avoid[ing] obstacles to the free movement of goods and services between Member States;*
(iii) *Attain[ing] the objective of a common market.*[5]

The EU VAT model, which is a harmonized VAT system adopted by EU Member States, has been referred to as "*the most prevalent form of VAT*".[6] The EU VAT model is based on the 'net VAT' method whereby "*tax is added at each stage of the*

Member States' revenue documents and literature and, therefore, will be used interchangeably with European Union and the abbreviation EU throughout this paper.

The abbreviation EC has also been defined by the Swedish Tax Agency in *The VAT Brochure SKV 552B Edition 10 ("Swedish VAT Brochure")*, p4. Available at http://www.skatteverket.se/download/18.6efe6285127ab4f1d2580008470/552B10svartvit.pdf [Accessed 9/12/2010].

[4]Pricewaterhouse Coopers offers the following description of VAT in the EU and the VAT Directives enacted:

> *The Sixth VAT Directive (77/388/EC) has represented for over twenty years the pillar of the common European framework for VAT. However, numerous amendments made it complicated to read and hard to access for practitioners.*
>
> *As from 1 January 2007, the new EC VAT Directive entered into force (2006/112/EEC), enhancing clarity, rationality and simplification without, however, entailing content changes.*
>
> *In clear, practical terms, A Guide to VAT in the EU of 27 Countries explains what the rules set out in the new EC VAT Directive entail in practice and how they are implemented in each of the 27 EU Member States.*

Available at http://www.pwc.com/be/en/publications/guide-to-vat-in-the-eu-of-27-countries.jhtml [Accessed 13/12/2010].

[5]European Commission Taxation & Customs Union. *VAT Directive 2 (01.01.2010) eLearning Course (Course on the VAT Directive).* Available at http://ec.europa.eu/taxation_customs/common/elearning/vat/index_en.htm [Accessed 13/12/2010].

[6]op cit Schenk, Alan & Oldman, Olivier, *Value Added Tax, A Comparative Approach* (2007), USA, p58.

supply chain"[7] and the VAT is determined "*on each transaction, based on the net amount of the transaction [and] taking into account the tax incurred on the prior transaction, for which deduction is allowed*".[8]

Implementing a harmonized VAT model in the EU is effected by the EU issuing either 'regulations' or 'directives'. It is essential to distinguish the difference between 'regulation' and 'directive' prior to considering this common VAT system. A 'regulation' "*becomes immediately enforceable as law in all Member States simultaneously*",[9] whereas a 'directive' "*requires Member States to achieve a particular result without dictating the means of achieving that result*".[10]

The initial two directives, the First and Second VAT Directives, merely set out the prevailing system structure, however, each member state was afforded the flexibility of determining its VAT rate structure, as well as the transactions[11] subject to VAT.[12] It was only with the adoption of the Sixth VAT Directive[13] that a consistent 'VAT base' was established throughout the European Union.[14] Several amendments to the Sixth VAT Directive were issued thereafter as additional provisions to the Sixth VAT Directive, and it was only in 2007 that the various provisions were brought together under one legislation when the VAT Directive 2006/112/EC ("VAT Directive") replaced the Sixth VAT Directive. The implementation of the VAT Directive allowed for a clearer and simplified VAT legislation.[15]

---

[7] loc cit European Commission Taxation & Customs Union *VAT Directive 2 (01.01.2010) eLearning Course (Course on the VAT Directive)*. Available at http://ec.europa.eu/taxation_customs/common/elearning/vat/index_en.htm [Accessed 13/12/2010].

[8] supra.

[9] supra.

[10] supra.

[11] The type of transactions subject to VAT is otherwise referred to as the 'VAT base'.

[12] European Commission Taxation & Customs Union. *General Overview – The History of VAT in the European Union until 1993* ["*EU VAT General Overview*"].

Available at http://ec.europa.eu/taxation_customs/taxation/vat/how_vat_works/index_en.htm [Accessed 05/06/2010].

[13] The Sixth VAT Directive was adopted in terms of Directive 77/388/EEC of 17 May 1977.

[14] op cit European Commission Taxation & Customs Union *General Overview – The History of VAT in the European Union until 1993*. Available at http://ec.europa.eu/taxation_customs/taxation/vat/how_vat_works/index_en.htm [Accessed 05/06/2010].

and

Makipaa, A *Value Added Tax (VAT) EN 4.18.2* (2008) p1. European Commission Taxation & Customs Union. Available at http://europarl.europa.eu/ftu/pdf/en/FTU_4.18.2.pdf [Accessed 14/12/2010].

[15] supra.

18.1.1.1 VAT System Applied: 'Destination Principle', 'Origin Principle', or 'Hybrid'

The EU VAT system typically operated on the 'destination principle' for the purpose of imposing VAT, however, *"[t]he realisation of the single market in 1993*[16] *resulted in the abolition of controls at the fiscal frontiers*".[17] In terms of the 'destination principle'[18] VAT was "*effectively charged at the rate of VAT applicable where the buyer [was] established*".[19] The 'destination principle' was administered in terms of 'physical frontier controls', for example, Customs Control at intra-community borders, however, with the "*abolition of controls at the fiscal frontiers*" it was no longer possible to administer the 'destination principle' effectively. In an attempt to correct this situation adoption of the 'origin principle'[20] was proposed. In terms of the 'origin principle' VAT would be "*charged at the rate in force where the*

---

[16]To achieve the "realisation of the single market" the European Union "*... Commission proposed moving from the pre-1993 "destination based" system, where VAT is effectively charged at the rate of VAT applicable where the buyer is established, to an "origin based" system, with VAT being charged at the rate in force where the supplier is established. This would have effectively abolished fiscal frontiers within the EU.*

This was, however, not acceptable to Member States as rates of VAT were too different and there was no adequate mechanism to redistribute VAT receipts to mirror actual consumption.

Therefore, until the conditions were right the Community adopted the ***Transitional VAT System*** *which maintains different fiscal systems but without frontier controls. The intention is still eventually to have a common system of VAT where VAT is charged by the seller of goods – an* ***origin*** *based VAT system. The transitional system is an origin based system for sales to private persons who can go and buy tax paid anywhere they like in the Union and take the goods home without having to pay VAT again. There are some exceptions to this general rule however (e.g. the purchase of new means of transport and distance selling). For transactions between taxable persons it is still a* ***destination*** *based VAT system".*

Available at http://ec.europa.eu/taxation_customs/taxation/vat/how_vat_works/index_en.htm [Accessed 31/05/2011].

[17]European Commission Taxation and Customs Union VAT: VAT and the Single Market – 1993 to now. Available at http://ec.europa.eu/taxation_customs/taxation/vat/how_vat_works/index_en.htm [Accessed 31/05/2011].

[18]The 'destination principle' was examined in, 16.2.1. *Basic Principles & Definitions,* Part V of this paper [p152]. Basically, in terms of the 'destination principle' VAT is imposed on the consumer in the country where the goods or services are consumed. Thus, with regard to the EU and intra-community transactions the VAT rate applicable in the consumer's country is effectively the VAT rate applied to the transaction.

[19]European Commission Taxation and Customs Union *EU VAT General Overview – History pre-1993.* EU Taxation and Customs, *General Overview – VAT and the Single Market – 1993 to now ["EU VAT General Overview – VAT & the Single Market post-1993"].*

Available at http://ec.europa.eu/taxation_customs/taxation/vat/how_vat_works/index_en.html [Accessed 21/01/2012].

[20]The 'origin principle' was examined in *Part V,* Chap. 16, 16.2.1 – *Basic Principles & Definitions,* page 152 of this paper. Basically, the 'origin principle' is effectively the opposite of the 'destination principle' whereby VAT is imposed in the jurisdiction "*where the goods are produced and services rendered*". Thus, with regard to the EU and intra-community transactions the VAT rate applicable in the supplier's country is effectively the VAT rate applied to the transaction.

supplier [was established]".[21] A move from the 'destination principle' to the 'origin principle', however, was not accepted by the EU Member States, and an alternative method had to be sought.

The 'transitional VAT system' was, therefore, adopted as a transitional regime until a 'definitive VAT system' could be devised and agreed upon. The initial intention was that the 'transitional system' should remain in effect until the end of 1996, whereafter a 'definitive system' would be adopted. However, by 1996 there was still no eligible 'definitive system' on the horizon. By the year 2000 the European Commission "*shifted its emphasis from a move to a 'definitive' system towards measures to improve the present 'transitional' arrangements*".[22,23] The 'transitional arrangement' is essentially an origin-destination hybrid system. In terms of this hybrid system the 'origin principle' is applied in respect of "*sales to individuals resident in the Community*".[24] Thus, sales to individual community residents would be taxed in the supplier's country at the applicable VAT rate within the supplier's country, even if the consumer was located in another EU Member State. Intra-community B2B sales, however, would be taxed in terms of the 'destination principle'; that is, taxable in the consumer's country. Furthermore, goods imported from non-EU Member States would also be subject to VAT in terms of the 'destination principle'.[25]

Germany submitted, in 2006, a proposal for the implementation of the 'reverse charge mechanism' for B2B intra-community transactions in respect of the supply of both goods and services exceeding € 5,000. However, in order to utilise the 'reverse charge mechanism'[26] the supplier would be obligated to confirm the purchaser's EU VAT identification number. Under such circumstances "*[t]he purchaser would have to declare the tax liability for all reverse charge supplies received . . .*".[27] Professor Michael Tumpel[28] described the German proposal as seemingly inappropriate for the following reasons:

---

[21]op cit European Commission Taxation & Customs Union *VAT: VAT and the Single Market – 1993 to now*. Available at http://ec.europa.eu/taxation_customs/taxation/vat/how_vat_works/index_en.htm [Accessed 31/05/2011].

[22]loc cit Makipaa, http://europarl.europa.eu/ftu/pdf/en/FTU_4.18.2.pdf. p2–3.

[23]supra.

[24]loc cit, Schenk and Oldman, p60.

[25]supra.

[26]The 'reverse charge mechanism' is discussed in 18.1.2. *The United Kingdom*', Part V of this paper [p188].

In terms of the 'reverse charge mechanism, the supply is "*treated as supplied in the country where the business customer is established, and the business customer will account for VAT under the reverse charge mechanism.*" – **[op cit HM Revenue & Customs: *VAT: Cross-Border VAT Changes 2010*.** http://www.hmrc.gov.uk/vat/cross-border-changes-2010.htm**].**

[27]op cit Tumpel, Michael, Professor, *A Hybrid VAT System in the European Union*, http://docs.google.com/viewer?a=v&q=cache:g5ZTN7J6sf8J:www.law.nyu.edu/...Y4eFA&pli=1. p15.

[28]The following is a brief biography of Professor Michael Tumpel:

> *... it creates additional compliance burdens for businesses and costs to control VAT for the tax authorities instead of extending the intra-Community tax status verification system and information exchange system to domestic supplies. If there are concerns regarding the functioning of these systems, it would be appropriate to consider improvements also for intra-Community trade.*[29]

There is, nevertheless, an interesting similarity between the German proposal and the EU amendments, issued in terms of the Council Directive 2008/8/EC[30] of 12 February 2008, concerning the place of supply of services. The Council Directive 2008/8/EC amended the VAT Directive[31] with an effective date of 1 January 2010. The Council Directive 2008/8/EC introduced two general rules[32] as follows:

(i) *The destination principle: "For supply of services to taxable persons already identified for VAT purposes the general principle is that the place of supply is where the customer's business is established."*[33] [Emphasis Added]
(ii) *The origin principle: "For supply of services to non-taxable persons the general principle is that the place of supply is where the supplier's business is established."*[34]

The destination principle and, therefore, the 'reverse charge mechanism', may only be applied in terms of B2B transactions. With regard to intra-Community acquisition of goods, the place of supply is "*where dispatch or transport of the goods to the buyer ends*"[35] and "*specific rules can apply when the acquiring company uses VAT identification numbers in other Member States*".[36] In other words, "*[f]or intra-Community acquisitions of goods, the place of acquisition is within the Member*

Michael Tumpel is full professor and head of the Department of Tax Management at the Johannes Kepler University Linz. He studied in Vienna and was visiting researcher at New York University (NYU). His special research interests are VAT, European Tax Law, corporate reorganisations and International Tax Law. He publishes in international journals and is the author of several books on European and International Tax Law. Available at http://www2.wu-wien.ac.at/sfb-itc/tumpel.html [Accessed 14/12/2010].

[29]op cit Tumpel, http://docs.google.com/viewer?a=v&q=cache:g5ZTN7J6sf8J:www.law.nyu.edu/...Y4eFA&pli=1. p16.

[30]Otherwise referred to as The Recast VAT Directive.

[31]Directive 2006/112/EC.

[32]The two general rules have already been incorporated into Member States legislation as noted in, 18.1.2. *The United Kingdom'*, Part V [p188] and the other EU countries, 18.1.4., Part V, examined in this paper [p195].

[33]loc cit European Commission Taxation & Customs Union. *VAT Directive 2 (01.01.2010) eLearning Course (Course on the VAT Directive).* http://ec.europa.eu/taxation_customs/common/elearning/vat/index_en.htm.

[34]supra.

[35]European Commission Taxation & Customs Union. *VAT Directive 2 (01.01.2010) eLearning Course (Course on the VAT Directive).* http://ec.europa.eu/taxation_customs/common/elearning/vat/index_en.htm.

[36]supra.

State which issued the VAT identification number used by the taxable person to acquire the goods".[37]

18.1.1.2 Taxable Transactions

The EU VAT Model encompasses four types of transactions, which may be subject to VAT in terms of Article 2 of the VAT Directive, namely:

(i) The supply of goods: "*...for consideration within the territory of a Member State by a taxable person acting as such*"[38];
(ii) The supply of services: "*...for consideration within the territory of a Member State by a taxable person acting as such*"[39];
(iii) Intra-Community acquisition of goods: "*...for consideration within the territory of a Member State by... a taxable person...*"[40]; and
(iv) The importation of goods in the Community.[41]

Prior to examining the impact of electronic commerce on the EU VAT Model and what provisions have been made by the EU in the matter of such transactions, it is important to first understand the four basic types of transactions and the accompanying definitions in respect of the VAT system.

For 'supply of goods', 'supply of services' and 'intra-Community acquisitions of goods', the transactions must, subject to exceptions, be for 'consideration' by a 'taxable person'. 'Consideration' is the price paid in regard to the transaction and it is important to note that the 'consideration' is not limited to monetary currency.

'Consideration' may also take a non-monetary form, for example, a barter transaction.[42] 'Consideration' has been highlighted as an important aspect in regard to the supply of services in eCommerce. The importance of 'consideration' for such transactions, as highlighted by Dr. Pernilla Rendahl, is because "*there are a lot of materials that can be downloaded to computers or cell phones free of charge*".[43] Several cases regarding 'consideration' have been heard by the Court of Justice of the European Communities ('ECJ') and 'consideration' criteria have been established as a consequence of these cases. Regardless of the form of the

---

[37] supra.

[38] Article 2(1)(a) of the VAT Directive 2006/112/EC.

[39] Article 2(1)(c) of the VAT Directive 2006/112/EC.

[40] Article 2(1)(b) of the VAT Directive 2006/112/EC.

[41] Article 2(1)(d) of the VAT Directive 2006/112/EC.

[42] loc cit European Commission Taxation & Customs Union. *VAT Directive 2 (01.01.2010) eLearning Course (Course on the VAT Directive)*. http://ec.europa.eu/taxation_customs/common/elearning/vat/index_en.htm.

[43] op cit Rendahl, p154.

'consideration' there must be "*a direct link between the services supplied and the consideration received*".[44,45]

The criterion for a 'direct link' was developed further by the ECJ whereby a 'legal relationship'[46] must also exist when:

"*... a supply of services is effected 'for consideration' within the meaning of Article 2(1) of the Sixth Directive, and hence is taxable, only if there is a legal relationship between the provider of the service and the recipient pursuant to which there is reciprocal performance...*"[47] [Emphasis Added]

'Taxable person' is defined under Article 9 of the VAT Directive as "*any person*[48] *who, independently, carries out in any place any economic activity, whatever the*

[44] supra.

[45] The criterion "*that there has to be a direct link between the service supplied and the consideration received*" was first established in the Case 154/80 Staatssecretaris van Financien v. Association Cooperatieve "Cooperative Aardappelenbewaarplaats GA" (1981) ECR I-044d, as discussed and analysed in Rendahl, p155. Furthermore, a synopsis of the case is given in Rendahl, p155:

> *The case concerned an agricultural cooperative association running a potato warehouse in the Netherlands. The members, equal shareholders in the cooperative, paid a storage charge at the end of the season, fixed by the cooperative. During two years there were no storage charges. Hence, the cooperative argued that there was no consideration for the service of storing potatoes, while the national fiscal authority claimed that the consideration consisted of a reduction of the value of the shares the members possessed... Where the consideration, as in this case, consists of an unfixed reduction in the value of shares, such a loss of value cannot be regarded as payment received by the cooperative that provides the service. Furthermore, the consideration is a subjective value that must be capable of being expressed in money, since it is the consideration actually received that is the basis of assessment and not a consideration based on objective criteria. Hence, no direct link between the service provided and the consideration received could be found.*

[46] Review of the 'legal relationship' was examined in the Case C-16/93 R. J. Tolsma v. Inspecteur der Omzetbelasting Leeuwarden (1994) ECR I-0743 (Tolsma). [op cit Rendahl, p157]. A synopsis of the case is given in Rendahl, p157:

> *Mr Tolsma played a barrel organ on the public highway in the Netherlands and offered passers-by the option of giving donations in a collecting-tin. The national Inspector of Turnover Taxes argued before the national court that there was a direct link between the donations and the service provided by Tolsma. The national court asked the ECJ for a preliminary ruling. With reference to its earlier case law, the ECJ emphasized the criteria of establishing a direct link between the services provided and the consideration received. In this case the passers-by do not request the music to be played for them and their donations, if any, depend on their subjective motives and not on the musical service. Hence, there is no necessary link between the donations and the service.*

[47] op cit Rendahl, p157.

[48] 'Any person', per A Guide to the European VAT Directives[AA], encompasses a variety of entities such as a legal person, co-operations joint ventures and partnerships, and individuals.

[AA] Terra, Ben and Kajus, Julie *A Guide to the European VAT Directives, Introduction to European VAT 2010, Volume 1* (2010), Netherlands, p331.

purpose or results of that activity".[49] The definition of 'taxable person' carries three criteria which must be satisfied in order to qualify as a 'taxable person':

(i) *Carrying out the economic activity of supplying goods or services;*
(ii) *Regularly; and*
(iii) *Independently.*[50]

Moral issues and ethical values are not pertinent to VAT: "*in principle VAT does not deal with questions of morality or ethics*".[51] VAT is a tax the sole purpose of imposition of which is the *plucking* of wealth by the empowered from the unempowered. In order to qualify as a 'taxable person' the above three criteria must be satisfied in respect of the activity carried on, regardless of "*the purpose or results of that activity*".[52] The relevance of this statement will be examined later in Chap. 20 of Part V of this paper in respect of the rampant availability of 'free downloading' in the eCommerce marketplace.

18.1.1.3 Place of Supply Rules

With the proliferation of cross-border transactions as a result of globalisation the doctrine of place of supply is becoming an increasingly decisive factor for determining whether the supply is taxable and within which jurisdiction the supply is subject to VAT.[53] Different place of supply rules apply with regard to each type of taxable transaction recognised by the EU VAT Model.

The place of supply of goods depends on the various circumstances of the supply, such as, whether the supply of goods is 'without transport',[54] is 'dispatched and transported',[55] is 'on board ships, aircraft or trains',[56] or is 'through distribution

---

[49]Article 9(1) of the VAT Directive 2006/112/EC.

[50]loc cit European Commission Taxation & Customs Union. *VAT Directive 2 (01.01.2010) eLearning Course (Course on the VAT Directive).* http://ec.europa.eu/taxation_customs/common/elearning/vat/index_en.htm.

[51]op cit, Terra and Kajus, Volume 1, p336.

[52]Article 9(1) of the VAT Directive 2006/112/EC.

[53]op cit, Terra and Kajus, Volume 1, p485.

[54]The place of supply of goods without transport is governed by Article 31 under Section 1, Chapter 1, Title V of the VAT Directive 2006/112/EC.

[55]The place of supply of goods with transport is governed by Articles 32 through to 36 under Section 2, Chapter 1, Title V of the VAT Directive 2006/112/EC.

[56]The place of supply of goods on board ships, aircraft or trains is governed by Article 37 under Section 3, Chapter 1, Title V of the VAT Directive 2006/112/EC.

With regard to the place of supply of goods on board ships, aircraft or trains, Article 37 deems the supply to be "*[w]here goods are supplied on board ships, aircraft or trains during the section of a passenger transport operation effected within the Community... the point of departure of the passenger transport operation*".

systems'.[57] The former two types of supply of goods are relevant to the purpose of this paper. The place of supply rules in respect of the supply of goods 'without transport' and 'with transport' are, respectively, as follows:

(i) "*. . . the place where the goods are located at the time when the supply takes place.*"[58]
(ii) "*. . . the place where the goods are located at the time when dispatch or transport of the goods to the customer begins.*"[59]

In the case of 'distance sales', which is the sale of goods across Community borders and between a taxable supplier and a non-taxable person (for example, a private individual), the place of supply is where the taxable supplier is established at the time the goods are supplied.[60] However, the provision that the place of supply is located where the supplier is established is subject to the provision that the annual sales to the member state of destination remain below a threshold of €35,000 or €100,000 (depending on the member state of destination). The diversity of threshold limit is in respect of the VAT rate applicable to the Member State of destination. Member States applying higher VAT rates typically enforce the lower threshold, whereas Member States applying lower VAT rates typically enforce the higher threshold. When a sales, by a taxable supplier, to another Member State exceeds the threshold, the distance sales become taxable in the other Member State, that is, in the State where the customer is located.[61] However, it should be noted that the taxable supplier is entitled to elect to register for VAT in another Member State even if sales to that Member State are below the threshold. In such circumstances, similar to the taxable supplier having exceeded the threshold, VAT becomes chargeable in the other Member State.[62]

---

[57]The place of supply of goods through distribution systems is governed by Articles 38 through to 39 under Section 4, Chapter 1, Title V of the VAT Directive 2006/112/EC.

With regard to the place of supply of goods through distribution systems, Article 38 deems the supply to be "*[i]n the case of the supply of gas through the natural gas distribution system, or of electricity, to a taxable dealer, . . . where that taxable dealer has established his business or has a fixed establishment for which the goods are supplied, or, in the absence of such a place of business or fixed establishment, the place where he has his permanent address or usually resides*".

Alternatively, in terms of Article 39, "*where such a supply is not covered by Article 38, the place of supply shall be deemed to be the place where the customer effectively uses and consumes the goods*".

[58]Article 31 of Section 1, Chapter 1, Title V of the VAT Directive 2006/112/EC

[59]Article 32 of Section 2, Chapter 1, Title V of the VAT Directive 2006/112/EC.

[60]European Commission *Distance Selling of Goods*. Available at http://ec.europa.eu/taxation_customs/taxation/vat/how_vat_works/distance_selling/index_en.htm [Accessed 05/06/2010].

[61]op cit, Terra and Kajus, Volume 1, p488.

[62]European Commission *Mail Order and Distance Purchasing*. Available at http://ec.europa.eu/taxation_customs/taxation/vat/consumers/mail_order_distance/index_en.htm [Accessed 05/06/2010].

In the furtherance of harmonizing indirect taxes in the EU the VAT Directive enshrines specific provisions in the matter of the place of supply rules for 'intra-Community acquisition of goods'. 'Intra-Community acquisition of goods' is defined as "*the acquisition of the right to dispose as owner of movable tangible property or transported to the person acquiring the goods, by or on behalf of the vendor or the person acquiring the goods, in a Member State other than that in which dispatch or transport of the goods began*".[63]

The place of supply rules in respect of 'distance sales', as discussed above, refers to the sale of goods between a taxable person and a non-taxable person and is governed by the provisions regarding place of supply of goods. The provisions regarding intra-Community acquisition of goods, on the other hand, apply to goods supplied between taxable persons located in different Member States.[64] The general rule in regard to 'intra-Community acquisition of goods' is that the place of supply "*shall be deemed to be the place where the dispatch or transport of the goods to the person acquiring them ends*".[65] There is, however, an exception, without prejudice, to the general rule whereby the place of supply shall be deemed to be in the purchaser's VAT identification issuing Member State unless the purchaser establishes that the acquisition is actually subject to VAT in terms of the general rule.[66]

The last type of taxable transaction in the matter of goods is the 'importation of goods'. The place of 'importation of goods' is simply "*the Member State within whose territory the goods are located when they enter the Community*".[67]

The assimilation of the place of supply of service rules into the VAT Directive, in terms of the Council Directive 2008/8/EC, is often referred to as the 'VAT package'.[68] The need for place of supply rules in the matter of services may be viewed as increasingly important in regard to cross-border transactions and determining the location of the supply. Without decisive rules which may be applied to determine the location of the supply of services, the potential for double taxation, non-taxation or even distortion of competition increases amongst the various Member States, and even globally.

> *It is a feature of services that the location of supply or of consumption is often elusive or even meaningless. This is particularly important for international trade in services, where two problems arise. First, rules must be devised to define what actually constitutes an export or import of a service; defining the location of a service supply is a prerequisite for effective treatment of traded items. Second, the*

[63]op cit, Terra and Kajus, Volume 1, p503.

[64]European Commission Taxation & Customs Union *General Overview – VAT on Goods Moving between Member States*. Available at http://ec.europa.eu/taxation_customs/taxation/vat/how_vat_works/index_en.htm [Accessed 05/06/2010].

[65]Article 40 of Chapter 2, Title V of the VAT Directive 2006/112/EC.

[66]op cit, Terra and Kajus, Volume 1, p504.

[67]Article 60 of Chapter 4, Title V of the VAT Directive 2006/112/EC.

[68]op cit Terra and Kajus, Volume 1, p510.

nontangibility of services makes it difficult to detect purchases of services by physical checks. at border points or inland.[69] [Emphasis Added]

Four crucial distinctions, which include the two general rules, between the place of supply provisions, incorporated in the VAT package, have been made in regard to determining the place of supply of services:

1. *Particular provisions... and when these do not apply, different main, or fall back, rules apply regarding:*
2. *Supplies to taxable persons [that is, the B2B general rule (refer below)]; or*
3. *Supplies to non-taxable persons [that is, the B2C general rule (refer below)]; unless*
4. *The use and enjoyment override rule applies.*[70] [Emphasis Added]

The 'particular provisions' are set out under Articles 46 through to 59b of the VAT Directive and are in respect of 10 specific types of services commanding specific place of supply rules. For the purpose of this paper, Articles 58, 59 and 59a, respecting electronic services, are relevant and will be examined further within the context of the two general rules and the 'use and enjoyment override rules'.

The two general rules, as set out in the VAT package, in respect of the place of supply of services, address B2B and B2C transactions and are in fact referred to as the 'B2B general rule' and the 'B2C general rule', as indicated above under the four distinctions defining the place of supply rule. The B2B and B2C general rules, as set out under Articles 44 and 45 of the VAT Directive respectively, are as follows:

(i) *"The place of supply of services to a taxable person acting as such shall be the place where that person has established his business. However, if services are provided to a fixed establishment of the taxable person located in a place other than the place where he has established his business, the place of supply of those services shall be in the place where that fixed establishment is located. In the absence of such place of establishment or fixed establishment, the place of supply of services shall be the place where the taxable person who receives such services has his permanent address or usually resides."*[71]

(ii) *"The place of supply of services to a non-taxable person shall be the place where the supplier has established his business. However, if those services are provided from a fixed establishment of the supplier located in a place other than the place where he has established his business, the place of supply of those services shall be the place where that fixed establishment is located. In the absence of such place of establishment or fixed establishment, the place*

[69]Kay & Davis *The VAT Services*, ch. 6 of Gillis, Shoup & Sicat, *Value Added Taxation in Developing Countries* 70–82, at 77 (World Bank 1990) as quoted and referenced in Schenk and Oldman, p189.

[70]op cit, Terra and Kajus, Volume 1, p510.

[71]Article 44 of Section 2, Chapter 3, Title V of the VAT Directive 2006/112/EC.

of supply of services shall be the place where the supplier has his permanent address or usually resides."[72]

The two general rules apply "*unless the use and enjoyment override rule applies*".[73] The 'use and enjoyment override rules' have been included in terms of Article 59a of the VAT Directive "*in order to prevent double taxation, non-taxation or distortion of competition*".[74] The 'use and enjoyment override rules' may be applied to various service transactions, including transactions governed by the two general rules and electronic services. In terms of such rules, EU Member States may:

(a) *Consider the place of supply of any or all of those services, if situated within [a Member State's] territory, as being situated outside the Community if the effective use and enjoyment of the services takes place outside the Community;*
(b) *Consider the place of supply of any or all of those services, if situated outside the Community, as being situated within [the Member State's] territory if the effective use and enjoyment of the services takes place within [the Member State's] territory.*

However, this provision shall not apply to the electronically supplied services where those services are rendered to non-taxable persons not established within the Community.[75] [Emphasis Added]

As electronically supplied services are a crucial aspect of this paper it should be noted that to the extent that the 'use and enjoyment override rules' may be applied to electronic services, such application may only be made until the year 2015. "[F]*rom 1 January 2015 there [will] no longer [be] the presumption that the place of supply of electronic services when supplied to non-taxable persons who are established outside the Community are used and enjoyed where the non-taxable person is established* ...".[76] Thus, Article 59(k) of the VAT Directive will be deleted as from 1 January 2015 and Article 58 of the VAT Directive will be replaced. Article 59 of the VAT Directive is in regard to the supply of services to non-taxable persons outside the Community:

> *The place of supply of the following services to a non-taxable person who is established or has his permanent address or usually resides outside the Community, shall be the place where that person is established, has his permanent address or usually resides:*
> *(k) electronically supplied services, in particular those referred to in Annex II* ...[77]

[72] Article 45 of Section 2, Chapter 3, Title V of the VAT Directive 2006/112/EC.

[73] op cit Terra and Kajus, Volume 1, p510.

[74] Article 59a of Section 10, Chapter 3, Title V of the VAT Directive 2006/112/EC.

[75] Article 59a(a), (b) and Proviso thereto of Section 10, Chapter 3, Title V of the VAT Directive 2006/112/EC.

[76] op cit Terra and Kajus, Volume 1, p577.

[77] Article 59(k) of Section 10, Chapter 3, Title V of the VAT Directive 2006/112/EC.

In terms of the Council Directive 2008/8/EC Article 58 of the VAT Directive will read as follows from 1 January 2015:

> ***Supply of telecommunications, broadcasting and electronic services to non-taxable persons***
>
> ***Article 58***
>
> *The place of supply of the following services to a non-taxable person shall be the place where that person is established, has his permanent address or usually resides:*
>
> (a) *Telecommunications services;*
> (b) *Radio and television broadcasting services;*
> (c) *Electronically supplied services, in particular those referred to in Annex II.*
>
> *Where the supplier of a service and the customer communicate via electronic mail, that shall not of itself mean that the services supplied is an electronically supplied service.*[78]

Annex II details the electronically supplied services as essentially those described in Annex L of the Sixth Directive.[79] The list of electronically supplied services described in Annex L is the exact same list detailed in the UK eCommerce guidelines examined later.[80]

With regard to the application of the 'use and enjoyment override rules' to the two general rules it has been submitted by Terra[81] and Kajus[82] "*that the discretionary*

---

[78]Terra, Ben and Kajus, Julie, *A Guide to the European VAT Directives, Integrated Texts of The Recast VAT Directive (Including the Implementing Regulation) and the former Sixth VAT Directive 2010 – Volume 2* (2010). Based on Directive 2008/8/EC, p37.

As of 2010, the current Article 58 of the VAT Directive reads as follows:

> ***Supply of electronic services to non-taxable persons***
>
> ***Article 58***
>
> *The place of supply of electronically supplied services, in particular those referred to in Annex II, when supplied to non-taxable persons who are established in a Member State, or who have their permanent address or usually reside in a Member State, by a taxable person who has established his business outside the Community or has a fixed establishment there from which the service is supplied, or who, in the absence of such a place of business or fixed establishment, has his permanent address or usually resides outside the Community, shall be the place where the non-taxable person is established, or where he has his permanent address or usually resides.*
>
> *Where the supplier of a service and the customer communicate via electronic mail, that shall not of itself mean that the service supplied is an electronically supplied service.*

[79]op cit, Terra and Kajus, Volume 1, p532.

[80]Annex L is examined in 18.1.2. The United Kingdom, Part V of this paper [p188].

[81]Ben Terra is one of the co-authors of the '*Guide to EU VAT Directives – Volume 1*'. The *Guide to EU VAT Directives – Volume 1* provides the following brief biography of Ben Terra:

> *Ben Terra Prof. ddr. h.c., is professor of law at the universities of Amsterdam, the Netherlands and of Lund, Sweden.*

[82]Julie Kajus is one of the co-authors of the '*Guide to EU VAT Directives – Volume 1*'. The *Guide to EU VAT Directives – Volume 1* provides the following brief biography of Julie Kajus:

> *Julie Kajus Advokat LLM, is indirect tax adviser specialized in European VAT.*

powers of each individual Member State to apply the use and enjoyment override rules for all or some supplies will result in a rather muddled allocation of the place of supply of services".[83] Terra and Kajus, furthermore, submit that "*[d]ue to the way in which the place of supply rules are (re)formulated, it will not be the contractual relationship (with the place of establishment) which determines the place of supply, but rather the establishment to [or from] which the service is supplied, introducing an economic criterion resulting ... in a paper-thin distinction between effective use and enjoyment rules and the main rules on the place of supply*".[84]

However, the adaptation of the provisions regarding the prevention of double taxation, non-taxation or distortion of competition, due to take effect 1 January 2015, removes the undisputed practice that electronic services to non-taxable persons are 'enjoyed within the Community'.[85] In terms of the adaptation Member States may consider the place of supply of telecommunications, broadcasting and electronic services as follows:

(i) *if situated within [the Member State's] territory as being situated outside the Community where the effective use and enjoyment of the services takes place outside the Community; [and]*
(ii) ... *if situated outside the Community, as being situated within [the Member State's] territory where the effective use and enjoyment of the services takes place within [the Member State's] territory.*[86]

For the purpose of determining where a non-taxable customer effectively uses and enjoys the supply of services, the place of supply shall be where the non-taxable customer 'is established', the location of the person's 'permanent address', or where the person 'usually resides'.[87] The OECD upholds the place of consumption to be where the consumer is resident or 'usually resides'.[88] Dr. Rendahl, however, submits that "*[i]n e-commerce three possible nexus[es] could be used:*

(i) *the address the consumer gives, if necessary;*
(ii) *the IP address the supply is made to; or*
(iii) *the country the payment is made from.*[89]

The OECD's recommendations may be less flexible than Dr. Rendahl's possible criteria. Furthermore, with the amelioration of technology, criteria such as "*the IP address the supply is made to*"[90] may prove to be a viable solution with regard

[83] op cit Terra and Kajus, Volume 1, p576.

[84] *supra.*

[85] *idem* Terra and Kajus, Volume 1, p535.

[86] *idem*, p534.

[87] Article 58 of the VAT Directive which will come into effect 1 January 2015.

[88] op cit Rendahl, p256.

[89] supra.

[90] supra.

to future technological developments. Furthermore, this may be an effective way to determine residence if the argument explored in Chap. 19 of Part II[91] were to stand. That is, if a person is able to meet the definition of 'being' physically present in cyberspace and, therefore, possibly resident in cyber worlds, such as Second Life, determining the IP address of the Second Life 'resident' may be a solution to determining place of supply.

Furthermore, as will be discussed later,[92] certain eRetailers are already using a consumer's IP address to determine the customer's downloading location which allows the eRetailer to determine whether specific digitised content should be blocked.[93] An example is Amazon.com. While Amazon.com requests the consumer's billing address prior to proceeding to payment and downloading pages, if the billing address is manipulated to provide a billing address in a jurisdiction other than that of the 'downloading' computer's actual location, Amazon.com will detect that the location of the 'downloading' computer and the billing address are inconsistent. For the purpose of testing whether Amazon.com relies on the IP address or the billing address, an account was set-up with Amazon.com whereby a United States of America billing address and phone number were provided. However, the 'downloading' computer was situated in South Africa. Upon attempting to download music from Amazon.com, with the use of a USA billing address, the download was blocked as "*[t]he sale of MP3 Downloads [are] currently available only to US[A] customers located in the 48 contiguous states, Alaska, Hawaii, and the District of Columbia*".[94] Thus, it is apparent that Amazon.com did not rely upon the USA billing address provided when determining that the 'downloading' computer was not a *"US[A] customer located in the*"[95] USA.

18.1.1.4 The EU VAT Model and Electronic Services

The implementation of the Recast VAT Directive, that is, the incorporation of Council Directive 2008/8/EC into the VAT Directive, affected the 'place of supply

---

[91] Refer to 8.1. *The Virtual World versus the Physical World*, Part II of this paper [p72].

[92] Discussed in 18.2.2. *South Africa'*, Part V of this paper [p205].

[93] In terms of Amazon.com's Terms and Conditions, Clause 6, territorial restrictions are imposed on the downloading of certain digitised content:

> *"As required by our Digital Content providers, Digital Content will, unless otherwise designated, be available only to customers located in the United States."*

Amazon.com *Amazon MP3 Music Service: Terms of Use*. Available at http://www.amazon.com/gp/help/customer/display.html?nodeId=200154280 [Accessed 8/01/2011].

[94] Per the Amazon Pop-up Screen which displays when the download is blocked due to territorial restrictions.

[95] The common pop-up screen which displays when the download is blocked due to territorial restrictions pertaining to the downloading of digital content:

rules' for electronically supplied services, as analysed earlier.[96] The classification of electronically supplied services, however, remains unchanged.[97]

The EU Regulation 1777/2005 defines 'electronically supplied services' as follows:

> *. . . include services which are delivered over the Internet or an electronic network and the nature of which renders their supply essentially automated and involving minimal human intervention, and in the absence of information technology is impossible to ensure.*[98]

The definition of 'electronic services' and details of electronically supplied services, per Annex L of the Sixth Directive, are examined later in 'Sect. 18.1.2. – *The United Kingdom',*[99] as well as in 'Sect. 18.1.3. – *Sweden'.*[100] Due to the harmonization of VAT rules by EU Member States, the definition and details in regard to electronically supplied services discussed under the United Kingdom and Sweden are in concert with the EU as both countries, in effect, have adopted the EU provisions in respect of the definition and details of electronically supplied services.[101]

It is, nevertheless, crucial to appreciate that the various types of software may entail various degrees of 'human intervention' and it has been submitted that "*[t]he degree of human intervention for a supply of software then also needs to be related to the objective of the purchase from a consumer perspective*".[102] In other words, electronically supplied services detailed in Annex II to the VAT Directive is not an exhaustive list and "*it is the degree of human intervention that is decisive for the classification of*"[103] electronically supplied services. Therefore, software which

---

"
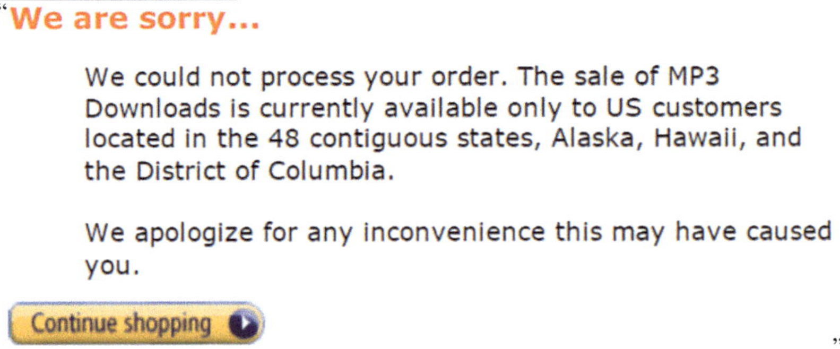

"

[96]Refer to 18.1.1.3. *Place of Supply Rules'*, Part V of this paper [p178].

[97]op cit Rendahl, p199.

[98]Article 11(1) of the EU Council Regulation (EC) No. 1777/2005.

[99]Refer to 18.1.2., Part V of this paper [p188].

[100]Refer to 18.1.3., Part V of this paper [p194].

[101]The definition and list of details relating to electronically supplied services are discussed in detail in 18.1.2. *The United Kingdom',* Part V of this paper [p188], as well as in 18.1.3. *Sweden',* Part V of this paper [p194].

[102]op cit Rendahl, p211.

[103]supra.

may not be included in the detailed list of electronically supplied services may still meet the definition of 'electronically supplied services' dependent on the degree of human intervention.[104]

The EU has shifted the place of supply rules from an origin/destination based principle to the 'destination based principle' which is in accordance with the OECD Ottawa Taxation Framework.[105] An important aspect of the changes, and further expected change, in *place of supply rules* which have occurred over the past few years especially in respect of electronically supplied services and distance sales, is the increased administrative burden for the supplier, whether an EU resident or not. If the 'destination principle' is applied, the taxable supplier may, potentially, have to register in multiple jurisdictions for VAT purposes as a result of the tax being payable in the jurisdiction in which the customer 'usually resides'. The EU has implemented a "one-stop-scheme" in an attempt to counteract the negative administrative burden imposed on non-EU established taxable suppliers as a result of the place of supply rule changes.

The 'one-stop-scheme' allows the non-EU established supplier to register in one EU jurisdiction of his choice in regard to taxable supplies occurring throughout the EU. The non-EU established supplier will, nevertheless, be required to levy VAT on electronically supplied services at the VAT rate applicable in the 'destination' jurisdiction.[106] For example, Amazon.com electronically supplies services to consumers located in multiple EU States. Amazon.com elects to register for VAT in Ireland. Electronically supplied services to non-taxable customers in Austria will still be subject to the Austrian VAT rate of 20 % and Amazon.com must levy and collect VAT accordingly. Electronically supplied services to non-taxable customers in Sweden are, however, subject to the Swedish VAT rate of 25 %, whereas electronically supplied services to non-taxable Irish customers will be subject to a VAT rate of 21 %.[107] Amazon.com must take care to levy and collect VAT accordingly, but will be entitled to declare supplies to the various EU Member States on one VAT return which must be submitted, in Ireland, the country of registration, on a quarterly basis. Amazon.com will have to declare total supplies per jurisdiction on the VAT return and pay the total VAT liability to the Irish Revenue Authority.

---

[104] op cit Rendahl, p211.

[105] idem, p189 & 255.

[106] idem, p257.

[107] EU Member State VAT Rates obtained from the *European Commission VAT Rates Applied in the Member States of the European Union.*

European Commission Taxation and Customs Union VAT Rates Applied in the Member States of the European Union. (Situation at 1st May 2010). Available at http://ec.europa.eu/taxation_customs/resources/documents/taxation/vat/how_vat_works/rates/vat_rates_en.pdf [Accessed 06/05/2010].

This is potentially a viable solution in regard to international electronically supplied services. However, the bid to satisfactorily register taxable suppliers in every jurisdiction precipitates an extensive administrative burden, and may become a significant point at issue in the eMarket Place, impeding globalisation. However, if international taxable suppliers were able to apply and turn to account a scheme similar to the EU 'one-stop-scheme', it would not only reduce their administrative burden but would probably increase VAT compliance internationally. Such a scheme could, potentially, be administered by an international organisation such as the OECD.

18.1.2 The United Kingdom[108]

The UK imposes VAT on the supply of goods and services, subject to conditions, affected by a 'taxable person' in the UK in the course of the 'taxable person's' business.[109] Her Majesty's Revenue & Customs ('HMRC') website provides the following definitions for 'taxable person' and 'taxable supplies' respectively:

- *any business entity that buys and sells goods or services and is required to be registered for VAT – this includes individuals, partnerships, companies, clubs, associations and charities.*
- *All goods and services sold or otherwise supplied by a taxable person which are liable to VAT at the standard, reduced or zero rate*[110]

As of the year 2010[111] a business is required to register for VAT if the business's turnover exceeded UK £73,000 in the previous 12 months or if the business's turnover will soon exceed this limit.[112] This is commonly referred to as the 'VAT

[108]As the UK is the first European country to be examined within this analysis, significant reference to, and quoting of, the EU VAT Directives will be made hereunder. Where the EU VAT Directives are referenced or quoted, same will not be reiterated under the sub-chapter relating to the European VAT.

[109]*Pricewaterhouse Coopers Worldwide Tax Summaries: United Kingdom – Corporate – Other Taxes*. Available at http://taxsummaries.pwc.com/uk/taxsummaries/wwts.nsf/ID/JDCN-89HU8E [Accessed 9/12/2010].

[110]HMRC Website. *HM Revenue & Customs: Introduction to VAT, VAT Glossary*. Available at http://www.hmrc.gov.uk/vat/start/introduction.htm [Accessed 9/12/2010].

[111]Comments provided herewith demonstrate the different registration threshold requirements which are, however, subject to change (i.e. the threshold value may increase or decrease or may even be removed altogether). The current applicable registration threshold requirements can be obtained from the HMRC website.

[112]HM Revenue & Customs *When to Register for UK VAT*. Available at http://www.hmrc.gov.uk/vat/start/register/when-to-register.htm [Accessed 05/10/2011].

threshold'.[113] A business is also entitled to register for VAT voluntarily; that is, a business may register for VAT if so desired even if the business has not exceeded the VAT threshold.[114] It is important to note that the requirement to register for VAT in terms of exceeding the VAT threshold is not limited to UK residents:

> *Taxable persons who are not normally resident in the UK, and do not have a business establishment in the UK and, in the case of companies, are not incorporated in the UK, but who make taxable supplies, sales to unregistered persons in the UK, or acquisitions of goods in the UK above the relevant limits, may be required to register and account for VAT [in the UK].*[115] [Emphasis Added]

A non-resident may be required to register[116] for VAT in the UK where taxable supplies have exceeded the VAT threshold and the 'place of supply' of those taxable supplies is within the UK. The principle of 'place of supply' rule applied by the UK is derived from the EC VAT Directives.[117] 'Place of supply' has been defined on the HMRC website as "*the country in which a supply of goods or services must be accounted for VAT purposes*".[118] The purpose of a 'place of supply rule' is to determine in which jurisdiction the supply correctly occurs apropos cross-border transactions. That is, where the supplier is located in one jurisdiction and the recipient in another, difficulty may arise in determining where the 'supply' correctly occurs. The 'place of supply' rule assists with eliminating this difficulty.[119] However, such rules may not be of assistance in regard to cross-border transactions if there is not a standardised 'place of supply' rule applied universally. As the 'place of supply' rule has been adopted from the EC VAT Law by all EC Member States the 'place of supply' rule has become standardised in the EU.[120]

---

[113]As discussed in 16.2.7. VAT Rates, Part V of this paper [p156], the VAT threshold is one of the desirable OECD factors which is required for a greater efficiency in the management and collection of consumption tax.

[114]Op cit HM Revenue & Customs Website. *HM Revenue & Customs: Introduction to VAT, When you must register for VAT.* Available at http://www.hmrc.gov.uk/vat/start/introduction.htm [Accessed 9/12/2010].

[115]loc cit *Pricewaterhouse Coopers Worldwide Tax Summaries: United Kingdom – Corporate – Other Taxes.* http://taxsummaries.pwc.com/uk/taxsummaries/wwts.nsf/ID/JDCN-89HU8E.

[116]Reference may also be made to Schedule 1 of the UK Value Added Tax Act 1994 c.23 (as amended) which addresses "registration in respect of taxable supplies".

[117]loc cit *Pricewaterhouse Coopers Worldwide Tax Summaries: United Kingdom – Corporate – Other Taxes.* http://taxsummaries.pwc.com/uk/taxsummaries/wwts.nsf/ID/JDCN-89HU8E.

[118]Loc cit HMRC Website. *HM Revenue & Customs: Introduction to VAT, VAT Glossary.* http://www.hmrc.gov.uk/vat/start/introduction.htm.

[119]HRMC Website, *Notice 741A Place of Supply of Services* (January 2010), p6.
Available at http://customs.hmrc.gov.uk/channelsPortalWebApp/channelsPortalWebApp.portal?_nfpb=true&_pageLabel=pageVAT_ShowContent&propertyType=document&id=HMCE_PROD1_029955#downloadopt [Accessed 12/12/2010].

[120]To the extent that each member state of the EU implements the EU VAT Directive, with specific emphasis on the place of supply rules, the EU Member States are, in effect, implementing a standardised 'place of supply' rule.

It should be noted that the supply rules regarding goods and services differ. The 'place of supply' of goods is, subject to exceptions, "*based on the physical location of the goods*".[121] The 'place of supply' of services, on the other hand, "*is the place where a service is treated as being supplied*".[122] Rules for determining the location of the 'place of supply' of services are:

(i) *Where the place of supply of services is in a Member State of the European Community (EC), that supply is subject to the VAT rules of that Member State and not those of any other country. If the Member State is not the UK, such supplies are said to be 'outside the scope' of UK VAT.*
(ii) *Where the place of supply of services is outside the EC, that supply is made outside the EC and is therefore not liable to VAT in any Member State (although local taxes may apply). Such supplies are said to be 'outside the scope' of both UK and EC VAT.*[123]

As from 1 January 2010, the general rule for the 'place of supply' of services was that services, subject to exceptions, "*provided to business customers [that is, B2B, which] will be treated as supplied in the country where the business customer is established, and the business customer will account for VAT under the reverse charge mechanism. [However,] [s]ervices provided to non-business customers [that is, B2C] will... generally be liable to VAT in the country of the supplier*".[124] The 'reverse charge mechanism' essentially "*treat[s] the recipient of the imported service as the supplier... The recipient is, therefore,... the one liable to account for any output tax on the supply...*".[125]

The general 'place of supply' rule for services is essentially two general rules, the B2B general rule and the B2C general rule. The two general rules, described in detail above, may be simply defined as:

(i) *The <u>B2B</u> general rule for supplies of services is that the <u>supply is made where the customer belongs</u>... [; and]*
(ii) *The <u>B2C</u> general rule for supplies of services is that the <u>supply is made where the supplier belongs</u>.*[126] **[Emphasis Added]**

---

[121]HRMC Website, HM Revenue & Customs. Main Rules: Structure and Application. *VAT-POSG3100 – Main Rules: Structure and Application, Introduction.* Available at http://www.hmrc.gov.uk/manuals/vatposgmanual/VATPOSG3100.htm [Accessed 9/12/2010].

[122]Loc cit *HMRC Notice 741A Place of Supply of Services* (January 2010). http://customs.hmrc.gov.uk/...pt. p4.

[123]supra.

[124]HM Revenue & Customs: *VAT: Cross-Border VAT Changes 2010.* Available at http://www.hmrc.gov.uk/vat/cross-border-changes-2010.htm [Accessed 9/12/2010].

[125]op cit McKenzie, Alastair, *GST – A Practical Guide*, New Zealand, p111.

[126]op cit *HMRC Notice 741A Place of Supply of Services* (January 2010). http://customs.hmrc.gov.uk/...pt. p4.

In terms of both general rules, the supply of services is either where the customer or supplier 'belongs'. A customer or supplier is defined as 'belonging' in the UK,[127] in the matter of receiving or making supplies of services respectively, when any one of the following criteria apply[128]:

(i) When the customer or supplier has either a 'business establishment' or 'fixed establishment' in the UK only; or
(ii) When the customer or supplier has either a 'business establishment' or 'fixed establishment' in other countries, but the establishment in the UK *"is most directly connected with [receiving or making] the supplies in question"*[129]; or
(iii) When the customer or supplier has a 'fixed establishment' in the UK and a 'business establishment' outside of the UK, but the 'fixed establishment' in the UK *"is most directly connected with [receiving or making] the supplies in question"*[130]; or
(iv) When the customer or supplier's 'usual place of residence' is the UK.

A 'business establishment' and 'fixed establishment' are simply the "*principal place of business*"[131] and "*an establishment other than the business establishment, which has the technical and human resources necessary for providing or receiving services permanently present*"[132] respectively. The 'usual place of residence', which applies when there is neither a 'business establishment' nor 'fixed establishment', is where the company is incorporated or is the individual's 'usual place of residence'.[133]

The UK VAT legislation allows for the zero rating of certain supply of goods or services. Services, subject to conditions and exceptions, may be zero rated where the place of supply is in the UK but internationally supplied, for example, the supply of services in respect of goods which are for export out of the UK and EC. Services rendered outside the UK are not zero rated because such services are viewed as outside the UK VAT scope because the place of supply is not in the UK.[134] The

[127]Similar to Registration requirements and threshold, place of supply rules may change and reference should be made to the HMRC website for updated place of supply rules, as well as section 7 of the UK Value Added Tax Act 1994 c.23 for updated comments. Individual EU jurisdictions are discussed to illustrate harmonization in respect of EU VAT Directive commentary and application. This principle applies to all EU Jurisdictions examined.

[128]op cit *HMRC Notice 741A Place of Supply of Services* (January 2010). http://customs.hmrc.gov.uk/...pt. p9.

[129]supra.

[130]supra.

[131]supra.

[132]supra.

[133]Refer to 9.2. Traditional Definition & Approach to 'Residence', Part III of this paper [p89] regarding a discussion on the 'residence' of a company or individual.

[134]op cit *HMRC Notice 741A Place of Supply of Services* (January 2010). http://customs.hmrc.gov.uk/...pt. p13–14.

South African VAT legislation, which will be examined later, differs in this regard. The South African VAT legislation lacks a 'place of supply' rule and consequently zero rates services which are rendered outside South Africa by a South African registered VAT vendor.

Certain supply of services, however, are subject to 'special rules' with respect to determining the 'place of supply'. Under such circumstances the 'place of supply' is not determined by the location of the supplier or customer but is rather dictated by the type of service supplied.[135]

UK HMRC has published guidelines, in accordance with the amendments to Article 9 of the EC Sixth VAT Directive (Directive 77/388) which was effected by the VAT on E-Commerce Directive (2002/38/EC) ('VAT on E-Commerce Directive'), regarding services constituting 'electronically supplied services'. The supply of goods or services excluded from the definition of 'electronically supplied services' is dealt with in terms of the general 'place of supply rules', subject to the 'special rules'. The HMRC has identified the following entities as being affected by the implementation of the 'place of supply rules' regarding 'electronically supplied services':

(i) *UK businesses supplying electronically supplied services.*
(ii) *Non-EU businesses supplying electronically supplied services to EU customers.*
(iii) *UK businesses and non-businesses' organisations receiving electronically supplied services from outside the UK.*[136]

An 'electronically supplied service' is defined as a service that is:

- *In the first instance ... delivered over the internet or an electronic network (in other words reliant on the internet or similar network for its provision); [and]*
- *The nature of the service in question is heavily dependent on information technology for its supply (in other words the service is essentially automated, involving minimal human intervention and in the absence of information technology does not have viability).*[137] [Emphasis Added]

In terms of the latter part of the definition, information relayed, transactions or trading facilitated electronically, such as emails, generally do not constitute 'electronically supplied services' as such communication relayed electronically does

[135]HM Revenue & Customs: *How to Work Out Your Place of Supply of Services for VAT.*
Available at http://www.hmrc.gov.uk/vat/managing/international/exports/services.htm [Accessed 9/12/2010].

[136]HM Revenue & Customs: *Electronically Supplied Services: A Guide to Interpretation* (April 2003). p1–2.
Available at http://customs.hmrc.gov.uk/channelsPortalWebApp/channelsPortalWebApp.portal?_nfpb=true&_pageLabel=oageVAT_ShowContent&id=HMCE_CL_000907?&propertyType=document#downloadopt [Accessed 12/12/2010].

[137]Idem, p3.

not *"involve minimal human intervention"*.[138] 'Electronically supplied services', therefore, include the following types of services:

- ***Digitised products*** *generally, such as software and changes to or upgrades of software;*
- ***A service*** *which provides, or supports a business or personal presence on an electronic network (for example website or webpage);*
- ***A service automatically generated from a computer****, via the Internet or an electronic network, in response to specific data input by the customer;*
- ***Services, other than those specifically mentioned in Annex L***[139] ***[to VAT on E-Commerce Directive], which are automated and dependent on the Internet or an electronic network for their provision.***[140] [Emphasis added]

The HMRC '*Electronically Supplied Services: A Guide to Interpretation*' (April 2003) provides the services specifically mentioned in Annex L to the VAT on eCommerce Directive, along with examples of such services, as well as examples of services which are not considered 'electronically supplied services', as illustrated in Table 1 (Appendix 2) and Table 2 (Appendix 3) respectively of the HMRC 'Electronically Supplied Services: A Guide to Interpretation'.[141]

Additional 'place of supply' rules may apply regarding 'electronically supplied services' in B2B transactions where the 'effective use and enjoyment' of the services is in a jurisdiction other than where the supply would have been, provided the supply was either outside the EC and effectively used or enjoyed within the EC or vice versa.[142] In other words, where *"the place of supply of services… [is] in*

---

[138]supra.

[139]Annex L of the EU VAT on E-Commerce Directive (2002/38/EC) provides an *"Illustrative List of Electronically Supplied Services…"*. Annex L lists five (5) categories of services which qualify as 'electronically supplied services'. The HMRC '*Electronically Supplied Services: A Guide to Interpretation*' (April 2003) lists the five (5) categories/items referred to in Annex L and also provides examples for each category/item, as well as examples of transactions which are not considered to be an 'electronically supplied service' with corresponding rationale for the non-inclusion. For the purpose of this paper, the tables provided in the HMRC '*Electronically Supplied Services: A Guide to Interpretation*' (April 2003) will be listed. The later subsection relating to the EU VAT analysis may refer back to these tables which are, in essence, based on Annex L of the EU VAT on E-Commerce Directive (2002/38/EC).

[140]Loc cit HM Revenue & Customs: *VAT: Cross-Border VAT Changes 2010*. http://www.hmrc.gov.uk/vat/cross-border-changes-2010.htm.

[141]Table 1 and Table 2 as set out in *HMRC Electronically Supplied Services: A Guide to Interpretation,* (April 2003). Available at http://customs.hmrc.gov.uk/channelsPortalWebApp/channelsPortalWebApp.portal?_nfpb=true&_pageLabel=oageVAT_ShowContent&id=HMCE_CL_000907?&propertyType=document#downloadopt [Accessed 12/12/2010]. Also, *Op cit* Europa, Annex L of the EU VAT on E-Commerce Directive (2002/38/EC), Available at http://eur-lex.europa.eu/LexUriServ/LexUriServ.do?uri=OJ:L:2002:128:0041:0044:en:PDF [Accessed 17/12/2014]. p4–8.

[142]op cit *HMRC Notice 741A Place of Supply of Services* (January 2010). http://customs.hmrc.gov.uk/...pt. p61–62:

the UK... [, in terms of the general 'place of supply rules',] but the services are effectively used and enjoyed [in a jurisdiction] outside of the EC",[143] or vice versa, where the 'place of supply' is outside the EC but the services are 'effectively used and enjoyed' within the EC. 'Effective use and enjoyment' has been defined by the HMRC as the "*place where the customer actually consumes the electronically supplied services irrespective of contract, payment or beneficial interest*".[144]

The additional 'place of supply' rule relating to the 'effective use and enjoyment' of the service only applies under such provisions described above and is viewed as only applying under such provisions "*where the EC position would otherwise be distortive*".[145]

18.1.3 Sweden

Sweden imposes VAT on, subject to exceptions, goods and services in terms of a multiple-tier VAT rate system which ranges from a standard rate of 25 % to reduced VAT rates of either 12 % or 6 %. All persons liable to charge VAT in Sweden are required to register for VAT regardless of annual turnover. A person becomes liable to charge VAT on the sale of goods or services provided each one of the following conditions are met:

The additional rules for electronically supplied services apply only where there is a B2B supply in either of the following situations:

- *The place of supply would be in the UK (because the supplier or the customer belongs in the UK, but the services are effectively used and enjoyed outside the EC); or*
- *The place of supply would be outside the EC (because the supplier or the customer belongs outside the EC), but the services are effectively used or enjoyed in the UK.*

In these circumstances, the place of supply of the electronically supplied services is where their effective use and enjoyment takes place. Where this is [in] the UK, the services are subject to UK VAT.

Consequently, they do not apply in any situation where:

- *B2C supplies of electronically supplied services are made. This is because most consumers are considered to use and enjoy the service in the same country in which they belong.*
- *The place of supply is the UK (because either the supplier or the customer belongs in the UK) and the service was effectively used and enjoyed in another Member State; or*
- *The place of supply is in another Member State (because either the supplier or the customer belongs there, but the supply is effectively used and enjoyed in the UK).*

[143] op cit *HMRC Notice 741A Place of Supply of Services* (January 2010). http://customs.hmrc.gov.uk/...pt. p61.

[144] op cit *HMRC Notice 741A Place of Supply of Services* (January 2010). http://customs.hmrc.gov.uk/...pt. p62.

[145] supra.

(i) Sells goods or services; ***and***
(ii) The turnover pertaining to the sale of goods or services is liable to VAT, which is, subject to exceptions, the sale of goods or services which occur in Sweden; ***and***
(iii) The turnover is in the course of commercial activities as defined under 'business operations' in the National Income Tax Act and if not defined there under, exceeds SEK 30,000; ***and***
(iv) The turnover occurs in Sweden.[146]

The Swedish 'place of supply' rules for services are identical to the UK's two general 'place of supply' rules for services examined above. Furthermore, the Swedish guide to interpreting 'electronically supplied services' is also identical to the UK's guide, including the two tables providing examples of services which do qualify and which do not qualify as 'electronically supplied'. The reason for this is that the Swedish VAT system, similar to the UK VAT system, is 'harmonised' with the EC VAT Law rules. The rules pertaining to the 'place of supply' and 'electronically supplied services' have been enacted into the Swedish VAT law in accordance with the EU Sixth VAT Directive.[147]

18.1.4 Other European Countries

The European countries of Austria, Ireland, Switzerland and Russia will be examined very briefly with reference to basic similarities and differences in respect of registration requirements, treatment of exports, etc. The latter two countries are not members of the European Union, whereas the former two are EU Member States. Ireland was examined in respect of the quantity of technology firms which have established headquarter companies in Ireland. Non-member countries of the European Union were also examined for the purpose of demonstrating the wide reaching lure of the VAT system and to determine whether there are any fundamental differences of note between taxation member and non-member countries. Russia and Switzerland were selected for discussion by reason of Russia's size and international status and Switzerland for the purpose of reviewing more than one non-European Union country which has implemented VAT.

---

[146]Swedish Tax Agency, *The VAT Brochure SKV 552B Edition 10*. Available at http://www.skatteverket.se/download/18.6efe6285127ab4f1d2580008470/552B10svartvit.pdf [Accessed 9/12/2010]. p5.

[147]Examination of the 'place of supply rules' and 'electronically supplied services' will, therefore, not be examined any further in 18.1.3. *Sweden*, Part V of this paper [p194], as it was extensively examined in 18.1.2. *The United Kingdom*, Part V of this paper [p188].

18.1.4.1 Austria

Austrian VAT, with a current standard rate of 20 % and reduced rates of 10 %, 12 % and zero per cent, is generally based on the EU 6th VAT Directive.[148] Certain transactions, such as the exporting of goods or services are exempt from Austrian VAT.[149] There is currently no VAT registration threshold in Austria, but persons qualifying as an 'entrepreneur' are required to register for VAT and levy VAT on the supply of goods or services to customers. An 'entrepreneur' is any company or individual "*carrying out an active business on a permanent basis*".[150,151] Situations which will give rise to an Austrian VAT registration obligation include:

- *Importing goods into the EU via Austria;*
- *Buying and selling goods within Austria;*
- *Holding goods in a warehouse in Austria as stock;*
- *Selling goods from Austria to other EU countries;*
- *Acquiring goods from other EU countries into Austria; and*
- *Distance selling to private individuals in Austria from another EU country; e.g. Internet retailing.*[152]

Non-resident companies or individuals qualifying as 'entrepreneurs' are not required to form a local company within Austria, but must, nevertheless, submit an application for registration as a VAT vendor within 30 days of making their first taxable supply.[153]

18.1.4.2 Ireland

Irish VAT, with a standard rate of 21 % and reduced rates of 13.5 %, 4.8 % and 0 %, "*comes under the EU VAT regime*".[154] VAT Directives issued by the EU essentially take precedence over local Member States' VAT legislations and, furthermore, "*lay*

---

[148]Pricewaterhouse Coopers Worldwide Tax Summaries. *Austria – Corporate – Other Taxes*. Available at http://taxsummaries.pwc.com/uk/taxsummaries/wwts.nsf/ID/JDCN-89HRKN [Accessed 3/12/2010].

[149]The significance of exported transactions being exempt rather than zero rated will be discussed further in the brief summary of Ireland's VAT system in 18.4.2. Ireland, Part V of this paper [p196].

[150]loc cit Pricewaterhouse Coopers Worldwide Tax Summaries *Austria – Corporate – Other Taxes*, http://taxsummaries.pwc.com/uk/taxsummaries/wwts.nsf/ID/JDCN-89HRKN.

[151]loc cit Pricewaterhouse Coopers Worldwide Tax Summaries *Austria – Corporate – Other Taxes*. http://taxsummaries.pwc.com/uk/taxsummaries/wwts.nsf/ID/JDCN-89HRKN.

[152]International VAT Services, TMF Group. *Austria VAT*. Available at http://www.tmf-vat.com/vat/austria-vat.html [Accessed 3/12/2010].

[153]supra.

[154]International VAT Services, TMF Group. *Irish VAT*. Available at http://www.tmf-vat.com/vat/ireland-vat.html [Accessed 3/12/2010].

out the principles of the VAT regime to be adopted by the Member States".[155,156] However, unlike Austria, registration is only required where the trader's turnover exceeds the VAT threshold which is, subject to exceptions, "*€ 37,500 for the supply of services, and € 75,000 for the supply of goods*".[157] However, the VAT registration threshold only applies to persons 'established' in Ireland. A 'non-established' supplier, that is a supplier "*who does not have a fixed place of business in [Ireland]*",[158] is required to register for VAT in Ireland, irrespective of the turnover amount, where suppliers[159]:

- *Import goods into [Ireland];*
- *Supply goods within [Ireland] ...;*
- *Engage in distance selling of goods to a person who is not a taxable person in [Ireland] ...;*
- *Engage in the supply of services connected with immovable goods located in [Ireland] ...;*
- *Engage in the supply of electronic services from outside the EU to a private individual whose usual place of residence is [Ireland]. These services include the following:*
  - *Website supply, web-hosting, distance maintenance of programmes and equipment,*
  - *Supply of software and the updating of it,*
  - *Supply of images, text and information, and making databases available,*
  - *Supply of music, films and games, including games of chance and gambling games and of political, cultural, artistic, sporting, scientific and entertainment broadcasts and events,*
  - *Supply of distance teaching.*[160]

Similar to Austria, non-resident companies or individuals are not required to form a local company within Ireland in order to register for VAT in Ireland.[161] However, unlike Austria, the exporting of most goods is zero rated for VAT purposes

---

[155] supra.

[156] The EU VAT Directives were discussed further in 18.1.1. *European Union VAT Law*, Part V of this paper [p171].

[157] Irish Tax and Customs Revenue website. *VAT Registration FAQs*. Available at http://www.revenue.ie/en/tax/vat/registration/index.html [Accessed 12/12/2010].

[158] Irish Tax and Customs Revenue website. *VAT Registration for Foreign Traders*. Available at http://www.revenue.ie/en/tax/vat/leaflets/vat-registration-foreign-traders.html [Accessed 12/12/2010].

[159] Only five (5) of the 11 listed activities carried on by a non-established supplier qualifying for VAT registration in Ireland are pertinent to and, therefore, noted for the purpose of this paper.

[160] loc cit Irish Tax and Customs Revenue website. *VAT Registration for Foreign Traders*. http://www.revenue.ie/en/tax/vat/leaflets/vat-registration-foreign-traders.html.

[161] TMF Group *International VAT Services – Irish VAT*. Available at http://www.tmf-vat.com/vat/ireland-vat.html [Accessed 31/05/2011].

as opposed to being exempt from VAT.[162] "*Zero rating is preferable to exemption because most VAT costs incurred in making a zero-rated supply can be recovered, while those incurred in making an exempt supply generally cannot*".[163]

18.1.4.3 Russia

The Russian VAT system, with a standard rate of 18 % and reduced rates of 10 % and 0 %, "*while not originally based on the EU model, [is] gradually…moving towards it*".[164] The Russian 'place of supply' rules for services is similar to the EU rules for purposes of determining where services are supplied.[165] Russia also applies the 'reverse charge mechanism' whereby VAT must be accounted for by the Russian company customer with regard to any payments made to non-residents not registered for VAT in Russia with regard to the sale of goods or services in Russia. Similar to Ireland, the Russian VAT system allows for the zero rating of goods exported out of Russia, including the services in regard to the exporting of goods from Russia.[166]

VAT registration is covered by the taxpayer registration provisions, and foreign suppliers making taxable supplies in Russia may be required to register for VAT should the requirements for registration as a taxpayer apply. A foreign supplier will not be required to register as a taxpayer and, therefore, for VAT "*if the period of business activities performed in Russia does not exceed 30 days*".[167] Business activities performed in Russia exceeding 30 days which would ordinarily give rise to an obligation to register for VAT include:

- *where goods are delivered within Russia;*
- *Where goods are imported into Russia;*
- *Export of goods from Russia;*
- *Supply of services where the place of supply is Russia.*[168]

[162]Irish Revenue Legislation Services, Indirect Taxes Division (11th Edition) *VAT Guide 2008*, Chapter Eight, p68. Link to the VAT Guide 2008 available at http://www.revenue.ie/revsearch/search.jsp [Accessed 31/05/2011].

[163]Pricewaterhouse Coopers Worldwide Tax Summaries. *Ireland – Corporate – Other Taxes*. Available at http://taxsummaries.pwc.com/uk/taxsummaries/wwts.nsf/ID/JDCN-89HSNF [Accessed 3/12/2010].

[164]Pricewaterhouse Coopers Worldwide Tax Summaries. *Russian Federation – Corporate – Other Taxes*. Available at http://taxsummaries.pwc.com/uk/taxsummaries/wwts.nsf/ID/JDCN-89HTPC [Accessed 3/12/2010].

[165]supra.

[166]supra.

[167]International VAT Services, TMF Group. *Russia VAT*. Available at http://www.tmf-vat.com/vat/russia-vat.html [Accessed 3/12/2010].

[168]supra.

18.1.4.4 Switzerland

The Swiss VAT system, with a standard rate of 7.6 % and reduced rates of 3.6 % and 2.4 %, has "*followed the EU template in terms of all fundamental principles*"[169] despite the fact that Switzerland is not an EU Member State. For example, the Swiss VAT legislation was amended in alignment with the EU VAT law amendments with regard to the 'place of supply' rule for services rendered. Thus, the 'place of supply of services', subject to exceptions, is deemed to be where the recipient of the services is located.[170]

Compulsory VAT registration is required where annual sales turnover exceeds CHF 100,000. A person may, nevertheless, register for VAT where their annual sales turnover is below the VAT registration threshold. A non-resident making taxable supplies in Switzerland may be required to register for VAT in Switzerland where the non-resident carries on similar business activities as listed under Russia, that is:

- *Where goods are delivered within Switzerland;*
- *If the foreign trader imports, installs or assembles goods in Switzerland;*
- *Export of goods from Switzerland;*
- *Supply of services, where the place of supply is determined as being in Switzerland ...*[171]

18.2 Southern Hemisphere

Examination of VAT in the Southern Hemisphere will include New Zealand, South Africa, Australia and Brazil. The South African VAT system, which was adopted from New Zealand, will be examined subsequent to that of New Zealand with special reference to similarity. While Australian VAT is relatively new compared to New Zealand and South African VAT, Australian tax authorities have published several guidelines regarding GST on electronically supplied services. Thus, an overview of the Australian GST and guidelines will be examined in regard to electronic supplies. Furthermore, the Australian GST model differs slightly from the New Zealand model. Brazil will be briefly examined for the purpose of providing a comparative analysis of VAT systems across the global spectrum.

[169]International VAT Services, TMF Group. *Switzerland VAT.* Available at http://www.tmf-vat.com/vat/switzerland-vat.html [Accessed 3/12/2010].

[170]supra.

[171]supra.

18.2.1 New Zealand

New Zealand implemented a Goods and Service Tax regime with effect from 1 October 1986, which imposes GST "*on the worldwide supplies of registered persons domiciled or resident in the taxing country*",[172] in this case, New Zealand. Taxing registered persons on their worldwide supplies is referred to as the 'global reach'. It is in this regard that the Australian GST model primarily differs, as will be discussed later.[173] The global approach, in terms of the New Zealand GST regime, determines the place of supply in terms of the residence of the seller as opposed to the location of the supply.[174] However, where goods are exported, while the place of supply is considered to be New Zealand, such transactions will be, subject to conditions, zero rated[175] for GST purposes. While New Zealand applies GST in terms of a global reach, New Zealand, nevertheless, imposes GST on the supply of goods or services which occur in New Zealand by a non-resident, provided the goods are within or services are rendered in New Zealand when supplied.[176] However, the supply of goods or services, which are supplied or rendered in New Zealand, by a non-resident to a New Zealand GST registered recipient, will, unless the supplier and customer otherwise agree, not be subject to GST as it will be deemed to have occurred outside New Zealand.[177]

For the purpose of analysing the interaction and evaluating the harmonisation between the various VAT systems, certain definitions and sections of the New Zealand GST Act will be examined. GST is imposed in New Zealand in terms of section 8(1) of the NZ GST Act, No. 141 of 1985 ("the GST Act") whereby "*tax... shall be charged in accordance with the provisions of [the GST Act] at the rate of 12.5 percent on the supply (but not including an exempt supply) in New Zealand of goods and services... by a registered person in the course or furtherance of a taxable activity carried on by that person...*".[178] The GST registration threshold is NZ $ 60,000.

Section 8 of the NZ GST Act also provides a 'place of supply' rule in terms of section 8(2) which states that "*[f]or the purposes of [the NZ GST Act], goods and services shall be deemed to be supplied in New Zealand if the supplier is resident in New Zealand, and shall be deemed to be supplied outside New Zealand if the supplier is a non-resident*".[179]

---

[172] op cit, Schenk and Oldman, p195.

[173] As discussed in 18.2.3. *Australia, Part V* of this paper [p208].

[174] op cit, Schenk and Oldman, p196.

[175] Zero rating is subject to exceptions.

[176] op cit, Schenk and Oldman, p197.

[177] op cit, Schenk and Oldman, p197.

[178] Section 8(1) of the New Zealand Goods and Services Tax Act, No. 141 of 1985 (as amended).

[179] Section 8(2) of the NZ GST Act, No. 141 of 1985 (as amended).

In terms of section 8(1) of the NZ GST Act, GST is only imposed on goods and services supplied in the course or furtherance of a 'taxable activity'. A 'taxable activity' is defined as:

> ... *Any activity which is carried on continuously or regularly by any person, whether or not for a pecuniary, and involves or is intended to involve, in whole or in part, the supply of goods and services to any other person for a consideration; and includes any such activity carried on in the form of a business, trade, manufacture, profession, vocation, association, or club* ... [180]

For purposes of the NZ GST Act, 'goods', 'services', 'resident', 'non-resident', and 'telecommunications services' are defined as follows under section 2 of the NZ GST Act:

> ***'Goods'*** *means all kinds of personal or real property; but does not include [choices] in action, money or a product that is transmitted by a non-resident to a resident by means of a wire, cable, radio, optical or other electromagnetic system or by means of a similar technical system,*
>
> ***'Services'*** *means anything which is not goods or money;*
>
> ***'Resident'*** *means resident as determined in accordance with ... the [New Zealand] Income Tax Act 2007:*
>
> *Provided that, notwithstanding anything in those sections, —*
>
> (a) *A person shall be deemed to be resident in New Zealand to the extent that that person carries on, in New Zealand, any taxable activity or any other activity, while having any fixed or permanent place in New Zealand relating to that taxable activity or other activity;*
>
> (b) *A person who is an unincorporated body is deemed to be resident in New Zealand if the body has its centre of administrative management in New Zealand.*
>
> ***'Non-resident'*** *means a person to the extent that the person is not resident in New Zealand;*
>
> ***'Telecommunications Services'*** *means the transmission, emission or reception, and the transfer or assignment of the right to use capacity for the transmission, emission or reception, of signals, writing, images, sounds or information of any kind of wire, cable, radio, optical or other electromagnetic system, or by a similar technical system, and includes access to global information networks but does not include the content of the telecommunication*[181]

New Zealand applies the reverse charge mechanism and, with effect from 1 January 2005, incorporated a 'place of supply' rule in regard to imported services. In terms of the amendment "*a person who receives imported services is required to self-assess GST on the value of those services*"[182] provided the necessary criteria have been satisfied. The criteria include, *inter alia*, that "*the services are supplied*

[180]Section 6(1)(a) of the NZ GST Act, No. 141 of 1985 (as amended).

[181]Section 2 of the NZ GST Act, No. 141 of 1985 (as amended).

[182]New Zealand *Goods and Services Tax Legislation 2010* (Edition 24), p18.

by a non-resident to a resident"[183] and that *"the supply of those services, if made in New Zealand by a registered person in the course or furtherance of a taxable activity, would be a taxable supply"*.[184]

Amendment of the GST legislation increased international harmonisation by aligning *"New Zealand's GST system with other countries which have a VAT... or GST system"*.[185] Furthermore, the amendment included a 'place of supply' rule for imported services which was *"perceived as necessary to protect against any further significant erosion of the GST base caused by increases in the volume of imported services as the result of the growth in electronic commerce"*.[186] In June 2001 the New Zealand Inland Revenue Department issued a discussion document ('NZ Discussion Document') attending to the issue of imposing GST on imported services. The conclusions reached within the NZ Discussion Document align with the OECD recommendations set out in the Ottawa Taxation Framework.

For New Zealand GST purposes, the 'copyright' relating to a software programme is, generally, considered a 'service' while the software programme is a 'good'.[187] However, in accordance with the OECD recommendations, New Zealand GST legislation treats all digitally supplied products as the supply of services. Thus, where digital products are 'downloaded' in New Zealand from a non-resident supplier via the Internet, such supply constitutes an 'imported service'.[188]

The NZ Discussion Document especially dealt with imported services arising as a result of eCommerce cross-border transactions.[189] The reverse charge mechanism was considered the most practical, cost efficient and readily enforceable. The New Zealand legislation restricts the reverse charge mechanism to B2B transactions, similar to the OECD Ottawa Taxation Framework recommendations and acknowledgement ofthe difficulties pertaining to B2C enforcement.[190]

---

[183]supra.

[184]supra.

[185]supra.

[186]New Zealand *Goods and Services Tax Legislation 2010* (Edition 24), p18.

[187]Refer to Footnotes 9 and 10 of this paper [p163]. An opposing school of thought to the OECD recommendations holds that on-line software may constitute a 'good' rather than a 'service'. However, despite opposition New Zealand applies the OECD recommended guidelines and treats digitised software as the supply of services.

[188]New Zealand Inland Revenue *E-Commerce and GST (E-Commerce and tax)*. Available at http://www.ird.govt.nz/ecommerce-tax/ecommerce-gst/business-australian-ecommerce-gst.html [Accessed 4/12/2010].

[189]New Zealand Inland Revenue *GST and Imported Services – a challenge in an electronic commerce environment; A Government Discussion Document* (June 2001). Policy Advice Division of the Inland Revenue Department, New Zealand. Available at http://taxpolicy.ird.govt.nz/sites/default/files/2001-dd-gst-imported-services.pdf [Accessed 05/10/2011].

[190]op cit *NZ GST and Imported Services Discussion Document*, http://taxpolicy.ird.govt.nz/sites/... pdf. p29–31.

Where a non-resident has a website in New Zealand, such a website will not result in the non-resident being deemed to be a resident for New Zealand GST purposes.[191] While this matter has not been specifically attended to in terms of GST, it has been attended to extensively in terms of income taxation provisions and whether a website constitutes a 'permanent establishment'.[192] In accordance with OECD issued commentary in regard to the matter, "*a website does not in itself constitute a permanent establishment. Neither does a website hosting arrangement through an internet service provider result in a permanent establishment*".[193] While income taxation provisions concerning the determining of a 'permanent establishment' differ from GST provisions in respect of 'residence', there is, nevertheless, an overlap between the two determination tests. In terms of the NZ Discussion Document "*the provision of on-line services by a non-resident will not fall within the definition of a fixed or permanent place of business in New Zealand, so no GST is payable*".[194] This, of course, does not preclude such services from being subject to the reverse charge mechanism.[195]

With regard to the exportation of goods, goods ordered on-line via an Internet website shop will be treated as the exportation of goods. The mere fact that the physical goods are supplied as a result of an on-line order does not, in itself, change the nature of the supply. The supply of physical goods, which are ordered on-line and then exported out of New Zealand, will remain the 'exportation of goods' and, usually, be zero-rated for GST purposes.[196]

In accordance with the OECD's neutrality principle, services exported by a New Zealand registered person will be, subject to conditions, zero rated for VAT purposes. Thus, services provided by a New Zealand registered business to a non-resident, via the Internet, will be zero rated analogousto non-Internet based

---

[191] New Zealand Inland Revenue *Guide to Tax Consequences of Trading Over the Internet* (May 2002), p12 Available at http://www.ird.govt.nz/resources/d/9/d902a3804bbe5893bc4bfcbc87554a30/internettaxguide.pdf [Accessed 4/12/2010].

[192] New Zealand Inland Revenue *Guide to Tax Consequences of Trading Over the Internet* (May 2002). http://www.ird.govt.nz/resources/d/9/d902a3804bbe5893bc4bfcbc87554a30/internettaxguide.pdf. p15.

[193] op cit McKenzie, p119.

[194] ibid, p120.

[195] ibid, p119–120.

[196] ibid, p118.

transactions.[197] Such services may usually be zero rated, subject to exceptions, if the services are:

- *Physically performed outside New Zealand*[198]
- *The arranging of services which are physically performed outside New Zealand*[199]
- *Provided directly in connection with real or personal property (other than [choices] in action) which are situated outside New Zealand at the time the services are performed,*[200] *or*
- *Supplied to a non-resident who is outside New Zealand at the time the services are performed (however, those services will not be zero-rated if they are received*

---

[197]supra.

[198]Section 11A of the NZ GST Act pertains to the zero-rating of services. Section 11A(1)(j) of the NZ GST Act, No. 141 of 1985 (as amended) reads as follows:

> *11A(1)* ***[Zero-rated services]*** *A supply of services that is chargeable with tax under section 8 must be charged at the rate of 0 % in the following situations: . . .*
>
> *(j) The services are physically performed outside New Zealand or are the arranging of services that are physically performed outside New Zealand; . . .*

(This is similar to section 11(2)(k) of the South African VAT Act, No. 89 of 1991 (as amended), which reads as follows:

> *11. Zero Rating. – (2) Where, but for this section, a supply of services would be charged with tax at the rate referred to in section 7(1), such supply of services shall, . . . be charged with tax at the rate of zero per cent where –*
>
> *(k) the services are physically rendered elsewhere than in the Republic . . .*)

[199]Also zero rated in terms of section 11A(1)(j) of the NZ GST Act, No. 141 of 1985 (as amended).

[200]Such services may be zero-rated in terms of section 11A(1)(f) of the NZ GST Act, No. 141 of 1985 (as amended), which reads as follows:

> *11A(1)* ***[Zero-rated services]*** *A supply of services that is chargeable with tax under section 8 must be charged at the rate of 0 % in the following situations: . . .*
>
> *(f) The services are supplied directly in connection with moveable personal property, other than [choices] in action, situated outside New Zealand when the services are performed; . . .*

(This is similar to section 11(2)(g) of the South African VAT Act, No. 89 of 1991 (as amended), which reads as follows:

> *11. Zero Rating. – (2) Where, but for this section, a supply of services would be charged with tax at the rate referred to in section 7(1), such supply of services shall, . . . be charged with tax at the rate of zero per cent where –*
>
> (g) the services are supplied directly in respect of –
> (i) moveable property situated in any export country at the time the services are rendered . . .)

by a third party who is in New Zealand unless that third party receives the services in the course of making taxable or exempt supplies.[201,202]

18.2.2 South Africa

As the South African VAT Act is essentially an espousal of the New Zealand GST Act, the New Zealand GST Act and commentary are often referenced when interpretation or case law regarding a specific matter is absent in South African commentary or case law. South African principles and provisions are, as a result, fairly similar to those of New Zealand. There are some dissimilarities which will be noted later, however, zero rating provisions, exportation of goods and services, etc are treated fairly similarly. South Africa's standard VAT rate is currently 14 % with a reduced rate of zero per cent. South Africa also has two different registration thresholds of R1 million or R50 000 whereby the former appertains to compulsory registration and the latter represents the minimum turnover a person must generate in order to voluntarily register.[203]

---

[201]Such services may be zero-rated in terms of section 11A(1)(k) of the NZ GST Act, No. 141 of 1985 (as amended), which reads as follows:

> *11A(1)* ***[Zero-rated services]*** *A supply of services that is chargeable with tax under section 8 must be charged at the rate of 0 % in the following situations: ...*
>
> *(k) Subject to subsection (2), the services are supplied to a person who is a non-resident and who is outside New Zealand at the time the services are performed, ...*

(This is similar to section 11(2)(l) of the South African VAT Act, No. 89 of 1991 (as amended), which reads as follows:

> *11. Zero Rating. – (2) Where, but for this section, a supply of services would be charged with tax at the rate referred to in section 7(1), such supply of services shall, ... be charged with tax at the rate of zero per cent where –*
>
> *(l) the services are supplied to a person who is not a resident of the Republic, not being services which are supplied directly –*
> *(i) in connection with land or any improvement thereto situated inside the Republic; or*
> *(ii) in connection with moveable property ... situated inside the Republic at the time the services are rendered, except moveable property which –*
> *(aa) is exported to the said person subsequent to the supply of such services ...*
> *(iii) to the said person or any other person, ... if the said person or such other person is in the Republic at the time the services are rendered ...* ")

[202]ibid, p118.

[203]It should be noted that in the earlier analysis of various European VAT systems, while some European countries may have a compulsory VAT registration threshold, no reference is found regarding a voluntary registration threshold.

South African VAT registration thresholds are legislated and may be found under section 23(1) and 23(3) of the VAT Act, No. 89 of 1991 (as amended) respectively.

There is limited South African literature or case law on the matter of electronically supplied services. New Zealand, unlike South Africa, has published commentaries on the subject of internet based transactions and has also amended the GST Act to incorporate certain provisions pertaining to telecommunications services and electronically supplied services. Therefore, it is beneficial to refer to New Zealand legislation regarding electronically supplied services when analysing commentaries or case law on provisions as South African legislation is limited in such literature.

As briefly mentioned earlier slight, but crucial, variations between the New Zealand GST Act and South African VAT Act (adopted in 1991) may be noted. One such difference is the lack of a 'place of supply rule' in the South African VAT legislation. Indeed, the 'place of supply rule' is a provision incorporated in most of the VAT/GST models examined, thus making South Africa an exception within the global VAT community.

Furthermore, New Zealand has enacted the reverse charge mechanism with regard to B2B transactions, whereas the South African VAT legislation does not restrict the reverse charge mechanism to registered persons only. In terms of the South African legislation, 'imported services', which require self-assessment for VAT purposes, is defined as "*supply of services . . . to a recipient who is a resident of the Republic*[204] . . . ".[205] Thus, the reverse charge mechanism has a broader application in South Africa compared to that of New Zealand (that is, the self-assessment obligation is also, theoretically, incumbent upon non-registered persons). However, the broadened scope and obligation placed on non-registered consumers to account for output tax on imported services is, generally, not enforced as the administrative costs are both unrealistic and impractical.

Theoretically, when a consumer downloads, for example, a music album for $ 7.99,[206] the consumer is obligated to account for the VAT on the purchase and downloading of this 'imported service' as the consumer has received "*a supply of services . . . to a recipient [that is, the non-registered consumer] who is resident of the Republic . . .*".[207] The only example[208] found within the South African Revenue

[204]Within South African legislation, South Africa is often referred to as "the Republic".

[205]Section 1 of the Republic of South Africa Value-Added Tax ('VAT') Act, No. 89 of 1991 (as amended) ("the SA VAT Act").

[206]The MP3 downloading purchase price for the album 'One Love' by David Guetta from Amazon.com as at 22 December 2010.

[207]'Imported services' as defined under Section 1 of the Republic of the SA VAT Act, No. 89 of 1991 (as amened).

[208]Per Chapter 10 of the South African Revenue Service VAT 404 – Guide for Vendors, Example 31 on page 70 reads as follows:

Example 31 – Imported Services (digital goods/electronic products)

Mrs Bookworm orders an electronic version of the latest "Harry Potter" novel from Virtual Books (an internet based business located in Belgium) and downloads the document on her personal computer. She pays € 20 for this service on her credit card. Digital products such as electronic books are regarded internationally as 'services' and not 'goods'. Therefore, as these 'services' are supplied by a non-resident (Virtual Books, Belgium) to

Service ('SARS') published guidelines on imported services with regard to digital 'goods' advises that VAT on the imported services must be declared to SARS within 30 days from the time of supply, but provides no further guidelines in respect of the practicality or enforceability of such a provision.

In a bid to investigate the manner in which SARS would respond to a South African consumer wishing to account for VAT on a USA $ 7.99 'imported service', an attempt was made to electronically purchase David Guetta's newest album, *One Love*, the downloading of which, however, was blocked by iTunes.[209] Upon attempting to download the same album from Amazaon.com, Amazon.com stated that the downloading of the digitised product is limited to the USA.[210] Thus, it would

---

a recipient who is resident in the RSA [Republic of South Africa] (Mrs Bookworm) for non-taxable (private) purposes, VAT will be payable by Mrs Bookworm in this situation. If €20 was equivalent to R200 on the date of the importation, the VAT payable would be calculated as follows:

VAT payable = R200 × 14 % = R28.00

The SARS VAT 404 – Guide for Vendors continues to provide the time period within which the VAT must be accounted:

The VAT on imported services must be declared on form VAT215 and paid to the local SARS branch office within 30 days from the time of supply.

[SARS *VAT 404 – Value-Added Tax Guide for Vendors*. p70. Available at http://www.sars.gov.za/home.asp?pid=4150&tid=65&s=pubs&show=1312 **[Accessed 22/12/2010]].**

[209] The iTunes pop-up notice reads as follows:

[210] The Amazon.com notice reads as follows:

You have selected to purchase: ***One Love (New Version) [Explicit]*** *by David Guetta (Amazon MP3 purchases are limited to U.S. customers.)*

Available at http://www.amazon.com/gp/dmusic/order/amd-get-interstitial.html?ie=UTF8&ASIN=B003FAE0OE&isTrack=0&tryInPlace=0 [Accessed 22/12/2010].

After trying to proceed with the purchase despite the above notice, the download was blocked and the following notice was posted:

We are sorry *...*

We could not process your order. The sale of MP3 Downloads is currently available only to US customers located in the 48 contiguous states, Alaska, Hawaii, and the District of Columbia.

We apologize for any inconvenience this may have caused you."

Available at http://www.amazon.com/gp/digital/order/geo-filter-note.html?ie=UTF8&glCode=340 [Accessed 22/12/2010].

appear that the large commercial Internet website shops, while abiding by digital content territorial restrictions, are at the same time inadvertently avoiding cross-border taxation problems by merely limiting the downloading of certain digitised products to certain jurisdictions.[211]

Attempting to resolve cross-border tax issues by avoiding the problem altogether merely inhibits globalisation and the growth of eCommerce. Furthermore, while academics, such as Dr. Rendahl, propose the taxing of websites allowing the illegal downloading of copyrighted material by advocating that "*enforcing VAT on these supplies, if all the criteria can be met, could... be a solution to the problem with enforcing intellectual property rights*",[212] the use of copyright infringing websites, such as The Pirate Bay,[213] is inadvertently encouraged when legitimate legal on-line website shops like iTunes and Amazon.com block the legal purchasing of music. This will, however, be discussed further in regard to VAT within an eCommerce environment.[214]

18.2.3 Australia[215]

The Australian GST system, only introduced in the year 2000, may still be in its infancy, but has, analogous to New Zealand and unlike South Africa, issued commentaries and notes on electronic commerce and GST. A brief study of relevant Australian GST legislation will expedite a review of the governance of electronic commerce in Australia. The Australian GST rate is currently 10 % with a registration threshold of Aus $ 75,000. A person must register for GST in Australia if the following two requirements are to be met:

(i) *...are carrying on an enterprise, and*

---

[211]Amazon.com identifying a customer's location was discussed briefly in 18.1.1.3. Place of Supply Rules, Part V of this paper [p178].

[212]op cit Rendahl, p164.

[213]The Pirate Bay is a website which operates using BitTorrent software. BitTorrent software is faster than Peer-to-Peer file sharing methods. BitTorrent software is described by How Stuff Works as follows: "*[u]nlike some other peer-to-peer downloading methods, BitTorrent is a protocol that offloads some of the file tracking work to a central server (called a tracker). Another difference is that it uses a principal called tit-for-tat. This means that in order to receive files, you have to give [files for downloading]... BitTorrent downloads different pieces of the file you want simultaneously from multiple computers...*"

How Stuff Works. How BitTorrent Works, What BitTorrent Does. Available at http://computer.howstuffworks.com/bittorrent2.htm [Accessed 08/10/2009].

[214]Refer to Chap. 21 – The Impact of Technology on Tax & VAT in the Virtual World, Part V of this paper [p257].

[215]Op cit, Schenk and Oldman, p196.

(ii) . . . *GST turnover from supplies, that are connected with Australia and made in the course of [a person's] enterprise, meets or exceeds the registration turnover threshold of Aus $75,000* . . .[216] [Emphasis Added]

Thus, where a non-resident supplier satisfies the registration requirements in Australia, the non-resident supplier will have to register for GST in Australia.

The Australian GST system, unlike New Zealand and South Africa which have a global reach, is described as territorial based. Due to the peculiarity of the Australian VAT system base, the Australian GST system, which will be reviewed later,[217] has been described by Alan Schenk has having a "*unique set of place of supply rules*".[218]

The Australian GST system recognises the OECD Ottawa Taxation Framework Conditions.[219] The Australian definition of 'telecommunication services'[220] is fairly similar to the definition provided in EU VAT law. In the matter of electronically supplied services, according to Dr. Rendahl, Australia may recognise digital supplies, in theory, as "*part of intangible personal property as well as services*".[221] Under such circumstances, the treatment of digital supplies, in theory, is similar

---

[216] Australian Taxation Office *GST Registration Information for a non-resident.* Available at http://www.ato.gov.au/print.asp?doc=/content/57758.htm [Accessed 3/12/2010].

[217] op cit, Schenk and Oldman, p196.

[218] supra.

Alan Schenk describes this "unique set of place of supply rules" as follows:

> *A supply of goods is connected with Australia if the goods are delivered or made available in Australia to the recipient of the supply, the goods are being removed from Australia, the goods are being imported or installed or assembled in Australia . . . Any other supply is connected with Australia if the thing (like a service) is done in Australia or the supplier makes the supply through an enterprise conducted in Australia . . . Although a business or other activity apparently does not have to be conducted in Australia to be an enterprise and therefore some supplies by a non-resident enterprise can be subject to the GST . . . definition of an enterprise, which does not require that the business be conducted in Australia. Supplies of anything other than goods or real property that are not done in Australia are taxable only if the enterprise is carried on in Australia . . . For this purpose, an enterprise is carried on in Australia if it is carried on through a permanent establishment . . . Thus, supplies of services through a permanent establishment in Australia or services rendered in Australia appear to come within the scope of the GST, but most or all would be zero rated.*

[219] op cit, Rendahl, p94.

[220] Defined in terms of section 85–10 of the Australian GST Act of 1999, reads as follows:

> *A telecommunication supply is a supply relating to the transmission, emission or reception of signals, writing, images, sounds or information of any kind by wire, radio, optical or other electromagnetic systems. It includes:*
>
> (a) *The related transfer or assignment of the right to use capacity for such transmission, emission or reception; and*
> (b) *Provision of access to global information networks.*

[op cit, Rendahl, p239].

[221] ibid, p134.

to the opposing school of thought to the OECD previously discussed under New Zealand.[222]

However, it would appear that Australia, in terms of the electronic commerce publications issued by the Australian Taxation Office ('ATO'), treats digitised products as the supply of services.[223] Again, this is similar to New Zealand where, in terms of case law and literature,[224] an opposing school of thought to the OECD is recognised, but despite such acknowledgement, the principles laid down by the OECD are followed for purposes of international VAT/GST harmonisation. The supply of digitised products by a non-resident supplier to an Australian resident consumer will only be considered 'connected with Australia' provided:

- *The thing is done in Australia,*
- *The supply is made through an enterprise carried on in Australia, or*
- *The supply is of a right to acquire something that would be connected with Australia.*[225]

Despite the above requirements to qualify as a supply subject to GST in Australia, where all the following criteria are met a supply may also be deemed a taxable supply and, therefore, subject to GST if:

- *The recipient of the supply acquires the thing supplied solely or partly for the purpose of an enterprise that the recipient carries on in Australia, but not solely for a creditable purpose;*
- *The supply is for consideration;*
- *The recipient is registered, or required to be registered;*
- *The supply is not a taxable supply to the extent that it is GST-free or input taxed.*[226]

The average non-registered private consumer will not satisfy the above requirements when acquiring digitised products from a non-resident and the acquisition, therefore, will not be subject to GST. However, where the above exception criteria are met, the reverse charge mechanism will apply and the supply will be subject to GST.[227]

---

[222]Refer to Footnote 187 of this paper [p202].

[223]Also supported by Dr. Rendahl's overview of Australian GST. While it may be recognised that digital supplies may comprise *"part of intangible personal property as well as services"*, within Australian GST legislation *"[d]igital supplies do not cover supplies of goods or real property . . ."*. However, it is further noted that *"[a]t first glance the possible classification alternatives for digital supplies in Australian GST appear as a middle way between EC VAT and Canadian GST"*.

[op cit, Rendahl, p237].

[224]Refer to Footnotes 10 and 187 of this paper [p163 & 202 respectively].

[225]Australian Taxation Office *Electronic Commerce Industry Partnership – Issues Register*, p6. Available at http://www.ato.gov.au/print.asp?doc=/content/18428.htm [Accessed 3/12/2010].

[226]supra.

[227]supra.

Where an Australian supplier is supplying digitised products to a non-resident, such supplies will, provided the supplier satisfies the registration requirements, be subject to GST. However, where the supply of services are 'consumed' outside Australia, the supply may be "*GST-free*".[228] The circumstances under which the supply of services are "*for consumption outside Australia*"[229] are fairly similar in both New Zealand and Australia.[230]

The ATO advocates minimal compliance and administration costs in accordance with the OECD eCommerce principle of 'efficiency'.[231] Furthermore, the ATO promotes consistent treatment, at an international level, in regard to eCommerce transactions and the imposition of GST in order to prevent double taxation and non-taxation.[232] Thus, Australia's principles and provisions regarding the imposition of GST on B2C transactions are aimed at not contradicting the OECD Ottawa Taxation

---

[228]"GST-free" has been defined by the Australian Tax Office as follows:

"The Australian GST law makes certain supplies of things GST-free. Broadly, the following are examples of GST-free supplies: . . . most educational services; . . . international travel and transport; . . . and exports of goods or services or other things from Australia if certain requirements are met."

[op cit ATO, *GST Registration Information for a non-resident*, http://www.ato.gov.au/...htm**].**

[229]op cit ATO, *Electronic Commerce Industry Partnership – Issues Register*, http://www.ato.gov.au/p...htm. p2.

[230]The Australian GST legislation provides five types of supplies which may qualify "*for consumption outside of Australia*" and be "*GST-free*":

1. "Supply connected with property outside Australia – a supply that is directly connected with goods or real property situated outside Australia;
2. Supply to non-resident outside Australia – a supply that is made to a non-resident who is not in Australia when the thing supplied is done, and:
  (a) The supply is neither a supply of work physically performed on goods situated in Australia when the work is done nor a supply directly connected with real property situated in Australia; or
  (b) The non-resident acquires the thing in carrying on the non-resident's enterprise, but is not registered or required to be registered.
3. Supplies used or enjoyed outside Australia – a supply:
  (a) That is made to a recipient who is not in Australia when the thing supplied is done; and
  (b) The effective use or enjoyment of which takes place outside Australia;
  Other than a supply of work physically performed on goods situated in Australia when the thing supplied is done, or a supply directly connected with real property situated in Australia.
4. Rights – a supply that is made in relation to rights if:
  (a) The rights are for use outside Australia; or
  (b) The supply is to an entity that is not an Australian resident and is outside Australia when the thing supplied is done.
5. Export of services used to repair, etc imported goods – a supply is constituted by the repair, renovation, modification or treatment of goods from outside Australia whose destination is outside Australia."

[op cit ATO, *Electronic Commerce Industry Partnership – Issues Register*, http://www.ato.gov.au/p...htm. **p2–3].**

[231]op cit, Rendahl, p99.

[232]supra.

Framework Conditions.[233] As will be examined later under the review of Canada, similar principles are applied in regard to the Canadian GST system.

The Australian GST legislation has incorporated subcategories of supplies, referred to as "*supplies of anything else*",[234] which specifically include the supply of advice or information, whereas the EU VAT and Canadian systems treat advice or information as consultancy services. All three systems have congruent criteria whereby "*services require human intervention even if parts of the supplies are able to be delivered in a digital form*",[235] however, Dr Rendahl submits that by incorporating "*an openly written rule... [such as] rules for supplies of anything else*"[236] within the Australian legislation, allows the Australian GST system to be "*indeed flexible and technology neutral*".[237] Indeed, the Australian GST system categorises digital supplies into three subcategories, namely 'telecommunication services', 'anything else' and 'financial services'.[238]

While the Australian GST may be considered "*flexible and technology neutral*",[239] it does differ in certain aspects from most of the other jurisdictions analyzed herein; that is, Australia utilises a territorial based system, as opposed to a global reaching system.

That being said, it would not appear that the Australian GST system hinders cross-border eTransactions to the point of rendering the VAT/GST an ineffective system requiring reconceptualisation.

In a VAT utopia environment, harmonization of the Australian GST principles, allowing the Australian GST to become globally reaching, would undoubtedly ease administrative difficulties and increase the effectiveness of GST. However, the significant point at issue here is that Australia illustrates, like the EU VAT and Canadian GST systems, VAT's flexibility and ability to co-exist felicitously alongside other VAT systems despite differences in principles, thus reasserting VAT's propitious attribute of "*flexib[ility] and technolog[ical] neutral[ity]*".[240]

---

[233]ibid, p107.

[234]ibid, p241.

[235]Idem, Rendahl, p244.

Dr. Rendahl provided an organogram of the supplies which constitute digital supplies. One such subcategory, also referred to as 'things', is "*supplies for anything else", which may include "advice or information, services related to rights like copyright*". **[op cit, Rendahl, p238 & 241].**

[236]ibid, p245.

[237]supra.

[238]Op cit, Rendahl, p238.

[239]ibid, p245.

[240]supra.

18.2.4 Brazil

Brazil, a country which is comprised of 26 states, has not implemented a national VAT system. Similar to the USA, each state implements its own indirect tax legislation and compliance rules. In fact, various indirect tax systems are even implemented in different states, including a VAT type system. This has resulted in indirect tax rates ranging from 7 to 25 % depending upon the Brazilian state. A significant point at issue is that Brazil does not have a registration threshold and, accordingly, any person making taxable supplies is required to register for VAT regardless of turnover.[241]

Non-resident suppliers may be required to register for VAT, depending on the state, when the non-resident carries on importation and exportation of goods to and from Brazil and, furthermore, when the place of supply of services is Brazil. While a non-resident may be required to register for VAT, a non-resident is required to form a permanent establishment in Brazil for registration purposes, which also means that the non-resident will then be required to adhere to the applicable permanent establishment regulations.[242]

Both Brazil and China (an overview of which will be provided and discussed on the page over under the Jurisdictional Analysis of Asia), while not discussed and analysed in depth within this paper are, nevertheless, of significance by reason of Brazil's powerful economic status in South America and China's powerful economic status in Asia and expanding influence in the international market.

Brazil and especially China may have posed significant problems in the future with regard to electronic cross-border transactions and the establishment of a plausible eTax solution should these two economic powerhouses have not implemented VAT systems.

While China's VAT system is relatively new compared to, for example, Europe it is significant that although China's VAT system is tailored to her current economic policies China, nevertheless, has implemented a consumption-based VAT system. Similarly, it is significant that Brazil has implemented a VAT system in the form of an indirect consumption-based tax system unique to Brazil in that it has not been implemented on a national level but rather on a provincial basis.

18.3 Asia

For the purpose of demonstrating the broad reach of the VAT system a cursory mention should be made of the Asian countries China and Japan. Basic facts, legislative differences and differences in practice should be mentioned. While China

---

241 International VAT Services, The TMF Group. *Brazil VAT, ICMS, IPI, GST*. Available at http://www.tmf-vat.com/global-vat/brazil-vat-icms-ipi-gst.html [Accessed 3/12/2010].

242 Loc cit International VAT Services, The TMF Group. *Brazil VAT, ICMS, IPI, GST*. http://www.tmf-vat.com/global-vat/brazil-vat-icms-ipi-gst.html.

and Japan will not be examined in depth it is, nevertheless, significant that China, a continuously flourishing commercial hub and industrial power, as well as Japan, which currently "*retains position as world's second largest economy*",[243] have both implemented a form of VAT system.

18.3.1 China

In 1994 China introduced a VAT system which was imposed on goods including, but not limited to, the importation of goods and services in respect of goods such as repairs, etc.[244] The initial VAT system introduced was production-based, however, in 2009 China switched to the consumption-based VAT system.[245] Prior to the switch in the VAT system base, fixed assets acquired for the purpose of carrying on business activities were often not recoverable. However, in terms of the consumption-based VAT system, input VAT credit may be claimed on fixed assets and such claims are "*fully recoverable except for situations specified in the VAT regulations*".[246]

The exportation of goods from China are not zero rated for VAT purposes as is practised in some countries. However, the exporter may qualify for a VAT refund on goods exported where the materials were purchased within China.[247] While the standard VAT rate is currently 17 % and the reduced VAT rate is 13 %, it should be noted that VAT refunds on exported goods range from zero percent to 17 %. Thus, an exporter may not receive a full VAT refund with regard to goods exported as a result of the refund percentage range and prescribed formula which must be applied for purposes of determining the allowable VAT refund.[248]

It is compulsory to register for VAT in China if taxable supplies are made regardless of the quantity or turnover of supplies. In other words, China does not utilise a VAT threshold for purposes of determining when a taxable person is liable to register.[249]

---

[243]MecroPress, South Atlantic News Agency. *Japan Retains Position as World' Second Largest Economy*. Available at http://en.mecropress.com/2010/02/15/japan-retains-position-as-world-second-largest-economy [Accessed 27/12/2010].

[244]International VAT Services, TMF Group. *China VAT/GST*. Available at http://www.tmf-vat.com/global-vat/china-vat-gst.html [Accessed 3/12/2010].

[245]Pricewaterhouse Coopers Worldwide Tax Summaries. *China, People's Republic of – Corporate – Other Taxes*. Available at http://taxsummaries.pwc.com/uk/taxsummaries/wwts.nsf/ID/JDCN-89HRZF [Accessed 3/12/2010].

[246]supra.

[247]supra.

[248]Loc cit Pricewaterhouse Coopers Worldwide Tax Summaries. *China, People's Republic of – Corporate – Other Taxes*. http://taxsummaries.pwc.com/uk/taxsummaries/wwts.nsf/ID/JDCN-89HRZF.

[249]loc cit International VAT Services, TMF Group. *China VAT/GST*. http://www.tmf-vat.com/global-vat/china-vat-gst.html.

18.3.2 Japan

Introduced in 1989,[250] consumption tax is levied on the supply of goods, services and the importation of goods at a current standard rate of five per cent.[251] The Japanese consumption tax system is similar to the European VAT system, however, there are essentially three differences between the two systems. A fundamental difference between the two systems is that the Japanese consumption tax does not require the issuing of tax invoices in regard to taxable supplies.[252] Despite not being required to issue tax invoices in regard to taxable supplies, it is important to note that this does not negate the requirement to substantiate a supply.[253] Registered consumption taxpayers are required to maintain sufficient documentation to substantiate a taxable supply. Consumption tax input credits may be denied where the taxpayer is unable to substantiate the supply.[254]

The Japanese consumption tax has, furthermore, been referred to as a unique consumption tax system and a further variation from the European VAT system is the manner in which input tax credits are determined.[255] As the first variation was the lack of tax invoices, determining input tax credits differs from the European style VAT system because the purchaser does not have recourse to a tax invoice. Thus, input tax credits are determined from the purchaser's purchase records and it is assumed that the consumption tax inclusive amount is recorded.[256]

The third variation to the European VAT system is that a registered seller is entitled to claim input tax credits on goods or services acquired in the course of making taxable supplies regardless of whether the goods or services were acquired from a registered or unregistered supplier.[257]

18.4 Canada

The USA has not implemented a consumption-based VAT system, however, eCommerce is efficiently transacted between the USA and Canada, proving GST/VAT and retail sales tax can co-exist felicitously. Furthermore, Canada, which imposes

[250]International VAT Services, TMF Group. *Japan Consumption Tax*. Available at http://www.tmf-vat.com/global-vat/japan-consumption-tax.html [Accessed 3/12/2010].

[251]Pricewaterhouse Coopers Worldwide Tax Summaries. *Japan – Corporate – Other Taxes*. Available at http://taxsummaries.pwc.com/uk/taxsummaries/wwts.nsf/ID/JDCN-89HSSD [Accessed 3/12/2010].

[252]op cit, Schenk and Oldman, p41.

[253]ibid, p68.

[254]ibid, p69.

[255]ibid, 41 & 67.

[256]op cit, Schenk and Oldman, p68.

[257]supra.

VAT on a federal level and retail sales tax on provincial levels, serves as a practical example of GST's ability to co-exist and operate efficiently in conjunction with retail sales tax.

Canadian residents are required to register for GST, subject to exceptions, where total taxable supplies exceed CAN "*$ 30,000 in a single calendar quarter*[258] ***or*** *in four consecutive calendar quarters*".[259] A non-resident, on the other hand, carrying on business in Canada, even if no permanent establishment exists, is required to register for GST/HST under the following circumstances:

- *[The non-resident] provide[s] taxable, including zero-rated, goods or services in Canada in the course of carrying on business in Canada and [the non-resident] [is] not a small supplier*[260]*;*
- *[The non-resident] make[s] taxable supplies of admissions in Canada to a place of amusement, a seminar, an activity, or an event held in Canada, even if [the non-resident] [is] a small supplier;*
- *[The non-resident] [is] a non-resident who enters Canada to charge admission directly to audiences at activities or events in Canada, and the admissions are not made by a resident promoter or ticket agent;*
- *[The non-resident] host[s] a convention in Canada, and more than 25 % of the delegates are residents of Canada; or*
- *[The non-resident] solicit[s] orders for publications to be delivered to customers by mail or courier in Canada and [the non-resident] [is] not a small supplier.*[261]

A variety of indirect taxes are imposed in Canada at both the federal level and provincial level.[262] Canada imposes GST at the federal level at a rate of 5 %. Certain

---

[258]'Calendar quarter' is defined as follows: "*[a] calendar quarter means a period of three consecutive months ending on the last day of any of the following months: March, June, September, or December.*"

Canadian Revenue Agency ('CRA') *Definitions for GST/HST*. Available at http://www.cra-arc.gc.ca/tx/bsnss/tpcs/gst-tps/glssry-eng.html#quarter [Accessed 13/01/2011].

[259]CRA *GST/HST Mandatory Registration*. Available at http://www.cra-arc.gc.ca/tx/bsnss/tpcs/gst-tps/rgstrng/mndtry-eng.html [Accessed 13/01/2011].

[260]'Small supplier' is defined as including "*charities, and other public service bodies, that are engaged in commercial activity with revenues from worldwide taxable supplies (not including sales of capital property and financial services) equal to or less than $ 50,000 in the current calendar quarter and over the preceding four consecutive calendar quarters. The threshold for businesses that are not public service bodies is $ 30,000. Charities are also small suppliers if they meet the gross revenue test of $ 250,000 or less.*"

CRA *Definitions for GST/HST*. Available at http://www.cra-arc.gc.ca/tx/bsnss/tpcs/gst-tps/glssry-eng.html#smallsupplier [Accessed 13/01/2011].

[261]CRA GST / HST *Mandatory Registration for Non-Resident Businesses*. Available at http://www.cra-arc.gc.ca/tx/bsnss/tpcs/gst-tps/rgstrng/rgstr/rgstrng/mndtry_nr-eng.html [Accessed 30/05/2011].

[262]ibid, p376.

provinces also impose retail sales tax at the provincial level generally ranging from 5 to 10 %.[263] The provincial retail sales tax is often referred to as the Provincial Sales Tax ('PST').

18.4.1 Various Indirect Taxes Imposed in Canada

The provinces of Nova Scotia, New Brunswick, Newfoundland and Labrador entered into a Harmonized Sales Tax ('HST') at a rate of 15 % for Nova Scotia[264] and 13 % for the others.[265] As of 1 July 2010 Ontario and British Columbia harmonized their PST with GST at an effective rate of 13 % and 12 % respectively.[266] The HST is effectively comprised of the GST, at a rate of 5 %, and a PST, at the respective provincial rate which currently ranges from 7 to 10 %, imposed together as one tax, collected and administered by the federal government.[267]

The federal government in turn remits the PST of eight per cent to each respective province in terms of a formula, which was jointly developed and based on consumption patterns.[268] Quebec, on the other hand, imposes the GST-Quebec QST whereby the provincial government of Quebec administers both the federal GST and the Quebec provincial tax, and then remits the federal GST to the federal government.[269] Apart from the HST and Quebec QST, the GST is administered by the federal government and the PST by the provincial government, both taxes co-existing.[270]

The structure of the Canadian indirect tax system appears to be a combination of a European style VAT and the retail sales tax system implemented in the USA both of which interact with each other to form a dual VAT model.[271] Within the USA, retails sales tax is imposed at state level which gives rise to rules and principles

[263]Pricewaterhouse Coopers, Worldwide Tax Summaries *Canada – Corporate – Other Taxes*. Available at http://taxsummaries.pwc.com/uk/taxsummaries/wwts.nsf/ID/JDCN-89HRUU [Accessed 28/12/2010].

[264]CRA *Goods and Services tax/harmonized sales tax (GST/HST)*. Available at http://www.cra-arc.gc.ca/tx/bsnss/tpcs/gst-tps/menu-eng.html?=slnk [Accessed 28/12/2010].

[265]CRA *What is HST?* Available at http://www.cra-arc.gc.ca/tx/bsnss/tpcs/gst-tps/gnrl/hst-tvh/wrks-eng.html [Accessed 30/04/2010].

[266]loc cit CRA *Goods and Services tax/harmonized sales tax (GST/HST)*. http://www.cra-arc.gc.ca/tx/...=slnk.

[267]op cit, Schenk and Oldman, p376.

[268]supra.

[269]supra.

[270]ibid, p377.

[271]op cit, Schenk and Oldman, p377.

with regard to interstate transactions.[272] Canada contends with interprovincial transactions as well, however, the dual VAT model is an added difficulty in respect of Canada's interprovincial transactions.[273] Despite the dual VAT model, Schenk and Oldman note the Canadian authors Bird and Gendron's[274] approach to the dual VAT problem, expanded from the federal GST-Quebec QST, "*where the federal and provincial VATs rely on the destination principle, and suggest that the dual VAT model may be exportable to other federal systems or the EU*".[275,276]

18.4.2 'Destination' or 'Origin' Principle

Canada generally applies the 'destination principle' in regard to international transactions, however, interstate transactions may be determined in accordance with either the 'destination principle' or a 'hybrid origin-destination principle' depending on the Canadian province.[277] A noted difficulty pertaining to the implemented indirect tax system is in respect of imports. The reason for the difficulty is that while exports may be easily zero rated for GST purposes despite the province of supply, taxing imports is problematic, especially when the province of entry is not the importing province.[278]

In terms of Bird and Gendron's dual VAT proposal interprovincial sales are zero rated similar to Canadian exports. Interprovincial imports are then subject to tax at the point of resale by the provincial importer, thereby bringing the interprovincial import back into the tax regime. This is achieved in terms of a dual VAT system. According to Schenk and Oliver, the proposed dual VAT system:

> *... is imposed on the destination principle with features of the Canadian federal Goods and Services Tax and provincial Quebec Sales Tax. [Bird and Gendron] suggest that the taxation of cross-border trade is alleviated if a nation has both a subnational and national VAT. Whereas, by zero rating interprovincial sales, the GST provides some opportunity for tax*

[272]The USA Retail Sales Tax system will be examined in further detail in 20.2. *The Indirect Tax System Employed in the United States of America,* Part V of this paper [p240].

[273]op cit, Schenk and Oldman, p376.

[274]As per the brief history of Richard M Bird and Pierre-Pascal Gendron provided in Bird and Gendron's paper, '*Sales Taxes in Canada: The GST-HST-QSR-RST "System"*', Richard M Bird is Professor Emeritus of the Rotman School of Management at the University of Toronto, and Pierre-Pascal Gendron is Professor of The Business School at the Humber College of Technology and Advanced Learning, Toronto. Available at http://www.americantaxpolicyinstitute.org/pdf/VAT/Bird-Gendron.pdf [Accessed 28/12/2010].

[275]op cit, Schenk and Oldman, p376.

[276]supra.

[277]supra.

[278]supra.

> *avoidance on mail order or e-commerce sales, [Bird and Gendron] claim that the national VAT can be used to control or monitor interjurisdictional trade. Indeed, [Bird and Gendron] raise the possibility of using a 'virtual VAT' in a place like the EU that does not have a central VAT.*[279]

The HST system was, nevertheless, deemed preferable in regard to the prevention of avoiding HST on certain purchases such as mail order. In terms of the HST system, HST is charged and remitted on all purchases to consumers residing in an HST province.[280] While the GST-QST system was assessed as a good VAT model there was, however, one weak element noted, namely that the reverse-charge mechanism applies to unregistered persons.[281] Most of the countries previously examined restrict the reverse-charge mechanism to B2B transactions only. South Africa, however, implemented the reverse-charge mechanism in respect of B2C transactions because such implementation is theoretically possible. However, the practicality of such implementation is viewed as a weak element from an enforcement and administrative perspective. However, despite this noted weakness, Bird and Gendron advocate the GST-QST model as the better system above the HST as "*the HST's uniform base and rates preclude any degree of fiscal autonomy for provinces to establish their independent rate or alter their tax bases without unanimous consent*".[282]

18.4.3 GST/HST and Place of Supply Rules

A person, including non-residents, who makes "*taxable suppl[ies] in Canada in the course of carrying on a business in Canada is required to register*[283] *for GST/HST*

[279]op cit, Schenk and Oldman, p379.

[280]ibid, p380.

[281]ibid, p379.

[282]ibid, p380.

[283]Subsection 132(2) of the Canadian Excise Tax Act, per the CRA published guidelines, provides that:

> *a non-resident person who has a permanent establishment in Canada is considered to be resident in Canada in respect of, but only in respect of, the person's activities carried on through that permanent establishment. As a result, a non-resident person who makes taxable supplies through a permanent establishment in Canada is required to register for GST/HST purposes under subsection 240(1) of the [Canadian Excise Tax] Act as a resident person, and to collect tax on its taxable (other than zero rated) supplies made in Canada, unless the person is a small supplier.*

Registration is not limited to non-residents with a permanent establishment in Canada. Non-residents without a permanent establishment in Canada may also be required to register for GST / HST in accordance with subsection 240(1) of the Canadian Excise Tax Act:

purposes".[284] 'Taxable supplies' refer to the supply of 'goods and services' which are subject to GST/HST and supplied in the course of a commercial activity.[285] 'Carrying on a business' is defined as a business activity which "*is done regularly or continually*".[286] Dr. Rendahl notes a difference between the Canadian GST/HST and EU VAT system in respect of the definition of taxable person which may be significant for purposes of ensuring a broad taxing net for digital supplies. A broader definition may, specifically, be of significance in regard to applying VAT on, for example, illegally downloaded copyrighted material as a means to combat such illegal supplies as advocated by Dr. Rendahl[287]:

> *The criteria of reasonable expectation of profit is more emphasized in the Canadian GST than in EC VAT… Hence, the definition of taxable person in EC VAT is wider than the Canadian comparable definition of commercial activity. This also means that the wider scope of EC VAT is likely to catch more digital supplies than Canadian GST. This could e.g. make a difference where distinctions between taxing legal and illegal supplies on-line are discussed…*[288]

For the purpose of Canadian GST, 'supply' is defined as "*the provision of property or a service in any way, including sale, transfer, barter, exchange, licence, rental, lease, gift, and disposition*".[289] The Canadian Revenue Agency ('CRA') has categorised 'property' into three categories as "*real property, tangible personal property and intangible personal property*".[290] 'Intangible personal property' is defined as including "*contractual rights… [,] intellectual property*

> *…every non-resident person who makes taxable supplies in Canada in the course of a business carried on in Canada (other than as a small supplier), is required to register for GST/HST purposes. As a registrant, the non-resident is required to collect tax on its taxable (other than zero-rated) supplies made in Canada.*

CRA, GST/HST Technical Information Bulletin *GST/HST and Electronic Commerce* (July 2002) p27.

Available at http://www.cra-arc.gc.ca/BBF6E666-8A29-47F6-7781B1517476/FinalDownload/DownloadId_F964750C245682CA22DA0BC295CE6E20/BBF6E666-8A29-47F6-BF42-7781B1517476/E/pub/gm/b-090/b-090_e.pdf [Accessed 30/04/2010].

[284]CRA *Non-Residents and Carrying on Business in Canada* Available at http://www.cra-arc.gc.ca/tx/bsnss/tpcs/cmm/gst-tps/nnrs-eng.html [Accessed 30/04/2010].

[285]CRA *Doing Business in Canada – GST/HST Information for Non-Residents*. p4. Available at http://www.cra-arc.gc.ca/E/pub/gp/rc4027/rc4027-09e.pdf [Accessed 30/04/2010].

[286]ibid, p6.

[287]Refer to the discussion regarding The Pirate Bay Case discussed in 18.2.1. *New Zealand*, Part V of this paper [p200].

[288]op cit, Rendahl, p166.

[289]loc cit CRA *Doing Business in Canada – GST/HST Information for Non-Residents*. http://www.cra-arc.gc.ca/E/pub/gp/rc4027/rc4027-09e.pdf. p4.

[290]CRA *GST/HST Memoranda Series, 3.1. Liability for Tax* (August 1999, Revised September 2000) p11. Available at http://www.cra-arc.gc.ca/E/pub/gm/3-1/3-1-e.pdf [Accessed 28/12/2010].

(patents, trade-marks, trade-names), and rights in relation to goods that are not in possession . . ."[291] of the holder.

'Service' is defined as having "*a broad meaning covering anything other than property, money and a supply of services rendered by a person who is or agrees to become an employee or an officer to an employer in the course of, or in relation to the employee's office of employment*".[292] While the Canadian and EU definitions of 'supply of service' similarities are similar in essence, a significant difference between the two is that the Canadian definition does not include 'intangible personal property'.[293] This slight difference is significant because digital supplies may, according to certain schools of thought, constitute both 'services' and 'intangible personal property'.[294]

A supply of intangible personal property which '*may be used*' in whole or in part in Canada, appertains to real property or tangible personal property ordinarily situated in Canada, or appertains to the performance of a service in Canada which is deemed to be provided in Canada.[295] 'May be used' is interpreted by the CRA to mean 'allowed to be used'.[296] Thus, "*[t]he fact that the supply may be made to a recipient who is outside Canada has no bearing on whether the supply is made in Canada*".[297]

Where the supply of intangible personal property does not relate to real property, tangible personal property or services, and is not subject to place of use restrictions, the Canadian province in which the negotiation of the supply occurred is considered to be the place of supply.[298] 'Place of negotiation', for purposes of determining the place of supply, is defined as "*the location of the supplier's permanent establishment at which the individual principally involved in negotiating an agreement for the supplier ordinarily works or to which that individual ordinarily reports in the performance of his or her duties relating to the supplier's activities in the course of which the supply is made. 'Negotiating' includes the making or acceptance of an offer.*"[299]

---

[291]loc cit CRA *GST/HST Memoranda Series, 3.1. Liability for Tax*. http://www.cra-arc.gc.ca/E/pub/gm/3-1/3-1-e.pdf. p11.

[292]loc cit CRA *GST/HST Memoranda Series, 3.1. Liability for Tax*. http://www.cra-arc.gc.ca/E/pub/gm/3-1/3-1-e.pdf. p12.

[293]op cit, Rendahl, p130.

[294]supra.

(As examined in 18.2.1. *New Zealand*, Part V of this paper [p200]. Certain jurisdictions are of the opinion that digital supplies may constitute the supply of both 'services' and 'goods' and jurisdictions such as New Zealand deem the supply to constitute services only.)

[295]loc cit GST/HST Technical Information Bulletin *GST/HST and Electronic Commerce*. http://www.cra-arc.gc.ca/B...90_e.pdf. p16.

[296]supra.

[297]ibid, p17.

[298]ibid, p20.

[299]loc cit GST/HST Technical Information Bulletin *GST/HST and Electronic Commerce*. http://www.cra-arc.gc.ca/B...90_e.pdf. p20.

A supply of service, where the service is or is to be performed either in whole or in part in Canada, is deemed to be made in Canada.[300] Where the service is performed wholly outside Canada, the service is deemed to be discharged outside Canada. "Performed" is not defined, *per se*, but the CRA provides guidance whereby "*the place where a service is performed is traditionally the place where the person physically doing the work is situated*".[301]

18.4.4 eCommerce in Canada

As previously discussed, technology provides new methods of performing service and the concept of the person's physical location has been debated. The CRA acknowledges the pertinent possibility of unavoidable complications precipitated by eCommerce, which effectively "*allows services to be provided remotely*",[302] in regard to determining the place of supply of services performed electronically. The CRA provides the following guidance for determining the place of supply of service in respect of a service which is performed, at least, in part in Canada[303]:

- *The service requires a person to perform a task (i.e. the supplier acts through one or more of its employees), and the person performing or physically carrying out the task situated in Canada at the time the activity is done;*
- *The service includes operations performed by a supplier's equipment (e.g., computer equipment), and the equipment is located in Canada;*
- *The supply involves doing something to or with a recipient's equipment by accessing it from a remote location, and the recipient's equipment is located in Canada (however, this does not apply to a service wholly performed outside Canada, where the results are subsequently delivered electronically to a recipient's computers in Canada, e.g., a programming service carried out at the supplier's location outside Canada and e-mailed to a recipient in Canada); or*
- *Any activity related to the performance of the service is undertaken in Canada.*[304]

'The place of negotiation' is also applied to services for the purpose of determining the province where theplace of supply occurs.[305]

---

[300]ibid, p17.

[301]supra.

[302]supra.

[303]ibid, p18.

[304]supra.

[305]loc cit GST/HST Technical Information Bulletin *GST/HST and Electronic Commerce*. http://www.cra-arc.gc.ca/B...90_e.pdf. p21.

The CRA has published a bulletin addressing the CRA's interpretation of legislation relevant to eCommerce. The CRA acknowledges that "*the technology underlying electronic commerce facilitates the delivery of products and services by suppliers to customers located throughout the world. [And that, furthermore,] [a] business will often have no physical presence in its customer's jurisdiction, or its only physical presence in that jurisdiction may be a server...*"[306]

A digital supply may either be a supply of services, a supply of telecommunication services or a supply of intangible personal property. The CRA has provided guidelines for purposes of identifying factors which indicate whether an electronic supply constitutes a supply of intangible personal property or a supply of services[307]:

Supply of Intangible Personal Property	*Supply of Services*
A right in a product or a right to use a product for personal or commercial purposes is provided, such as:	The supply does not include the provision of rights (e.g. technical know-how), or if there is a provision of rights, the rights are incidental to the supply
Intellectual property or a right to use intellectual property (e.g. copyright); or	
Rights of a temporary nature (e.g. a right to view, access or use a product while on-line)	
A product is provided that has already been created or developed, or is already in existence	The supply involves specific work that is performed by a person for a specific customer; and
A product is created or developed for a specific customer, but the supplier retains ownership of the product; and	There is human involvement in making the supply.
A right to make a copy of a digitized product is provided	

[306]ibid, p2.

[307]ibid, p4 – The table is an exact extract from the GST/HST Technical Information Bulletin *GST/HST and Electronic Commerce*. http://www.cra-arc.gc.ca/B...90_e.pdf.

Upon applying the above criteria to the various examples[308] provided in the CRA guidelines, downloading of digitized products is considered intangible personal property. According to the CRA *"[t]he customer is provided with a copy of the*

[308]The CRA bulletin examined various examples pertaining to electronic commerce and examined whether such supplies constitute intangible personal property or services. The examples, along with brief comments, read as follows:

I. "Electronic Ordering and Downloading of Digitized Products

... A limitation with respect to the frequency, even to a single occurrence, or period of use of a downloaded copy of a digitized product, even to a single occurrence, does not alter the nature of the supply... The customer is provided with a copy of the product, as well as the right to use the product... Similarly, the supply of the updates and add-ons is characterized as a supply of intangible personal property...

II. Software Maintenance Contracts

These supplies typically involve the provision of software updates with technical support. Technical support may be provided on-line, through the use of a trouble-shooting database, or by communications (e.g., telephone or e-mail) with technicians. These supplies are characterized either as supplies of intangible personal property or of services, depending upon the principal object of the supply... As the principal object of the supply [of software maintenance] is the provision of a software update delivered electronically, the supply is characterized as one of intangible personal property... if the technical support [in regard to customer support over a computer network] is essentially the supply of a right to use existing technical information in the form of on-line documentation and access to a trouble-shooting database, and the interaction with the technician is incidental, the supply would be characterized as one of intangible personal property. If technical support is provided through interaction with technicians, and the provision of any rights to documentation or databases is incidental, the supply would be characterized as a supply of a service, since it is of specific work performed for a specific customer.

III. Application Hosting, Web site hosting, and data warehousing

These supplies include remote access and use of software, space on and access to servers to store data or run software, and technical support. They are characterized as either intangible personal property or services... [Where] [t]he host entity is essentially providing the space to store and run the software application on its equipment, as well as technical support... [such hosting is consequently] characterized as a supply of a service... [Under circumstances where] the host entity (rather than the customer) is the copyright holder for the software, the customer is being provided with the right to use the software... [and] is characterized as a supply of intangible personal property...

[With regard to web site hosting, where the] agreement between the supplier and the customer is to host the customer's Web site on a server maintained by the supplier, and the customer maintains all rights in the site[, there] is no supply of rights or of property between the supplier and the customer, and therefore the supply is characterized as a supply of a service... [Similarly, where the agreement relates to the storage of the] customer's computer data on a server maintained by the supplier[,]... there is no provision of rights or property, the supply is characterized as a supply of a service.

IV. Supplies Related to On-Line Sales

These supplies include advertising, referral, and representation on behalf of on-line suppliers of goods or services. The suppliers provide a means of bringing consumers and merchants together on-line, but do not supply the goods or services being advertised or marketed. These supplies are generally characterized as supplies of services...

V. Subscriptions to Databases and Web sites

These supplies typically involve a provider making digitized content available to customers for search, retrieval and use. They are generally characterized as supplies of intangible personal property...

product, as well as the right to use the product".[309] This is a significant dissimilarity to the EU VAT system whereby the downloading of digitized products is considered electronically to be supplied *services*. A further variation from the EU VAT system is in regard to the 'human involvement' criterion. In terms of Canadian GST/HST a supply of a service includes the factor of human intervention, for example, technical support, whereas minimal human involvement is required in order to qualify as an electronically supplied service in terms of the EU VAT.[310] The EU VAT model distinguishes between traditionally supplied services and electronically supplied services.[311]

Similar to other VAT jurisdictions, 'telecommunication services' has been specifically defined in the Canadian legislation and reads as follows:

(a) *the service of emitting, transmitting or receiving signs, signals, writing, images or sounds or intelligence of any nature by wire, cable, radio, optical or other electromagnetic system, or by any similar technical system, or*

VI. Information Provided by Electronic Means

These supplies range from professional advisory services to the periodic electronic delivery of data to subscribers in accordance with their personal preferences. If the supply is of an existing product or a product created for a group of customers who receive rights to the product (e.g., subscriptions for data delivered on a periodic basis), it is characterized as a supply of intangible personal property. If there is human involvement in the making of the supply, or specific work is performed by a person for a specific customer, and the supply does not involve the transfer of rights, it is characterized as a supply of a service . . . The supply of . . . advice to clients, delivered by electronic means, is a supply of a service, as it involves specific work that is performed for a specific client, and does not involve a supply of rights to an existing product . . . [If the] supply is one of a right to customized information[, t]here is no human involvement on the part of the supplier in the making of the supply. Consequently, the supply is characterized as one of intangible personal property . . . "

[loc cit GST/HST Technical Information Bulletin *GST/HST and Electronic Commerce*. http://www.cra-arc.gc.ca/B...90_e.pdf. **p5–p11].**

[309]ibid, p5.

[310]op cit, Rendahl, p230.

[311]supra.

Also, refer to the discussion and examination of the EU VAT model in 18.1.1 *European Union VAT Law*, Part V of this paper [p171].

(b) *making available for such emission, transmission or reception telecommunication facilities*[312] *of a person who carries on the business of supplying services referred to in paragraph (a)*[313] [Emphasis Added]

There is a distinction between the supply of a telecommunication service and the use of telecommunications for the purpose of supplying services and other property.[314] It is important to establish whether there is a supply of telecommunication services or merely the use thereof. E-mail, internet access service provided by an ISP, data transmission, web-based broadcasting and voice telephony services provided through the Internet are a few examples of telecommunication services.[315]

While telecommunication service has been specifically defined in concordance with other VAT jurisdictions, a distinctive difference between the EU VAT model and the Canadian GST/HST is that the latter examines where the telecommunication service is made preparatory to determining place of supply, whereas the EU determines the location of the supplier and the residency of the purchaser with the intent of determining the place of supply.[316]

For the purpose of performing a jurisdictional analysis it is relevant to emphasize significant differences between Canadian GST (which demonstrates the ability to effectively co-exist with retail sales tax) and the European VAT system (which demonstrates harmonization of VAT systems across international borders). The differences illustrate possible 'functional problems'[317] which may exist within the European VAT system. For example, the European VAT system's "place-of-supply" rules provide certainty in regard to cross-border trade, but predominantly only in respect of cross-border transactions between European Union Member States. However, despite potential functional problems,[318] the European Union bears testimony to the ability of VAT to operate effectively in an harmonized state.

[312]'Telecommunication facilities' is defined in subsection 123(1) of the Canadian Excise Tax Act as follows:

> *any facility, apparatus or other things (including any wire, cable, radio, optical or other electromagnetic system, or any similar technical system, or any part thereof) that is used or is capable of being used for telecommunications*

[loc cit GST/HST Technical Information Bulletin *GST/HST and Electronic Commerce.* http://www.cra-arc.gc.ca/B...90_e.pdf**. p12].**

[313]Subsection 123(1) of the Canadian Excise Tax Act.
[ibid, p12].

[314]ibid, p13.

[315]loc cit GST/HST Technical Information Bulletin *GST/HST and Electronic Commerce.* http://www.cra-arc.gc.ca/B...90_e.pdf. p13–p16.

[316]op cit, Rendahl, p280.

[317]op cit Jean Monnet Center for International & Regional Economic Law & Justice, *Chapter III: Shortcomings of the Present European VAT System with Respect to Electronic Supplies, Classification of E-Commerce Transactions.* Available at http://centers.law.nyu.edu/jeanmonnet/papers/01/013301-03.html [Accessed 05/10/2011].

[318]supra.

Similarly, Canada (as previously discussed) illustrates the ability of VAT to operate effectively with retail sales tax. As will be discussed later,[319] VAT is not without its flaws and areas requiring improvement as, in its current state, certain cross-border transactions may be subject to double VAT or double non-VAT. VAT, nevertheless, remains a system which is flexible enough to adapt to the needs of eCommerce transactions. However, in order to move towards a VAT utopia the differences between the various VAT systems, especially in respect of eCommerce transactions, should be identified and understood.

The supply of property, specifically intangible personal property pertinent to digital supplies, or services made to a non-registered non-resident person will be subject to Canadian GST/HST if made in Canada, but at the rate of zero per cent.[320] The zero rating provisions were in point of fact expanded to incorporate the supply of intangible personal property to a non-resident on account of the outcome of the Canadian case *Canada v. Dawn's Place Ltd.*[321] ("Dawn case").[322]

The Dawn case appertains to a Canadian run website which allowed the downloading of imageries available to subscribers. The use and access of the website was not geographically restricted and could be accessed internationally. Due to the international usage of the website, the place of supply was queried. To ensure that subscriptions would be subject to Canadian GST/HST it was held that "*a supply is deemed to be made in Canada if it is a supply of intangible personal property that may be used in whole or in part in Canada*".[323] The subscription agreement did not grant ownership of the imageries, but merely the right to view and download for personal use. As held by the court, "*the question [was] whether access to an internet website operated by a Canadian enterprise (which is a supply of intangible personal property) is a zero-rated supply to any non-resident recipient (who is not a GST registrant), because the recipient has the right to download and retain a copy of copyrighted material accessed on the website*".[324]

Dawn's Place Ltd. ("Dawn's Place") operated a website containing a collection of copyright material to which users could subscribe in order to access the copyright contents of the website.[325] In terms of the subscription agreement "[*t]he subscriber has the right to download and retain for the subscriber's own use, on one computer, any image or video file on the website*".[326] Despite not being able to determine where its subscribers were located Dawn's Place submitted that a minimum of 90 %

[319]Refer to 21.3.3. *Is VAT Perfect in its Current Form?* Part V of this paper [p270].

[320]loc cit GST/HST Technical Information Bulletin *GST/HST and Electronic Commerce*. http://www.cra-arc.gc.ca/B...90_e.pdf. p25.

[321]Canada v Dawn's Place Ltd. [2006] G.S.T.C. 137 [Canada].

[322]op cit, Rendahl, p283.

[323]Her Majesty the Queen v Dawn's Place Ltd [2006] FCA 349 at para 3 [Canada]. Available at http://decisions.fca-caf.gc.ca/en/2006/2006fca349/2006fca349.html [Accessed 05/10/2011].

[324]ibid at para 9.

[325]ibid at para 10.

[326]ibid at para 13.

of its subscribers were non-residents of Canada based on the tracking of the source of payments.[327] Dawn's Place submitted, and was upheld by the Tax Court, that "*because copyright subsist[ed] in the contents of the website and the copyright [was] owned by Dawn's Place, it necessarily follow[ed] that Dawn's Place was supplying its subscribers with a right, licence or privilege to use the copyright in the website contents... [which lead to the conclusion] that the supplies in issue were prima facie within the scope of...*"[328] the GST zero rating provisions in regard to supplies to non-residents.

The Appellate Court, however, held that further analysis was required in respect of the characterization of the supply and that "*[t]he fact that the copy is made by the subscriber himself through his own computer is a necessary incident of the supply. Indeed, there is no other way to access and retain material on a website. However, that incidental copying does not change the essential nature of the supply*"[329] [Emphasis Added].

The place of supply was determined to be Canada in consideration of the subscription agreement. However, the Canadian court ruled that the supply of intangible personal property did not fall within the scope of the zero rating provisions legislated at the time in relation to the supplies made to the non-resident subscribers.[330] The Appellate Court held that "*a transaction that in essence is an acquisition of data or images transmitted electronically, any incidental copying is merely the means by which the data is captured and stored. The essential consideration for the payment in that case is the data, not the use of the copyright, even though the copyright is incidentally used... [and, therefore,] the reasoning underlying the OECD commentary is sound*"[331] [Emphasis Added].

The limited zero rating provisions gave rise, potentially, to double taxation as the supply was subject to Canadian GST/HST and possibly VAT or GST in

[327] ibid at para 14.

[328] ibid Her Majesty the Queen v Dawn's Place Ltd [2006] FCA 349 at para 3 [Canada], http://decisions.fca-caf.gc.ca/en/2001/2001fca260/2001fca260.html. at para 17.

[329] ibid at para 20.

[330] op cit, Rendahl, p281–p282.

[331] op cit Her Majesty the Queen v Dawn's Place Ltd. [2006] FCA 349 at para 3 [Canada]. http://decisions.fca-caf.gc.ca/en/2001/2001fca260/2001fca260.html. at para 29.

the customer's jurisdiction if, for example, the destination principle applied,[332] thus illustrating the impact technology has had on the 'doctrine of neutrality'.[333] However, as previously stated, this was overcome by merely expanding the zero rating provisions to incorporate the supply of intangible personal property to a non-resident, thereby overcoming the inequity which arose as a result of such eCommerce transactions. This did not require 'reconceptualisation' of the GST principles, but merely expression of the zero rating provisions.

It has been suggested that access to Second Life, labelled as an online game with regard to Canadian users, is deemed to be made in Canada because the online game "*can be wholly or partly used in Canada*".[334,335] As an alternative, the Canadian user may be liable for GST/HST in terms of the reverse charge mechanism as the provisions pertaining to the importation of taxable supplies may also apply.[336] While two possible taxing solutions have been suggested in respect of supplies to Canadian consumers, Dr. Rendahl underscores the potential unintentional double non-taxation which may occur if a proper evaluation of the supplying company's structure and the location of the servers is not executed.[337]

---

[332] op cit, Rendahl, p282.

[333] An argument was submitted that "*the correct interpretation of [the relevant zero rating provision] must respect the doctrine of neutrality, which is the notion that tax should not provide an incentive or disincentive it determining the manner in which business is conducted*". Interpreting and applying the legislation in a manner which may give rise to double taxation may be viewed as a contradiction of the doctrine of neutrality. The double taxation may discourage foreign recipients from utilising services supplied by Dawn's Place causing Dawn's Place to suffer a competitive disadvantage.

Both the Crown and Dawn's Place attempted to argue the doctrine of neutrality to support their cases respectively: "*the Crown argued that if the supply of copyrighted material in electronic form is zero-rated, then the supply of electronic versions of copyrighted material would have an advantage over the supply of the same content in the form of a magazine. Dawn's Place agreed that neutrality was important, but argued that the supply of electronic material to non-residents is the functional equivalent of the export of magazines, so that if the supply in this case is not zero-rated, the export of magazines would have an advantage over the supply of electronic material to non-resident*".

The Appellate Court held, however, that "*the submissions on neutrality [were] of no assistance, given the record of this case. The doctrine of neutrality generally is a guideline for the development of tax policy, which in turn may inform the drafting and enactment of tax legislation. However, except for what may be inferred from the language of [the relevant zero rating provision/s] and the relevant elements of the statutory scheme, [the Judge had] no basis for determining the policy underlying [the zero rating provisions]. In particular, [the Judge had] no basis for determining whether, or to what extent, [the zero rating provisions were] intended to give effect to the doctrine of neutrality*".

op cit Her Majesty the Queen v Dawn's Place Ltd. [2006] FCA 349 at para 3 [Canada]. http://decisions.fca-caf.gc.ca/en/2001/2001fca260/2001fca260.html. at para 30–31.

[334] ibid, p285.

[335] supra.

[336] supra.

[337] ibid, p285–p286.

Bibliography

Primary Sources

Cases

Canadian Cases

Canada v Dawn's Place Ltd. 2006. G.S.T.C. 137. Available at http://reports.fja.gc.ca/eng/2007/2006fca349.html. Accessed 22 Jan 2012.

Her Majesty the Queen v Dawn's Place Ltd. 2006. FCA 349. Available at http://decisions.fca-caf.gc.ca/en/2006/2006fca349/2006fca349.html. Accessed 05 Oct 2011.

Statutes

Australian Goods and Services Tax Act, No. 55 of 1999 (as amended)

Europa. *Official Journal of the European Communities. VAT on E-Commerce Directive (2002/38/EC).* Available at http://eur-lex.europa.eu/LexUriServ/LexUriServ.do?uri=OJ:L:2002:128:0041:0044:en:PDF. Accessed 17 Dec 2014.

European Union VAT Directive 2006/112/EC

New Zealand Goods and Services Tax Act, No. 141 of 1985 (as amended)

South Africa Value-Added Tax Act, No. 89 of 1991 (as amended)

UK Value Added Tax Act 1994 c.23 (as amended)

Secondary Sources

Amazon.com. *Amazon MP3 music service: Terms of use.* Available at http://www.amazon.com/gp/help/customer/display.html?nodeId=200154280. Accessed 8 Jan 2011.

Amazon.com. *Further notice.* Available at http://www.amazon.com/gp/digital/order/geo-filter-note.html?ie=uUTF8&glCode=340. Accessed 22 Dec 2010.

Amazon.com. *The notice.* Available at http://www.amazon.com/gp/dmusic/order/amd-get-interstitial.html?ie=UTF8&ASIN=B003FAE0OE&isTrack=0&tryInPlace=0. Accessed 22 Dec 2010.

Australian Taxation Office. *Electronic commerce industry partnership – Issues register.* Available at http://www.ato.gov.au/print.asp?doc=/content/18428.htm. Accessed 3 Dec 2010.

Australian Taxation Office. *GST registration information for a non-resident.* Available at http://www.ato.gov.au/print.asp?doc=/content/57758.htm. Accessed 3 Dec 2010.

Bird, Richard M., and Pierre-Pascal Gendron. *Sales taxes in Canada: The GST-HST-QSR-RST 'system'.* Available at http://www.americantaxpolicyinstitute.org/pdf/VAT/Bird-Gendron.pdf. Accessed 28 Dec 2010.

Canadian Revenue Agency. *Definitions for GST/HST.* Available at http://www.cra-arc.gc.ca/tx/bsnss/tpcs/gst-tps/glssry-eng.html#quarter. Accessed 13 Jan 2011.

Canadian Revenue Agency. *Definitions for GST/HST.* Available at http://www.cra-arc.gc.ca/tx/bsnss/tpcs/gst-tps/glssry-eng.html#smallsupplier. Accessed 13 Jan 2011.

Canadian Revenue Agency. *Doing business in Canada – GST/HST information for non-residents.* Available at http://www.cra-arc.gc.ca/E/pub/gp/rc4027/rc4027-09e.pdf. Accessed 30 Apr 2010.

Canadian Revenue Agency. *Goods and services tax/harmonized sales tax (GST/HST).* Available at http://www.cra-arc.gc.ca/tx/bsnss/tpcs/gst-tps/menu-eng.html?=slnk. Accessed 28 Dec 2010.

Canadian Revenue Agency. *GST/HST mandatory registration for non-resident businesses.* Available at http://www.cra-arc.gc.ca/tx/bsnss/tpcs/gst-tps/rgstrng/rgstr/rgstrng/mndtry_nr-eng.html. Accessed 30 May 2011.

Canadian Revenue Agency. *GST/HST mandatory registration.* Available at http://www.cra-arc.gc.ca/tx/bsnss/tpcs/gst-tps/rgstrng/mndtry-eng.html. Accessed 13 Jan 2011.

Canadian Revenue Agency. *GST/HST memoranda series, 3.1. Liability for tax* (August 1999, Revised September 2000). Available at http://www.cra-arc.gc.ca/E/pub/gm/3-1/3-1-e.pdf. Accessed 28 Dec 2010.

Canadian Revenue Agency. 2002, July. GST/HST Technical Information Bulletin. *GST/HST and electronic commerce*. Available at http://www.cra-arc.gc.ca/BBF6E666-8A29-47F6-7781B1517476/FinalDownload/DownloadId_F964750C245682CA22DA0BC295CE6E20/BBF6E666-8A29-47F6-BF42-7781B1517476/E/pub/gm/b-090/b-090_e.pdf. Accessed 30 Apr 2010.

Canadian Revenue Agency. *Non-residents and carrying on business in Canada*. Available at http://www.cra-arc.gc.ca/tx/bsnss/tpcs/cmm/gst-tps/nnrs-eng.html. Accessed 30 Apr 2010.

Canadian Revenue Agency. *What is HST?* Available at http://www.cra-arc.gc.ca/tx/bsnss/tpcs/gst-tps/gnrl/hst-tvh/wrks-eng.html. Accessed 30 Apr 2010.

Europa. *The EU at a glance – The history of the European Union*. Available at http://europa.eu/abc/history/index_en.htm. Accessed 2 July 2010.

European Commission. *Distance selling of goods*. Available at http://ec.europa.eu/taxation_customs/taxation/vat/how_vat_works/distance_selling/index_en.htm. Accessed 05 June 2010.

European Commission. *Mail order and distance purchasing*. Available at http://ec.europa.eu/taxation_customs/taxation/vat/consumers/mail_order_distance/index_en.htm. Accessed 05 June 2010.

European Commission Taxation & Customs Union. *General overview – VAT on goods moving between member states*. Available at http://ec.europa.eu/taxation_customs/taxation/vat/how_vat_works/index_en.htm. Accessed 05 June 2010.

European Commission Taxation & Customs Union. *General overview – The history of VAT in the European Union until 1993*. Available at http://ec.europa.eu/taxation_customs/taxation/vat/how_vat_works/index_en.htm. Accessed 05 June 2010.

European Commission Taxation & Customs Union. *VAT directive 2 (01.01.2010) eLearning course (Course on the VAT directive)*. Available at http://ec.europa.eu/taxation_customs/common/elearning/vat/index_en.htm. Accessed 13 Dec 2010.

European Commission Taxation & Customs Union. *VAT rates applied in the member states of the European Union.* (Situation at 1st May 2010). Available at http://ec.europa.eu/taxation_customs/resources/documents/taxation/vat/how_vat_works/rates/vat_rates_en.pdf. Accessed 06 May 2010.

European Commission Taxation & Customs Union. *VAT: VAT and the single market – 1993 to now*. Available at http://ec.europa.eu/taxation_customs/taxation/vat/how_vat_works/index_en.htm. Accessed 31 May 2011 and 21 Jan 2012.

HM Revenue & Customs. *When to register for UK VAT*. Available at http://www.hmrc.gov.uk/vat/start/register/when-to-register.htm. Accessed 05 Oct 2011.

HM Revenue & Customs Website. *HM revenue & customs. Main rules: Structure and application. VATPOSG3100 – Main rules: Structure and application, introduction*. Available at http://www.hmrc.gov.uk/manuals/vatposgmanual/VATPOSG3100.htm. Accessed 9 Dec 2010.

HM Revenue & Customs Website. *HM revenue & customs: Introduction to VAT, VAT glossary*. Available at http://www.hmrc.gov.uk/vat/start/introduction.htm. Accessed 9 Dec 2010.

HM Revenue & Customs Website. 2010, January. *Notice 741A place of supply of services*. Available at http://customs.hmrc.gov.uk/channelsPortalWebApp/channelsPortalWebApp.portal?_nfpb=true&_pageLabel=pageVAT_ShowContent&propertyType=document&id=HMCE_PROD1_029955#downloadopt. Accessed 12 Dec 2010.

HM Revenue & Customs Website. *HM revenue & customs: Introduction to VAT*. Available at http://www.hmrc.gov.uk/vat/start/introduction.htm. Accessed 9 Dec 2010.

HM Revenue & Customs. 2003, April. *Electronically supplied services: A guide to interpretation*. Available at http://customs.hmrc.gov.uk/channelsPortalWebApp/channelsPortalWebApp.portal?_nfpb=true&_pageLabel=oageVAT_ShowContent&id=HMCE_CL_000907?&propertyType=document#downloadopt. Accessed 12 Dec 2010.

HM Revenue & Customs. *How to work out your place of supply of services for VAT*. Available at http://www.hmrc.gov.uk/vat/managing/international/exports/services.htm. Accessed 9 Dec 2010.

HM Revenue & Customs. *VAT: Cross-border VAT changes 2010*. Available at http://www.hmrc.gov.uk/vat/cross-border-changes-2010.htm. Accessed 9 Dec 2010.

How Stuff Works. *How BitTorrent works, what BitTorrent does*. Available at http://computer.howstuffworks.com/bittorrent2.htm. Accessed 08 Oct 2009.

Irish Revenue Legislation Services, Indirect Taxes Division (11th Edition). *VAT guide 2008*. Chapter Eight. Link to the VAT guide 2008. Available at http://www.revenue.ie/revsearch/search.jsp. Accessed 31 May 2011

Irish Tax and Customs Revenue Website. *VAT registration FAQs*. Available at http://www.revenue.ie/en/tax/vat/registration/index.html. Accessed 12 Dec 2010.

Irish Tax and Customs Revenue Website. *VAT registration for foreign traders*. Available at http://www.revenue.ie/en/tax/vat/leaflets/vat-registration-foreign-traders.html. Accessed 12 Dec 2010.

The Jean Monnet Center for International & Regional Economic Law & Justice, The NYU Institutes on the Park. *Chapter III: Shortcomings of the present European VAT system with respect to electronic supplies, classification of e-commerce transactions*. Available at http://centers.law.nyu.edu/jeanmonnet/papers/01/013301-03.html. Accessed 05 Oct 2011.

Makipaa, A. 2008. *Value added tax (VAT) EN 4.18.2*. European Commission Taxation & Customs Union. Available at http://europarl.europa.eu/ftu/pdf/en/FTU_4.18.2.pdf. Accessed 14 Dec 2010.

McKenzie, Alastair. 2008, August. *GST – A practical guide*, 8th ed. CCH New Zealand Limited, A Wolters Kluwer Business, Auckland, New Zealand

MecroPress, South Atlantic News Agency. *Japan retains position as world' second largest economy*. Available at http://en.mecropress.com/2010/02/15/japan-retains-position-as-world-second-largest-economy. Accessed 27 Dec 2010.

New Zealand Inland Revenue. *E-commerce and GST (E-commerce and tax)*. Available at http://www.ird.govt.nz/ecommerce-tax/ecommerce-gst/. Accessed 4 Dec 2010.

New Zealand Inland Revenue. *E-commerce and GST (E-commerce and tax)*. Available at http://www.ird.govt.nz/ecommerce-tax/ecommerce-gst/business-australian-ecommerce-gst.html. Accessed 4 Dec 2010.

New Zealand Inland Revenue GST and Imported Services. 2001, June. A challenge in an electronic commerce environment. A Government discussion document. Policy Advice Division of the Inland Revenue Department, New Zealand. Available at http://taxpolicy.ird.govt.nz/sites/default/files/2001-dd-gst-imported-services.pdf. Accessed 5 Oct 2011.

New Zealand Inland Revenue. 2002, May. *Guide to tax consequences of trading over the internet*. Available at http://www.ird.govt.nz/resources/d/9/d902a3804bbe5893bc4bfcbc87554a30/internettaxguide.pdf. Accessed 4 Dec 2010.

Pricewaterhouse Coopers. *Description of VAT in the EU and the VAT directives*. Available at http://www.pwc.com/be/en/publications/guide-to-vat-in-the-eu-of-27-countries.jhtml. Accessed 13 Dec 2010.

Pricewaterhouse Coopers Worldwide Tax Summaries. *Austria – Corporate – Other taxes*. Available at http://taxsummaries.pwc.com/uk/taxsummaries/wwts.nsf/ID/JDCN-89HRKN. Accessed 3 Dec 2010.

Pricewaterhouse Coopers Worldwide Tax Summaries. *Canada – Corporate – Other taxes*. Available at http://taxsummaries.pwc.com/uk/taxsummaries/wwts.nsf/ID/JDCN-89HRUU. Accessed 28 Dec 2010.

Pricewaterhouse Coopers Worldwide Tax Summaries. *China, People's Republic of – Corporate – Other taxes*. Available at http://taxsummaries.pwc.com/uk/taxsummaries/wwts.nsf/ID/JDCN-89HRZF. Accessed 3 Dec 2010.

Pricewaterhouse Coopers Worldwide Tax Summaries. *Ireland – Corporate – Other taxes*. Available at http://taxsummaries.pwc.com/uk/taxsummaries/wwts.nsf/ID/JDCN-89HSNF. Accessed 3 Dec 2010.

Pricewaterhouse Coopers Worldwide Tax Summaries. *Japan – Corporate – Other taxes*. Available at http://taxsummaries.pwc.com/uk/taxsummaries/wwts.nsf/ID/JDCN-89HSSD. Accessed 3 Dec 2010.

Pricewaterhouse Coopers Worldwide Tax Summaries. *Russian Federation – Corporate – Other taxes*. Available at http://taxsummaries.pwc.com/uk/taxsummaries/wwts.nsf/ID/JDCN-89HTPC. Accessed 3 Dec 2010.

Pricewaterhouse Coopers Worldwide Tax Summaries. *United Kingdom – Corporate – Other taxes*. Available at http://taxsummaries.pwc.com/uk/taxsummaries/wwts.nsf/ID/JDCN-89HU8E. Accessed 9 Dec 2010.

Rendahl, Pernilla. 2009. *Cross-border consumption taxation of digital supplies*. Amsterdam: IBFD.

Bird, Richard M., and Pierre-Pascal Gendron. 2009, May 29. *Sales taxes in Canada: The GST-HST-QSR-RST "system"*. Available at http://www.americantaxpolicyinstitute.org/pdf/VAT/Bird-Gendron.pdf. Accessed 28 Dec 2010.

Roosevelt, Franklin D. Available at http://thinkexist.com/search/searchquotation.asp?search=tax&page3. Accessed 8 May 2008.

Schenk, Alan, and Oliver Oldman. 2007. *Value added tax: A comparative approach*. New York: Cambridge University Press.

South African Revenue Service. *VAT 404 – Value-added tax guide for vendors*. South African Revenue Service, SA. Available at http://www.sars.gov.za/home.asp?pid=4150&tid=65&s=pubs&show=1312. Accessed 22 Dec 2010.

The Swedish Tax Agency. *The VAT brochure SKV 552B edition 10*. Available at http://www.skatteverket.se/download/18.6efe6285127ab4f1d2580008470/552B10svartvit.pdf. Accessed 9 Dec 2010.

Terra, Ben, and Julie Kajus. 2010a. *A guide to the European VAT directives: Introduction to European VAT 2010*, vol. 1. Amsterdam: IBFD.

Terra, Ben, and Julie Kajus. 2010b. *A guide to the European VAT directives, integrated texts of the recast VAT directive (including the implementing regulation) and the former sixth VAT directive 2010*, vol. 2. Amsterdam: IBFD.

TMF, International VAT Services, The TMF Group. *Austria VAT*. Available at http://www.tmf-vat.com/vat/austria-vat.html. Accessed 3 Dec 2010.

TMF, International VAT Services, The TMF Group. *Brazil VAT, ICMS, IPI, GST*. Available at http://www.tmf-vat.com/global-vat/brazil-vat-icms-ipi-gst.html. Accessed 3 Dec 2010.

TMF, International VAT Services, The TMF Group. *China VAT/GST*. Available at http://www.tmf-vat.com/global-vat/china-vat-gst.html. Accessed 3 Dec 2010.

TMF, International VAT Services, The TMF Group. *Irish VAT*. Available at http://www.tmf-vat.com/vat/ireland-vat.html. Accessed 3 Dec 2010.

TMF, International VAT Services, The TMF Group. *Japan consumption tax*. Available at http://www.tmf-vat.com/global-vat/japan-consumption-tax.html. Accessed 3 Dec 2010.

TMF, International VAT Services, The TMF Group. *Russia VAT*. Available at http://www.tmf-vat.com/vat/russia-vat.html. Accessed 3 Dec 2010.

TMF, International VAT Services, The TMF Group. *Switzerland VAT*. Available at http://www.tmf-vat.com/vat/switzerland-vat.html. Accessed 3 Dec 2010.

TMF Group. *International VAT services – Irish VAT*. Available at http://www.tmf-vat.com/vat/ireland-vat.html. Accessed 31 May 2011.

Tumpel, Professor Michael A Hybrid VAT System in the European Union (Draft 04/24/2007). New York University. Available at http://docs.google.com/viewer?a=v&q=cache:g5ZTN7J6sf8J:www.law.nyu.edu/idcplg?IdcService%3DGET_FILE%26dDocName%3DECM_DLV_013830%26RevisionSelectionMethod%3DLatestReleased+The+common+framework+for+VAT+created+in+1967+for+the+EU&hl=en&pid=bl&srcid=ADGEESig8c6y5AwqvxSipGHOW8-aslQcrIqfbzM1dwHa6pTbqOQbLX60f8_nx3d-UlY3vjQQg2BR8zYGevnpGPnM9rt5H2Q4RkiAHe0Pl_tR6xZFjyqhxg0yx3ZcnIdwyatBM51Kdeyp&sig=AHIEtbSZXkC370HMugv4EdOPt6e-bY4eFA&pli=1. Accessed 14 Dec 2010.

Chapter 19
VAT Jurisdictions vs. Non-VAT Jurisdictions

Abstract The point at issue is whether it is possible for VAT jurisdictions to effectively interact with non-VAT jurisdictions in regard to eCommerce.

VAT and retail sales tax are without doubt the two prevailing indirect tax systems within the global community. 130 jurisdictions as of the year 2010 adopted and implemented a VAT system. Other jurisdictions of significance, for example, the USA, utilize a retail sales tax system.

While VAT and retail sales tax differ in terms of the principles of neutrality and the manner in which tax is imposed and implemented, the primary discrepancy between the two systems may, arguably, be the contention as to whether the destination or origin principle is applied and the manner in which the place of supply is determined and, furthermore, the interpretation of 'physical presence'.

As cross-border transactions are exacerbated by the easy access and use of the eMarket, there has been increased urgency to harmonize principles and definitions globally. The OECD has recommended the use of the destination principle, and the USA Streamlined Sales Tax Program (SSTP) encourages a shift to the destination principle in regard to cross-border transactions, especially in regard to eCommerce.

Both GST and retail sales tax are applied in Canada. GST is imposed on a national level and retail sales tax on a provincial level. The provincial sales tax and GST have been operating in conjunction since 1991, serving as testament that non-VAT jurisdictions need not have a devastating impact on eCommerce when transacting with VAT jurisdictions.

The inability of VAT jurisdictions to effectively operate in conjunction with retail sales tax jurisdictions would doubtless precipitate problematic imposition of indirect taxation within the virtual world. Furthermore, the impact of countries not following a VAT system in regard to eCommerce is a point at issue which posits the challenge as to whether it is possible for VAT jurisdictions to effectively interact with non-VAT jurisdictions.[1]

A pivotal point at issue is that whether a jurisdiction utilises a retail sales tax system or a VAT system, both are indirect taxes. While there may be other types of

[1]Extensively discussed in the previous chapter with reference to jurisdictional analysis, Chap. 18, Part V of this paper [p169–229].

A.M. Bardopoulos, *eCommerce and the Effects of Technology on Taxation*,
Law, Governance and Technology Series 22, DOI 10.1007/978-3-319-15449-7_19

indirect tax systems utilised in the global community, VAT and retail sales tax (while the former is more prevalent than the latter) are without a doubt the two prevailing indirect tax systems within the global community. As previously mentioned, 130 jurisdictions currently, as of the year 2010, have adopted and implemented a VAT system. Other jurisdictions of significance, for example, the USA, utilise a retail sales tax system.

Professor Michael Tumpel maintains that *"[s]ales tax seems to fulfil all principles of VAT as a consumption tax on the one hand and, on the other hand, the tax applies to only the last transaction in the chain of production and distributions... But in reality, sales taxes largely deviate from the principle of neutrality."*[2] While sales tax may deviate from the principle of neutrality and may not be considered a 'general consumption tax'[3] as is VAT, it is, nevertheless, consumption tax principle based similar to VAT.

While VAT and retail sales tax differ in terms of the principles of neutrality and the manner in which each tax is imposed and implemented, the primary discrepancy between the two systems may, arguably, be the contention as to whether the destination or origin principle is applied and the manner in which the place of supply is determined and, furthermore, the interpretation of 'physical presence'. However, this is a conflict which may also exist between VAT jurisdictions. The contemporaneous actuality of the two indirect tax systems and, moreover, additional VAT systems, necessitates a common global recognition of tax and technology definitions and principles.

As cross-border transactions are exacerbated by the easy access and use of the eMarket, there has been increased urgency to harmonize principles and definitions globally. The OECD has recommended the use of the destination principle which, although it may or may not be applied by all member states, demonstrates global recognition of a need for common applications. Furthermore, the USA SSTP encourages a shift to the destination principle in regard to cross-border transactions, especially in regard to eCommerce.

Examining examples of cross-border transactions between retail sales tax jurisdictions and VAT jurisdictions is a satisfactory means of ascertaining whether retail sales tax and VAT can be co-efficient. However, it may be submitted that a perfect example of this point at issue is the Canadian indirect tax system. As examined previously under Canada,[4] both GST and retail sales tax are applied in Canada. GST is imposed on a national level and retail sales tax on a provincial level. GST was introduced into Canada in 1991, and the provincial sales tax and GST have been operating in conjunction for 20 years. A few provinces have even implemented a

[2]op cit Tumpel, Michael, Professor *A Hybrid VAT System in the European Union* (Draft 04/24/2007). New York University. Available at http://docs.google.com/...8J:www.law.nyu.edu/... 4eFA&pli=1 [Accessed 14/12/2010], p31.

[3]supra.

[4]As discussed in 18.4. Canada, Part V of this paper [p215]

harmonized tax whereby the GST and the provincial sales tax are levied, collected and remitted together.

Harmonizing GST and provincial sales tax allows for more efficient administration of the two indirect taxes. If the two indirect taxes could not be co-efficiently enforced, it may be presumed that GST and the provincial sales tax would not still be in co-existence. The effective co-existence of provincial retail sales tax and GST in Canada for 20 years serves as testament that non-VAT jurisdictions need not have a devastating impact on eCommerce when transacting with VAT jurisdictions.

Bibliography

Secondary Sources

Tumpel, Michael, Professor. *A hybrid VAT system in the European Union* (Draft 04/24/2007). New York University. Available at http://docs.google.com/viewer?a=v&q=cache:g5ZTN7J6sf8J:www.law.nyu.edu/idcplg?IdcService%3DGET_FILE%26dDocName%3DECM_DLV_013830%26RevisionSelectionMethod%3DLatestReleased+The+common+framework+for+VAT+created+in+1967+for+the+EU&hl=en&pid=bl&srcid=ADGEESig8c6y5AwqvxSipGHOW8-aslQcrIqfbzM1dwHa6pTbqOQbLX60f8_nx3d-UlY3vjQQg2BR8zYGevnpGPnM9rt5H2Q4RkiAHe0Pl_tR6xZFjyqhxg0yx3ZcnIdwyatBM51Kdeyp&sig=AHIEtbSZXkC370HMugv4EdOPt6e-bY4eFA&pli=1. Accessed 14 Dec 2010.

Chapter 20
United States of America

Abstract The USA provides significant insight in the matter of taxing electronic transactions and adapting tax principles to effectively apply indirect tax in eCommerce between states, and in respect of the issues of privacy.

The revenue loss arising from eCommerce transactions occurring across state borders has been estimated to have reached US$ 52 billion between April 2009 and 2012.

In the USA suppliers can supply customers in multiple diverse states without the need to establish a 'nexus'. The lack of nexus and, therefore, inability to impose and collect sales tax arising from inter-state sales has been exacerbated by the Internet.

The Streamlined Sales Tax Program was a direct response to the vast revenue loss arising from the proliferation of the Internet and accompanying inter-state transactional complications (Lowtax *United States Sales Tax Site: Sales on the Internet* Available at http://www.usa-sales-use-tax-e-commerce.com/sales_on_internet.asp [Accessed 2/12/2010]).

The Streamlined Sales and Use Tax Agreement offers the first solution to interstate Internet transactions, but the sales tax implications of Internet transactions with regard to digitised products occurring from non-USA retailers is relatively uncertain (supra).

To contend with eCommerce, tax definitions should be synchronous with technology industry definitions. In regard to the Amazon tax, (Refer to discussion and explanation of the 'Amazon tax', which is not specific law in itself but rather a tax 'coined' as the 'Amazon tax', in 6.1.7., Chap. 6, Part II, pages 60–64 of this paper) legislators have attempted to establish a nexus in the State of New York. Economic activity is the primary factor in the establishment of this nexus, as the 'physical presence' of Amaxzon.com itself has been disregarded. However, if 'presence' were defined in congruence with the technology industry, it may be contended that eRetailers, such as Amazon.com, are 'physically present' in states such as New York through the means of the Internet.

A.M. Bardopoulos, *eCommerce and the Effects of Technology on Taxation*,
Law, Governance and Technology Series 22, DOI 10.1007/978-3-319-15449-7_20

20.1 Introduction

Prior to reviewing the application of VAT to the virtual world it is imperative to review, analyze and understand the indirect tax system implemented in the USA as the USA is a major commercial hub in relation to electronic transactions.

The USA, furthermore, provides significant insight in the matter of taxing electronic transactions and adapting tax principles in order to effectively apply indirect tax in eCommerce occurring between states, as well as the matter of issues of privacy which, depending upon administrative regulations imposed for purposes of effectively collecting indirect tax, may occur and are of concern.

20.2 The Indirect Tax System Employed in the United States of America

The USA sales tax system differs from the VAT model and is a single-stage tax model which, furthermore, varies between the USA states.[1] Each state applies its own sales tax rates and rules which often vary in definition. With the exception of five states a general sales tax is imposed at state level. The five states which do not impose general sales tax at state level are Alaska, Delaware, Montana, New Hampshire and Oregon.[2] Despite not imposing a general sales tax, some of the latter do impose sales tax on specific products and, furthermore, general sales tax may still be imposed by localities within these five states.[3]

Sales tax is generally imposed where the seller's 'nexus' is located.[4] "*Nexus, or substantial physical presence, is established if a business maintains a temporary or permanent presence of people (employees, service people or independent sales/service agents) or property (inventory, offices, warehouses) in a given locality*".[5] As different states' sale tax definitions vary the USA sales tax regime lacks overall commonality. Varying definitions and varied application of definitions, for example, the manner in which 'nexus' may be defined is problematic for sellers operating in multiple states.[6] Sales tax is generally imposed on retail sales, that is

[1]op cit Rendahl, Pernilla, *Cross-Border Consumption Taxation on Digital Supplies*, Netherlands, p17.

[2]supra.

[3]supra.

[4]Lowtax *United States Tax Site: Introduction*. Available at http://www.usa-sales-use-tax-e-commerce.com/Intro_sales.asp [Accessed 2/12/2010].

[5]supra.

[6]Loc cit Lowtax *United States Tax Site: Introduction*, http://www.usa-sales-use-tax-e-commerce.com/Intro_sales.asp.

on the end-purchase, however, retail sale is defined broadly by most states and may also vary between states.[7]

Typically sales tax is imposed on moveable property, that is tangible personal property, and excludes real estate and intangible property. Thus, services were often excluded from sales tax, however, the sales tax scope has broadened in recent years and depending upon the state may now capture services.[8]

A state's authority to impose and collect tax does not extend beyond the relevant state and authority is restricted to within state borders. To prevent loss of tax revenue state authorities have often attempted to extend their authority beyond state borders, and the proliferation of eCommerce has created greater motivation for states to harmonize the sales tax regime and definitions due to increasing revenue loss. Several states, in an attempt to circumvent revenue loss arising from cross-state border transactions, have implemented a 'use' tax in conjunction with the sales tax.[9] The 'use' tax commonly applies to "*use, storage, or other consumption within the state where the tangible personal property is located*".[10] The revenue loss arising from eCommerce transactions occurring across state borders has been estimated to have reached US $52 billion between April 2009 and 2012.[11]

The delivery of physical goods from a non-USA supplier to a USA customer, that is international transactions relating to physical moveable property, will be subject to USA sales tax where the supplier is resident in a DTA jurisdiction and has a 'permanent establishment' in the USA in accordance with the DTA agreement. If the sale of physical moveable property from a supplier resident in a non-DTA jurisdiction to a USA customer is "*effectively connected with the conduct of a US[A] trade or business*",[12] then such products will be subject to sales tax upon arrival in the USA.[13]

The proliferation of eCommerce not only caused the USA to question and re-examine the current structure of the sales and 'use' tax regimes,[14] but may be considered a major contributing factor to the Streamlined Sales Tax Program. Difficulties pertaining to inter-state transactions and attempts to overcome such difficulties were discussed previously with regard to the Amazon tax[15] instituted

[7]Loc cit Lowtax *United States Tax Site: Introduction*, http://www.usa-sales-use-tax-e-commerce.com/Intro_sales.asp.

[8]supra.

[9]supra.

[10]supra.

[11]supra.

[12]supra.

[13]supra.

[14]Loc cit Lowtax *United States Tax Site: Introduction*, http://www.usa-sales-use-tax-e-commerce.com/Intro_sales.asp.

[15]Refer to discussion and explanation of the 'Amazon tax', which is not specific law in itself but rather a tax 'coined' as the 'Amazon tax', in 6.1.7., Chap. 6, Part II, pages 55–59 of this paper.

by the State of New York.[16] The states of Iowa, Alabama and New York will be examined briefly for the purpose of demonstrating the USA sales tax regime whereby all states are, effectively, independent of each other in regard to sales tax. However, prior to examining the three sample states the Streamlined Sales Tax Project/Program ('SSTP') and transactions occurring over the internet in the USA will be discussed.

20.2.1 Streamlined Sales Tax Program

The sales tax regime in the USA allows cross-border transactions to occur free of sales tax, because suppliers can supply customers in multiple diverse states without the need to establish a 'nexus'. A further hurdle which had to be overcome was a 1992 Supreme Court ruling[17] "*that states could not force business outside their borders to collect their sales taxes unless the companies have stores or headquarters (nexus[es]) in those states*".[18] Where the supplier has established a nexus in the state of delivery, the supplier will be required to register for sales tax, impose the sales tax on the sales, collect and remit to the applicable state's revenue authority. The lack of nexus and, therefore, inability to impose and collect sales tax arising from inter-state sales has been exacerbated by the Internet:

> *. . . in many, perhaps most cases, an internet sale will not involve nexus in the receiving state, and the Supreme Court has prevented states from imposing sales tax on out-of-state supplies in that situation. Arguably, use tax provisions should then step in and impose tax on the sale, but the reality is that the operation of such consumption taxes depends heavily on the ability of the taxing authority to find traces or records of transactions . . .* [19]

The SSTP was a direct response to the vast revenue loss arising from the proliferation of the internet and accompanying inter-state transactional complications.[20]

In accordance with the Streamlined Sales and Use Taxes, 'delivered electronically' and 'electronic' are defined respectively as:

---

[16]Discussed in 6.1.7. Amazon.com and 8.1. The Virtual World versus The Physical World, Part II of this paper [p55 and 72 respectively].

[17]USA Supreme Court Quill Corp. v. North Dakota, 504 U.S. 298 (1992) [USA].

Also, Mazerov, Michael *Amazon's Arguments Against Collecting Sales Taxes Do Not Withstand Scrutiny* (29 November 2010) Center on Budget and Policy Priorities. Available at http://www.cbpp.org/cms/index.cfm?fa=view&id=2990#_edn2 [Accessed 05/10/2011].

[18]Lowtax *United States Tax Site: The Streamlined Sales Tax Program* Available at http://www.usa-sales-use-tax-e-commerce.com/streamlined_sales.asp [Accessed 2/12/2010].

[19]loc cit Lowtax *United States Sales Tax Site: Sales on the Internet,* http://www.usa-sales-use-tax-e-commerce.com/sales_on_internet.asp.

[20]loc cit Lowtax *United States Tax Site: The Streamlined Sales Tax Program,* http://www.usa-sales-use-tax-e-commerce.com/streamlined_sales.asp

- *means all delivered to the purchaser by means other than tangible storage media.*[21]
- *means relating to technology having electrical, digital, magnetic, wireless, optical, electromagnetic, or similar capabilities.*[22]

As previously discussed in respect of the USA and the imposition of sales tax, there are two primary restrictions which states are required to adhere to and Iowa abides by these two restrictions:

(i) *the due process clause and commerce clause of the United States Constitution; and*
(ii) *Public Law … passed by the United States in 1959 … if a corporation's only Iowa business activity consists of soliciting orders for the purchase of tangible personal property, Public Law … prohibits Iowa from imposing a corporate income tax …*[23]

By the year 2009 22 states had adopted the Streamlined Sales and Use Tax Agreement ('SSUTA').[24] In terms of the SSUTA, harmonised definitions and uniformed state-wide sales tax rates (single rate per product type) were adopted and implemented by participating states.[25] On-line suppliers' sales tax reporting requirements were also simplified by the SSTP.[26] Furthermore, on-line retailers present in SSTP participating states, and in agreement, would commence collecting and remitting sales taxes originating from any of the participating states at the applicable sales tax rate in an attempt to circumvent the non-payment and non-collection of sales taxes due to internet sales.[27] On-line retailers not present in SSTP participating states are not, however, excluded from participating in the collection and remittance scheme in regard to Internet transactions.[28]

[21] 'Delivered electronically' as defined under Definitions of Sub-chapter I, Chapter 423.10 of Division XIV, Streamlined Sales and Use Taxes. Available at http://www.iowa.gov/tax/taxlaw/Ch423.pdf [Accessed 2/12/2010].

[22] 'Electronic' as defined under Definitions of Sub-chapter I, Chapter 423.10 of Division XIV, Streamlined Sales and Use Taxes. Available at http://www.iowa.gov/tax/taxlaw/Ch423.pdf [Accessed 2/12/2010].

[23] Iowa Department of Revenue – Iowa Taxes *Requirement (Nexus) for Out-of-State Businesses*. Available at http://www.iowa.gov/tax/business/nexus.html [Accessed 2/12/2010].

[24] loc cit Lowtax *United States Sales Tax Site: Sales on the Internet,* http://www.usa-sales-use-tax-e-commerce.com/sales_on_internet.asp

[25] loc cit Lowtax *United States Tax Site: The Streamlined Sales Tax Program,* http://www.usa-sales-use-tax-e-commerce.com/streamlined_sales.asp

[26] supra.

[27] loc cit Lowtax *United States Tax Site: The Streamlined Sales Tax Program,* http://www.usa-sales-use-tax-e-commerce.com/streamlined_sales.asp

[28] supra.

20.2.2 USA and Internet Sales

The SSUTA currently offers the first solution to inter-state internet transactions, but the sales tax implications of internet transactions in regard to digitised products occurring from non-USA retailers is still relatively uncertain.[29] Where internet sales result in physical moveable goods being delivered to the USA, such sales are taxed in accordance with the DTA, if one is in place.[30] If the foreign on-line retailer resides in a DTA jurisdiction, such internet sales will only be subject to sales tax if the on-line retailer has a "permanent establishment"[31] in the USA. If the foreign on-line retailer resides in a non-DTA jurisdiction, the sale of physical moveable goods will be subject to sales tax upon importation into the USA.[32] The downloading of software is regarded as a delivery and is treated similarly to the delivery of physical products depending upon the specific state in which the software is downloaded.[33]

It has been suggested that while the location of the server may not constitute a 'permanent establishment' in the USA, the server's host may constitute an 'agent' in certain circumstances.[34] The presence of an agent may give rise to a 'permanent establishment'.[35] However, the overall complexities arising from international cross-border eCommerce are relatively uncertain and are amplified by presumption and supposition devoid of substantiating support.

20.2.3 Solution to Inter-state Internet Transactions Implemented by the State of New York

The State of New York widened the sales tax scope in terms of legislation dubbed the 'Amazon tax', as was previously discussed in the analysis as to whether it is possible to establish physical presence through the Internet.[36] When the State of New York widened the sales tax net in order to impose sales tax on supplies made to New York resident customers, that is, to create an obligation for out-of-state eRetailers

[29]Lowtax *United States Sales Tax Site: International Internet Sales* Available at http://www.usa-sales-use-tax-e-commerce.com/international_internet.asp [Accessed 2/12/2010].

[30]supra.

[31]"Permanent establishment" was discussed in *12.2. Permanent Establishment*, Part IV of this paper [p121].

[32]loc cit Lowtax *United States Sales Tax Site: International Internet Sales,* http://www.usa-sales-use-tax-e-commerce.com/international_internet.asp

[33]supra.

[34]supra.

[35]supra.

[36]Discussed in 6.1.7. Amazon.com and 8.1. The Virtual World versus The Physical World, Part II of this paper [p55 and 72 respectively].

to comply with New York sales tax requirements, the Amazon tax "*created a presumption that an out-of-state seller was… 'soliciting business [in New York] through an independent contractor or other representative if the seller enters into an agreement with a resident of [New York] state under which the resident, for a commission or other consideration, directly or indirectly refers potential customers, whether by a link on an internet website or otherwise, to the seller, if the cumulative gross receipts from sales by the seller to customers in the state who are referred to the seller by all residents with this type of an agreement with the seller is in excess of ten thousand dollars during the preceding four quarterly periods…'*".[37] Thus, in such circumstances the out-of-state retailer will have a nexus in the State of New York.

Amazon.com argued, in terms of 'facial challenges' and 'due process and commerce clauses', the constitutionality of this legislation. The challenge was initially dismissed. However, the complaint has been reinstated for further proceedings following Amazon.com's appeal of the matter to the Supreme Court. The Supreme Court did, however, establish that the legislation was not unconstitutional in terms of Amazon.com's 'facial challenges' argument and that further proceedings were only required in terms of due process and commerce clauses. In accordance with the opinion in United States v Salerno[38] "*a plaintiff can only succeed in a facial challenge by establish[ing] that no set of circumstances exists under which the Act would be valid', i.e., that the law is unconstitutional in all of its applications*".[39] In other words, "*[l]egislative enactments enjoy a strong presumption of constitutionality… [and] parties challenging a duly enacted statute face the initial burden of demonstrating the statute's invalidity beyond a reasonable doubt*".[40]

However, the Supreme Court held that in respect of a state's taxing rights and the Commercial and Due Process clauses:

> *…the US[A] Constitution expressly authorizes Congress to 'regulate Commerce with foreign Nations, and among the several States.' While the Constitution 'says nothing about the protection of interstate commerce in the absence of any action by Congress… the Commerce Clause is more than an affirmative grant of power; it has a negative sweep as well' ([per the] Quill Corp. v North Dakota*[41] *[case]…).*

[37]Amazon.com, LLC v New York State Department of Taxation & Finance 2010 NY Slip Op 07823 (November,4 2010) at para 3 [USA].

Available at http://www.courts.state.ny.us/reporter/3dseries/2010/2010_07823.htm [Accessed 4/12/2010].

[38]United States v Salerno 481 US 739, 745 [1987] [USA].

[39]*ibid* Amazon.com, LLC v New York State Department of Taxation & Finance 2010 NY Slip Op 07823 (November,4 2010) at para 3 [USA].

Also, Washington State Grange *v*. Washington State Republican Party et al. [2008] at para II [USA]. Available at http://caselaw.lp.findlaw.com/scripts/getcase.pl?court=US&vol=000&invol=06-713 [Accessed 30/05/2011].

[40]LaValle v Hayden, 98 NY2d 155, 161 [2002] [USA].

[41]*Quill Corp. v North Dakota [case]…, 504 US[A] 298, 309 [1992]* [USA].

'[B]y its own force', [it] prohibits certain state actions that interfere with the interstate commerce (id. quoting South Carolina State Highway Dept. v Barnwell Bros., Inc..[42]*.).*

In Moran Towing Corp., the Court of Appeals outlined the four-prong test for determining whether a state tax violates the Commerce Clause. The court stated that the tax will be upheld '[1] when the tax is applied to an activity with a substantial nexus with the taxing State, [2] is fairly apportioned, [3] does not discriminate against interstate commerce, and [4] is fairly related to the services provided by the State' (99 NY2d at 449, quoting Complete Auto Tr., Inc. v Brady[43] *...)...*

The sine qua non for the finding that a party has a substantial nexus with New York, and is thus required to collect sales or use taxes, is that it have a physical presence[44] *within the state (id. At 449, citing Matter of Orvis Co.*[45] *... Nevertheless, '[w]hile a physical presence of the vendor is required, it need not be substantial' (Orvis Co. at 178). While it must constitute more than a 'slightest presence" (id. quoting National Geographic v California Equalization Bd.*[46]*), 'it may be manifested by the presence in the taxing State of the vendor's property or the conduct of economic activities in the taxing State performed by the vendor's personnel or on its behalf' ...*

...In upholding the tax, the court [in Washington v J.C. Penney Co.[47]*] framed the threshold inquiry as 'whether the state has given anything for which it can ask return'" (id. at 562, quoting Washington v J.C. Penney Co...)...*

Amazon['s argument]... challenge[s] the fairness of requiring [Amazon] and other out-of-state retailers like them to collect sales tax from New York residents referred to [Amazon] by their New York-based Affiliates.

In [the] Quill [case]... the Supreme Court [held] that the Due Process Clause implicates fundamentally different concerns from the Commerce Clause (id. at 306 – 18). The Court stated:

'[d]ue process centrally concerns the fundamental fairness of governmental activity. Thus, at the most general level, the due process nexus analysis requires that we ask whether an individual's connections with a State are substantial enough to [legitimise] the State's exercise of power over him... In contrast, the Commerce Clause and its nexus requirement are informed not so much by concerns about fairness for the individual... as by structural concerns about the effects of state regulation on the national economy.'

... thus, the Commerce Clause operates to 'limit the reach of state taxing authority so as to ensure that state taxation does not unduly burden interstate commerce'..., while the Due Process Clause ensures that there is 'some definite link, some minimum connection, between a state and the person, property or transaction it seeks to tax, and that the income

---

[42]*South Carolina State Highway Dept. v Barnwell Bros., Inc., 3030 US[A] 177, 185 [1992]* [USA].

[43]*Complete Auto Tr., Inc. v Brady, 430 US[A] 274, 279 [1977]* [USA].

[44]With reference to the discussion and analysis in 6.1.7. Amazon.com and 8.1. The Virtual World versus The Physical World, Part II of this paper [p55 and 72 respectively], it was argued that internet companies or eRetailers, such as Amazon.com, do indeed have a physical presence in, for example, New York state achieved through and by the means of the internet. Examining whether eRetailers, for example Amazon.com, have established a physical presence in New York through the internet has not been explored as the preferment was the nexus analysis, that is, to establish a nexus by examining the use of 'agents', etc.

[45]*Matter of Orvis Co. v Tax Appeals Trib. of State of N[ew] Y[ork], 86 NY2d 165 [1995], cert denied 516 US[A] 989 [1995]* [USA].

[46]*National Geographic v California Equalization Bd., 430 US[A] 551, 556 [1997]* [USA].

[47]*Washington v J.C. Penney Co., 311 US[A] 435, 444 [1940]* [USA].

attributed to the State for tax purposes [is] rationally related to values connected with the taxing state'...[48] [Emphasis Added]

As previously discussed, to prevail over taxing complexities caused by new technology, tax definitions should be synchronous with technology industry definitions. In regard to the Amazon tax, legislators have attempted to create or establish a nexus in the State of New York, whereby a nexus, "*while it must constitute more than a 'slightest presence'*",[49] "*may be manifested by the presence in the taxing State of the vendor's*... *conduct of economic activities in the taxing State performed by the vendor's personnel or on its behalf*".[50]

It is submitted that economic activity is the primary factor in the establishment of a nexus within the State of New York, as the 'physical presence' of Amazon.com itself, and not 'agents', has been disregarded as the primary contention for nexus. "*The sine qua non for the finding that a party has a substantial nexus with New York, and is thus required to collect sales or use taxes, is that it have a physical presence within the state* ... *Nevertheless, '[w]hile a physical presence of the vendor is required, it need not be substantial'*..."[51] However, if 'presence' were defined in congruence with the technology industry, it may be contended that eRetailers, such as Amazon.com, are in fact 'physically present' in states such as New York through the means of the internet.[52]

20.2.4 State of New York

The New York State sales tax rate is based on the destination principle.[53] Thus, the point of delivery of the taxable supply generally determines the applicable sales tax rate.[54] The sales tax rate comprises the applicable sales tax rate in the New York State jurisdiction of delivery, as well as the local sales tax rate of the delivery jurisdiction.[55] Taxable products, including tangible personal property, and services supplied in the State of New York will be subject to sales or use tax. Tangible personal property has been defined as "*physical personal property, of any nature,*

[48]idem Amazon.com, LLC v New York State Department of Taxation & Finance 2010 NY Slip Op 07823 (November,4 2010) at para 23 through to 34. [USA].

[49]idem Amazon.com, LLC v New York State Department of Taxation & Finance at para 25. [USA].

[50]supra.

[51]idem Amazon.com, LLC v New York State Department of Taxation & Finance at para 25.

[52]Refer to 8.1. Virtual World versus the Physical World, Part II of this paper [p72].

[53]New York State Department of Taxation and Finance *Is the New York State sales tax rate based on the point of sale or point of delivery?* Available at http://nystax.custhelp.com/app/answers/detail/a_id/958/related/1 [Accessed 4/12/2010].

[54]supra.

[55]supra.

that has a material existence and is perceptible to the human senses. Tangible personal property includes a variety of goods ... [which includes, but not limited to,] computers [and] prewritten (canned/off-the-shelf/standard) computer software (whether transferred by CD-ROM, Internet download, remote access, etc.) ... ".[56] It is important to note that 'internet downloaded software' is considered tangible personal property in the State of New York which is in contradistinction to the Ottawa Framework where all digital supplies are considered services. Not all services supplied in New York are subject to sales tax and in terms of the New York State guide to sales tax the provision of "*certain information services*" is included in the list of certain services subject to sales tax.[57]

An out-of-state supplier is entitled to register for sales tax voluntarily if the supplier's connection with the State of New York is insufficient to make registration obligatory.[58] A supplier is required to register as a vendor with the New York State Department of Taxation and Finance if any of the following conditions are satisfied in regard to the supply of taxable tangible personal property or services:

- *[the supplier] maintain[s] a place of business in the state [of New York[, such as a store, office, or warehouse, and sell[s] taxable, tangible personal property or services to persons within the state; or*
- *[the supplier] solicit[s] business in New York State through employees, independent contractors, agents, or other representatives, and through these persons, sell[s] taxable, tangible personal property or services in New York State; or*
- *[the supplier] solicit[s] business through catalogs or other advertising material, and [has] some additional connection with the state, and through the catalogs [the supplier] sell[s] taxable, tangible personal property or services; or*
- *[the supplier] make[s] sales of taxable products to customers within the New York State, and regularly (at least 12 times a year) deliver[s] the products in [the supplier's] own vehicles.*[59]

In terms of the above criteria, "*[i]f the only connection [the supplier] has with New York State is the delivery of [the supplier's] product into the state by U.S.[A.] Postal Service or common carrier, [the supplier is] not required to register or collect sales tax*".[60] It is in this regard that some out-of-state mail-order companies do not satisfy the obligatory requirements to register as a vendor and collect sales tax.[61] However, in terms of the above criteria the out-of-state supplier may still

[56]New York State Department of Taxation and Finance *A Guide to Sales Tax in New York State (Publication 750)* p17. Available at http://www.tax.state.ny.us/pdf/publications/sales/pub750.pdf [Accessed 5/12/2010].

[57]idem p18.

[58]idem p9.

[59]New York State Department of Taxation and Finance: Taxpayer Guidance Division *Do I Need to Register for Sales Tax?* Available at http://www.tax.state.ny.us/pdf/tg_bulletins/sales/b10_175s.pdf [Accessed 4/12/2010].

[60]loc cit New York State Department of Taxation and Finance *A Guide to Sales Tax in New York State (Publication 750),* http://www.tax.state.ny.us/pdf/publications/sales/pub750.pdf, p8.

[61]supra.

be presumed to satisfy the vendor requirements.[62] For example, where the out-of-state supplier delivers taxable products to customers in New York at least 12 times a year in the supplier's own vehicles, that is, not through the U.S.A. postal system. Furthermore, where the out-of-state supplier solicits business through advertising located in or connected with New York. It is in the latter circumstances that Amazon.com potentially falls within the New York sales tax net.

The 'presumption rule' may be "*rebutted where the seller is able to establish that the only activity of its resident representatives in New York State on behalf of the seller is placing a link on the resident representatives' Web sites to the seller's Web site*".[63] A primary reason for Amazon.com potentially not falling within the rebuttal of the presumption rule is because Amazon.com reportedly pays commissions to the "resident[64] representatives".

Analogous to the other states examined, where an out-of-state supplier is not required to register, collect or remit sales tax on taxable supplies to New York customers, the New York customers will be responsible for the payment of sales or use tax on the taxable supplies upon bringing the taxable supply into New York State.[65]

The State of New York has entered into a sales tax agreement with the state of New Jersey with the express purpose of simplifying tax submissions and expediting tax compliance. Certain aspects of the agreement are similar to the 'one-stop-scheme' implemented by the EU, however, in the EU the vendor is entitled to register for VAT in only one jurisdiction despite the fact that taxable supplies

---

[62]supra.

[63]New York State Department of Taxation and Finance: Office of Tax Policy Analysis Taxpayer Guidance Division *Additional Information on How Sellers May Rebut the New Presumption Applicable to the Definition of Sales Tax Vendor as Described in TSB-M-08(3)S* (TSB-M-08(3.1)S, Sales Tax, June 30, 2008). Available at http://www.tax.ny.gov/pdf/memos/sales/m08_3_1s.pdf [Accessed 7/01/2011].

[64]"*For sales and use tax purposes, the definition of resident may include a person who may not be considered a resident for personal income tax purposes. For example, a person maintaining a permanent place of abode in New York who does not spend more than 183 days a year in the state, a college student, and military personnel may all be residents for sales and use tax purposes even if they are not residents for income tax purposes. For sales and use tax purposes, an individual is a resident of the state and of any locality in which he or she maintains a permanent place of abode. A permanent place of abode is a dwelling place maintained by a person, or by another for that person to use, whether or not owned by such person, on other than a temporary or transient basis....*

A corporation incorporated under the laws of New York is a resident of New York State. A corporation, association, partnership (including an LLP). LLC, or other entity doing business in New York State and of any locality in which it is doing business or maintaining a place of business... ".

New York State Department of Taxation and Finance *Purchaser's Obligations to Pay Sales and Use Taxes Directly to the Tax Department Questions and Answers (Publication 774).* Available at http://www.tax.ny.gov/pdf/publications/sales/pub774.pdf [Accessed 07/01/2011].

[65]loc cit New York State Department of Taxation and Finance *A Guide to Sales Tax in New York State (Publication 750),* http://www.tax.state.ny.us/pdf/publications/sales/pub750.pdf, p8.

are made in several jurisdictions. The vendor is then required to collect VAT, at the applicable rate according to the location of the customer, and submit a return reflecting a breakdown of all the taxable supplies regarding each respective VAT jurisdiction. The submission, as well as remittance of VAT, need only be made to the revenue authorities in the jurisdiction of registration. In terms of the New Jersey – New York sales tax agreement a vendor qualifying for registration in both states is still required to register in both states. However, the vendor need submit only a single sales tax return in respect of payment for taxes owing in both states and a breakdown reflecting how much pertains to which state to only one revenue authority, namely the vendor's home state.[66]

It is important to note that the State of New York, as of January 2011, is currently not listed as either a full member or associate member of SSUTA.[67] In October 2006 the New York Department of Taxation and Finance issued a publication wherein difficulties with complying with SSUTA were identified. In order to conform with SSUTA the State of New York would have to effect numerous changes including non-uniformity of exemptions and tax rates with reference to common product types.[68] The October 2006 publication emphasized that *"[a] large number of the changes necessary to conform would exclusively impact New York's counties and cities that impose sales tax. For example, all localities would be required to impose tax on an identical base. As a result, the practice of granting local options for participation in sales tax exemptions would no longer be permissible ... New York City's unique sales tax base would also need to be aligned with the State and local tax base in the rest of the state. This would affect the taxation of a variety of services which are taxable only by New York City."*[69]

Despite New York State not having conformed to SSUTA, *"New York participated in the Streamlined Sales Tax Project as the Project developed the provisions*

[66]loc cit New York State Department of Taxation and Finance *A Guide to Sales Tax in New York State (Publication 750)* p14.

[67]*"Legislation enacted in 2003 increased the level of official New York State participation. It authorized delegates from the Senate, Assembly, Governor and Tax Commissioner to represent New York State before the member states. However, no legislation has been introduced to incorporate the provisions of the Agreement into New York's sales tax law to make the State a member of the multi-state compact. New York's State and local sales tax does not comply with a large number of the Agreement's provisions. A broad-based revision of the Tax Law would be needed before New York could document compliance with the Agreement."*

New York State Department of Taxation and Finance: Office of Tax Policy Analysis (October 2006) *Streamlining New York's Sales Tax: Examining Requirements for Compliance with the Streamlined Sales and Use Tax Agreement* p6. Available at http://www.tax.ny.gov/pdf/stats/policy_special/streamlining_new_yorks_sales_tax_october_2006.pdf [Accessed 7/01/2011], pg. ii.

[68]idem.

[69]idem p6.

now contained in the Agreement[, that is, the SSUTA]".[70] The analysis published in October 2006 concludes that:

> *[s]ome of these changes could promote a simpler tax structure; others may limit the flexibility of the State [of New York] in crafting its annual financial plan and providing for the revenue needs of localities ...*
>
> *Legislation to modernize and simplify the New York sales tax would be worthwhile, but it is unclear if the proposal developed by the Streamlined project would yield net benefits to New York's taxpayers and local businesses. The likelihood of the State and its localities generating vast amounts of "new" sales tax revenue from taxing mail order and e-commerce sales is low. As the Streamlined project moves forward, New York's policymakers may wish to consider a number of options, including the option of adopting some, but not all, of the Agreement's provisions to realize some benefits of simplification short of full conformity.*[71]

20.2.5 State of Iowa

While the State of New York addresses eCommerce transactions and is a participating state of SSUTA, as analysed and discussed above, it is not the only state which has identified eCommerce transactions as an area requiring attention and the reason for the need to harmonise inter-state retail sales tax systems.

Iowa defined nexus, for the purpose of determining whether a company should register for Sales or Use Tax, as "*presence in Iowa*".[72] The State of Iowa is a participating state of SSUTA.[73] As such, and in accordance with the streamlined objectives, the destination principle is applied with regard to tangible physical goods delivered via post. Therefore, the local sales tax rate at the applicable destination is applied.[74] Previously the sales tax rate applicable in the seller's location was applied.[75] Internet sales which give rise to the delivery of taxable goods in Iowa will be subject to sales and use tax in accordance with SSUTA.[76] Information downloaded from the internet may be considered a 'service' and is exempt from

---

[70]supra.

[71]op cit New York State Department of Taxation and Finance: Office of Tax Policy Analysis (October 2006) *Streamlining New York's Sales Tax: Examining Requirements for Compliance with the Streamlined Sales and Use Tax Agreement,* http://www.tax.ny.gov/pdf/stats/policy_s..._2006.pdf, p98–99.

[72]Iowa Department of Revenue – Iowa Taxes *Requirement (Nexus) for Out-of-State Businesses.* Available at http://www.iowa.gov/tax/business/nexus.html [Accessed 2/12/2010].

[73]Iowa Department of Revenue – Iowa Taxes *Streamlined Sales Tax: An Introduction.* Available at http://www.iowa.gov/tax/educate/SLSTIntro.html [Accessed 2/12/2010].

[74]Iowa Department of Revenue *Iowa Sales Tax Changes Effective July 1,* 2004. Available at http://www.iowa.gov/tax/educate/SLSTLetter.pdf [Accessed 2/12/2010].

[75]supra.

[76]Iowa Department of Revenue – Iowa Taxes *Taxable?* Available at http://www.iowa.gov/tax/educate/internetsales.html [Accessed 2/12/2010].

sales and use tax in Iowa.[77] "*Unlike tangible personal property, which is subject to sales/use tax unless specifically exempted by Iowa law, services are subject to sales/use tax only when specified by Iowa law. Iowa sales tax is due when the taxable service is rendered, furnished, or performed*".[78]

20.2.6 State of Alabama

The Alabama Department of Revenue ('ADOR') specifically provides that goods sold over the Internet, from eRetailers located outside the State of Alabama, will be treated synonymously with traditional inter-state supplies.[79] In other words, "*[t]he retail sale of goods made over the Internet that are delivered into Alabama from an out-of-state seller are treated the same as the retail sale of tangible personal property made through more traditional channels, with the same 'nexus' rules applying to both*".[80] Thus, tangible personal property delivered to an Alabama customer located in Alabama from an out-of-state supplier will be subject to Use Tax at the applicable Alabama rate provided the supplier does not have a 'nexus' in Alabama. Where the supplier does have a 'nexus' in Alabama, the supply of tangible personal property will be subject to Sales Tax which must be imposed and collected by the supplier.[81]

'Nexus' is established if the retailer has 'physical presence' in Alabama. The ADOR lists 'physical presence' as including "*a retail store, warehouse, inventory, or regular presence of travelling salespeople or agents, or has established remote entity nexus*". A detailed list of conditions which will establish 'remote entity nexus' include:

- *The out-of-state business and the in-state business maintaining one or more locations within Alabama are related parties'*[82] *and one or more of the following conditions are met:*
  - *The out-of-state business and the in-state business use an identical or substantially similar name, tradename, trademark, or goodwill, to develop, promote, or maintain sales; or*

[77] supra.

[78] Iowa Department of Revenue – Iowa Taxes *Services*. Available at http://www.iowa.gov/tax/educate/78524.html [Accessed 2/12/2010].

[79] Alabama Department of Revenue: Sales, Use & Business Tax Division. *Frequently Asked Questions* p2. Available at http://www.revenue.alabama.gov/salestax/faq.html [Accessed 1/12/2010].

[80] supra.

[81] idem p3.

[82] An out-of-state and in-state related party will exist where a minimum of one of the following three requirements exist:

- *One or both entities is a corporation, and one entity and any party related to that entity in a manner that would require an attribution of stock from the corporation under*

- *The out-of-state business and the in-state business pay for each other's services in whole or in part contingent upon the volume or value of sales; or*
- *The out-of-state business and the in-state business share a common business plan or substantially coordinate their business plans, or*
- *The in-state business provides services to, or that inure to the benefit of, the out-of-state business related to developing, promoting, or maintaining the in-state market.*[83]

Where none of the above conditions are met, a remote entity nexus will not exist in the State of Alabama. The other 'physical presence' requirements may still apply and each one will have to be examined depending upon the facts. This point of issue pertains to 'physical presence' which has already been discussed.[84]

Bibliography

Primary Sources

Cases

United States of America Cases

Amazon.com. 2010, November 4. LLC v New York State Department of Taxation & Finance 2010 NY Slip Op 07823. Available at http://www.courts.state.ny.us/reporter/3dseries/2010/2010_07823.htm. Accessed 12 April 2010.

Complete Auto Tr., Inc. v Brady, 430 US[A] 274, 279 [1977]. Available at http://caselaw.lp.findlaw.com/scripts/getcase.pl?court=us&vol=430&invol=274. Accessed 22 Jan 2012.

LaValle v Hayden, 98 NY2d 155, 161 [2002]. Available at http://caselaw.findlaw.com/ny-supreme-court/1202700.html. Accessed 22 Jan 2012.

Matter of Orvis Co. v Tax Appeals Trib. of State of N[ew] Y[ork], 86 NY2d 165 [1995], cert denied 516 US[A] 989 [1995]. Available at http://www.mtc.gov/uploadedFiles/Multistate_Tax_Commission/Nexus_Program/Training/Nexus_Cases/Orvis%20v%20Tax%20Appeals%20NY.pdf. Accessed 22 Jan 2012.

---

the attribution rules of Section 318 of the IRC owns directly, indirectly, beneficially, or constructively at least 50 percent of the value of the corporation's outstanding stock; or

- *One or both entities is a limited liability company, partnership, estate, or trust and any member, partner or beneficiary, and the limited liability company, partnership, estate, or trust and its members, partners or beneficiaries own directly, indirectly, beneficially, or constructively, in the aggregate, at least 50 percent of the profits, or capital, or stock, or value of the other entity or both entities; or*
- *An individual stockholder and the members of the stockholder's family, as defined in Section 318 of the IRC, owns directly, indirectly, beneficially, or constructively, in the aggregate, at least 50 percent of the value of both entities' outstanding stock.*

Alabama Department of Revenue: *Notice, Remote Entity Nexus, Act #2003-390, Alabama State*. Available at http://www.revenue.alabama.gov/salestax/remotenexus073103.html [Accessed 6/01/2011].

[83]loc cit Alabama Department of Revenue: *Notice, Remote Entity Nexus, Act #2003-390, Alabama State,* http://www.revenue.alabama.gov/salestax/remotenexus073103.html

[84]As discussed in 8.1. The Virtual World Versus The Physical World, Part II of this paper [p72].

National Geographic v California Equalization Bd., 430 US[A] 551, 556 [1997]. Available at http://caselaw.lp.findlaw.com/scripts/getcase.pl?court=us&vol=430&invol=551. Accessed 22 Jan 2012.

South Carolina State Highway Dept. v Barnwell Bros., Inc., 3030 US[A] 177, 185 [1992]. Available at http://www.lawnix.com/cases/sc-highway-barnwell.html. Accessed 22 Jan 2012.

United States v Salerno 481 US 739, 745 [1987]. Available at http://caselaw.lp.findlaw.com/cgi-bin/getcase.pl?court=us&vol=481&invol=739. Accessed 22 Jan 2012.

USA Supreme Court Quill Corp. v. North Dakota (91-0194), 504 U.S. 298 (1992) [USA]. Available at http://www.law.cornell.edu/background/internet/Quill.htm. Accessed 12 Sept 2010. Available at http://www.ct.gov/drs/cwp/view.asp?A=1514&Q=268516. Accessed 12 Sept 2010.

Washington State Grange v. Washington State Republican Party et al. [2008]. Available at http://caselaw.lp.findlaw.com/scripts/getcase.pl?court=US&vol=000&invol=06-713. Accessed 30 May 2011.

Washington v J.C. Penney Co., 311 US[A] 435, 444 [1940]. Available at http://statecasefiles.justia.com/documents/washington/files/271951.unp.doc.pdf. Accessed 22 Jan 2012.

Statutes

State of Iowa of the United States of America Definitions, Subchapter I of Chapter 423, Division XIV, Streamlined Sales and Use Taxes. Available at http://www.iowa.gov/tax/taxlaw/Ch423.pdf. Accessed 2 Dec 2010.

Secondary Sources

Alabama Department of Revenue: *Notice, Remote Entity Nexus, Act #2003-390, State of Alabama*. Available at http://www.revenue.alabama.gov/salestax/remotenexus073103.html. Accessed 6 Jan 2011.

Alabama Department of Revenue: Sales, Use & Business Tax Division. *Frequently asked* questions. Available at http://www.revenue.alabama.gov/salestax/faq.html. Accessed 1 Dec 2010.

Iowa Department of Revenue. *Iowa sales tax changes effective July 1, 2004*. Available at http://www.iowa.gov/tax/educate/SLSTLetter.pdf. Accessed 2 Dec 2010.

Iowa Department of Revenue – Iowa Taxes. *Requirement (Nexus) for out-of-state businesses*. Available at http://www.iowa.gov/tax/business/nexus.html. Accessed 2 Dec 2010.

Iowa Department of Revenue – Iowa Taxes. *Services*. Available at http://www.iowa.gov/tax/educate/78524.html. Accessed 2 Dec 2010.

Iowa Department of Revenue – Iowa Taxes. *Streamlined sales tax: An introduction*. Available at http://www.iowa.gov/tax/educate/SLSTIntro.html. Accessed 2 Dec 2010.

Iowa Department of Revenue – Iowa Taxes. *Taxable?* Available at http://www.iowa.gov/tax/educate/internetsales.html. Accessed 2 Dec 2010.

Lowtax. *United States sales tax site: International internet sales*. Available at http://www.usa-sales-use-tax-e-commerce.com/international_internet.asp. Accessed 2 Dec 2010.

Lowtax. *United States sales tax site: Sales on the internet*. Available at http://www.usa-sales-use-tax-e-commerce.com/sales_on_internet.asp. Accessed 2 Dec 2010.

Lowtax. *United States tax site: Introduction*. Available at http://www.usa-sales-use-tax-e-commerce.com/Intro_sales.asp. Accessed 2 Dec 2010.

Lowtax. *United States tax site: The streamlined sales tax program*. Available at http://www.usa-sales-use-tax-e-commerce.com/streamlined_sales.asp. Accessed 2 Dec 2010.

Mazerov, Michael. 2010, November 29. *Amazon's arguments against collecting sales taxes do not withstand scrutiny*. Center on Budget and Policy Priorities. Available at http://www.cbpp.org/cms/index.cfm?fa=view&id=2990#_edn2. Accessed 5 Oct 2011.

New York State Department of Taxation and Finance. *A guide to sales tax in New York State (Publication 750).* Available at http://www.tax.state.ny.us/pdf/publications/sales/pub750.pdf. Accessed 5 Dec 2010.

New York State Department of Taxation and Finance. *Is the New York State sales tax rate based on the point of sale or point of delivery?* Available at http://nystax.custhelp.com/app/answers/detail/a_id/958/related/1. Accessed 4 Dec 2010.

New York State Department of Taxation and Finance. *Purchaser's obligations to pay sales and use taxes directly to the tax department questions and answers (Publication 774).* Available at http://www.tax.ny.gov/pdf/publications/sales/pub774.pdf. Accessed 7 Jan 2011.

New York State Department of Taxation and Finance: Office of Tax Policy Analysis. 2006, October. *Streamlining New York's sales tax: Examining requirements for compliance with the streamlined sales and use tax agreement.* Available at http://www.tax.ny.gov/pdf/stats/policy_special/streamlining_new_yorks_sales_tax_october_2006.pdf. Accessed 7 Jan 2011.

New York State Department of Taxation and Finance: Office of Tax Policy Analysis Taxpayer Guidance Division. *Additional information on how sellers may rebut the new presumption applicable to the definition of sales tax vendor as described in TSB-M-08(3)S* (TSB-M-08(3.1)S, Sales Tax, June 30, 2008). Available at http://www.tax.ny.gov/pdf/memos/sales/m08_3_1s.pdf. Accessed 7 Jan 2011.

New York State Department of Taxation and Finance: Taxpayer Guidance Division. *Do I need to register for sales tax?* Available at http://www.tax.state.ny.us/pdf/tg_bulletins/sales/b10_175s.pdf. Accessed 4 Dec 2010.

Rendahl, Pernilla. 2009. *Cross-border consumption taxation of digital supplies.* Amsterdam: IBFD.

Chapter 21
The Impact of Technology on Taxation & VAT in the Virtual World

> *"[T]he digital revolution is not the first to affect the flow of commerce and the actual and potential tax base. The transportation and communications revolutions of earlier centuries come to mind, for example . . . " (op cit Bird, Richard Taxing Electronic Commerce: A Revolution in the Making. Available at http://www.cdhowe.org/pdf/commentary_187.pdf [Accessed 16/09/2010], p15) "The rise of mass industry and the development of the financial system, led to the dominance of withholding at source on income tax and then to the consumption-tax equivalent – the VAT." (supra) "'In 1831, a British member of Parliament asked Michael Faraday, a pioneer of electrical theory, what use his discovery might be. Mr. Faraday replied that he did not know, but that he was sure governments would one day tax it. The Internet may be rather harder to tax, but someone, somewhere will find a way.'"('The End of Taxes?' The Economist, Survey on The New Economy, September 23, 2000, p.30" as cited in Bird, http://www.cdhowe.org/pdf/commentary_187.pdf, p15)*

Abstract Second Life is relevant to any discussion apropos VAT and the virtual world. Where the Second Life user earns 'real world' income as an individual and not through the means of a company, determining residence is problematic. The user of Second Life may be subject to income tax in the country of his residence. However, earning income within the virtual world is easily manipulated to avoid taxation, for example, by forming a business, which in turn exacerbates the problem of double taxation or double non-taxation in international transactions.

Second Life has been labelled an online game and in terms of the various VAT guidelines and provisions, online games constitute an electronically supplied service. Digitised products qualify as the supply of services or may also qualify as the supply of goods, 'goods' such as virtual property, do not meet the attributes of real property.

Despite commonalities between jurisdictions applying VAT, a *consensus omnium* is essential to international harmonization if a correlative framework of basic principle, rules and effective application is to be achieved. Essential points at issue include:

- Application of the destination principle;
- Application of a global based approach and the zero rating of exports;

A.M. Bardopoulos, *eCommerce and the Effects of Technology on Taxation*,
Law, Governance and Technology Series 22, DOI 10.1007/978-3-319-15449-7_21

- Digital supplies to be treated as the supply of services;
- Registration threshold for persons carrying on taxable activities within the relevant jurisdiction.

The primary inadequacies of VAT are in respect of the collection and monitoring of VAT, which are points at issue in traditional cross-border transactions, and are issues which have been exacerbated by the virtual eMarket.

21.1 Introduction

Technology has undeniably impacted taxation and the manner in which it is effectively imposed. As previously discussed income tax principles may have to be 'reconceptualised' in order to be effectively applied to eCommerce transactions as income tax principles, in their current form, are not conducive to cross-border eCommerce transactions. The intellectual basis of this paper is the submission that the indirect consumption-based VAT system is the most amenable taxation system for the purpose of effectively imposing tax on cross-border eCommerce transactions. While VAT is not perfect and requires modification if it is to be effectively applied to the virtual world, and although administrative difficulties pertaining to cross-border transactions do require resolution, it is submitted that VAT is, nevertheless, more effective than income tax, is based primarily on the flexibility of VAT principles compared to the inflexible principles of income tax. Furthermore, while VAT may require amendment to allow for a more conducive global application, the various systems examined demonstrate that:

(a) It is possible for countries to harmonize their VAT systems to allow for a more efficient application and administration of VAT (as demonstrated by the European Union); and
(b) VAT is capable of co-existing with an indirect consumption-based retail tax system as is demonstrated by USA, and Canada which has implemented a federal VAT system and also a provincial retail sales tax systems.

It is of paramount importance that the retail tax system utilised by the USA, the largest commercial hub, especially in respect of eCommerce transactions, can effectively operate in conjunction with VAT. Indeed, the USA is a critical point at issue when determining an effective global taxing system.

The intellectual basis of this paper is the submission that VAT is the most amenable tax system for application in eCommerce, because VAT's inherently flexible nature enables it to adapt to technical amelioration and the unprecedented and unexplored terrain of a seamless, borderless virtual world.

21.2 The Impact of Technology

Several points at issue proceed from the virtual world and the impact technology has had on taxation, however, technology has not impacted taxation alone. A contentious issue raised in respect of the Internet and the new founded virtual world is in regard to privacy. Within the realm of this paper discussion of privacy issues is confined to various taxing methods proposed to combat tax evasion. While the overall privacy issues regarding the Internet fall outside the scope of this paper, it should be noted that the issue of privacy persists as a highly debated topic which in itself precipitates dissension in regard to various taxation methods, for example, identifying a consumer's location with his IP address. While the need for the protection of privacy is not disputed, and this paper does not support in any way the introduction of 'Big Brother'[1] into the virtual world, the Internet has provided consumer's with a certain degree of heightened privacy not afforded in the physical world. Elements of privacy issues in respect of taxation, which have been raised and discussed briefly throughout this paper, will be examined further.

The various contentions regarding privacy issues as a result of eCommerce were discussed in Part II of this paper.[2] One such contention raised was that a consumer is capable of maintaining anonymity in the physical world by purchasing an item with cash, a luxury not afforded in the virtual world where eRetailers collect and retain full details of the eConsumer including a description of the item purchased. Further contention relates to the enforcement of taxation in the virtual world whereby eRetailers may be required to release the purchase details of customers should an audit be conducted. Tax authorities have retorted that such detailed information is not necessary for purposes of an audit. An eRetailer does not need to release specific details regarding the name of a book acquired and details regarding the eConsumer in order for revenue authorities to conduct, say, a VAT audit.

An eVAT audit would require the vendor to substantiate the value of sales, the location of the eConsumer and the total tax imposed, collected and remitted on the sale. Details required for the purpose of conducting an eVAT audit do not differ greatly from the information required in order to conduct a tax audit on credit card purchases in the physical world. The only real significance is that the eConsumer's location would need to be identified and that *"[p]erhaps... the real danger of e-*

---

[1]Richard Bird held that *"[i]t is important... to distinguish such a transparent world from the big-brother world envisaged by some commentators as emerging from current security concerns. Unlike the nightmare of secretive central control, not all the effects of living in a glass bowl will necessarily be evil, and not just because an important side effect would be to reduce the ease of tax evasion... "*.

[op cit Bird, http://www.cdhowe.org/pdf/commentary_187.pdf**, p18]**.

[2]As discussed in 7.3.2. Privacy, Part II of this paper [p68].

commerce's effect on taxation may lie not so much in the erosion of the tax base as in the erosion of privacy as governments take defensive action ...".[3]

That being said, it is noted that privacy issues remain a contentious topic and must be borne in mind when any tax solution is proposed in the virtual world. However, for the purpose of this paper the impact of technology on taxation, needless to say, is of primary importance. But the impact of technology on other matters, such as privacy, cannot be ignored and a balance between the effective imposition of tax and the protection of privacy should be sought. Analyzing such a balance and providing recommendations on how a balance may be reached falls outside the scope of this paper and would in fact constitute a study on its own, however, the principle remains that whichever tax is recommended as the eTax solution, privacy must be borne in mind when devising effective administrative methods.[4]

---

[3]op cit Bird, http://www.cdhowe.org/pdf/commentary_187.pdf, p17.

[4]Refer to 6.1.7. Amazon.com, Part II of this paper [Pages 55 to 59]. Extract thereof provided hereunder:

> *Implementation of the Amazon tax has whipped up a fury of outrage and contention concerning not least of all the issue of internet privacy. It is contended that to comply with the Amazon tax requirements, Amazon will be forced to release customers' details and customers' "private content choices"*[A] *to the revenue authorities should the latter wish to conduct, for example, an audit to measure Amazon's compliance.*
>
> *Revenue authorities argue that there will be no violation of internet privacy as such detailed information is not necessary for the assessment of Amazon's compliance in the collection of sales tax. Revenue authorities argue that they "...have too much data. The last thing [they] need is data [they] don't need"*[B].
>
> *Amazon has collected a treasure trove of data detailing "who is reading what"*[C]. *If Amazon released to the government data detailing customers' reading choices such data could be embarrassing and injurious to the customer. Consider "what the government could do with 'Converting to Islam for Dummies' or 'Plant Your Own Marijuana Field'"*[D].
>
> *In the real world it is possible for a consumer to maintain anonymity when making a cash purchase, however, consumer anonymity is not possible in the virtual marketplace as the eConsumer's personal information, including a detailed description of the item purchased is necessary to effect a sale.*

[A] Loc cit Cohen, Noam *In a State's Search for Sales Tax, Amazon Raises Privacy Concerns* (2010). The New York Times. Available at http://www.nytimes.com/2010/05/03/business/media/03link.html?ref=sales_tax&pagewanted=print [Accessed 7 July 2010], p1.
[B] supra.
[C] Loc cit Cohen, http://www.nytimes.com/2010/05/03/business/media/03link.html?ref=sales_tax&pagewanted=print, p2.
[D] supra.
Refer to 7.3. Electronic Transactions Law, Part II of this paper [p65].
Refer to 7.3.2. Privacy, Part II of this paper [p68–69]. Extract thereof provided hereunder:

> *Privacy and information protection rules and regulations differ in diverse jurisdictions. However, with the Internet, there is an increasing need for standardised regulations relating to privacy because the virtual world is borderless and, in effect, jurisdictionless.*
>
> *The EU has a very strict policy regarding privacy and information protection, whereas other countries, such as the USA, have adopted the self-regulatory approach towards privacy and information protection. That being said, if a country wishes to transact*

While this paper is aimed at supporting the contention that VAT is the eTax solution, income tax issues relating to 'residence' versus 'source' have also been addressed. As submitted by Richard Bird, "*[n]o one and no country appears as yet to have found the silver bullet that will solve all the fiscal problems to which*

---

commercially with an EU member State, that country must comply with the EU's privacy laws and regulations. A latterly focus of interest is the protection of data within the virtual world. Protection of an individual's personal information is necessary as the "processing [of] personal info[rmation] threatens [an] individual in [two] ways: [1] compilation and distribution of personal information creates a direct threat to the individual's right to be left alone without interference; [2] the acquisition and disclosure of false or misleading information may lead to an infringement of identity" [E].

Several countries view privacy as a constitutional right which must be protected. It is important to note, however, that privacy and protection of 'identity' should not be restricted to individuals alone. Companies, while juristic persons, also have privacy concerns. It is important to note that while some countries view privacy as a constitutional right, certain courts have recognised that this 'constitutional right' to privacy is not an absolute right and there can be exceptions.

Regardless of the controls utilised by diverse countries for privacy protection, that is self-regulatory or by implementation of strict rules, privacy protection has become an increasing concern with the advent of the Internet era. As discussed earlier[F]*, opponents to the Amazon tax attempted to prevent the promulgation of the Amazon tax act alleging that it threatened privacy. Opponents contended that possible compliance checks pertaining to the collection of Internet sales tax could entail disclosure of sales records, giving government unrestricted access to detailed descriptions of eConsumers' purchases and personal information.*

Threat of infringement of privacy within the domain of the virtual world is an explosive issue. If, for example, Microsoft, registered in Ireland, provided USA revenue authorities with all relevant records pertaining to USA on-line sales, such compliance to an audit would provoke furious debate apropos of Microsoft's failure to protect USA customers' personal data from a USA perspective, and Microsoft's alleged contravention of the strict privacy regulations of the EU. The Internet's borderless environment has made it increasingly imperative to adopt standardised definitions and regulations in all spheres of the law. Within the context of this paper, informed scrutiny of diverse perspectives of privacy laws is advocated as being essential to the successful imposition of taxing systems within the virtual world. The essence of the problem is not the tax itself but the means of successful imposition and implementation of the tax while yet respecting the axiom of privacy protection.

[E]Hofman, Julien eLaw 1, Topic 10: Data Privacy [Lecture slides] (2005) Department of Commercial Law, University of Cape Town.

[F]Refer to 6.1.7. Amazon.com, Part II of this paper [p55].

Refer to Ecommerce Transactions: OECD Commentary, Chap. 17, Part V of this paper [p161].

Refer to 20.1. Introduction, Part V of this paper [p240].

Refer to 21.2. Impact of Technology, Part V of this paper [p259]. Extract thereof provided hereunder:

Several issues arise in the matter of the virtual world and the impact technology has had on taxation, however, technology has not impacted taxation alone. A contentious issue raised in regard to the Internet and the new founded virtual world pertains to privacy.

While the need for the protection of privacy is not disputed, and this paper does not support in any way the introduction of 'Big Brother'[G] *into the virtual world, the Internet has provided consumer's with a certain degree of heightened privacy not afforded in the physical world. Thus, elements of privacy issues relating to taxation, which have been raised and discussed briefly throughout this paper, will be examined further.*

the growth of the borderless economy of cyberspace potentially gives rise".[5] It is unlikely that such a 'silver bullet' will be configured and one of the fundamental underlying principles of this paper is that instead of focusing on achieving an eTax that will ensnare all the various taxes, it may be more efficacious to focus on one type of taxing system that will facilitate the most practical and efficient way of imposing, collecting and enforcing tax in the virtual world. While VAT is a lower taxing percentage than, say, income tax, the varying income tax principles are less flexible than VAT, and while VAT may be the 'lesser tax', it is possibly more achievable than the 'higher tax' earner.

21.3 Applying VAT to the Virtual World

Richard Bird submitted that "*if one believes, as [he is so] inclined to, that necessity is the mother of invention, a workable technological solution of the fiscal problems arising from new technology may loom in the not too distant future*".[6] Indeed, it has been submitted by the archaeologist Gunter Dreyer that the advent of "*writing emerged as an innovation because of economic necessity*".[7,8] However, the exigent necessity here is not necessarily to devise a workable technological solution to the

Contention pertains to the enforcement of taxation in the virtual world whereby eRetailers may be required to release the purchase details of customers should an audit be conducted. Tax authorities have retorted that such detailed information is not necessary for purposes of an audit. An eRetailer does not need to release specific details regarding the name of a book acquired and details regarding the eConsumer in order for revenue authorities to conduct, say, a VAT audit.

An eVAT audit would require the vendor to substantiate the value of sales, the location of the eConsumer and the total tax imposed, collected and remitted on the sale. Details required for the purpose of conducting an eVAT audit do not differ greatly from the information required in order to conduct a tax audit on credit card purchases in the physical world. The only real significance is that the eConsumer's location will need to be identified.

[G] Richard Bird held that "*[i]t is important ... to distinguish such a transparent world from the big-brother world envisaged by some commentators as emerging from current security concerns. Unlike the nightmare of secretive central control, not all the effects of living in a glass bowl will necessarily be evil, and not just because an important side effect would be to reduce the ease of tax evasion ...*"

[op cit Bird, http://www.cdhowe.org/pdf/commentary_187.pdf**, p18]**.
Refer to 21.5. Collection and Monitoring, Part V of this paper [p277].

[5] op cit Bird, http://www.cdhowe.org/pdf/commentary_187.pdf, p2.

[6] op cit Bird, http://www.cdhowe.org/pdf/commentary_187.pdf, p16–17.

[7] op cit, Lymer, Andrew & Hasseldine, John *The International Taxation System* (2002), U.S.A, p21.

[8] As discussed in 2.2. History of Taxation. Globalisation and International Trade, Part I of this paper [p22].

fiscal problems arising from technology, but to check international political conflicts which inhibit all potential workable solutions.

"How does one mark territory in a seamless, digital world? How does one map nations and taxing jurisdictions in a world that is not based on geography? This throws the application of tax laws into disarray?"[9] This challenge to tax may relate primarily to income tax laws more so than indirect tax laws. However, consumption tax laws are also thrown into disarray in regard to identifying the location of the consumer and, therefore, the place of supply in terms of the destination principle for the purpose of imposing the consumption tax. Furthermore, virtual worlds such as Second Life, if physical presence is acknowledged in the virtual world, throw the application of tax laws into further disarray due to the complexities of identifying a supplier or consumer's jurisdictional residence and location. However, for the purpose of imposing an indirect tax such as VAT, the consumer's place of consumption may possibly be determined with greater ease than applying income tax principles by identifying the consumer's IP address as the final place of consumption, use and enjoyment.

Application of VAT within the virtual world does not differ significantly from traditional application. The primary difference appears to pertain to determining the place of supply, but apart from such determination the VAT principles and concepts can be applied with relative ease within the virtual world. Income tax laws, on the other hand, have deemed certain technology to constitute, for example, permanent establishment when required and, furthermore, the vast conflict in source and resident based systems implemented globally creates further complexities. Further, income tax utilising, for example, a residence basis system increases the motivation of suppliers to move their business operations to tax havens. Of course this may also be experienced with the 'origin principle' in VAT law, however, there is an increased departure from the 'origin principle' in lieu of the 'destination principle'. Thus, if a supplier were to relocate its business operations to an 'origin principle' based jurisdiction in an attempt to operate from a jurisdiction with a lower VAT rate, it would potentially result in double taxation as so many jurisdictions apply the destination principle. Furthermore, there is less motivation for suppliers to take such action as the indirect tax is essentially borne by the consumer.

eCommerce has not impacted VAT laws to the extent it has income tax laws, but has impelled an exponential increase in cross-border transactions, for which tax laws, depending on the jurisdiction, attend to by zero-rating exports and taxing imports. Technology has, however, impacted the current retail sales tax systems in effect in the USA instigating an increased urgency to streamline the retail sales tax system. Several administrations and lobbyists have campaigned for the streamlining and harmonization of the indirect tax system implemented in the various states of the USA for decades to no avail until the Internet forced the hand of co-operation. Technology has contributed vastly to the implementation and inter-state co-operation in regard to the SSTP and SSUTA. And from an international

---

[9]Thakkar, Ajay, as quoted in Bird, http://www.cdhowe.org/pdf/commentary_187.pdf, p4–5.

harmonization perspective, it is doubtful that the global community objects to the USA aligning their indirect tax principles with the rest of the world. However, whether the streamlining of the USA retail sales tax system is a good or bad thing falls outside the scope of this paper as it is a highly contentious topic in its own right.

To reiterate, the substantial impact of technology on VAT has not been in regard to the application of VAT, but rather to the determination of the place of supply, enforcement, collection and overall administrative aspect of the imposition of VAT. This is evident from the eCommerce guidelines published by the several jurisdictions and the OECD wherein the issues in respect of the place of supply determination and administrative aspect have been discussed and debated, more so than the need to change the actual laws.

Income tax has been examined and debated in detail, and while 'source-based' taxation has been supported as the best income tax method, application of the 'source-based' method in its current form carries a wide range of complexities and inefficiencies. Application of the 'residence-based' tax system with regard to eCommerce remains problematic as the virtual world has allowed for the manipulation of the place of 'effective management'. Furthermore, as concluded within the Australian Review of International Taxation Arrangements Constitution Paper "*it is clear that legislative reform is the only option*"[10] in regard to applying the 'residence-based' tests for determining income tax.[11]

As previously discussed, it is apparent that traditional criteria relevant to 'presence', 'fixed' and 'agent' cannot be effectively applied in an eCommerce environment. It has, furthermore, been submitted that deliberation of 'fixed', a concept pertinent to traditional criteria for determining 'source', may no longer be apposite to an eCommerce environment. However, as previously stated this paper does not advocate the total abandonment of the 'source-based' taxation in its entirety, but "*that the way in which source is defined for active income may need*

[10]loc cit Dirkis, Micahel *Still a Problem Child: Central Management and Control After RITA* (2005). Available at http://www.austlii.edu.au/au/journals/RevenueLJ/2005/7.pdf [Accessed 14 July 2010].

[11]Application of traditional 'residence' definition was discussed and analysed in Part III of this paper. For the purpose of convenience, the concluding paragraph of Part III of this paper [p103], is recapitulated below:

> ...*Indeed, it may be argued that legislative reform for determining 'residency' in the virtual world for income tax purposes should presuppose provisions especially structured to accommodate flexibility of application. In the traditional business world, the 'effective management' test is principle based in that an examination of the facts and circumstances of each case is a requisite for determining jurisdiction of residency of a company. However, determining place of 'effective management' within the virtual world has proved to be more rule based than principle driven. Thus, it may be contended that rather than attempting to adapt traditional 'residence' tests to the virtual world for income tax purposes, it may be more expedient to devise provisions more apposite to the virtual world business model.* [Emphasis Added]

to be reconceptualised...".[12] The "*reconceptualization*" [13] of the 'source-based' tax system, as supported and advocated by Dr Pinto in his doctorial thesis, may be requisite for effective imposition of income tax on eCommerce.

While this paper may not advocate the abandonment of income tax principles in their entirety, upon examining income tax based principles and the VAT laws implemented in the various jurisdictions, the virtual world may be more amenable to the application of VAT than to income tax principles. Income tax, however, appears to be the primary focus of much research, debate and discussion impelled by the quantity of tax revenue connected with effective imposition of income tax. VAT, on the other hand, may be regarded as the lesser tax revenue as VAT is generally a much lower tax percentage than income tax. However, the global community may be at the stage where it may be more beneficial to collect peanuts rather than attempting the collection of walnuts and ending up with nothing.

Case studies of Amazon.com and Second Life will be used as examples in an analysis of VAT application in the virtual world in support of the intellectual basis of this paper. Furthermore, application of income tax principles will be briefly perused to emphasize by contradistinction the efficacy of VAT.

21.3.1 Amazon.com

Acknowledgement of physical presence in the virtual world, or through means of the virtual world, is not an absolute necessity for application of VAT. If to be 'physically present' in or through the virtual world is acknowledged it merely supports the argument that eRetailers, such as Amazon.com, may meet the requirements to register as a vendor in the jurisdiction where the place of supply occurs for indirect tax purposes.

Alternatively, if the physical presence argument is not supported, eRetailers may still have to register for indirect tax depending on the particular jurisdiction's registration requirements, and failing the requirement to register, the eRetailers' supplies, subject to exceptions and conditions, remain taxable in the consumer's jurisdiction. 'Physical presence' does not impact on the taxability of a supply in terms of indirect tax but more readily, tax administration, that is, it affects whether the eRetailer is required to register, impose the indirect tax, collect and remit same to the applicable revenue authority, or if the eConsumer, subject to conditions and jurisdictional limitations, is responsible for accounting for the applicable indirect tax. 'Physical presence', for the purpose of applying a source-based income tax system, is a critical point at issue.

---

[12]**op cit Pinto, Dale** ***E-Commerce and Source-Based Income Taxation*** (2003)**, Netherlands, p63**. This was discussed in Part IV of this paper and is an extract of Dr Pinto's summation of the impact of technology on 'physical presence' and, therefore, 'source' as quoted on p109–110 of this paper.

[13]As discussed in Chap. 14, Part IV of this paper [p137].

Amazon.com's eSales to eConsumers resident in New York State is, as discussed earlier,[14] a significant point at issue. Amazon.com does not satisfy the physical presence requirements for the purpose of the application of 'source-basis' income tax. Even if the previously submitted contention that it is possible to achieve 'physical presence' through the means of the virtual world is upheld, it is doubtful that Amazon.com will satisfy the permanent establishment requirement whereby "*a fixed place of business through which the business of an enterprise is wholly or partly carried on*".[15]

While 'physical presence' in the internet may be within the realm of possibility, Amazon.com may fail to satisfy the 'fixed' requirement due to the innovation and structure of the virtual world. In the application of indirect tax to Amazon.com's supplies to New York eConsumers, the New York customers will be responsible for the payment of sales or use tax on the taxable supplies upon importation of the taxable supply into New York State, whereas the out-of-town eRetailer is not required to register as a vendor. Various submissions have been made as to why out-of-state eRetailers, such as Amazon.com, may qualify as vendors in the State of New York, however, presupposing that none of these submissions hold, the impact of Amazon.com meeting the definition of 'physical presence' in New York through the means of the Internet would effectuate a liability to register as a vendor. In such circumstances, Amazon.com would be liable to impose, collect and remit the sales tax on all taxable supplies made to New York eConsumers. Thus, whether or not 'physical presence' is satisfied for indirect tax purposes, the taxable supplies themselves are, nevertheless, subject to New York sales tax.

21.3.2 Second Life

As discussed earlier, Second Life is relevant to any discussion on application of VAT in the virtual world.[16] While Second Life has been described as a 'game' it has, nevertheless, resulted in the earning of "real world" income. In the year 2006 "*over 3,000 residents reportedly [made] an excess of 20 thousand US Dollars (USD) per year running businesses in Second Life. Most of them sell objects they've created that other residents want. One Second Life resident landed a Business Week cover story for earning a three-figure income – that's real world dollars – selling virtual real estate*".[17]

---

[14]As discussed in Chap. 6, Part II of this paper [p49].

[15]op cit, OECD *OECD Model Tax Convention on Income and on Capital, Condensed Version – July 2005* (2005), France, p26.

[16]As discussed in 6.1.6. Second Life, Part II of this paper [p54].

[17]loc cit www.wisegeek.com *What is Second Life?* Available at http://www.wisegeek.com/what-is-second-life.htm [Accessed 11 July 2010].

The conducting of business in a virtual world, such as Second Life, which results in the earning of "real world" income emphasizes the predicament of how best to tax such income. *If the 'residence based' taxation system is applied, is it applied to the Second Life 'user' resident within the virtual world, that is, the Second Life avatar resident that earned the income, or is it applied to the 'physical world' 'user' resident? Is the income earned within the virtual world of Second Life, or the physical world residence of the 'gaming' company, Linden Labs?* (The possibility of achieving presence in the virtual world is here presupposed as discussed in Part II, Chap. 8.)

As previously discussed in Part III of this paper,[18] traditional income tax provisions dismally lack the flexibility to be effectively applied to the virtual world. In the traditional business world the 'effective management' test is principle based, in that the examination of the circumstances and facts of each case is a requisite for determining the residence of a company. Determining the place of effective management within the virtual world, however, has proved to be more rule based than principle driven. Thus, with regard to income earned as a result of Second Life, application of the 'residence based' tax system for the purpose of determining the jurisdiction entitled to tax income earned is complicated, in that more than one jurisdiction could potentially claim residence for the purpose of taxing the income earned within Second Life by reason of the problem of determining 'place of effective management', that is, where business operations took place, etc. Furthermore, technology enables management to be physically located in several diverse jurisdictions and still effectively manage a company with the aid of teleconferencing or videoconferencing. Furthermore, Second Life facilitates the hosting of board meetings and even shareholders' meetings within the virtual world.

In circumstances where the Second Life user earns 'real world' income as an individual and not through the means of a company, etc., determining 'residence' is problematic. *Whose 'residence' is pertinent – that of the individual user located in the physical world, or that of the avatar resident in the virtual world?* Assuming that residence in the virtual world is not recognised, then the user of Second Life may be subject to income tax in the country of his residence depending on his country's tax policy. However, earning income within the virtual world is easily manipulated to evade taxation, for example, by forming a business, which in turn exacerbates the problem of double taxation or double non-taxation in international transactions.

Determining the 'source' of the income carries the same complexities as discussed under Amazon.com,[19] if not more. In short, if 'physical presence', or 'residence' within the virtual world is acknowledged and recognised, the complexities of determining the taxing jurisdiction in respect of income earned increases exponentially. However, even attempting to apply traditional taxing principles to income earned is proving increasingly difficult on account of the inflexibility of

[18] As discussed in 10.3. Conclusion, Part III of this paper [p103].

[19] As discussed in 21.3.1. Amazon.com, Part V of this paper [p265].

income tax principles. Indirect tax such as VAT, on the other hand, may be applied with greater ease regardless of whether the ability to be 'physically present' within the virtual world is acknowledged or not.

Second Life has been labelled an online game and in terms of the various VAT guidelines and provisions, online games constitute an electronically supplied service. While it is debatable as to whether digitised products qualify solely as the supply of services or may also qualify as the supply of goods, "*goods*" such as virtual property, do not meet the attributes of real property.[20] Digital products are, excluding exceptions, globally accepted as the supply of services. The type of services supplied may be debatable and Dr Rendahl examines the various forms the service supplied may take in Second Life:

(i) The user pays Linden Labs a subscription fee for access to the Second Life game, as well as exchange services pertaining to Linden dollars which enables the user to buy and maintain virtual property, including other services.[21] As purchasing, for example, virtual property, is part of the game, it may be considered part-and-parcel of the subscription fees.[22]
(ii) On the other hand, it may be contended that the additional supplies constitute separate supplies.[23] That is, the subscription fees for the on-line game constitute one supply and the additional B2C supply of digitised products, for example, virtual property, constitute a second supply. However, even this second supply constitutes an electronically supplied service.[24] As held by Dr Rendahl, *"[t]he additional supplies made within the game are, either way, dependent on the original supply – to get access to the game*".[25] The additional supplies, while debatably separate from the original supply, contribute to the enjoyment of the game.[26]
(iii) C2C supplies may also occur within Second Life as the virtual world has created an economic environment enabling users to contract with each other and "*buy and sell rights they have earned or created within the game . . .* ".[27, 28] in order for such supplies to be subject to tax, at least one of the consumers must be responsible for imposition of VAT or be subject to the reverse charge mechanism. In several jurisdictions the reverse charge mechanism is restricted to taxable persons only. Thus it is possible for C2C supply of services to be

[20] op cit Rendahl, Pernilla, *Cross-Border Consumption Taxation on Digital Supplies,* Netherlands, p194.

[21] supra.

[22] supra.

[23] op cit Rendahl, p194.

[24] supra.

[25] idem p195.

[26] supra.

[27] supra.

[28] supra.

free of tax, however, if the consumer does not qualify as a taxable person, it is irrelevant if the supply occurs in the virtual world or the traditional world.

(iv) Certain supplies involve greater human involvement than others.[29] Where the human involvement is substantial, such supply will not constitute an 'electronically supplied service'[30] as defined by the EU, or a supply of intangible personal property as recognised by Canada. This may, depending on the jurisdiction, change the nature of the service supplied but is, nevertheless, the supply of a service. An example of such services includes Second Life's ability to provide a platform for educational seminars and lectures, as well as conferences and board meetings.

Regardless of the type of service, the virtual environment does not inhibit the application of VAT on taxable services. Second Life's VAT policy,[31] however, provides that only EU resident 'users' will be subject to VAT where the user is not an EU VAT registered person. Thus, the supply of Second Life's gaming service is not subject to VAT if the 'user' is, for example, a Canadian resident. Access to online games which are "*wholly or partly used in Canada*" may qualify as a taxable service if a wide interpretation is placed on the Canadian Excise Taxation Act.[32] Under such

---

[29] supra.

[30] supra.

[31] Second Life's VAT policy statement reads as follows:

> *In accordance with the sales tax regulations of European Union countries in which our Residents live, we must collect and remit Value Added Tax, or VAT, from Residents.*
>
> Who should be charged VAT?
>
> *Currently, only Residents who live in the European Union are charged VAT. The EU allows people and companies to register for VAT exemption, which we abide by.*
>
> How does Linden Lab determine who to charge VAT for?
>
> *When you registered your account, you told us what country you live in. If that country is in the EU, then VAT is applied.*
>
> *If you say that you come from a different country that doesn't charge VAT, it's very likely that discrepancies between your IP address and your declared country would get caught in our risk detection system and may cause your account to be flagged for review or even suspended.*
>
> What are the items for which Linden Lab charges VAT?
>
> *Anything that you pay Linden Lab for will have VAT applied. This includes:*
>
> - *Premium account registration*
> - *Purchases from the Land Store*
> - *Land use fees (tier)*
> - *Private Region fees*
> - *Land auctions*
> - *LindeX™ transaction fees . . .*
>
> *What are the items for which Linden Lab doesn't charge VAT? Transactions in L$ between individual Residents are not subject to VAT . . .*

Second Life *Value Added Tax*. Available at http://secondlife.com/corporate/vat.php **[Accessed 13/01/2011]**.

[32] op cit Rendahl, p285.

circumstances Second Life, carrying on a business in Canada, would be required to register and impose VAT/GST on the supply of services to Canadian 'users'. As Second Life has categorically stated that only services rendered to EU Member State residents will be subject to VAT,[33] the assumption has been made that Second Life has adopted a bold approach by applying a narrower interpretation to the Canadian Excise Taxation Act. Second Life's approach is, needless to say, debatable and depending on the jurisdiction, Second Life may qualify as a VAT vendor in jurisdictions other than the EU. However, despite Second Life not imposing GST on the rendering of services to, for example, Canadian users does not exclude such supplies from the Canadian GST net. While Second Life may, questionably, not be required to impose, collect and remit Canadian GST on services rendered to Canadian users, such supplies would qualify as 'imported taxable supplies' and may be subject to the reverse charge mechanism.

New Zealand GST legislation, unfortunately, has restricted mandatory registration to, *inter alia*, 'residents' or the carrying on of a taxable activity while having any fixed or permanent place in New Zealand. Thus, Second Life's VAT policy statement does not contradict the application of the New Zealand GST legislation provided Second Life does not qualify as carrying on a taxable activity while having a fixed or permanent place in New Zealand. However, analogous to Canada, the services rendered by Second Life may qualify as 'imported taxable supplies'. Each and every VAT jurisdiction could be analysed in relation to Second Life's VAT policy and the statement may hold true for certain jurisdictions and may not for others depending on the registration requirements in each jurisdiction. It is, nevertheless, a bold statement to have made considering that 130 countries have implemented a VAT system and, therefore, it is questionable that Second Life qualifies as a taxable person in the EU only.

Regardless of the administrative aspect and the global compliance of Second Life, the above analysis demonstrates that the services supplied in or through Second Life, subject to exceptions and conditions, in theory qualify as taxable services and subject to VAT/GST in the jurisdiction where the 'user' consumes such services, whether in terms of self-assessment or directly imposed by Second Life.

21.3.3 Is VAT Perfect in Its Current Form?

VAT is not without defect and perplexities relative to both the traditional and virtual worlds. For example, imputable to Australia's inharmonious territorial approach to VAT application, the supply of online gaming services, such as SecondLife, could potentially be deemed subject to VAT in both Australia and another jurisdiction

[33] loc cit Second Life *Value Added Tax*, http://secondlife.com/corporate/vat.php

which practices global application of VAT.[34] It is strongly submitted, therefore, that VAT in its current form (that is, any of the current models discussed within this paper, for example, the Canadian, New Zealand, European Union, etc.) stands in need of amendment for the purpose of achieving international harmonization of principles and definitions. Thus, VAT cannot be said to be perfect in its current form.

Globally, the changes requisite for international harmonization are for the most part relatively minor within the compass of diverse VAT legislations. However, a few jurisdictions do occur where necessary change may be significant. For example, jurisdictions requiring significant amendment may be those not applying the destination principle. The destination principle is well supported by VAT jurisdictions and recommended by the OECD. While the EU may apply a hybrid system whereby the destination and origin principles are utilised, in terms of the jurisdictional analysis effectuated in this paper[35] there does not appear to be any jurisdiction which applies only the 'origin principle'. However, assuming hypothetically that out of the 130 countries applying a VAT model there is a jurisdiction that applies only the 'origin principle', a global standard of harmonization would undoubtably necessitate a significant amendment within such a jurisdiction.

The 'place of supply' rules is a significant point at issue. South Africa is one of the few countries that does not have a 'place of supply' rule. While it may be argued that absence of a 'place of supply' rule allows greater flexibility for determining jurisdiction of supply, it has precipitated uncertainty within the traditional world. The 'place of supply' rule is succinctly propounded in the New Zealand legislation and commentary.

Both New Zealand and South Africa afford pragmatic discussion in the matter of the application of the consequences pertaining to the 'place of supply rules'. The 'place of supply' rule relies on the 'residence' of the supplier which is where the inflexibility may arise as examined in Part III of this paper. Section 8(2) of the New Zealand GST Act pertains to the 'place of supply' rule which reads as follows:

---

[34]This point is discussed by Dr Rendahl in her discussion regarding place of supply with reference to Australia:

> *Supplies of games like Second Life and War of Warcraft could be held to be effectively used and enjoyed in Canada if supplied to Australian residents, thus these supplies also could be taxed under Australian GST. There are, however, too many issues left uncertain for making a full evaluation of these supplies, since the placement of the servers and the organisation of the supplying company also affect whether these supplies can be deemed to be made in Australia or not. Thus, as for Canadian GST, a case of unintentional or intentional double or non-taxation could be at hand, depending on the suppliers' location and applicable tax law in that state as well as the perspective of the Australian state.*
>
> **[op cit Rendahl, p321]**.

[35]Jurisdictional Analysis: Summary, per Appendix 1 of this paper [p362].

> **"Section 8 Imposition of Goods and Services Tax on Supply**
> **8(2) [Supply in New Zealand]** For the purposes of this Act, goods and services shall be deemed to be supplied in New Zealand if the supplier is resident in New Zealand, and shall be deemed to be supplied outside New Zealand if the supplier is a non-resident."[36]

However, while the determination of residence may relate back to the criteria applied for income tax purposes, 'residence' may also be deemed for GST purposes to be where *"[a]n overseas person . . . makes supplies in New Zealand in the course of a taxable activity and those supplies exceed the registration threshold*".[37] It is submitted that jurisdictions lacking a 'place of supply' rule may, theoretically, be applying a more flexible VAT model than jurisdictions that have incorporated a 'place of supply' rule, because of the 'residence' requirement which has proven to be inefficient for income tax purposes when applied to the virtual world. However, where the place of supply rule includes a deeming residence provision which pertains to the "*supplies [made] in New Zealand in the course of a taxable activity . . .*",[38] such application should not inhibit the effectiveness of applying GST to the virtual world.

The New Zealand guide to GST describes the rules as applying "*to the supply of goods which are in New Zealand at the GST time of supply, to the supply of services physically performed by any person in New Zealand, and to some cross-border supplies of telecommunication services*".[39] For the purpose of eliminating difficulties with regard to determining the place of supply in respect of the supply of 'telecommunication services', New Zealand has gone one step further and incorporated additional 'place of supply' rules specifically appertaining to 'telecommunication services':

> **"Section 8 Imposition of Goods and Services Tax on Supply**
> **8(6) [Telecommunications Services Deemed Supplied in New Zealand]** Despite subsection (2), telecommunications services are treated as being supplied in New Zealand if the supplier is a non-resident and a person, physically in New Zealand, initiates the supply from a telecommunications supplier, whether or not the person initiates the supply on behalf of another person . . ."

(continued)

[36]Section 8(2) of the New Zealand Goods and Services Tax Act as at February 2010.

[37]op cit McKenzie, Alastair. *GST – A Practical Guide* (Edition 8) (2008), New Zealand, p82.

[38]supra.

[39]idem p6.

"**Section 8A Certain Supplies of Telecommunications Services**

8A(1) [Place of supply where determination of physical location is impractical] Despite section 8(2), if a telecommunications supplier cannot apply section 8(6) because it is impractical for the supplier to determine the physical location of a person due to the type of service or to the class of customer to which the person belongs, the supplier must treat a supply of telecommunications services as being supplied in New Zealand if the person's address for receiving invoices from the supplier is in New Zealand."[40]

Within the compass of the above rules the supply of services are either deemed to take place in New Zealand when the "*initiator*" of the supply is either physically located in New Zealand or has a New Zealand 'billing address'.[41] New Zealand has recognised the potential difficulty of determining the physical location of a person using the Internet, however, of especial interest is the person to whom the services are rendered. The New Zealand GST guide defines the '*initiator*' as *"the party who satisfies the highest factor listed for present purposes. The factors are listed in the following order: the party who controls the commencement of the supply, the payer, or the person who contracts for the service*".[42]

If one applies the above definition to *'Illustrative Example Alpha'* on page vii of this paper, the initiator of the supply is Kosta. Kosta controlled the commencement of the supply by logging onto Amazon.com and selecting the desired DVD, initiated the contract of service by ordering the desired DVD and was the payer. If Kosta was either physically located in New Zealand or had a New Zealand billing address, in terms of the New Zealand 'place of supply' rules, the supply occurred in New Zealand. As previously discussed,[43] however, the 'billing address' can be easily manipulated by the user but the IP address of the 'initiator's' 'initiating' computer can be determined to ascertain the location of the 'initiator'.

Problems and application difficulties created as a result of legislation lacking a 'place of supply rule' is one of the primary reasons why New Zealand amended its GST legislation to incorporate a 'place of supply rule'. The 'place of supply' rule is not a required amendment for the application of VAT to the virtual world, but is required for traditional cross-border transactions. The 'place of supply' rules

[40]Sections 8(6) and 8A(1) of the New Zealand GST Act respectively as at February 2010.

[41]op cit McKenzie, p103.

[42]idem p102.

[43]Refer to the analysis of South Africa under 'Jurisdictional Analysis', 18.2.2., Part V of this paper regarding the manipulation of a billing address tested for the purpose of downloading music restricted to USA territory [p205–208].

introduced regarding virtual cross-border transactions assist with simplifying the application of VAT/GST and, as seen above, are principle based as opposed to the rule based amendments inherent to income tax legislation. And this, it may be argued, is a major contradistinction between application of income tax principles and application of VAT to the virtual world. Requisite to application of income tax is either legislative reform or reconceptualization if it is to be effectively applied to eCommerce, whereas the legislative 'reform' or amendments requisite to VAT are necessary to traditional application of VAT and not exclusively necessary to eCommerce. VAT reform essential to effective application of VAT in the virtual world pertains exclusively to administrative points at issue such as determining the location of the user.

Despite commonalities between jurisdictions applying VAT, a *consensus omnium* is essential to international harmonization if a correlative framework of basic principles, rules and effective application is to be achieved. Essential points at issue include:

(i) Application of the destination principle;
(ii) Application of a global based approach and the zero rating of exports;
(iii) Digital supplies to be treated as the supply of services;
(iv) Registration threshold for persons carrying on taxable activities within the relevant jurisdiction.

Complying with recommended guidelines for the international harmonization of VAT principles, rules and application of VAT may perfect VAT as an effective eTax in several respects, the submission of which precipitates a discussion of VAT as an effective eTax.

21.4 VAT as an Effective eTax

VAT as an effective eTax can be applied to the virtual world in a manner analogous to traditional application precluding administrative difficulties. Inherent to indirect taxes such as VAT, the capacity to expedite eCommerce and facilitate the general operation, management and control of the virtual world is testament to the latter's potentiality as an effective eTax.

Harmonization of global tax systems is typically problematic, the primary point at issue being diverse political agendas, however, escalating globalization has impelled the urgency for intensified co-ordination and co-operation between jurisdictions. Despite the impact of globalisation on international taxation, disputes pertaining to diverse political agendas predominate most specifically in respect of application of income tax principles. For example, a point at issue is the harmonization of income tax principles with regard to the 'source-based' approach in respect of which countries such as the USA would have to forfeit their right to impose tax on a citizenship basis. It may be argued that the political aspect of income tax is the primary inhibitory factor of global harmonization of income tax principles, rules and law. It is not to be implied, however, that indirect taxes such as VAT are insusceptible to disputes extant to conflicting political agendas, however, existing similarities have promoted harmonization of indirect taxes on account of cross-border transactions.

Indeed, SSUTA is testament to the possibility of attaining harmonization and cross-border co-ordination and co-operation expedited by the virtual world and eRetailers such as Amazon.com.[44] Proliferating technology has undoubtedly contributed to harmonisation and increased global co-operation. The comparative ease with which VAT legislation, converse to income tax, has adapted to harmonization extols VAT as an effectual eTax solution.

As mentioned previously VAT may facilitate the control of copyright infringement. The Pirate Bay website endorses the downloading of copyrighted material. Taxation is distinct from moral issues and within the compass of taxation the suitability of imposition and enforcement of taxation and not the morality of the activity should be scrutinized. Indeed, Dr Rendahl submits that imposition of VAT on illegal activities may be applied as an effective tool for eradicating illegal activities. The Pirate Bay practices the *quid pro quo* principle of payment in respect of which consumers do not fiscally reimburse The Pirate Bay for the downloading of files, but instead The Pirate Bay users are "*encouraged to upload as many files as [they] download*",[45] the uploading of which qualifies as 'consideration'. In respect of the *quid pro quo* practice Dr Rendahl submits that:

> *The consequences for the tax authorities could be considerable administrative costs for enforcing the VAT on these supplies and determining if deductions for input VAT would be required to uphold the functioning of the VAT without causing further distortions on the market. However, enforcing VAT on these supplies, if all criteria can be met, could also be a solution to the problem with enforcing intellectual property.* [Emphasis Added]

From a neutral fiscal perspective, in the hypothetical case of imposition of VAT on such supplies input VAT would be admissible despite the illegality of the activity. However, in actuality it is implausible that illegal websites would qualify for many input credits. With reference to The Pirate Bay, it is improbable that consumers would qualify as taxable persons and, therefore, The Pirate Bay would not be able to claim input credits in respect of illegal copyright material.

[44] Discussed previously in Chap. 20 – United States of America, Part V of this paper [p240]:

"Proliferation of eCommerce has caused the USA to question and examine the current structure of the sales, and 'use', tax regimes, and may be attributed as one of the major contributing reasons for the Streamlined Sales Tax Program... The SSTP was a direct response to the vat revenue loss arising from the proliferation of the internet and accompanying inter-state transactional complications."

[45] op cit Rendahl, p161

Historically the enforcement of taxation has proved to be an effective tool for curbing illegal activities. The infamous Al Capone[46] was finally brought to justice not for Prohibition[47] violations but for tax evasion. Therefore, VAT as an eTax solution is endowed with the capacity to effectively combat the deluge of illegal copyright exacerbated by the proliferation of the Internet.

Imposition of VAT on illegal downloads would stifle the economic advantage of websites like The Pirate Bay over legitimate copyright downloads. However, as previously discussed under the *Jurisdictional Analysis of South Africa,*[48] it is imperative that in respect of territorial copyright restrictions jurisdictions do not inadvertently encourage and promote illegal websites by blocking legitimate downloads. Therefore, if VAT is to be an effective eTax solution, copyright and tax laws should be *en rapport* with each other.

---

[46]The USA Federal Bureau of Investigation provides the following biography of Al Capone:

> *Born of an immigrant family in Brooklyn, New York in 1899, Al Capone quit school after the sixth grade and associated with a notorious street gang, becoming accepted as a member...*
>
> *In 1925, Capone became boss... Capone had built a fearsome reputation in the ruthless gang rivalries of the period, struggling to acquire and retain "racketeering rights" to several areas of Chicago. That reputation grew as rival gangs were eliminated or nullified, and the suburb of Cicero became, in effect, a fiefdom of the Capone mob...*
>
> *On February 28, 1931, Capone was found guilty in federal court on [a] contempt of court charge and was sentenced to six months in Cook County Jail. His appeal on that charge was subsequently dismissed.*
>
> *Meanwhile, the U.S. Treasury Department had been developing evidence on tax evasion charges...*
>
> *On November 16, 1939, Al Capone was released after having served seven years, six months and fifteen days, and having paid all fines and back taxes.*

The FBI Federal Bureau of Investigation *Al Capone, Famous Cases & Criminals*. Available at http://www.fbi.gov/about-us/history/famous-cases/al-capone **[Accessed 17/01/2011]**.

[47]Prohibition, as defined by the Oxford English Dictionary, is "*the prevention by law of the manufacture and sale of alcohol, especially in the US[A] between 1920 and 1933.*"

'Prohibition', Oxford Dictionaries. Available at http://english.oxforddictionaries.com/view/entry/m_en_gb0665350?rskey=UcwQWR&result=2#m_en_gb0665350.004 [Accessed 17/01/2011].

[48]Discussed briefly in 18.2.2. South Africa, Part V of this paper [p205–208]:

> *... the use of copyright infringing websites, such as The Pirate Bay, is inadvertently encouraged when legitimate legal on-line website shops like iTunes and Amazon.com block the legal purchasing of music...*

21.5 Collection and Monitoring

VAT is not the "*silver bullet that will solve all the fiscal problems to which the growth of the borderless economy of cyberspace potentially gives rise*".[49] Further taxation problems arise with the proliferation of eCommerce which may not be effectively resolved with the application of VAT, such as transfer pricing, which will be briefly discussed in Part VII of this paper. VAT, furthermore, carries its own fallibilities in regard to effective application. For the purpose of examining the effectiveness of VAT as the eTax solution it is important to understand the deficiencies of VAT and the proposals to combat such deficiencies. Implicit to this paper the primary inadequacies of VAT are in respect of the collection and monitoring of VAT, which are points at issue in traditional cross-border transactions, and are issues which have been exacerbated by the virtual eMarket.

The various aspects of the collection and monitoring of the application of eVAT in diverse jurisdictions has been previously discussed. Methods of determining the eCustomer's location have been examined and debated by, including others, the OECD and proposals pertinent to this point at issue have been submitted. Other points significant to this issue to be considered are:

(i) Privacy issues have become an increasing concern globally and location determining methods should guard against infringing upon a customer's privacy. Measures should be taken to guard against 'Big Brother' tyranny in the virtual world the consequences of which would be the inhibiting of the growth and development of the virtual world, technology and eCommerce.
(ii) Technological amelioration may precipitate current or suggested methods being rendered useless and/or obsolete. Therefore, recommendations should not pertain too strictly to current technology but should be sufficiently flexible to facilitate adaptation to new technology.
(iii) Recommended solutions should be practically effective and realistically feasible to implement.

The practicality of a recommendation is of pre-eminent significance. A solution may be flawless in principle, but flawed in practicability. A hypothetical solution to the problem of determining the eConsumer's location in respect of cross-border eTransactions is to implant a general satellite positioning ('GSP') chip into every person worldwide which would unequivocally communicate the exact location of each users' eTransaction. This radically hypothetical solution would incontrovertibly solve the problem of eTransactions, locations and eUsers. However, in practicality it is currently beyond the realm of possibility and, furthermore, would be globally administratively exorbitant and would detonate the privacy issue.

It is essential that recommended methods are not too closely linked to specific technological paradigms at risk of possible obsoletion in the face of technological amelioration. Bit-tax has been proffered as a solution to taxing the virtual world. Imposition of 'bit-tax' taxation is defined by the measure of bits which relate to

---

[49] op cit Bird, http://www.cdhowe.org/pdf/commentary_187.pdf, p2.

the transmission of information.[50] Prolongation of the efficacy of bit-tax would necessitate the utilisation of binary digits for transmitting information, even so, 'quantum computing'[51] is already superseding 'bit-tax'. The life span of binary data

---

[50]op cit Bird, http://www.cdhowe.org/pdf/commentary_187.pdf, p4.

[51]'Quantum computing' is an example of how technology may develop. As an analysis and explanation of quantum computing falls outside the scope of this paper, a full explanation has not been provided within the body of this paper. However, for the purpose of illustrating the capabilities of technology and how such technology may develop, extracts from IT Engineer Roy Johnson's article, '*Quantum computing is based on different mathematics and different hardware from conventional, binary computing*', are set-out hereunder to provide a relevant overview of quantum computing and its capabilities:

> *... The mathematical limitations are being tackled with a new maths that will only be familiar to quantum physicists and 'quants' in the stockbroking field who use very advanced statistical models and analyses.*
>
> *This is the core of quantum computing and it is as 'new' as binary systems were when they replaced previous, unwieldy machines that were designed to work in decimal.*
>
> *Quantum computers already exist, in one form or another, and they work with qbits, not the usual 1/10 bits. A qbit is, mathematically, a state vector in a two-level quantum system or a vector that applies to complex numbers. Putting it simply and practically, a qbit can have the value 1,0 or both. In quantum language the simultaneous 1/10 value is called a superposition ...*
>
> *...Quantum states also have the unique property of entanglement. This is a non-local property of quantum states (qbits, for example) whereby two sets will have higher correlation than is possible in classical mathematics. Simply and somewhat inaccurately expressed, this allows quantum machines to work quickly on problems that a conventional machine can solve – but only with impossible time scales.*
>
> *Just on a 'fun' note, the fact that entanglement is a non-local property opens up the possibility of building something akin to the Star Trek transporter – one day ...*
>
> *... Apart from being more efficient on many problems, quantum computers have unique abilities to handle complexity, thanks again to the opaque mathematics of probability that govern their operation ...*
>
> *... By 1998, the first working machines were demonstrated – only using two or three qbits, but a start nonetheless ... In 2009, the first universal programmable quantum computer was demonstrated and, this year, a quantum machine simulated a hydrogen molecule with accurate results. Google has demonstrated a quantum algorithm that could be used for very fast searches on enormous data volumes. Microsoft Research is also working on quantum.*
>
> *Quantum computing is not just theoretical – it is a commercial opportunity and the major players are already moving on this ...*
>
> *... Yes, quantum computing is still new, still in development – and any discussion of its future will have a question mark attached ... It might be ten years before quantum computing is commonplace. Even then, it will be invisible to the end user, running data centres, server farms and, probably, a significant amount of internet infrastructure ... [Q]uantum computing will generally remain an invisible, enabling technology. For highly specialised users in science, engineering and complex financial analyses, it will become essential.*
>
> *It also goes hand-in-hand with some radical innovations in hardware and technology that will have a huge impact in communications systems and control systems of almost any kind as these breakthroughs move from the laboratory to the IT world and beyond.* [Emphasis Added]

is provisional. Therefore, 'bit-tax' as a recommended system of taxation which has not as yet been implemented is already courting superannuation. However, it may be surmised *"that binary data will continue to be the way of the future for at least another decade until quantum computing matures"*.[52] However, the exigent point at issue is that if a taxing system is directly linked to current technology, such taxing system will have to be reconceptualised or even completely reformed if it is to have an effective impact upon a rapidly proliferating technology.[53]

The OECD has studied diverse proposals in regard to taxing cross-border eTransactions, (as discussed in Chap. 17, Part V of this paper) by way of illustration, the benefit of a third party for the purpose of imposing, collecting and administering VAT on all virtual world consumption. The OECD acknowledged the efficacy of the proposed system but rejected the proposal on account of the administrative cost to establish such a system. However, the long term benefit and administrative effectiveness would surely outweigh start-up costs involved and such a programme could potentially be managed by the OECD. The current agreement between New York and New Jersey of the USA and the EU 'one-stop-scheme', as well as the Canadian HST, demonstrates the ability for shared tax revenue to be collected and effectively divided between respective parties.

The manner in which VAT would be divided between participating jurisdictions has been demonstrated as administratively possible by Canada with regard to HST, the USA states New York and New Jersey ('NY-NJ') with regard to their sales tax agreement and the EU with regard to the 'one-stop-scheme'. Where an amount is directly attributable to a specific jurisdiction said amount is remitted to that jurisdiction, such as the EU 'one-stop-scheme' and the NY-NJ sales tax agreement. Where the VAT quantity determination is less clear, the Canadian HST has proved an effective system with regard to determining the provinces' PST portion of tax collected in terms of a formula based on consumption patterns.

Such a collection method would resolve several problems in respect of complicated issues pertaining to the recognition of 'physical presence' within the virtual world. The benefit of a third party would assist in determining 'place of consumption'.

However, the most practicable solution is VAT registration thresholds in respective VAT jurisdictions, utilisation of a 'one-stop-scheme' framework coupled with determining a user's location by ascertaining the user's IP address, and the Canadian HST framework of dividing revenue where the 'location' is recognised as existing within the virtual world, all of which is administered by a third party.

Johnson, Roy Engineer IT. What is a qbit?: *Quantum computing is based on different mathematics and different hardware from conventional, binary computing.* (5 April 2010) Available at http://mybroadband.co.za/news/hardware/11987-What-qbit.html?print [Accessed 19/01/2011].

[52]Kontos, Kosta BSc (CompSci) (UCT), MBA (UCT). Managing Director (MD) of Kontos Technologies. (19 January 2011).

[53]Idem Kontos.

Incontrovertible evidence of user location defined by user IP address detonates privacy points at issue, however, eRetailers such as iTunes and Amazon.com are currently availing themselves of technology to determine a customer's location for the purpose of enforcing territorial copyright restrictions. The vigorously debated copyright topic is a critical point at issue which would be significantly alleviated by application of such technology to facilitate imposition and collection of VAT. However, privacy issues are debated with proportionate vigour and would have to be equitably resolved or blatantly disregarded to expedite enforcement of copyright in a manner commensurate with that practised by such eRetailers.

Bibliography

Primary Sources

Statutes

New Zealand Goods and Services Tax Act, No. 141 of 1985 (as amended).

OECD. 2005. *OECD model tax convention on income and on capital, condensed version – July 2005*. Paris: OECD Publishers.

Secondary Sources

Bird, Richard. 2003, September. *Taxing electronic commerce: A revolution in the making*. Toronto: C.D. Howe Institute Commentary. Available at http://www.cdhowe.org/pdf/commentary_187.pdf. Accessed 16 Sept 2010.

Cohen, Noam. 2010. *In a state's search for sales tax, Amazon raises privacy concerns*. The New York Times. Available at http://www.nytimes.com/2010/05/03/business/media/03link.html?ref=sales_tax&pagewanted=print. Accessed 7 July 2010,

Dirkis, Micahel. 2005. *Still a problem child: Central management and control after RITA*. Available at http://www.austlii.edu.au/au/journals/RevenueLJ/2005/7.pdf. Accessed 14 July 2010.

FBI Federal Bureau of Investigation, The Al Capone, Famous Cases & Criminals. Available at http://www.fbi.gov/about-us/history/famous-cases/al-capone. Accessed 17 Jan 2011.

Hofman, Julien. 2005. *eLaw 1, Topic 10: Data privacy* [Lecture slides]. Department of Commercial Law, University of Cape Town

Johnson, Roy, Engineer IT. 2010, April 5. What is a qbit?: *Quantum computing is based on different mathematics and different hardware from conventional, binary computing*. Available at http://mybroadband.co.za/news/hardware/11987-What-qbit.html?print. Accessed 19 Jan 2011.

Kontos, Kosta, BSc (CompSci) (UCT), MBA (UCT). Managing Director (MD) of Kontos Technologies.

Lymer, Andrew, and John Hasseldine. 2002. *The international taxation system*. Boston/Dordrecht/London: Kluwer Academic Publishers.

McKenzie, Alastair. 2008, August. *GST – A practical guide* (Edition 8). Auckland: CCH New Zealand Limited, A Wolters Kluwer Business.

Oxford Dictionaries, *Prohibition*. Available at http://english.oxforddictionaries.com/view/entry/m_en_gb0665350?rskey=UcwQWR&result=2#m_en_gb0665350.004. Accessed 17 Jan 2011.

Pinto, Dale. 2003. *E-Commerce and source-based income taxation*. Amsterdam: IBFD Publications.

Rendahl, Pernilla. 2009. *Cross-border consumption taxation of digital supplies*. Amsterdam: IBFD.

Second Life. *Value added tax*. Available at http://secondlife.com/corporate/vat.php. Accessed 13 Jan 2011.

Wisegeek.com. *What is second Life?* Available at http://www.wisegeek.com/what-is-second-life.htm. Accessed 11 July 2010.

Part VI
Practical Examples

This part will take cognizance of diverse case studies the VAT legislations of which (namely New Zealand, South Africa and the EU VAT Directive where possible) may be appraised in terms of efficacy and practicality of VAT application within an eCommerce environment. Furthermore, Part VI will also include a comparative study of the effectiveness of income tax versus VAT imposition on the equivalent transaction. A further case study will be included citing only VAT implications by reason of the thought challenging technology circumstances pertaining to that case study.

While imposition of income tax devolves upon the supplier and VAT upon the end consumer (even if the supplier is obligated in certain circumstances to collect the VAT), a comparative study affords an incisive perception of the tax complications inherent to technology.[1]

Transfer pricing, thin capitalisation and controlled foreign company provisions will not be included in the analysis as same falls outside the scope of this paper, but will be discussed briefly under Part VII of this paper. Where an income tax analysis is performed, the analysis will be limited to 'residence' and 'source' principles as discussed under Parts III and IV of this paper. Accordingly, 'residence' and 'source' principles will both be applied regardless of whether the jurisdictions being analysed utilise 'residence' or 'source' based principles.

Where the analysis demonstrates the possibility of double taxation, the OECD Double Tax Agreements principles may be applied for the purpose of establishing which country has taxing rights under such circumstances.

---

[1]As previously stated, this chapter will examine diverse legislations (including definitions and relevant legislative sections) within the compass of application of those legislations to diverse case studies. Scrutiny of diverse case studies affords the opportunity of examining application of VAT in diverse circumstances.

Chapter 22
Case Study: Google AdWords

Abstract A Google office located in, for example, Ireland, provides 'AdWords' programming services for eRetailers located in, for example, New Zealand.

To determine location of 'central management and control', requisites established by the De Beers case (De Beers Consolidated Mines Ltd v Howe (Surveyor of Taxes) (1906) AC 455 [UK]. The De Beers case was discussed in 9.2.2., Part III of this paper [p92]) may be applied to Google. The USA applies place of incorporation to determine residence of a company, deeming Google Ireland propter hoc a USA resident company. As Google is a global company, residence of shareholders would presumably be in multiple jurisdictions.

With the amelioration of technology business operations are carried on in multiple jurisdictions through and within the virtual world. Google's operations are globally extensive making it difficult to restrict its 'economic nexus' to a single jurisdiction. Minute books are reduced to mere record keeping and no longer serve as evidence of a meeting's location. In terms of 'permanent establishment', programmers may be physically located anywhere in the world and may carry out income earning activities within Second Life for, exempli gratia, Google Ireland. The OECD issued commentary that the location of the ISP may constitute a 'permanent establishment'. However, through 'load shedding' Google servers may be located in numerous jurisdictions.

The sustained inconstancy of facts reflecting the unstoppable amelioration of technology precipitates increasing difficulty in the determining of 'residence' and 'source'.

22.1 Background Facts

Google's headquarters are located in California, USA, but due to Google's growth and dominance as an Internet search engine, Google has extended its offices globally.[1] eRetailers, or any user for that matter, may contract with Google

[1]Google's offices span over six continents. *"[C]orporate headquarters, fondly nicknamed the Googleplex, is located in Mountain View, California. Today it's one of [Google's] many offices around the globe."*

[Google *The Google Culture* Available at http://www.google.com/corporate/culture.html **[Accessed 19/01/2011]**].

A.M. Bardopoulos, *eCommerce and the Effects of Technology on Taxation*,
Law, Governance and Technology Series 22, DOI 10.1007/978-3-319-15449-7_22

with regard to the use of Google 'AdWords'[2] which is a form of electronic advertising.

AdWords assist with directing, for example, eConsumers to eRetailers' websites where the eRetailers' commodities match the eConsumers' Google search. Google, in turn, invoices the eRetailer for the cost of 'AdWord' advertising.

Situations may arise whereby a Google office located in, for example, Ireland, provides 'AdWord' programming services for eRetailers located in, for example, New Zealand or South Africa. In such circumstances, while Google may have an office in New Zealand or South Africa, Google Ireland is providing the service.

The following assumptions have been made for the purpose of illustrating income tax and VAT implications consequent to such an eventuality:

(i) For the purpose of this case study, only AdWords programmed for eRetailers will be examined. eRetailers carrying on business activities in both New Zealand and South Africa whereby the eRetailers are registered VAT/GST vendors in each respective country will be examined. Google Ireland, on the other hand, is a registered VAT vendor in Ireland only.
(ii) Board meetings do not necessarily occur in one venue and Google may utilise technology for the purpose of hosting management meetings pertaining to the 'effective management' of Google. Due to the global size of Google, it is assumed that the directors rarely meet in one location for the purpose of making management decisions, and, furthermore, meetings may take place primarily via means of teleconference, videoconference, and possibly even in Second Life.
(iii) The Google branch located in Ireland will be referred to as Google Ireland and the Google Headquarters located in the USA will be referred to as Google.
(iv) It is assumed that Google Ireland is merely a branch of Google USA and is, therefore, a USA incorporated company. Google Ireland is not effectively managed in Ireland nor is it incorporated in Ireland.
(v) Google utilises numerous servers located globally.

---

[2]The following extract is from Google's explanation as to what a Google AdWord is:

> *AdWords ads are displayed along with search results when someone searches Google using one of your keywords. Ads appear under 'Sponsored links' in the side column of a search page, and may also appear in additional positions above the free search results. That way, you'll be advertising to an audience that's already interested in your business. You can also choose to display your ads on Display Network sites in the growing Google Network. And, you can choose the exact Display Network placements where you'd like your ad to appear, or you can let contextual targeting match your keywords to content.*
>
> *You can choose from a variety of ad formats, including text, image, and video ads, and easily track your ad performance using the reports available in your account.*
>
> *There's no minimum monthly charge with AdWords – just a nominal activation fee. Learn more about the cost of advertising with Google AdWords. Alternatively, you can watch this short, online course now and get step-by-step instructions on how to create an AdWords account…*

Google *What is Google AdWords?* Available at http://adwords.google.com/support/aw/bin/answer.py?hl=en&answer=6084 [Accessed 19/01/2010].

(vi) Google Ireland develops the Google 'AdWords' in Ireland for each eRetailer. That is, the physical work is carried out in Ireland. It is assumed that Google Ireland utilises Google's global servers.

(vii) The eRetailer 'initiates' the supply by contracting with Google Ireland to develop the desired 'AdWords'. Regardless of how the consideration is determined, consideration is paid to Google Ireland in return for the 'AdWords'.

The below illustrates the structure and background facts:

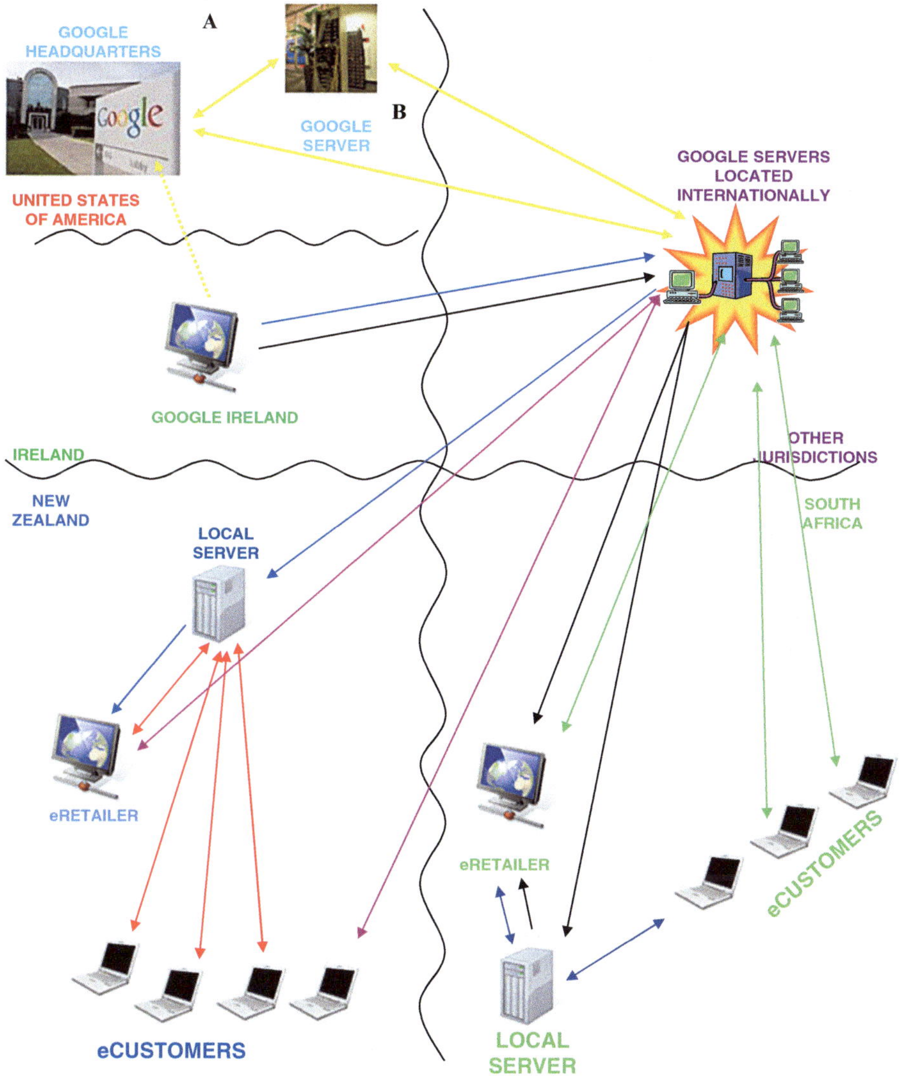

A = Picture of Google's headquarter offices in California, USA. Available at http://blogs.sfweekly.com/thesnitch/2010/08/google_protest_net_neutrality.php [Accessed 20/01/2011]. B = Picture of a Google Server. Available at http://www.destination360.com/google/google-server [Accessed 20/01/2011].

22.2 Income Tax Implications of Residence and Source

Prior to examining the application of traditional 'residence' or 'source' base principles, the income tax implication of 'residence' and 'source' will be examined. For imposition of income tax on basis of residence, the residence of Google Ireland must be determined. As examined in Part III of this paper various tests may be applied for the purpose of determining residence of a company, the points at issue being the place of incorporation, the place of effective management or the place where the actual business operations are carried on. The USA applies place of incorporation to determine residence of a company, deeming Google Ireland *propter hoc* a USA resident company. Ireland applies either place of incorporation or place of central management and control. The latter is also supported by the OECD for the purpose of determining 'residence' of a company.

The 'central management and control' "*ordinarily coincides with the place where the directors of the company exercise their power and authority (which will generally be where they meet)*".[3] Thus, in determining the location of 'central management and control' of Google Ireland, the various factors, as established by the De Beers case,[4] are examined and applied:

(i) *"Place of incorporation"*[5]

This has already been established as the USA.

(ii) *"Place of residence of shareholders and directors"*[6]

As Google is a global company, applying the residence of shareholders test would presumably result in multiple jurisdictions qualifying as the residence of Google Ireland. Owing to the structure of Google and the manner in which Google operates, the residence of the directors should not be a decisive factor in determining the residence of Google. The exact country of residence of each director is uncertain, and while it may be assumed that the majority of the directors reside in the USA, Google may have non-USA resident directors as well.

(iii) *"Where the business operations take place"*[7]

"*Where the business operations take place*"[8] is an alternative test to determine the jurisdiction based on the location of where the 'central management and control'

---

[3]op cit OECD *Taxation and Electronic Commerce, Implementing the Ottawa Taxation Framework Conditions* (2001), France p146.

[4]De Beers Consolidated Mines Ltd v Howe (Surveyor of Taxes) (1906) AC 455 [UK]. The De Beers case was discussed in 9.2.2., Part III of this paper [p92].

[5]supra.

[6]supra.

[7]De Beers Consolidated Mines Ltd v Howe (Surveyor of Taxes) (1906) AC 455 [UK].

[8]supra.

occurs. The location of where the "*directors of the company exercise their power and authority*", while a well supported principle in terms of the De Beers case and various other international cases which upheld the De Beers case principle, may become an increasingly difficult test to apply by reason of the ability of directors to exercise their power and authority while in multiple jurisdictions.

The location of where actual business operations are carried on was held by the Northern Australia Pastoral case as being the location of residence for a company despite directors' meetings being held in a different location. However, due to the structure of Google, it is plausible that the business operations of Google Ireland are carried on in both Ireland and the USA. Programming, management, administration, etc. relating to Google Ireland may be carried on in the virtual world by programmers, administrators, etc. located in the USA. For argument's sake, however, it will be assumed that as Google Ireland is a branch located in Ireland, all Google Ireland business operations are carried on in Ireland, therefore qualifying Ireland as the jurisdiction of residence. But while such an assumption may be made for argument's sake it is, nevertheless, important to bear in mind that with the amelioration of technology it will become increasingly plausible for business operations to be carried on in multiple jurisdictions through and by the means of the virtual world and within the virtual world itself.

(iv) *"Where the financial dealings of the company occurred"*[9]

Determining the jurisdiction in which Google boasts the strongest 'economic nexus' may be an effective means of determining the residence of Google. However, such a means of determining residence can only be transient if not already becoming obsolete owing to the rapidly ameliorating globalisation of Google's business operations. Indeed, Google's operations are globally extensive and continue to globally unfurl at an exponential rate, making it increasingly difficult to restrict Google's 'economic nexus' to a single jurisdiction.

(v) *"Where the seal and minute books of the company [are] kept"*[10]

Prior to the daunting amelioration of precocious technology which facilitates the phenomenon of the concurrent multijurisdictional meeting, the location of the minute books constituted unarguable evidence of the location of 'central management and control' meetings. However, the location of the minute books no longer dictates the location of effective management meetings as meetings and decisions may occur via teleconference, videoconference or even in Second Life. The minute books have been reduced to mere record keeping and no longer serve as evidence of a meeting's location.

In terms of the above, Google Ireland is incorporated in the USA, but the business operations, for the sake of argument may be assumed, at the present juncture, to take place in Ireland. In such circumstances Google Ireland will be considered a USA

---

[9]supra.

[10]De Beers Consolidated Mines Ltd v Howe (Surveyor of Taxes) (1906) AC 455 [UK].

resident and an Irish resident. Assuming a standard OECD double tax agreement were in effect between the USA and Ireland, application of the OECD tie-breaker clause may not prove to be of much assistance as the tie-breaker examines the 'place of effective management' of the company. As discussed above, it may become ever increasingly difficult to determine Google's' place of effective management or even location of where actual business operations occur as same may occur virtually within the virtual world, thus rendering 'residence basis' for determining income taxation useless and ineffective.

Application of the 'source-based' principle may ostensibly be more effective and efficient in comparison to the 'residence basis' test, it is, however, ineffective in its own right. As examined in Part IV[11] of this paper, Vogel deems 'source' to be the "*state that in some way or other is connected to the production of the income in question, to the state where value is added to a good*".[12] Other definitions include the "*place of income generating activity*"[13] and "*the country in which the business conducts its trade and earns its income is usually referred to as the 'source country*'".[14] In terms of Google, AdWord programmes provided to the New Zealand and South African eRetailers may be adapted and tailored by programmers in Ireland, however, the AdWord programming is only possible because of the manner in which Google conducts its trade, which is not located solely in Ireland. However, in terms of the 'entitlement theory' "*it is the source country as the 'place of income-generating activity' rather than the country where the income-producer resides... that economically contributes to the production of income...* ".[15] Regardless of the 'entitlement theory', the 'origin' of the income needs to be determined and application of the 'permanent establishment' concept is a well supported method of attributing profits of an enterprise to the 'source' country.

In terms of application of 'permanent establishment' to the current set of facts and circumstances, Google Ireland satisfies the 'permanent establishment' requirement in Ireland as Google Ireland has a 'place of business' which is fixed and through which business is 'carried out'. However, for argument's sake, assuming that by reason of the proliferation of technology Google conducts all its activities in Second Life, would such a migration have an impact on establishing whether a 'permanent establishment' is located in Ireland? Google may continue to have a physical work location for programmers, *et cetera*, however, such programmers may just as well be physically located anywhere in the world and may carry out income earning activities within Second Life for, *exempli gratia*, Google Ireland.

[11]Refer to 12.1., Part IV of this paper [p115].

[12]op cit Pinto, Dale *E-Commerce and Source-Based Income Taxation* (2003), Netherlands, p48.

[13]supra.

[14]Op cit Pinto, p48.

[15]idem p36.

Second Life also creates the opportunity for programmers to 'work from home' as the 'office' is within Second Life which may be accessed anywhere. Assuming 'permanent establishment' cannot be determined in the traditional sense, the OECD has issued commentary that the location of the ISP may constitute a 'permanent establishment'. Applying such commentary to the above facts and circumstances, Google Ireland utilises Google servers located in numerous jurisdictions. In terms of 'load-shedding' the same server may not be used each time the New Zealand or South African eRetailers' AdWords are accessed.

22.3 Efficacy of Applying Income Tax 'Residence' or 'Source' Provisions

In the application of the traditional 'residence' or 'source' based principles to the current set of facts and circumstances, both 'residence' and 'source' may still be ascertainable, however, 'residence' is less effective and efficient than 'source' principles. It is, nevertheless, crucial to be cognizant of the assumption that Google's business operations will adapt to technological amelioration. Present difficulty to determine the location of 'effective management' may be imputed to current communication technology. Furthermore, determining 'residence' in terms of traditional principles may be achieved by applying 'residence' tests other than location of 'effective management'. The sustained inconstancy of facts reflecting the unstoppable amelioration of technology precipitates increasing difficulty in the determining of 'residence' or 'source'.

Cognizance should be taken of the divergent manner in which businesses such as Google may operate in the future due to technological amelioration. Google, on account of company principles and staff policy may continue to utilise physical buildings in order to provide employees with a 'Google environment'. However, an employee working for Google Australia may no longer need to relocate to Australia to carry out his employment duties as work may be performed within the virtual world. The establishment of the 'Google environment' comprising provision of food, entertainment and overall ambience located in a physical building may not be sufficient to justify residence or source of income earning activities. However, that being said, this point at issue can only be debated hypothetically and cannot at the present juncture be satisfactorily resolved as it is contingent upon ameliorating technology.

22.4 Applying VAT to the Google AdWord Services

For the purpose of analysing the VAT implications the supply must be examined, and it must be determined whether the supply constitutes a service or good and whether such supply is taxable. The EU VAT Directive will be applied for the purpose of determining the VAT implication in Ireland. In other words, the assumption will be made that the Irish VAT system is identical to the EU VAT Directive with no variances for the purpose of this case study. Thereafter the New Zealand GST and South African VAT implications will be examined with regard to the supply each respective eRetailer is receiving from Google Ireland.

The application of VAT in respect of the Google AdWords sequence of events may be illustrated as follows:

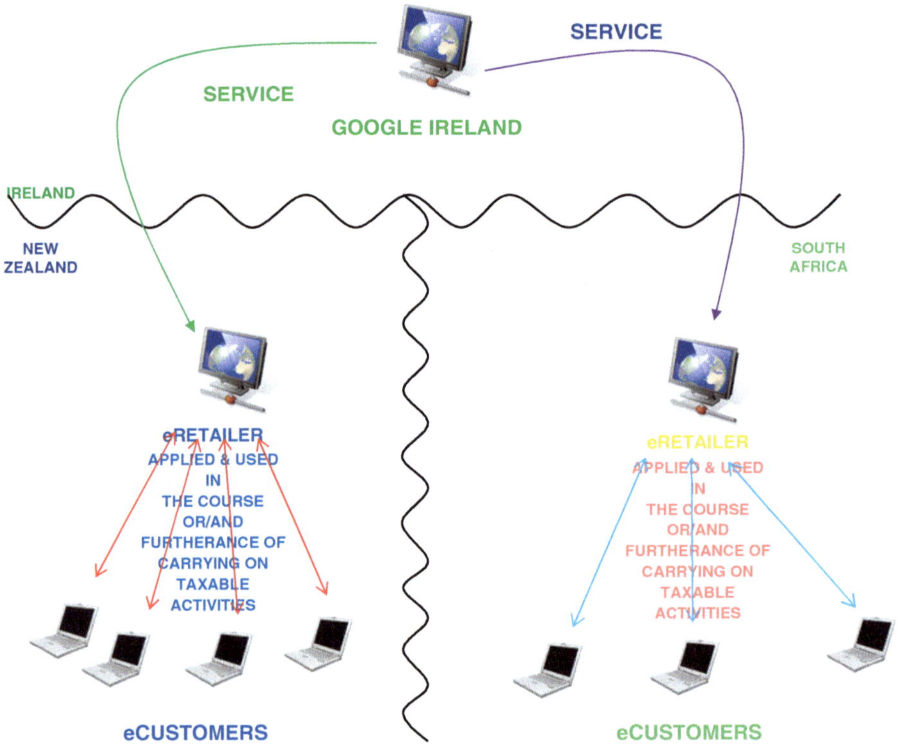

22.4.1 Application of the EU VAT Directive

AdWords, a form of advertising space, constitutes electronically supplied services in terms of Annex II of the EU VAT Directive. The service meets the criteria of a taxable transaction as the service is procured for a consideration and, assuming Google Ireland is registered for VAT, is made by a taxable person. Application of the EU place of supply rules assists with determining where the supply occurs and, therefore, where the service will be subject to EU VAT. As indicated previously,

Google Ireland is supplying the services to registered vendors in New Zealand and South Africa. Therefore, the supply constitutes B2B transactions internationally, but not within the EU community.

The B2B general rule as set out under Article 44 of the EU VAT Directive states that *"[t]he place of supply of services to a taxable person acting as such shall be the place where that person has established his business . . . "*.[16] However, if the perspective adopted is that the supply is not to a 'taxable person'[17] in that the New Zealand and South African eRetailers are not registered for VAT within the EU, then the B2C general rule, as set out under Article 45 of the EU VAT Directive, may apply whereby *"[t]he place of supply of services to a non-taxable person shall be the place where the supplier has established his business . . . "*.[18] It is unlikely that the former approach would be applied, but both rules will, nevertheless, depending on the circumstances, apply "*unless the use and enjoyment override rule applies*".[19]

Current provisions in respect of electronically supplied services to non-taxable persons not established within the Community, namely Article 59(k)[20] of the EU VAT Directive, will be replaced by Article 58 of the EU VAT Directive as from 1 January 2015. As such, Article 58 of the EU VAT Directive will be applied to the above point in question due to the pending 'obsoletion' of the current provisions. In terms of Article 58 of the EU VAT Directive, *"[t]he place of supply of ['electronically supplied services, in particular those referred to in Annex II . . . '] to a non-taxable person shall be the place where that person is established, has his permanent address or usually resides.... "*.[21] Currently the location of the two eRetailers may be determined by traditional methods, however, assuming that both eRetailers adapt their business structures to technology causing increasing difficulty in traditional determining of the recipient's permanent address or residence, the IP addresses of both eRetailers would assist in demonstrating that both are established outside the EU community. Thus, the electronically supplied services, the AdWords programmes, will not be subject to VAT in the EU or alternatively will be subject to VAT at the rate of zero per cent.

---

[16] Article 44 of the EU VAT Directive 2006/112/EC.

[17] 'Taxable person', as defined under Article 9 of the EU VAT Directive 2006/112/EC, is "*any person who independently, carries out in any place any economic activity, whatever the purpose or results of that activity*".

[18] Article 45 of the EU VAT Directive 2006/112/EC.

[19] loc cit Terra, Ben and Kajus, Julie *Guide to EU VAT Directives – Volume 1*, Amsterdam, p510.

[20] Article 59(k) of the EU VAT Directive: "*[t]he place of supply of ['electronically supplied services, in particular those referred to in Annex II . . . '] to a non-taxable person who is established or has his permanent address or usually resides outside the Community, shall be the place where that person is established, has his permanent address or usually resides . . . "*.

[21] Article 58 of the EU VAT Directive 2008/8/EC.

22.4.2 Application of the New Zealand GST Legislation

As the provision of AdWords programs is an "*. . . activity which is carried on continuously or regularly . . . and involves . . . the supply of . . . services to any other person for a consideration . . .*",[22] the supply constitutes a 'taxable activity' as defined by the New Zealand legislation. New Zealand GST is imposed "*. . . on the supply . . . in New Zealand of goods and services . . . by a registered person in the course or furtherance of a taxable activity carried on by that person . . .*".[23] Furthermore, "*. . . goods and services shall be deemed to be supplied in New Zealand if the supplier is resident in New Zealand . . .*".[24]

If Google carries on any taxable activity in New Zealand "*while having any fixed or permanent place in New Zealand relating to that taxable activity*"[25] and the supply of taxable services exceeds the GST registration threshold, Google would be required to register for GST in New Zealand and impose GST on the supply of AdWords programs. If the supply was, however, "*made in New Zealand by a registered person in the course or furtherance of a taxable activity, [such supply] would be a taxable supply*".[26] If the AdWords program was supplied by a New Zealand registered supplier in New Zealand, such supply would constitute a taxable activity subject to GST. Therefore, in the circumstances where the non-resident supplier does not qualify to register for GST and, therefore, is not required to impose GST on the supply, the New Zealand eRetailer is required to account for the GST in terms of the reverse charge mechanism.[27]

In terms of section 5B of the NZ GST Act the "*supply of services that is treated . . . as being made in New Zealand is treated as being made by the recipient of the supply in the course or furtherance of a taxable activity carried on by the recipient*". Within the parameters of the current set of facts, it may be assumed that the New Zealand eRetailer is a registered GST vendor. However, if the supply was to a non-registered vendor, and the supply to the New Zealand recipient exceeded the registration threshold, then the New Zealand recipient would be required to

[22]Section 6(1)(a) of the NZ GST Act, No. 141 of 1985 (as amended).

[23]Section 8(1) of the NZ GST Act, No. 141 of 1985 (as amended).

[24]Section 8(2) of the NZ GST Act, No. 141 of 1985 (as amended).

[25]Definition of '***resident***' as defined in Section 2 of the NZ GST Act, No. 141 of 1985 (as amended).

[26]op cit *New Zealand Goods and Services Tax Legislation 2010* (Edition 24), New Zealand, p18.

[27]Reverse Charge Mechanism: "*a person who receives imported services is required to self-assess GST on the value of those services*" provided that "*the services are supplied by a non-resident to a resident [and that] the supply of those services, if made in New Zealand by a registered person in the course or furtherance of a taxable activity, would be a taxable supply*".

[op cit *New Zealand Goods and Services Tax Legislation 2010* (Edition 24), p18].

register for GST and account for the output tax in accordance with the reverse charge mechanism.[28]

Thus, the imported services used by the New Zealand eRetailer in the course or furtherance of his enterprise will be subject to NZ GST, accountable by the eRetailer. Regardless of the manner in which the AdWords are provided or programmed, for example, whether in Ireland or the virtual world, a New Zealand eRetailer is consuming or using the services for which GST is correctly imposed and accounted for with certainty as the 'place of supply' is provided by the 'place of supply' rules. The GST/VAT rules, regulations and laws in terms of this supply have allowed for an equitable application, imposition and collection of taxation.

22.4.3 Application of the South African VAT Legislation

As previously discussed, South Africa is one of the few countries without a place of supply rule. Furthermore, in terms of New Zealand legislation a 'resident' carrying on taxable activities exceeding the registration threshold is required to register for GST. In terms of the SA legislation any person carrying on an "enterprise" which exceeds the compulsory registration threshold is required to register for VAT.

"Enterprise" is defined as *"... any ... activity which is carried on continuously or regularly by any person in the Republic [of South Africa] or party in the Republic [of South Africa] and in the course or furtherance of which goods or services are supplied to any other person for a consideration ...".*[29] Therefore, unlike NZ where the recipient is required to register where the 'imported services' exceed the registration threshold in terms of the 'reverse charge mechanism', the 'reverse charge mechanism' applies until such time that the supplier is liable to register for VAT in SA. However, comparable to NZ, SA applies the reverse charge mechanism but with wider scope is that applied in NZ. That is, SA applies the reverse charge mechanism to both B2B and B2C transactions, including services provided the services qualify as "imported services".

"Imported services" are defined under section 1 of the SA VAT Act as "*a supply of services that is made by a supplier who is resident or carries on business outside the Republic [of South Africa] to a recipient who is a resident of the Republic [of South Africa] to the extent that such services are utilised or consumed in the Republic [of South Africa] otherwise than for the purpose of making taxable supplies*".[30]

Therefore, within the parameters of this Google case study, the supply of the AdWords program is to a registered South African VAT vendor who utilises or

[28]op cit McKenzie, Alastair. *GST – A Practical Guide* (Edition 8) (2008), New Zealand, p111.

[29]Section 1 of the SA VAT Act, No. 89 of 1991 (as amended).

[30]Section 1 of the SA VAT Act, No. 89 of 1991 (as amended).

consumes the service for the purpose of making taxable supplies. The AdWords are used to advertise the South African eRetailer's business. As such, the services fall outside the scope of the VAT legislation as they do not meet the definition of "imported services". Therefore, the South African eRetailer will not be accountable for the output VAT on the supply, but by the same token the eRetailer will not be entitled to a VAT input claim as the expense does not qualify as a taxable expense.

The practicality of the exclusion of such services from the definition of 'imported services' is that it does not result in a financial loss for the fiscus as no money would actually pass across to the revenue authorities. If such supplies were not excluded the eRetailer would be accountable for the output tax on his VAT return, and on the very same VAT return claim the corresponding input tax claim resulting in an 'in-and-out', which in itself would constitute simply a paper trail record of the transaction.

If, for argument's sake, the South African eRetailer were not a registered VAT vendor, such supply from Google Ireland would constitute a defined "imported service". The eRetailer would then be obligated to account for the output tax arising on the 'imported service' supply. The VAT rules, regulations and laws in terms of this supply have allowed for an equitable application, imposition and collection of taxation.

22.5 Effectiveness of Applying VAT Provisions

Application of traditional income tax provisions may, to a certain extent, still be effectively applied depending upon the facts and circumstances. However, 'residence' provisions may be easily manipulated and the slightest change in any facts or circumstances engenders increasing difficulty in the application of both 'residence' and 'source' income tax provisions.

However, the application of VAT/GST was relatively unaffected by changes or the technological means by which the supply was made. In each respective circumstance in respect of the supply of services to New Zealand and South Africa, the supply would be, depending upon the EU jurisdiction where the supply was made, either not subject to VAT or else zero rated for VAT purposes in the EU. The supply of services would then be subject to the reverse charge mechanism in Ireland, assuming Google Ireland did not qualify to register for GST, and would be subject to GST where the recipient is a registered, or required to be registered, GST vendor. The supply of services to the South African eRetailer would be subject to the reverse charge mechanism, regardless of whether the recipient is registered or not, where the supply qualifies as an "imported service" and to the extent that Google Ireland is not required to register for VAT. If Google Ireland were required to register for VAT in South Africa, then the supply of services would still be subject to VAT but Google Ireland, and not the recipient, would be required to impose, collect and account for the VAT.

Bibliography

Primary Sources

Statutes

European Union VAT Directive 2006/112/EC.

European Union VAT Council Directive 2008/8/EC.

New Zealand Goods and Services Tax Act, No. 141 of 1985 (as amended).

New Zealand. *Goods and services tax legislation 2010* (Edition 24), Auckland: CCH A Wolters Kluwer Business.

South Africa Value-Added Tax Act, No. 89 of 1991 (as amended).

Secondary Sources

Google. *The Google culture.* Available at http://www.google.com/corporate/culture.html. Accessed 19 Jan 2011.

Google. *What is Google AdWords?* Available at http://adwords.google.com/support/aw/bin/answer.py?hl=en&answer=6084. Accessed 19 Jan 2010.

McKenzie, Alastair. 2008, August. *GST – A practical guide* (Edition 8). Auckland: CCH New Zealand Limited, A Wolters Kluwer Business.

New Zealand. 2010. *Goods and services tax Legislation 2010* (Edition 24). Auckland: CCH A Wolters Kluwer Business.

OECD. 2001. *Taxation and electronic commerce, implementing the Ottawa taxation framework conditions.* Paris: OECD Publications.

Picture of a Google Server. Available at http://www.destination360.com/google/google-server. Accessed 20 Jan 2011.

Picture of Google's headquarter offices in California, USA. Available at http://blogs.sfweekly.com/thesnitch/2010/08/google_protest_net_neutrality.php. Accessed 20 Jan 2011.

Pinto, Dale. 2003. *E-Commerce and source-based income taxation.* Amsterdam: IBFD Publications.

Terra, Ben and Julie Kajus. 2010. *A guide to the European VAT directives, Introduction to European VAT 2010*, vol 1. Amsterdam: IBFD Publishers.

Chapter 23
Case Study: Software Consultant

Abstract A South African software consultant (X) enters into a business transaction with a Swedish company (Z). Z develops copyright software. X performs tests on the software to ensure that the program functions correctly.

Z obstructs extraneous downloading of the software. X accesses the software by logging into Z's network. The following assumptions are made apropos this case study:

- X is a registered VAT vendor in South Africa.
- Z is a registered VAT vendor in Sweden
- X's consulting fee does not exceed the Swedish registration threshold and X has performed no other consulting work in Sweden or Europe.

Through the Internet X discharges his services to the Swedish Company's network while being physically present in South Africa.

Section 11(2)(l) of the South African VAT Act, No. 89 of 1991 (as amended) necessitates administrative burden of proof which is complicated by technology in that the service is rendered electronically. Section 11(2)(k) of the SA VAT Act (1991) states that "*a . . . supply of services . . . [will] be charged with tax at the rate of zero percent where . . . the services are physically rendered elsewhere than in the Republic . . .*" (Section 11(2)(k) of the South African VAT Act, No. 89 of 1991 (as amended)).

If services 'physically rendered' outside South Africa are zero rated for VAT purposes in terms of traditional application, then if 'physical presence' in or through the virtual world is acknowledged the same must apply. *Consensus omnium* of physical presence in or through the virtual world would be commensurate with current business and technological amelioration and demonstrates VAT's ability to adapt to technology rather than forcing technology to adapt to tax.

23.1 Background Facts [Structure A]

A South African software program consultant enters into a business transaction with a Swedish company with regard to copyrighted material. The Swedish Company develops copyrighted software for business clients. The South African consultant,

A.M. Bardopoulos, *eCommerce and the Effects of Technology on Taxation*, Law, Governance and Technology Series 22, DOI 10.1007/978-3-319-15449-7_23

Kosta, performs a string of tests on the software to ensure that the programme functions correctly before the programme is released to the Swedish Company's business clients.

To guarantee the security of the copyrighted programs, the Swedish company unmitigatedly obstructs the downloading of the software onto any computer or server extraneous to the Swedish Company. *Id est*, Kosta is unable to save the programme, or a part thereof, on his local network and all work is performed on the Swedish Company's server and network at all times. Kosta gains access to the software by logging onto the Swedish network. The cross-border transaction may be illustrated by the following brief organogram:

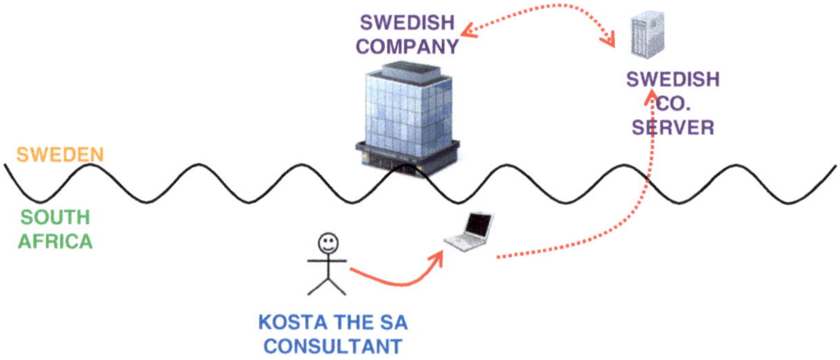

The following assumptions have been made in respect of this case study:

(i) The South African consultant is a registered VAT vendor in South Africa.
(ii) The Swedish Company is a registered VAT vendor in Sweden.
(iii) The consulting fee received with regard to the services rendered does not exceed the Swedish registration threshold and the South African consultant has preformed no other consulting work in Sweden or Europe.

23.2 Applying VAT to the Cross-Border Electronic Consulting Fee

The point at issue in this case study is not whether the Swedish Company is carrying on an enterprise in South Africa in respect of VAT, because in this case Kosta is the supplier and the Swedish Company is the recipient. Because Kosta is an independent consultant carrying on such activity continuously in South Africa in the course or furtherance of which activity services are supplied for a consideration, Kosta is by definition carrying on an 'enterprise' in South Africa. The mere fact that Kosta meets the 'enterprise' definition in South Africa does not preclude him from qualifying as a vendor in Sweden. As previously discussed, it is possible for a person to qualify as a vendor in numerous jurisdictions.

The point at issue in this case study is that services rendered are unique to recently current technology. In the absence of Internet and a virtual world, Kosta would have to physically travel to Sweden to perform his services. However, by means of the Internet and the virtual world Kosta discharges his services to the Swedish Company's network while being present in body in South Africa. All the services are '*physically performed*'[1] in Sweden as nothing may be downloaded onto the South African hard drive, network or server as all services may only be executed on the Swedish network located in Sweden. Therefore, it may be submitted that Kosta achieves *'physical presence'* in Sweden through the Internet as his action constitutes "*an object of action ... pertaining to the object or end as the cause or action*".[2]

However, to apply VAT legislation within the parameters of such circumstances technology related principles should be acknowledged. Although this paper submits that taxation principles should be adapted to technology and not technology that should be adapted to taxation principles, traditional application of VAT legislation will be examined first for the purpose of determining VAT implications with regard to supply of services to the Swedish Company.

23.2.1 Traditional Application of SA VAT in Cross-Border Transactions

Kosta, a South African VAT vendor is providing services from South Africa to Sweden. Therefore, Kosta is 'exporting' his services to Sweden. 'Exported services' may be zero rated for VAT purposes as provided in terms of section 11(2) of the SA VAT Act. Section 11(2)(l) of the SA VAT Act provides that "*a ... supply of services ... be charged with tax at the rate of zero per cent where ... the services are supplied to a person who is not a resident of the Republic [of South Africa], not being services which are supplied directly ... to the said person or any other person ... if the said person or such other person is in the Republic [of South Africa] at the time the services are rendered ...*".[3]

For the purpose of the SA VAT Act, 'resident' is defined in terms of the SA Income Tax Act[4] as follows: "*[p]rovided that any other person or any other company shall be deemed to be a resident ... to the extent that such person or company carries on in [SA] ... any enterprise or other activity and has a fixed*

[1]Refer to discussion regarding 'physical presence' and 'physically performed' in Parts II [p39–83] and IV [p109–139] of this paper.

[2]op cit *Shorter Oxford Dictionary on Historical Principles* (1986), p1426.

[3]Section 11(2)(l) of the SA VAT Act, no. 89 of 1991 (as amended).

[4]SA Income Tax Act, No. 58 of 1962 (as amended).

or permanent place in [SA]... relating to such enterprise or other activity".[5] The assumption has been made that the Swedish Company does not qualify as a South African 'resident' for VAT purposes and was not in South Africa at the time Kosta provided his services. If the Swedish Company, for example a director, is present in South Africa at the time Kosta renders his consulting services, and the director's presence relates to the consulting services, there is argument that the services are in fact consumed in South Africa in such circumstances and would be subject to VAT at the South African standard rate.

In such circumstances the consulting fee would be subject to South African VAT at the rate of zero per cent. However, application of section 11(2)(l) of the VAT Act necessitates administrative burden of proof which is complicated by technology in that the service is rendered electronically. Verification of the Swedish Company's status and location in regard to cross-border eCommerce transactions is problematic. Indeed, the administrative aspect is a crucial point at issue in cross-border eCommerce and is possibly the greatest inhibiting constraint in the global growth of VAT as the eTax solution. However, as previously discussed, identifying and verifying locations of supplier and recipient may be achieved through verification of both parties' IP addresses.

23.2.2 Alternative Application of VAT in Cross-Border Transactions Occurring in an eCommerce Environment

Recognition of 'physical presence' in the virtual world or through the virtual world presupposes acquiescence of Kosta physically rendering consulting services in a jurisdiction other than South Africa. In terms of section 11(2)(k) of the SA VAT Act "*a... supply of services... [will] be charged with tax at the rate of zero per cent where... the services are physically rendered elsewhere than in the Republic [of South Africa]...* ".[6] If services 'physically rendered' outside South Africa are zero rated for VAT purposes in terms of traditional application, then if 'physical presence' in or through the virtual world is acknowledged the same must apply. *Consensus omnium* of physical presence in or through the virtual world would be commensurate with current business and technological amelioration and demonstrates VAT's ability to adapt to technology rather than forcing technology to adapt to taxation.

[5]'Resident of the Republic' as defined in section 1 of the SA VAT Act, No. 89 of 1991 (as amended).

[6]Section 11(2)(k) of the SA VAT Act, No. 89 of 1991 (as amended).

23.2.3 Other Possible South African VAT Implications Which Could Arise

The mere fact that the Swedish Company is allowing Kosta to access and utilise its network does not in itself constitute supply of services by the Swedish Company to Kosta. However, assuming the action of connecting to and utilising the Swedish Company's network and server constituted a supply of services by the Swedish Company to Kosta, such supply could constitute 'importing of services' from the Swedish Company. In such circumstances Kosta would be required to account for the output VAT on the supply, provided the supply qualified as an imported service.

However, in terms of the facts provided, Kosta is utilising the service for the purpose of making taxable supplies and, therefore, the supply does not qualify as an 'imported service' and is not subject to VAT in South Africa. If Kosta were not utilising the supply with the intention of making taxable supplies, then Kosta would be required to account for the VAT, provided the supply was made for a consideration.

23.2.4 Swedish VAT Implications

The Swedish 'place of supply' rules are identical to the UK, both emulating the EU VAT Directive as previously discussed under the Jurisdictional Analysis of this paper.[7] In terms of traditional application of VAT provisions the Swedish Company, as the recipient, 'belongs' in Sweden if the Company's "*principal place of business*"[8] is located in Sweden, or if the Swedish Company has "*an establishment other than [a] business establishment, which [nevertheless] has the technical and human resources necessary for providing or receiving services permanently present*",[9] is established as being located in Sweden. Thus, a traditional supply of services to the Swedish Company by a non-EU member state resident will be subject to the general 'place of supply' rules.

The place of supply of services in respect of services provided to business customers "*will be treated as supplied in the country where the business customer is established, and the business customer will account for the VAT under the reverse charge mechanism*".[10] Thus, in terms of the above provision, the Swedish Company,

[7]Refer to 18.1.3. Sweden, Part V of this paper [p194].

[8]loc cit HMRC, *Notice 741A Place of Supply of Services* (2010). Available at http://customs.hmrc.gov.uk/channelsPortalWebApp/channelsPortalWebApp.portal?_nfpb=true&_pageLabel=pageVAT_ShowContent&propertyType=document&id=HMCE_PROD1_029955#downloadopt [Accessed 12/12/2010], p9.

[9]Supra.

[10]loc cit HMRC *VAT: Cross-Border VAT Changes 2010*. Available at http://www.hmrc.gov.uk/vat/cross-border-changes-2010.htm [Accessed 9/12/2010].

'belonging' in Sweden when receiving the supply of services and being the recipient of the service, will be "*liable to account for any output tax on the supply* . . .".[11]

The provision of 'electronically supplied services' is subject to 'special rules' for the fixed purpose of determining the 'place of supply'. Therefore, it must be determined if Kosta's consulting services constitute an 'electronically supplied service' in terms of the following definition:

(i) *"In the first instance [the service] is delivered over the Internet or an electronic network (in other words reliant on the internet or similar network for its provision)"*[12]

Kosta's 'consulting services', which are essentially the testing and accessing of the Swedish Company's software, are reliant on the internet or similar network to provide such service.

(ii) *"The nature of the service in question is heavily dependent on information technology for its supply (in other words the service is essentially automated involving minimal human intervention and in the absence of information technology does not have viability)."*[13]

Accessing the Swedish Company's software would not be viable in the absence of information technology, however, the degree of human intervention may cause the services to fall outside the scope of an 'electronically supplied service'; in which case the general 'place of supply' rules will apply. To determine the level of human intervention in Kosta's consultation it is essential to acquire a comprehensive understanding of the service. If Kosta's consulting services imply indisputable review and examination of program language, then such services would be dependent on human intervention. However, if Kosta's services include assessment of the software by running automated tests, etc., argument could be submitted that the services require 'minimal human intervention'.

Kosta's 'consulting services' cannot be conveniently catalogued in terms of the list of 'supplies covered by the legal text' as provided by the EU VAT Directive. Item 2 of Annex L to the EU VAT Directive covers the supply of '*software and updating thereof*'.[14] The type of services offered by Kosta are not covered by the list of examples accompanying Item 2 of Annex L. However, '*online automated*

[11]op cit McKenzie, Alastair. *GST – A Practical Guide* (Edition 8) (2008), New Zealand p111.

[12]loc cit HMRC *Electronically Supplied Services: A Guide to Interpretation* (April 2003). Available at http://customs.hmrc.gov.uk/channelsPortalWebApp/channelsPortalWebApp.portal?_nfpb=true&_pageLabel=oageVAT_ShowContent&id=HMCE_CL_000907?&propertyType=document #downloadopt [Accessed 12/12/2010], p3.

[13]loc cit HMRC *Electronically Supplied Services: A Guide to Interpretation,* http://customs.hmrc....opt, p3.

[14]Item 2 of Annex L to the EU VAT Directive, Table 1. loc cit HMRC *Electronically Supplied Services: A Guide to Interpretation,* http://customs.hmrc....opt

installation of filters on websites'[15] is included under the list of examples and Kosta's services may be described as 'online automated testing'. However, if the definition of 'electronically supplied services' is applied to the description of Kosta's services then such services may be deemed comparable to Item 2 of Annex L. Furthermore, Annex L does cater for services which are not explicitly listed in terms of Item 6.

Annex L also provides an example list of services which do not meet the definition of 'electronically supplied services' such as the "*supply of services of lawyers and financial consultants and so on, who advise clients through email*"[16] due to the fact that such services rely on "*substantial human intervention and the Internet or electronic network is only used as a means of communication*".[17] Kosta's services may be described as consulting services, however, in terms of the nature of the 'consulting' services 'advice' is not delivered electronically. In terms of the facts provided, Kosta's 'consulting services' should satisfy the definition of 'electronically supplied services'. If the services do not satisfy the definition of 'electronically supplied services' the traditional general 'place of supply' rules will apply as previously stated. In such circumstances, provided the Swedish Company 'belongs' to Sweden, the services will be subject to Swedish VAT and the Swedish Company will be liable to account for the VAT. Alternatively, if it is accepted that the services constitute 'electronically supplied services' the 'place of supply' will be where the services are 'effectively used and enjoyed'.

As defined by the UK HMRC 'effective use and enjoyment' is the "*place where the customer actually consumes the electronically supplied services irrespective of contract, payment or beneficial interest*".[18] Due to the similarities between the UK VAT system and the Swedish VAT system, for the purpose of analysing this case study, it has been assumed that Sweden accepts and applies a similar definition for 'effective use and enjoyment'. It is, therefore, the Swedish Company which is effectively using and enjoying the services rendered by Kosta. Comparable to application of the general 'place of supply' rules, the reverse charge mechanism will apply, provided that Kosta is not liable to register for VAT in Sweden.

23.3 Effectiveness of VAT Provisions

Regardless of whether section 11(2)(l) of the SA VAT Act or section 11(2)(k) of the SA VAT Act is applied, the services rendered by Kosta qualify as 'exported services' subject to VAT at the rate of zero per cent. The services, whether in terms

[15] supra.

[16] Example 2(a) of Table 2 idem.

[17] supra.

[18] op cit HMRC, *Notice 741A Place of Supply of Services*, http://webarchive.nationalarchives.gov.uk/20100202144103/ http://customs.hmrc.gov.uk/channelsPortalWebApp/channelsPortalWebApp.portal?_nfpb=true&_pageLabel=pageVAT_ShowContent&propertyType=document&id=HMCE_PROD1_029955.

of the reverse charge mechanism or because Kosta is required to register for VAT in Sweden, are subject to VAT in Sweden regardless of whether or not the services constitute 'electronically supplied services'. The diverse implications engendered by the above are whether Kosta or the Swedish Company as the recipient is required to account for the VAT and whether the general 'place of supply' rules or the special supply rules apply.

23.4 Income Tax Implications

An examination of income tax implications illustrates the inflexibility of income tax principles in comparison to VAT, thus accentuating the ineffectiveness of income tax in comparison to VAT.

The facts of the current case study allow for the relatively easy application of 'residence' principles for the purpose of determining income tax implications. Application of the 'source' principle is also relatively easy if physical presence in Sweden through the means of the virtual world is not recognised. The ability to be physically present in Sweden through the means of the virtual world may, furthermore, create complications with regard to applying 'source' principles for the fixed purpose of determining income tax.

Furthermore, the above case study is relatively elementary and for the purpose of examining effective application of income tax provisions to the virtual world examination of a more complicated structure is advantageous.

23.4.1 Income Tax Implications of Current Circumstances

Kosta's company is incorporated in South Africa, all the business operations occur in South Africa, and South Africa is Kosta's company's place of effective management. In terms of the current facts and structure, Kosta is defined as a South African resident and as such is taxable in South Africa on his worldwide income. However, while 'residence' is clearly South African, 'source' may be debatable. However, if the ability to be 'physically present' in Sweden through the virtual world is not recognised, then the 'source' of the 'income-generating activity' is South African as that is where Kosta is located and that is where he conducts his consulting services.

However, there is potential to argue that the 'source' is in fact Sweden as Kosta 'physically renders' his service in Sweden through the virtual world, provided such services are carried on through a permanent establishment in Sweden. As previously discussed for the purpose of determining whether the 'income-earning activity' is sourced within a jurisdiction, 'physical presence', an academic point at issue, is an important criterion supported by the OECD for the purpose of determining whether there is a 'permanent establishment' within a jurisdiction. As supported by case law "*permanent [is] a relative term that [is] not synonymous with everlasting*"[19] and "*permanence does not mean that the right to use the place of business must be perpetual*".[20] Kosta will be utilising the Swedish Company's network and server, which is fixed, in "*relationship or connection to a geographical area... [which] suffices to create a permanent establishment if the activity is regularly repeated over a long period of time in the same location, if the work is being performed for the same principal as part of one project...*".[21]

Determining 'source' depends upon the facts of each case and in this case there is potential to support the contention that Sweden is the 'source' of the consulting fees. However, argument supporting Sweden as the 'source' jurisdiction is contentious as it is dependent upon the recognition of the technology industry's virtual world and the ability to be 'physically present' in or through the means of the virtual world.

23.5 Income Tax Implications in Terms of a New-Age Business Structure [Structure B]

A change in business structure will have greater impact on income tax provisions than VAT. For the purpose of demonstrating this point, the facts and framework pertaining to the Case Study – *Software Consultant* will be altered to create a more complicated structure, as illustrated in the organogram provided below.

Kosta no longer provides his services from his South African incorporated and resident company. Kosta forms and incorporates a company, Consulware Co., in Second Life with three other software consultants each located in different jurisdictions. All board, decision and control meetings occur in Second Life in Consulware Co.'s virtual building. If effective management within Second Life is not acknowledged, determining jurisdiction of 'effective management' is impossible. All four directors carry equal authority in all business operations which occur in Second Life or through Second Life.

As in the previous structure all consulting work performed for the Swedish Company is carried out on the Swedish Company's server and network located in Sweden to guarantee protection of copyrighted software being tested, however, in the altered structure Kosta and Connie perform equal amount of tests on the software. All the 'test programmes' utilised by Consulware Co., for the purpose of providing 'consulting services' to clients globally, were discussed and written by all four consultants within Consulware Co.'s virtual offices.

[19] op cit Pinto, Dale *E-Commerce and Source-Based Income Taxation* (2003), Netherlands, p110.

[20] supra.

[21] idem p109.

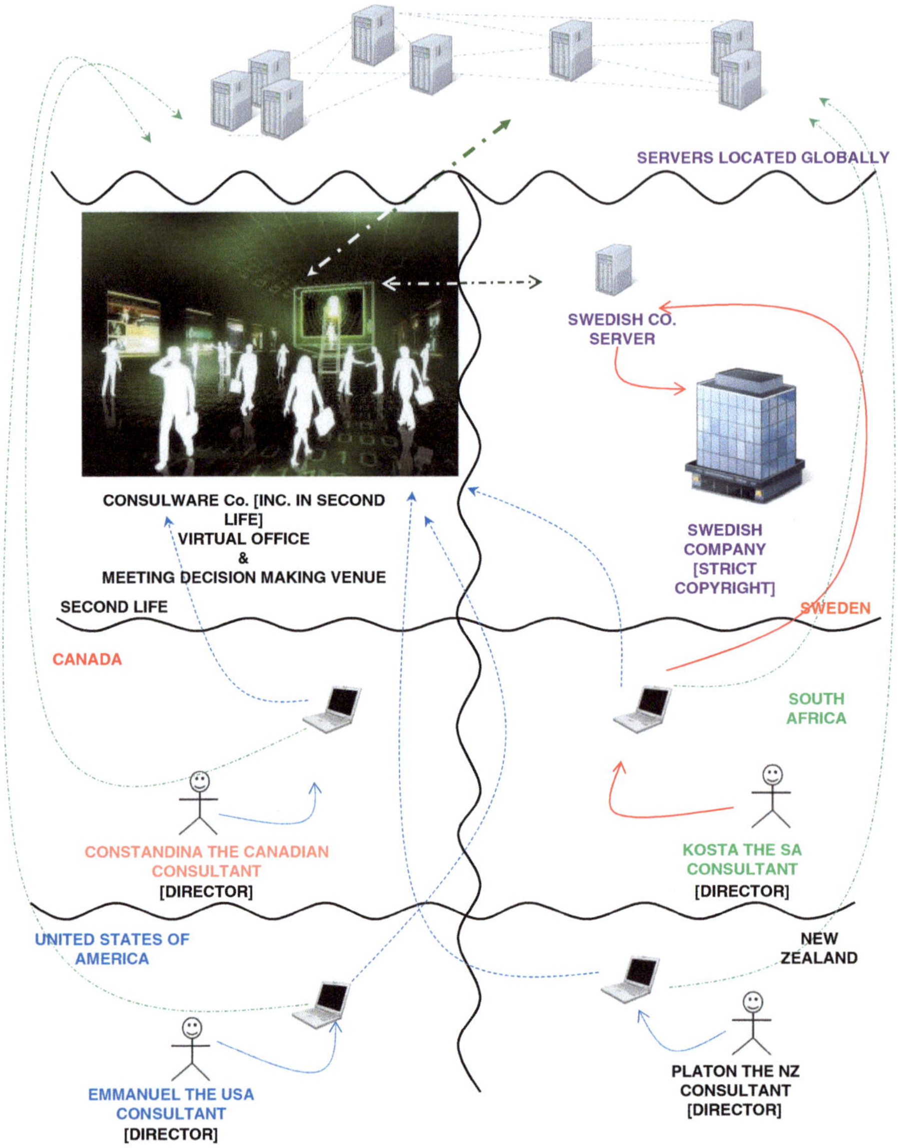

23.5.1 *Income Tax Implication of Change in Business Structure*

Attributable to the diversity of the business structure 'residence' cannot be limited to one jurisdiction. Indeed, the place of management, 'place of effective management', and the place of incorporation are all located within Second Life. The four directors and four shareholders are each located in a different jurisdiction.

Attempting to determine place of residence by determining the location where actual business operations are carried on is not facilitated by the new-age business structure. Consultants provide services of testing and assessing software programmed by other companies. Typically actual business operations are carried on within Second Life. Alternatively, business operations may be performed through the Internet and networks in which case if 'physical presence' in the Internet is acknowledged then actual business operations may be deemed to be carried on globally. If the traditional approach to 'physical presence' is espoused, then actual business operations are deemed to be carried on equally in four diverse jurisdictions thereby rendering application of the 'actual business operation' test obsolete and ineffective.

As illustrated above, application of the 'residence basis' principle to the new-age business structure is problematic and effectually impracticable if 'residence' within the virtual world is not recognised and is, furthermore, not deemed a taxable jurisdiction in its own right.

Attempting to apply 'source basis' principles to a new-age business structure proves to be equally doubtful and impractical in terms of effectiveness. "*[S]ource of income is not the quarter from which it comes but rather the originating cause of its receipt*",[22] however, the 'originating cause' may not necessarily be restricted to one location. Under such circumstances, global case law holds that 'dominant source' will indicate the 'source location'. For the fixed purpose of determining the 'dominant cause', when there is more than one 'originating cause' regarding the generation of income, a distinction must be made between the 'dominant' cause and the 'incidental' cause.[23] The inconvenience of applying 'source basis' to a new-age business structure is the problem of identifying which cause may be viewed as the *'dominant cause'*. The 'dominant cause' may be viewed as the employment of Consulware Co.'s capital which constitutes the test programs utilised in providing the necessary services to clients. Thus, in terms of case law, as the 'dominant cause' relates to the software programs applied by Consulware Co., the location where the software programme was written may constitute the 'source location'. However, the software programming was discussed and written in Consulware Co.'s virtual offices located in Second Life. Failure to recognise technology's virtual world entails agreeing that the software was 'written' in four diverse jurisdictions. Either way, determining the 'source location' in terms of the 'dominant cause' is effectually impractical.

A further test for determining 'source location' is the 'entitlement theory' where "*the source country ... [is] the 'place of [the] income-generating activity'*

---

[22]op cit CIR v Lever Brothers & Unilever 1946 AD 441 [RSA].

[23]ibid Transvaal Associated Hide and Skin Merchants v Collector of Income Tax, Botswana 29 SATC 97 1967 (BCA) [Bots]. As highlighted and discussed in Chap. 12, Part IV of this paper [p115].

rather than the country where the income-producer resides ... that economically contributes to the production of income ...".[24] With regard to the new-age business structure illustrated above there are essentially four income-producers residing in four diverse jurisdictions. The location of the 'income-generating activity' is located within the virtual world.

An alternative test is the location of the server utilised by Consulware Co. to determine the geographical location of Consulware Co.'s 'fixed place of business' and, therefore, Consulware Co.'s 'permanent establishment' and 'source location'. However, in order to ensure effective, accurate, uninterrupted and timeous software testing for clients, Consulware Co., unless otherwise stipulated, utilises several servers located in various jurisdictions to ensure 'load-balancing'. It is only when services are performed for clients with stringent copyright protection regulations that 'a' server may be easily located, as in the case of the Swedish Company's server. Consulware Co. accesses the Swedish Company's server via the 'load-balancing' servers utilised by Consulware Co., however, Consulware Co.'s presence on the Swedish Company's server is for a limited period of time only, the duration of which is the 'testing' of the software and, therefore, may not satisfy the required "*degree of permanence*".[25] Needless to say, application of the current 'source basis' principles is effectually impractical and convoluted.

23.5.2 VAT Implication of a New-Age Business Structure

Application of VAT in South Africa and Sweden has been discussed within the parameters of the original business structure. Regardless of the number of consultants employed by Consulware Co. for the purpose of carrying out the required services, the supply of services will be taxable in Sweden either through Consulware Co., should Consulware Co. qualify to register for VAT in Sweden, or through the Swedish Company in terms of the reverse charge mechanism. The change in the business structure will not impact the Swedish VAT implications previously examined as the services still constitute 'imported services' where the place of supply is located in Sweden; regardless of whether the place of supply is determined in terms of the general supply rule or the special supply rules (depending on whether the services constitute 'electronically supplied services').

From a South African VAT perspective, the new-age business structure may impact VAT application. Formerly Kosta was supplying services to the Swedish Company and his activities qualified as carrying on an 'enterprise' in South Africa. Furthermore, the services were zero rated in terms of SA VAT being defined as

---

[24]op cit Pinto, p36.

[25]op cit OECD *OECD Model Tax Convention on Income and on Capital, Condensed Version – July 2005* (2005), France p85.

'exported services'. However, the services are now being rendered by Consulware Co. and examination of Consulware Co.'s enterprise activities in South Africa, and other jurisdictions, is mandatory.

23.5.2.1 South Africa

Re-examination of the definition of 'enterprise' is requisite for the analysis of the new-age business structure. 'Enterprise' is defined as "*in the case of any vendor, any enterprise . . . which is carried on continuously or regularly by any person in the Republic [of South Africa] or partly in the Republic [of South Africa] and in the course or furtherance of which goods or services are supplied to any other person for a consideration . . .*".[26] While Consulware Co. is managed by four directors located in four different jurisdictions and Consulware Co.'s offices are located in the virtual world it is, nevertheless, possible for Consulware Co. to qualify as an 'enterprise' in South Africa for VAT purposes. Carrying on an 'enterprise' in South Africa has not been clearly defined by legislation, however, "*a person would not be regarded as carrying on a business or other activity in a country unless he either has a physical presence in the country or he provides goods or performs services there, whether personally or through an agent . . .*".[27] To carry on an 'enterprise' partly within South Africa "*refers to an activity which is carried on in an export country . . . as well as in [South Africa] . . . [, however, there is no] minimum scope of activity in [South Africa which] is required*".[28]

The lack of place of supply rules in South Africa has been noted as creating uncertainty in of "*the South African VAT status of international businesses making supplies to South Africans by way of electronic commerce*".[29] In the current case study the supplies are not being made to South African recipients, however, it is debatable as to whether Consulware Co. is 'physically present' in South Africa by reason of Kosta's presence in South Africa. Furthermore, assuming that the technology enabling physical presence elsewhere through the virtual world is not recognised, then Consulware Co. may be deemed to be performing services within South Africa. However, should this be the case and Consulware Co. meets the VAT registration requirements, then the VAT provisions, examined and discussed in terms of the previous basic business structure, will apply. That is, the services will be zero rated for VAT purposes.

[26]Section 1 of the SA VAT Act, No. 89 of 1991 (as amended).

[27]Botes, MC & De Wet, CG (General Editor) *Juta's Value Added Tax* (Revision Service 5, 2008), South Africa, 1 enterprise-6.

[28]supra.

[29]supra.

23.5.2.2 Canada

Second Life, despite being utilised as a business tool and despite being the location of Consulware Co.'s virtual offices, is viewed in Canadian commentary as a game. If Second Life is viewed as a game in all circumstances, then the Canadian director, Constandina, may be liable for GST in terms of the reverse charge mechanism as accessing Second Life will be viewed as an 'importation of services'. A similar concept was examined in terms of the basic business structure in regard to South African VAT implications. However, in terms of the basic business structure, Kosta was utilising or consuming such imported services in the course or furtherance of making taxable supplies. If such imported services had indeed been subjected to VAT Kosta would have been entitled to claim an input credit. If Consulware Co. were to register for Canadian GST and accessing Second Life was viewed as a Consulware Co. business expense, then Consulware Co. would be entitled to claim an input credit. However, if Consulware Co. is not registered for Canadian GST or the 'imported services' were viewed as being supplied to Constandina and not Consulware Co., accessing Second Life may be subject to Canadian GST.

The possibility of Constandina being subjected to GST as a result of accessing Second Life is not so much imputable to VAT principles being unable to adapt to technology but rather because of Canadian *parti pris* towards Second Life. Within the context of the new-age business structure, Second Life is not an on-line game but is a portal to Consulware Co.'s virtual offices which are used for business purposes.

Consulware Co. would be required to register for Canadian GST if Consulware Co. makes "*taxable suppl[ies] in Canada in the course of carrying on a business in Canada*",[30] where 'carrying on a business' is defined as a business activity which "*is done regularly or continually*".[31] The definition of 'taxable person' is narrower in terms of the Canadian GST legislation due to "*[t]he criteria of reasonable expectation of profit [which] is more emphasized in the Canadian GST than in the EC VAT...*". If Consulware Co. satisfies all these requirements, Consulware Co. would be required to register for Canadian GST.

As previously held, "*[t]he fact that the supply may be made to a recipient who is outside Canada has no bearing on whether the supply is made in Canada*".[32] Examination as to whether services rendered to the Swedish Company fall within the scope of the Canadian GST legislation is compulsory. The supply of intangible personal property which 'may be used' in whole or in part in Canada and which relates to the performance of a service in Canada is deemed to be made in Canada. Thus, this circles back to the debate regarding the interpretation of physical

[30]loc cit CRA *Non-Residents and Carrying on Business in Canada* Available at http://www.cra-arc.gc.ca/tx/bsnss/tpcs/cmm/gst-tps/nnrs-eng.html [Accessed 30/04/2010].

[31]loc cit CRA *Doing Business in Canada – GST/HST Information for Non-Residents.* Available at http://www.cra-arc.gc.ca/E/pub/gp/rc4027/rc4027-09e.pdf [Accessed 30/04/2010], p6.

[32]loc cit CRA GST/HST Technical Information Bulletin *GST/HST and Electronic Commerce* (July 2002). Available at http://www.cra-arc.gc.ca/BBF6... 090_e.pdf [Accessed 30/04/2010], p16.

presence. If Constandina is regarded as performing her services elsewhere than in Canada through the means of the virtual world, then 'performance of the service' is not in Canada. However, in terms of the Canadian guidelines "*the place where a service is performed is traditionally the place where the person physically doing the work is situated*".[33] If the traditional approach is supported, then as the service was performed in Canada, even if only in part, the supply of the service is deemed to be Canada.

The supply may constitute either the supply of intangible personal property or the supply of services. In terms of the latter, the supply constitutes services if the "*supply involves specific work that is performed by a person for a specific customer, and there is human involvement in making the supply*".[34] In terms of the former, the supply constitutes intangible personal property where "*a product is provided that has already been created or developed, or is already in existence[, or] a product is created or developed for a specific customer, but the supplier retains ownership of the product*".[35] In terms of the facts of this case study, Consulware Co. is supplying intangible personal property as Consulware Co. either utilises testing software which has already been developed, or if special testing software is required, Consulware Co. would retain ownership of such software. There is, however, scope for arguing that Consulware Co. is supplying services to the Swedish Company as the supply may also meet the requirements of 'services'.

Thus, while Consulware Co. may be required to register for Canadian GST, and the supply of intangible personal property, or the supply of services, to the Swedish Company may fall within the scope of the GST legislation, as the supply is made to a non-registered non-resident person the supply will be zero rated for GST purposes.

In terms of new-age business structure Consulware Co. may be required to register for GST/VAT in multiple jurisdictions, and the supply may be subject to VAT/GST in multiple jurisdictions, but generally the supply is zero rated in the jurisdictions where the supply is considered to have been made and subject to VAT in the jurisdiction of consumption at that jurisdiction's standard rate. Thus, despite the complicated structure and the various debates regarding physical presence the supply is subject to taxation at a standard rate once, whereas application of the income tax provisions results in double taxation or non-taxation.

23.5.2.3 New Zealand

For the purpose of providing a complete analysis, New Zealand GST implications will also be examined. The point in question as to whether Consulware Co. would be required to register for GST in New Zealand is dependent upon whether Con-

[33]loc cit CRA *GST/HST and Electronic Commerce*, http://www.cra-arc.gc.ca/BBF6...090_e.pdf, p17.

[34]ibid p4. Refer to page 223 of this paper for the entire list of 'supply of services'.

[35]supra Refer to page 223 of this paper for the entire list of 'supply of intangible personal property'.

sulware Co. is carrying on taxable activities as defined in New Zealand. 'Taxable activity' being "*...any activity which is carried on continuously or regularly by any person, whether or not for a pecuniary, and involves or is intended to involve, in whole or in part, the supply of goods and services to any other person for a consideration...*".[36] In terms of the New Zealand 'place of supply' rules, "*...goods and services shall be deemed to be supplied in New Zealand if the supplier is resident in New Zealand, and shall be deemed to be supplied outside New Zealand if the supplier is a non-resident*".[37] Thus, Consulware Co.'s residence status in New Zealand necessitates scrutiny to determine whether Consulware Co. is required to register for GST in New Zealand and, if so, what the GST implications are for Consulware Co.

The definition of New Zealand 'resident' for GST purposes refers back to the NZ Income Tax Act. Interestingly even New Zealand revenue authorities acknowledge, for income tax purposes, that "*internet business[es]...operat[ing] through [the businesses'] own server[s] located overseas*"[38] may result in "*[t[he business operations...be[ing] considered to be completely carried out on the site, and the profits liable for tax in the country where the server is located*".[39] As previously discussed in Part III of this paper, application of 'residence' provisions within a virtual context may be effectually impracticable, however, from a GST perspective application of 'residence' has an administrative impact. In other words, if Consulware Co. does not satisfy the 'resident' definition, then the supply of services to the Swedish Company will fall outside the scope of the New Zealand GST net. However, if Consulware Co. does satisfy the 'resident' definition and the services fall within the scope of the NZ GST legislation, then such services would be zero rated provided the recipient is not in NZ at the time the services are rendered in terms of section 11A(1)(k) of the NZ GST Act, which would be the situation in the case of the Swedish Company.

The definition of 'resident' as defined in the NZ GST Act, cited *from the NZ Income Tax Act*, includes two further deeming provisions of which one may be relevant for the purpose of the new-age business structure illustrated in this case study. For GST purposes "*a person shall be deemed to be resident in New Zealand to the extent that that person carries on, in New Zealand, any taxable activity or any other activity, while having any fixed or permanent place in New Zealand relating to that taxable activity or other activity*".[40] There is plausible scope for arguing that Platon's physical presence in New Zealand, any services physically performed by

---

[36]Section 6(1)(a) of the NZ GST Act, No. 141 of 1985 (as amended).

[37]Section 8(2) of the NZ GST Act, No. 141 of 1985 (as amended).

[38]New Zealand Inland Revenue *Example C (E-commerce and tax)*. Available at http://www.ird.govt.nz/ecommerce-tax/ecommerce-incometax/incometax-bus-model-c.html [Accessed 4/12/2010].

[39]supra.

[40]Proviso (a) of the definition of 'Resident', Section 2(1) of the NZ GST Act, No. 141 of 1985 (as amended).

Platon on his laptop located in New Zealand, and any activities carried out for and on behalf of Consulware Co. may create a 'permanent place' in New Zealand for Consulware Co. However, the New Zealand revenue authority has stated in published guidelines that "*the provision of on-line services by a non-resident will not fall within the definition of a fixed or permanent place of business in New Zealand...*".[41] While Platon may perform some of his duties for Consulware Co. while located in New Zealand, Consulware Co. is a non-resident business providing on-line services. By the same token, Platon is in fact 'logging into' Consulware Co. virtual offices which are hosted on international servers and he performs any necessary services on-line for Consulware Co..

Needless to say, determining whether a new-age business would qualify as a 'resident' for GST purposes in NZ would undoubtedly depend upon the facts of each case which should be separately debated. However, as emphasized above, determining whether a company like Consulware Co. would be required to register for GST in NZ revolves primarily around the administrative aspect of GST as the supply to the Swedish Company would either fall outside the scope of the NZ GST net or subject to GST at the rate of zero per cent. Therefore, in terms of this case study, it may be submitted that the supply currently continues to be subject to VAT/GST at a standard rate in only one jurisdiction, that is, Sweden.

23.5.2.4 United States of America

Application of the USA retail sales implications is limited to the information sourced with regard to the USA and separate states of the USA. Downloaded software is deemed analogous to physical moveable goods delivered to the USA and taxable in the state where the software is downloaded. Physical moveable goods delivered to the USA as a result of internet sales are subject to sales tax in accordance with the DTA if such is in place as discussed previously in Part V of this paper. Physical moveable goods are subject to sales tax upon importation into the USA where the foreign on-line retailer resides in a non-DTA jurisdiction. As previously discussed, accessing Second Life may be deemed by some jurisdictions as a supply which the Second Life user receives. However, for the purpose of studying the new-age business structure, if Emmanuel, the USA director, assisted with the services provided to the Swedish Company, then examining 'place of supply' from a USA perspective is mandatory.

The presence of an agent may give rise to a 'permanent establishment' in the USA. Assuming Emmanuel resides in the State of New York, as an employee and director of Consulware Co. Emmanuel may satisfy the requirements of 'agent'. Registration for sales tax is required if a person satisfies various conditions, all of which require the sale or supply of service in New York to clients or customers located in New York, because New York State sales tax is based on the destination principle.

[41] op cit McKenzie. p120.

If services are supplied to New York clients, then Emmanuel's presence in New York State may result in Consulware Co. having a 'permanent establishment' in New York State, thus, giving rise to registration liability. Even without Emmanuel's presence in New York State, depending on the circumstances it is possible for Consulware Co.'s New York clients to effectuate registration liability for Consulware Co.

However, in terms of the facts of the current case either services or tangible personal property are supplied to the Swedish Company which is not located in New York, and neither services nor tangible personal property are used in New York and, therefore, there should be no New York State sales tax implications in this case.

23.6 Effectiveness of Applying VAT Provisions

Regardless of whether or not Consulware Co. is required to register for VAT/GST in various jurisdictions, the net result appears to remain the same whereby the service/digital supply is subjected to VAT/GST at a standard rate only once. If Consulware Co. meets the requirements to register for VAT/GST in jurisdictions other than the destination/use jurisdiction the supply generally qualifies for zero rating. Therefore, it may be submitted that the application of VAT in the context of this case study is more effective than application of income tax which either resulted in double non-taxation due to the inability to determine residence, or double taxation due to more than one jurisdiction claiming source.

However, the new-age business structure accentuates, as previously discussed, the administrative inefficiencies pertaining to VAT, specifically in regard to the possibility of registration in multiple jurisdictions despite the supply being consumed and taxed at the standard rate in one jurisdiction. Furthermore, the provision of Consulware Co.'s consulting services in multiple jurisdictions may give rise to registration in multiple jurisdictions where the jurisdiction applies registration thresholds in respect of the carrying on of taxable activities within that jurisdiction. Therefore, administrative inefficiencies constitute a critical point at issue and must be resolved if effective application of VAT is to be achieved and inhibition of eCommerce and globalisation is to be prevented.

Bibliography

Primary Sources

Cases

Republic of South African Cases

CIR v Lever Brothers & Unilever 1946 AD 441, *14 SATC 441*.

Other Cases
Transvaal Associated Hide and Skin Merchants v Collector of Income Tax, Botswana 29 SATC 97 1967 (BCA) [Botswana].

Statutes
New Zealand Goods and Services Tax Act, No. 141 of 1985 (as amended).
OECD. 2005. *OECD model tax convention on income and on capital, condensed version – July 2005*. Paris: OECD Publishers.
South Africa Value-Added Tax Act, No. 89 of 1991 (as amended).
South African Income Tax Act, No. 58 of 1962 (as amended).

Secondary Sources

Botes, M.C., and C.G. De Wet (General Editor) *Juta's value added tax* (Revision Service 5, 2008) Juta & Co. Ltd, Cape Town, South Africa.
Canadian Revenue Agency. *Doing business in Canada – GST/HST information for non-residents*. Available at http://www.cra-arc.gc.ca/E/pub/gp/rc4027/rc4027-09e.pdf. Accessed 30 April 2010.
Canadian Revenue Agency. *Non-residents and carrying on business in Canada*. Available at http://www.cra-arc.gc.ca/tx/bsnss/tpcs/cmm/gst-tps/nnrs-eng.html. Accessed 30 April 2010.
Canadian Revenue Agency GST/HST Technical Information Bulletin. 2002, July. *GST/HST and electronic commerce*. Available at http://www.cra-arc.gc.ca/BBF6E666-8A29-47F6-7781B1517476/FinalDownload/DownloadId_F964750C245682CA22DA0BC295CE6E20/BBF6E666-8A29-47F6-BF42-7781B1517476/E/pub/gm/b-090/b-090_e.pdf. Accessed 30 April 2010.
HM Revenue & Customs. *VAT: Cross-border VAT changes 2010*. Available at http://www.hmrc.gov.uk/vat/cross-border-changes-2010.htm. Accessed 9 Dec 2010.
HM Revenue & Customs. 2003, April. *Electronically supplied services: A guide to interpretation*. Available at http://customs.hmrc.gov.uk/channelsPortalWebApp/channelsPortalWebApp.portal?_nfpb=true&_pageLabel=oageVAT_ShowContent&id=HMCE_CL_000907?&propertyType=document#downloadopt. Accessed 12 Dec 2010.
HM Revenue & Customs. 2010, January. *Notice 741A place of supply of services*. Available at http://customs.hmrc.gov.uk/channelsPortalWebApp/channelsPortalWebApp.portal?_nfpb=true&_pageLabel=pageVAT_ShowContent&propertyType=document&id=HMCE_PROD1_029955#downloadopt. Accessed 12 Dec 2010.
McKenzie, Alastair. 2008, August. *GST – A practical guide* (Edition 8). Auckland: CCH New Zealand Limited, A Wolters Kluwer Business.
New Zealand Inland Revenue. *Example C (E-commerce and tax)*. Available at http://www.ird.govt.nz/ecommerce-tax/ecommerce-incometax/incometax-bus-model-c.html. Accessed 4 Dec 2010.
Pinto, Dale. 2003. *E-Commerce and source-based income taxation*. Amsterdam: IBFD Publications.
The Shorter Oxford English Dictionary on Historical Principles. 1986. Oxford: University Printing House.

Chapter 24
Case Study: Server Warehousing

Abstract Classification of technological services is crucial to the regulation of VAT implications of technological services. VAT implications pertinent to each type of hosting are dictated by the particularities of the hosting arrangement. In shared hosting the client 'rents' pure virtual storage space shared by multiple users. The client may not change the core technologies, but may store any form of data and may download or install software provided that such installation conforms with the storage restrictions applicable to the 'shared hosting' server.

The dedicated server is a form of virtual 'safety deposit box' in respect of which the physical server equipment is merely a device which facilitates the provision of secure virtual storage. Colocation is merely the 'parking lot' for fully owned servers.

The prime focus of this Case Study is to discuss in detail the distinguishing features of the diverse types of 'server hosting' and the relative VAT implications which are contingent upon the defining features of each classification. Furthermore, this Case Study makes clear the practicality and effectiveness of VAT application in eCommerce. In every circumstance discussed in this Case Study VAT/GST was levied at a standard rate in only a single jurisdiction and the raison d'étre for no levy in any jurisdiction was that the supply was specifically exempt or excluded from the VAT/GST net for administrative purposes, and not because of inability to effectively apply VAT/GST provisions.

The classification of technological services is crucial to the regulation of the VAT implications of technological services as is made clear in this Case Study. As the essential condition of this Case Study is an appraisal of the regulation of VAT implications applicable to the particularity of the diverse technological services pertaining to server hosting, a comparative analysis between income tax provisions and VAT provisions will not be included.

24.1 Background Facts

Server hosting and server data warehousing is a common service within the virtual technology world. Various types of hosting prevail and the VAT implications pertinent to each type of hosting are dictated by the particularities of the hosting

A.M. Bardopoulos, *eCommerce and the Effects of Technology on Taxation*,
Law, Governance and Technology Series 22, DOI 10.1007/978-3-319-15449-7_24

arrangement. Kosta Tech Ltd, located in South Africa, offers server hosting services to clients located in the United Kingdom and New Zealand. Each client enters into a server hosting agreement with Kosta Tech Ltd dependent upon the individual client's needs. Kosta Tech Ltd is a registered VAT vendor in South Africa and the following organogram illustrates the current state of affairs:

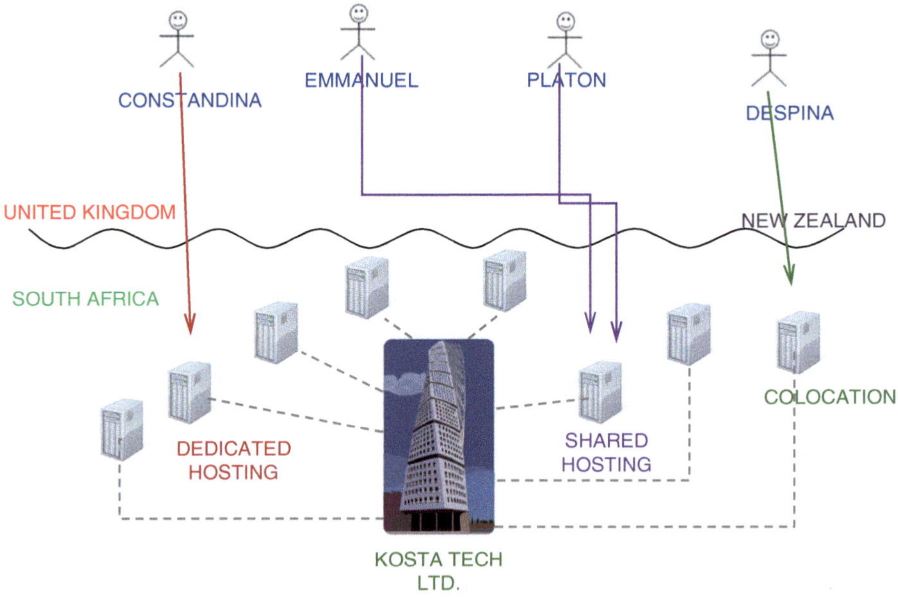

Kosta Tech Ltd provides three different types of server hosting, namely, dedicated hosting, shared hosting and collocation, each of which is briefly described below. Dedicated[1] hosting entails Kosta Tech Ltd retaining ownership of the server and

[1] TechTarget/WhatIs.com provides the following definition of 'dedicated hosting':

> *In the Web hosting business, a dedicated server refers to the rental and exclusive use of a computer that includes a Web server, related software, and connection to the Internet, housed in the Web hosting company's premises. A dedicated server is usually needed for a Web site (or set of related company sites) that may develop a considerable amount of traffic – for example, a site that must handle up to 35 million hits a day. The server can usually be configured and operated remotely from the client company. Web hosting companies claim that the use of a dedicated server on their premises saves router, Internet connection, security system, and network administration costs.*
>
> *In renting a dedicated server, the client company may be required to use a specified computer system or may be offered a choice of several systems. Some host providers allow a client company to purchase and install its own computer server at the host provider's location, a service known as colocation.*
>
> *Typically, a dedicated server is rented that provides a stated amount of memory, hard disk space, and bandwidth (here meaning the number of gigabytes of data that can be*

being responsible for maintaining the hardware, but it is utilised by only one client who is entitled to install any desired software and who retains the rights to the software installed. Shared hosting,[2] on the other hand, is used by multiple clients but Kosta Tech Ltd retains ownership of both the hardware and basic software required for operation. Colocation[3] refers to situations where the client purchases the server hardware, retains ownership and control of the hardware and software and merely pays a monthly rental for the physical space the server occupies.

Cognizance of the type of server hosting is significant in that it is pertinent to the determining of whether the 'rent' pertains to the physical property or pertains to virtual space. Shared hosting and colocation are relatively well-defined respectively. Dedicated hosting, however, may present problems in respect of VAT application attributable to misconception of the qualitative features of dedicated hosting. The qualitative features and VAT implications of each type of server hosting will be discussed below.

---

delivered each month). Some hosting companies allow the renter of a dedicated server to do virtual hosting, in turn renting services on the server to third parties for their Web sites. Domain name system, e-mail, and File Transfer Protocol (FTP) capabilities are typically included and some companies provide an easy-to-use control interface.

SearchSOA.com Definitions (Powered by WhatIs.com) *What is Dedicated Server?* Available at http://searchsoa.techtarget.com/definition/dedicated-server [Accessed 27/01/2011].

[2]TechTarget/WhatIs.com provides the following definition of 'shared hosting':

Shared hosting is Web hosting in which the service provider serves pages for multiple Web sites, each having its own Internet domain name, from a single Web server. Most Web hosting companies provide shared hosting. Although shared hosting is a less expensive way for businesses to create a Web presence, it is usually not sufficient for Web sites with high traffic. These sites need a dedicated Web server, either provided by a Web hosting service or maintained in-house.

SearchSOA.com Definitions (Powered by WhatIs.com) *What is Shared Hosting?* Available at http://searchsoa.techtarget.com/definition/shared-hosting [Accessed 27/01/2011].

[3]TechTarget/WhatIs.com provides the following definition of 'colocation hosting':

In general, collocation is moving or placing things together, sometimes implying a proper order. On the Internet, this term (often spelled "colocation" or "co-location") is used to mean the provision of space for a customer's telecommunications equipment on the service provider's premises. For example, a Web site owner could place the site's own computer servers on the premises of the Internet service provider (ISP). Or an ISP could place its network routers on the premises of the company offering switching services with other ISPs. The alternative to collocation is to have the equipment and the demarcation point located at the customer's premises.

SearchSOA.com Definitions (Powered by WhatIs.com) *What is Colocation?* Available at http://searchsoa.techtarget.com/definition/collocation [Accessed 27/01/2011].

24.1.1 Shared Hosting[4]

In shared hosting the client 'rents' pure virtual storage space shared by multiple users. A 'shared server' is comparable to storage space rented for gold shares acquired on the stock market, where the actual gold is held at Fort Knox, presupposing that Fort Knox holds privately owned gold rather than USA Federal gold reserves.[5] In such an hypothesis the gold owner never has access to Fort Knox and has control over neither the manner in which the gold is stored nor the security systems protecting the gold housed within Fort Knox. Multiple investors own shares in the gold housed within Fort Knox, and while the investors retain the rights to, and ownership of, their investments they have no actual say in the manner in which it is stored, protected or maintained. Furthermore, the investor may not dictate the type of valuable stored in Fort Knox. The investor may store any type of gold bullion, but it may only be gold bullion and not, for example, diamonds. Fort Knox in turn provides secure storage for the gold investment.

---

[4]The diverse analogies in respect of server hosting and the case study have been confirmed, from a technological perspective, with Kontos, Kosta BSc (CompSci) (UCT), MBA (UCT). Managing Director (MD) of Kontos Technologies. (15th February 2011).

[5]GobalSecurity.org provides a description and historical account of Fort Knox, extracts of which have been reiterated hereunder for sake of convenience. While Fort Knox holds gold reserves for the USA Federal Government and not privately held gold, for the purpose of this example Fort Knox is hypothetically redefined as privately owned secure storage providing safe custody for privately owned gold.

> ***Fort Knox Bullion Depository***
>
> *A large amount of the United States' gold reserves is stored in the vault of the Fort Knox Bullion Depository, one of the institutions under the supervision of the Director of the United States Mint. The remaining gold reserves are held in the Philadelphia Mint, the Denver Mint, the West Point Bullion Depository and the San Francisco Assay Office, also facilities of the United States Mint.*
>
> *... The only gold removed has been very small quantities used to test the purity of gold during regularly scheduled audits. Except for these samples, no gold has been transferred to or from the Depository for many years ...*
>
> *The Depository was completed in December 1936 at a cost of $560,000. Building materials used included ... granite, ... concrete, ... reinforcing steel, and ... structural steel. It is located ... [in] Louisville, Kentucky, on a site which was formerly a part of the Fort Knox military reservation ...*
>
> *... The Gold Vault was also used to store and to safeguard the English crown jewels and the Magna Carta, along with the gold reserves of several of the countries of occupied Europe ... [and also] the Declaration of Independence ...*
>
> *At each corner of the structure on the outside, but connected with it, are four guard boxes. Sentry boxes, similar to the guard boxes at the corners of the Depository, are located at the entrance gate ...*
>
> *The gold stored in the Depository is in the form of standard mint bars of almost pure gold or coin gold bars resulting from the melting of gold coins ...*

GobalSecurity.org *Military: Fort Knox Bullion Depository*. Available at http://www.globalsecurity.org/military/facility/fort-knox-depository.htm [Accessed 27/01/2011].

'Shared hosting' is a virtual equivalent of such warehouse storage, however, instead of gold the client stores data and programmes. The client may not change the core technologies, being "*the most prevalent 'stack' of technologies in hosting*".[6] The "*core stack of technologies*"[7] which is essentially comprised of the "*operating system*",[8] "*website application server software*",[9] "*the database server software*"[10]

---

[6]Kontos, idem footnote 4 of this chapter.

The "*four pieces of software, namely Linux, Apache, MySQL and PHP, are the most prevalent 'stack; of technologies in hosting, and together are commonly referred to as LAMP (an acronym formed from the first letter of each component, respectively).*"

LAMP, as discussed by Dale Dougherty of O'Reilly Media, Inc., "*. . . represents the open source web platform. Most importantly, LAMP is the platform of choice for the development and deployment of high performance web applications. It is solid and reliable, and if Apache is any indicator, then LAMP sites predominate . . . .*"

Dougherty, Dale *LAMP: The Open Source Web Platform* (01/26/2001). O'Reilly Media, Inc. Available at http://onlamp.com/lpt/a/566 [Accessed 16/03/2011].

[7]Kontos, idem footnote 4 of this chapter.

[8]*Supra.*

Kontos provides the following description of an "*operating system*":

> *The operating system, generally speaking, serves as a software foundation that coordinates a computer's underlying hardware, and acts as an interface between this hardware and all other software applications installed on the computer.*

Dougherty offers the following comments regarding Linux:

> *Too often, the market identifies open source with Linux, and Linux is already well covered on many sites. . . . [O'Reilly Media, Inc. feel] that the market has ignored the tools that make Linux a great applications development platform, especially for robust web applications that run on Linux servers.*

loc cit Dougherty, http://onlamp.com/lpt/a/566.

[9]Kontos, *idem* footnote 4 of this chapter.

Kontos, Kosta provides the following description of a "*website application server*":

> *The website application server, generally speaking, is responsible for housing website applications and servicing requests to these applications.*

[10]*Supra.*

Kontos provides the following description of a "*database server*":

> *The database server, generally speaking, is responsible for storing* ***dynamic*** *data – namely variable data used to both configure website applications as well as to furnish website application users with content.*

Charles Babcock of InformationWeek, offers the following comments with regard to MySQL:

> *MySQL is the speedy, open source, Web-page-serving database that's used by Facebook, Google, Slashdot, and other giants of the Web . . .*
>
> *Regardless of operating system choice . . . .[the CEO of Sun Mircrosystems] asserted that with MySQL, Sun [Microsystems] has a set of software that more directly competes with Microsoft's Windows Server and SQL Server database . . .*

and "*language*"[11] of the server system may not be changed by the client or alternative "*core stack of technologies*"[12] downloaded or installed.[13] This is comparable with Fort Knox storage restrictions whereby any form of gold bullion may be stored, but not diamonds. In this example, the 'gold bullion' in Fort Knox is the "*core stack*". Thus, the client may store any form of data and may download or install software provided that such installation conforms with the storage restrictions applicable to the 'share hosting' server.

> *As developers build out Web applications that interact with individual site visitors, answer questions with fresh product information and data, and conduct transactions, Sun [Microsystems] wants to be the supplier to the enterprise for the network's next phase. Sun [Microsystems] plans to buy additional open source companies, but it clearly views MySQL as the cornerstone of its campaign ...*

Babcock, Charles *Sun Locks Up MySQL, Looks to Future Web Development* (26/02/2008) InformationWeek. Available at http://www.informationweek.com/shared/printableArticleSrc.jhtml;jsessionid=02I05L2K1EMIRQE1GHPSKHWATMY32JVN?articleID=206900327 [Accessed 16/03/2011].

[Brief description and overview of Sun Microsystems as published by Carolyn Tajnai in *From the Valley of Heart's Delight to the Silicon Valley: A Study of Standford University's Role in the Transformation*:

> *Sun Microsystems was founded in 1982 by Andreas Bechtolsheim, an electrical engineering PhD student in the Computer Systems Laboratory (CSL), Scott McNealy and Vinod Khosla, roommates at Stanford's Graduate School of Business, and Bill Joy, a PhD student in computer science at the University of California, Berkeley.*
>
> *Sun's first product was the brainchild of Bechtolsheim. He built his first workstation out of spare parts scrounged from the Department of Computer Science and Silicon Valley supply houses. In 1982, he teamed with McNealy, Khosla and Joy to found Sun which is an acronym for Stanford University Network, the communications project for which Bechtolsheim designed his workstation.*
>
> *Oracle completed its acquisition of Sun Microsystems in 2010.*

Tajnai, Carolyn *From the Valley of Heart's Delight to the Silicon Valley: A Study of Standford University's Role in the Transformation* Standford University. Available at http://www.stanford.edu/group/wellspring/sun_spotlight.html [Accessed 19/03/2011]].

[11] Kontos, *idem* footnote 4 of this chapter.

Kontos provides the following description of "*language*":

> *The application library, generally speaking, is a set of pre-defined,* ***reusable*** *variables and functions that can be leveraged by website applications installed on the server in order to perform common tasks.*

[12] *supra.*

[13] *supra.*

24.1.2 Dedicated Server

A dedicated server may be compared to a safety deposit box held within a bank. A client 'rents' a safety deposit box in a Swiss bank which allows the client to store anything he desires within his box as long as it fits. If his items are too large he can acquire a larger box. His rent entitles him to a 'dedicated' storage space for his personal items which are kept separate from the bank's other clients' items. However, despite the extended storage freedom compared to 'shared' storage space, the client has no ownership or control over the actual physical box. In other words, the client does not reserve the right to put his own lock onto the box neither is he entitled to mark nor paint the box. Furthermore, the client has no control over the physical storage of the box nor the manner in which the box is physically protected as this is a service historically offered by banks and over which banks retain strict control.

In order to provide 'dedicated space' the bank utilises physical equipment, for example, the safety deposit box. Despite the use of the safety deposit box, the client is 'renting' storage space and not physical property of the bank. The 'safety deposit box' is not the object of the service but the equipment required to provide the object of the service – separate and safe storage.

The dedicated server is a form of virtual 'safety deposit box' in respect of which the physical server equipment is merely a device which facilitates the provision of secure virtual storage.

24.1.3 Colocation

Colocation may be compared to parking your car in a privately owned parking lot. The car belongs to you and you are entitled to do whatever you please with your car, for example, change its colour, add special features, overhaul the engine, add specialised bucket seats, etc. The privately owned parking lot is merely a place where you can safely store your car and the 'fee' you pay relates to the storage of your car because you choose not to leave your vehicle parked on the public streets. 'Parking lots' may offer additional services to make their parking space more attractive than other parking lots, for example, a car wash service. The fact that the parking lot may wash your car does not mean that they have control or retain any rights over your car.

The acquisition of physical server equipment requires a 'parking space' similar to the needs of the vehicle, but the fact that the server is being 'parked' at Kosta Tech Ltd does not prevent the server owner from doing as he wishes to the physical hardware just as the vehicle owner may overhaul the engine of the vehicle. In terms of colocation Kosta Tech Ltd is merely the 'parking lot' for fully owned 'servers'. Kosta Tech Ltd may 'service' the physical hardware and ensure that the server operates, but such service is additional service analogous to the additional service offered by the parking lot.

24.2 VAT/GST Implications Relating to Colocation

Despina, located in New Zealand, enters into a 'colocation' server agreement with Kosta Tech Ltd. Despina pays Kosta Tech Ltd a monthly 'rack-space' fee for storing her physical server equipment. The server hardware and software have been designed to Despina's specifications. Kosta Tech Ltd maintains the server equipment for Despina, the cost of the maintenance is included in the 'rack-space' fee.

24.2.1 New Zealand GST Implications

If Kosta Tech Ltd satisfies the New Zealand registration requirements, Kosta Tech Ltd will be obligated to register for GST in New Zealand. If, however, Kosta Tech Ltd does not satisfy the registration requirements but the supply is still considered a taxable supply in New Zealand, Despina, assuming she is registered or required to register, will be liable to account for the necessary output tax in terms of the reverse charge mechanism. However, in terms of the 'place of supply' rules the supplies are not deemed to be within New Zealand, nor are the supplies imported at any point which would give rise to a taxable event. Thus, the 'colocation' services offered in South Africa will not be subject to New Zealand GST.

Assuming that the supply is considered taxable in New Zealand it would satisfy at least two zero rating provisions. If the supply is taxable "*the services are supplied directly in connection with moveable personal property . . . situated outside New Zealand when the services are performed*"[14] and "*the services are physically performed outside New Zealand . . .*".[15]

24.2.2 South African VAT Implications

VAT is imposed "*on the supply by any vendor of goods or services supplied by him . . . in the course or furtherance of any enterprise carried on by him*" .[16] Kosta Tech Ltd is carrying on an 'enterprise' in South Africa whereby "*any enterprise or activity which is carried on continuously or regularly . . . and in the course or furtherance of which goods or services are supplied to any other person for a consideration*".[17] The 'rack-space' is one of many services offered by Kosta Tech

[14]Section 11A(1)(f) of the NZ GST Act, No. 141 of 1985 (as amended).

[15]Section 11A(1)(j) of the NZ GST Act, No. 141 of 1985 (as amended).

[16]Section 7(1) of the SA VAT Act, No. 89 of 1991 (as amended).

[17]'Enterprise' as defined under section 1 of the SA VAT Act, No. 89 of 1991 (as amended).

Ltd for which a 'fee' is charged. There is no dispute that Kosta Tech Ltd is making a 'taxable supply' (as defined above) which will be subject to VAT in South Africa, however, it must be determined if the supply will be subject to VAT at the standard rate or zero rated.

The services rendered by Kosta Tech Ltd relate to 'moveable property' which is "*situated inside [South Africa] at the time the services are rendered*".[18] There is wide debate regarding the interpretation of 'directly in connection with moveable property' which has created much uncertainty when attempting to determine whether a supply qualifies for zero rating. New Zealand case law holds that where "*the tools and equipment [are] aids to . . . [the services supplied] and not the objects thereof*",[19] then the supply will not be 'directly in connection with moveable property'. However, in terms of colocation hosting, the service relates to providing 'rack-space' and maintenance of the physical server, which is the 'object' of the supply. Thus, the supply will be subject to SA VAT at the standard rate.

24.3 VAT/GST Implications Pertaining to Shared Hosting

Platon, located in New Zealand, and Emmanuel, located in the United Kingdom, both enter into 'shared server hosting' agreements with Kosta Tech Ltd. Platon and Emmanuel both store data on the same server which utilises Kosta Tech Ltd software.

24.3.1 New Zealand GST Implications

Assuming that Kosta Tech Ltd does not satisfy the New Zealand GST registration requirements, the supply of shared server hosting will be taxable in New Zealand in terms of the reverse charge mechanism if the supply qualifies as an 'imported service' and assuming Platon is, or is required to be, registered for GST in New

[18] Section 11(2)(l)(ii) of the SA VAT Act, No. 89 of 1991 (as amended).

[19] op cit Botes, MC & De Wet CG (General Editor) *Juta's Value Added Tax* (Revision Service 5, 2008), South Africa, 11–26.

The New Zealand case referenced is New Zealand Case T54 (1998) 18 NZTC 8,410 [NZ], a synopsis of which is given in *Juta's Value Added Tax*:

> *. . . it was held that the production of videos of Japanese tourists holidaying in New Zealand was zero-rated, as the services were not supplied directly in connection with video camera or tape used – the tools and equipment were aids to the production of the video and not objects thereof. As the resultant video cassette did not come into existence until after the relevant services had been performed, it was not situated inside New Zealand at the time the services were performed . . .*

Zealand. In order to qualify as 'imported services' the services must be supplied by a non-resident to a resident and "*the supply of those services, if made in New Zealand by a registered person in the course or furtherance of a taxable activity, would be a taxable supply*".[20]

Digitally supplied services are treated as the supply of services in New Zealand and may, therefore, qualify as a supply of 'imported services'. As previously examined,[21] New Zealand legislation has incorporated provisions relating to digitally supplied services defined under 'telecommunication services'. 'Telecommunication services', as defined in the NZ GST Act, are considered widely defined and include "*website and server hosting*".[22,23] The 'supply of services' is deemed to occur in New Zealand if the recipient, physically in New Zealand, "initiates" the supply of telecommunication services from a non-resident supplier not in New Zealand.[24] The "initiator" of the supply "*is the party who satisfies the highest factor listed for present purposes. The factors are listed in the following order: the party who controls the commencement of the supply, the payer, or the person who contracts for the service*".[25] Platon satisfies all these factors and, therefore, is the "initiator" of the supply which means that the "*website and server hosting*"[26] is deemed to be supplied in New Zealand.

Thus, Platon will be liable for GST at the standard rate for the server hosting services received provided Platon is a registered vendor. However, in terms of a further NZ GST provision the supply of such 'telecommunication services' will be deemed to occur outside New Zealand and, therefore, will not be subject to New Zealand GST, if the registered recipient is entitled to claim an input tax credit in regard to the supply, and provided both parties do not agree otherwise.[27]

As will be discussed later,[28] the supply will be zero rated for VAT purposes in South Africa and, in terms of the NZ GST provisions, and will not be subject to GST in New Zealand. However, where such circumstances prevail, the supply should not be considered as being subject to double non-taxation as the exclusion from the New Zealand GST scope is merely for administrative purposes. In other words, if Platon, a registered vendor, accounted for the GST on such 'imported service' and was entitled to claim an input tax credit in respect of the service acquired, it would result in a pure "in-and-out" on, most likely, the same GST return. The

[20]op cit *New Zealand Goods and Services Tax Legislation 2010* (Edition 24), CCH A Wolters Kluwer Business, New Zealand, p18.

[21]Refer to 18.2. Jurisdictional Analysis: Southern Hemisphere, Part V of this paper [p199].

[22]op cit McKenzie, Alistair, *GST – A Practical Guide*, New Zealand, p102.

[23]supra.

[24]idem p103.

[25]idem p102.

[26]op cit McKenzie, p102.

[27]idem p103.

[28]Discussed in 24.2.2 *South African VAT Implications*, Part VI of this paper [p326].

possible double non-taxation may occur, however, where the services are provided to a non-registered New Zealand recipient who is not subject to the reverse charge mechanism.

24.3.2 United Kingdom/EU VAT Implications

Kosta Tech Ltd may be required to register for VAT in the UK where taxable supplies made by Kosta Tech Ltd exceed the registration threshold and the 'place of supply' of the supplies is or is deemed to be in the United Kingdom. In terms of the applicable general 'place of supply' rules, services "*provided to business customers will be treated as supplied in the country where the business customer is established and the business customer will account for VAT under the reverse charge mechanism*".[29] Thus, where the 'place of supply' is deemed to be the UK and Kosta Tech Ltd is not required to be a registered vendor in the UK, then assuming Emmanuel is a registered UK vendor, Emmanuel may be liable to account for the VAT on the 'shared hosting server' supply.

However, 'electronically supplied services' are subject to special 'place of supply' rules. In terms of the special 'place of supply' rules where "*the place of supply of services would have been in the UK ... [, in terms of the general 'place of supply' rules,] but the services are effectively used and enjoyed [in a jurisdiction] outside the*"[30] UK, as an EU country, and vice versa, the 'place of supply' will be where the services are 'effectively used and enjoyed'. The place where the supply is 'effectively used and enjoyed' being "*the place where the customer[, that is, Emmanuel,] actually consumes the electronically supplied services irrespective of contract, payment or beneficial interest*".[31]

"*Website hosting and web page hosting*"[32] and "*online data warehousing*"[33] are considered electronically supplied services. While 'server hosting' may consist of more than just web page hosting or on-line data warehousing, 'server hosting' is not specifically listed under examples of services electronically supplied. But provided

[29]loc cit HMRC *VAT: Cross-Border VAT Changes 2010*. Available at http://www.hmrc.gov.uk/vat/cross-border-changes-2010.htm [Accessed 9/12/2010].

[30]op cit HMRC, *Notice 741A Place of Supply of Services* (2010). Available at http://customs.hmrc.gov.uk/channelsPortalWebApp/channelsPortalWebApp.portal?_nfpb=true&_pageLabel=pageVAT_ShowContent&propertyType=document&id=HMCE_PROD1_029955#downloadopt [Accessed 12/12/2010], p61.

[31]idem p62.

[32]Item 1 of Table 1, Annex L to the EU VAT Directive. Loc cit HMRC *Electronically Supplied Services: A Guide to Interpretation* (April 2003). Available at http://webarchive.nationalarchives.gov.uk/20100202144103/ http://customs.hmrc.gov.uk/channelsPortalWebApp/channelsPortalWebApp.portal?_nfpb=true&_pageLabel=pageVAT_ShowContent&propertyType=document&id=HMCE_PROD1_029955 [Accessed 12/12/2010], p4–8.

[33]supra.

'server hosting' meets the definition of an electronically supplied service, then same should be considered an electronically supplied service unless specifically excluded. In terms of the 'electronically supplied service' definition a 'shared server hosting' is "*delivered over the internet or an electronic network*"[34] and "*the nature of the service in question is heavily dependent on information technology for its supply.... involving minimal human intervention* ...".[35] Any software update or maintenance performed by Kosta Tech Ltd falls within the example list of services that qualify as 'electronically supplied services'.[36]

In terms of the general supply rule Emmanuel, assuming he is a registered UK VAT vendor, will be liable to account for the VAT on the supply. Furthermore, Emmanuel will be using and enjoying the 'shared server hosting' services in the UK, assuming the server is utilised for his UK business. Thus, 'place of supply' is, furthermore, confirmed as being in the UK in terms of the 'special place of supply rules'.

Double non-taxation may arise if Emmanuel were not a registered UK VAT vendor and Kosta Tech Ltd were not obligated to register for VAT in the UK. Such potential double non-taxation was also observed in New Zealand, however, it should be noted that in terms of the 'reverse charge mechanism' restrictions, jurisdictions appear to have made a conscious decision to not include the supply of services to non-registered customers under 'reverse charge mechanism' by reason of the administration required to enforce such application. This is an important distinction to make because when compared to income tax provisions, double taxation or double non-taxation arises primarily due to the inability to effectively apply 'residence' or 'source' principles, and not because the revenue authority made a conscious decision to exclude such supply from its taxing net owing to administrative reasons.

24.3.3 South African VAT Implications

Similar to 'colocation' services the provision of 'shared server hosting' is a 'taxable supply' made by Kosta Tech Ltd in the course or furtherance of its enterprise for which it receives a consideration in return. The 'shared server hosting' does, however, differ from colocation as Kosta Tech Ltd is providing pure virtual storage space services and not physical storage space in respect of the actual server equipment.

In terms of the 'shared server hosting' the server equipment is merely "*the tools and equipment*"[37] which aid the supply of virtual storage space "*and not objects*

[34] idem p3.

[35] supra.

[36] idem p4–8.

[37] op cit Botes & De Wet, 11–26.

thereof".[38] The storage service supply does not fall into the provisos or restrictions with regard to the zero rating provision and the supply may, therefore, be zero rated in terms of section 11(2)(l) of the SA VAT Act whereby "*the services are supplied to a person who is not a resident of... [South Africa]...* ",[39] provided further that the non-resident is not in South Africa at the time the services are rendered.[40]

24.4 VAT/GST Implications Relating to 'Dedicated Server'

The VAT implications in regard to the 'dedicated server' service will not actually differ from the 'shared hosting server' services. However, if the concept of 'dedicated server' hosting is misunderstood Kosta Tech Ltd may be inclined to regard the 'dedicated server' hosting as being comparable to colocation.

It is, therefore, important to fully comprehend the concept of 'dedicated server' hosting and to understand that although Constandina is the sole user of the server and may store and install anything she chooses, it does not alter the assertion that

---

[38]supra.

[39]Section 11(2)(l) of the SA VAT Act, No. 89 of 1991 (as amended).

[40]Investigation of whether the non-resident Emmanuel is not in South Africa at the time the services are rendered falls outside the scope of the case study discussed as it is assumed that Emmanuel is utilising the 'shared server hosting' services for his UK business and that Emmanuel remains in the UK at all times. However, a brief discussion regarding the requirement that the non-resident must not be in South Africa at the time the services are rendered will be discussed briefly for the sake of erudition.

There is much debate as to what is meant by "*not being services which are supplied directly... to the said person or any other person, ... if the said person or such other person is in... [South Africa] at the time the services are rendered...*"[A] The purpose of such inclusion is to ensure that where the 'consumption' occurs in South Africa then such service will not be zero rated.[B] Thus, it is "*considered that the presence of the recipient or other person in... [South Africa] must relate to the supply of the services before the zero-rating would be denied*"[C]. For example, if Emmanuel came to South Africa for a holiday, his presence in South Africa would not automatically result in Emmanuel being considered to be in South Africa "*at the time the services are rendered*", especially as Kosta Tech Ltd may not even be aware of the fact that Emmanuel was in South Africa.[D] However, if Emmanuel came to South Africa for a meeting with Kosta Tech Ltd and was charged for the meeting, the meeting fee may not be zero rated as the consumption will be considered to have occurred within South Africa.

Guidelines regarding persons other than a natural person are unclear as to how such person may be considered to be in South Africa at the time the services are rendered.[E] There is opinion that under such circumstances a director's presence, depending on the reason for the visit or presence in South Africa, may cause the foreign company to be considered to be in South Africa at the time the services are rendered.

[A] Section 11(2)(l)(iii) of the SA VAT Act, No. 89 of 1991 (as amended).

[B] op cit Botes & De Wet, 11–28.

[C] supra.

[D] supra.

[E] supra.

the physical equipment is not the object of the service but rather "*the tools and equipment*"[41] which expedite the supply of virtual storage space.

The general misconception in respect of 'dedicated servers' is that the physical equipment is being rented. In terms of the legal definition of "lease", a lease is "*a contract under which an owner of property . . . grants another person . . . exclusive possession of the property . . . The lessee must have exclusive possession, i.e. the right to control the property and to exclude everyone else from it . . . If possession is not exclusive, there is no lease . . .*".[42] The hardware remains within the exclusive control of Kosta Tech Ltd and Kosta Tech Ltd remains responsible for the physical equipment. At no time does Kosta Tech Ltd grant Constandina exclusive possession of the physical equipment. Constandina is only entitled to the "*exclusive possession*" of the virtual space analogous to the exclusive rights to the space provided by a safety deposit box within the bank's safe.

24.5 Effectiveness of Applying VAT Provisions

The prime focus of this Case Study is the distinguishing features of the diverse types of 'server hosting' and the relative VAT implications which are contingent upon the defining features of each classification. Furthermore, this Case Study makes clear the practicality and effectiveness of VAT application in eCommerce. In every circumstance discussed in this Case Study VAT/GST was levied at a standard rate in only a single jurisdiction and the *raison d'être* for no levy in any jurisdiction was that the supply was specifically exempt or excluded from the VAT/GST net for administrative purposes, and not because of inability to effectively apply VAT/GST provisions.

Bibliography

Primary Sources

Statutes

New Zealand Goods and Services Tax Act, No. 141 of 1985 (as amended).

New Zealand *Goods and Services Tax Legislation 2010* (Edition 24), CCH A Wolters Kluwer Business, New Zealand.

South Africa Value-Added Tax Act, No. 89 of 1991 (as amended).

Cases

New Zealand

New Zealand Case T54 (1998) 18 NZTC 8,410.

[41]op cit Botes & De Wet, 11–26.

[42]Martin, Elizabeth A. (Editor) *Oxford Dictionary of Law (Fifth Edition)* (2003), definition of 'lease'.

Secondary Sources

Babcock, Charles. 2008, February 26. *Sun locks up MySQL, looks to future web development.* InformationWeek. Available at http://www.informationweek.com/shared/printableArticleSrc.jhtml;jsessionid=02I05L2K1EMIRQE1GHPSKHWATMY32JVN?articleID=206900327. Accessed 16 Mar 2011.

Botes, MC & De Wet, CG (General Editor). *Juta's Value Added Tax* (Revision Service 5, 2008). Cape Town: Juta & Co. Ltd.

Dougherty, Dale. 2001, January 26. *LAMP: The open source web platform.* O'Reilly Media, Inc. Available at http://onlamp.com/lpt/a/566. Accessed 16 Mar 2011.

GobalSecurity.org. *Military: Fort Knox Bullion depository.* Available at http://www.globalsecurity.org/military/facility/fort-knox-depository.htm. Accessed 27 Jan 2011.

HM Revenue & Customs. *VAT: Cross-border VAT changes 2010.* Available at http://www.hmrc.gov.uk/vat/cross-border-changes-2010.htm. Accessed 9 Dec 2010.

HM Revenue & Customs. 2003, April. *Electronically supplied services: A guide to interpretation.* Available at http://customs.hmrc.gov.uk/channelsPortalWebApp/channelsPortalWebApp.portal?_nfpb=true&_pageLabel=oageVAT_ShowContent&id=HMCE_CL_000907?&propertyType=document#downloadopt. Accessed 12 Dec 2010.

HM Revenue & Customs Website. 2010, January. *Notice 741A Place of supply of Services.* Available at http://customs.hmrc.gov.uk/channelsPortalWebApp/channelsPortalWebApp.portal?_nfpb=true&_pageLabel=pageVAT_ShowContent&propertyType=document&id=HMCE_PROD1_029955#downloadopt. Accessed 12 Dec 2010.

Kontos, Kosta BSc (CompSci) (UCT), MBA (UCT). Managing Director (MD) of Kontos Technologies.

Martin, Elizabeth A. (ed.). 2003. *Oxford Dictionary of Law*, 5th ed. Oxford: Oxford University Press.

McKenzie, Alastair. 2008, August. *GST – A practical guide* (Edition 8). Auckland: CCH New Zealand Limited, A Wolters Kluwer Business.

New Zealand. *Goods and services tax legislation 2010* (Edition 24). Auckland: CCH A Wolters Kluwer Business.

SearchSOA.com Definitions (Powered by WhatIs.com). *What is colocation?* Available at http://searchsoa.techtarget.com/definition/collocation. Accessed 27 Jan 2011.

SearchSOA.com Definitions (Powered by WhatIs.com). *What is dedicated server?* Available at http://searchsoa.techtarget.com/definition/dedicated-server. Accessed 27 Jan 2011.

SearchSOA.com Definitions (Powered by WhatIs.com). *What is shared hosting?* Available at http://searchsoa.techtarget.com/definition/shared-hosting. Accessed 27 Jan 2011.

Tajnai, Carolyn. *From the valley of heart's delight to the Silicon valley: A study of Stanford University's role in the transformation.* Stanford University. Available at http://www.stanford.edu/group/wellspring/sun_spotlight.html. Accessed 19 Mar 2011.

Part VII
Other Taxing Issues Emanating from eCommerce

In accordance with a comprehensive manuscript, Part VII is a brief synopsis of significant points at issue implicated by taxation and the virtual world. Pertinent issues encompass tax avoidance, tax evasion and compelling compliance in respect of tax in eCommerce, as well as compliance and administrative costs incurred by the taxation of eTransactions versus the benefits of imposition and enforcement of eTax. A significant aspect of eCommerce is that it transacts across borders and a single transaction can engage diverse jurisdictions. To compel tax compliance in such a situation may present a challenge. Therefore, a flexible taxing system operating in combination with an uncontrolled technological environment in diverse jurisdictions is essential, as has been submitted as a fundamental proposition throughout this paper.

Furthermore, while this paper submits VAT to be the eTax solution, such submission is mitigated by the concession that eVAT will not resolve all taxing issues which have been impacted by the proliferation of modern technology. Transfer pricing is a point at issue which will not be resolved by VAT. Concerns and issues regarding transfer pricing application with regard to cross-border transactions occurring within the virtual world will be discussed later.

Chapter 25
Tax Avoidance and Tax Evasion

Abstract Tax avoidance is a highly debatable moral issue, on the one hand in the Commissioner of Tax v Ferera (Former Rhodesia (Zimbabwe case) Commissioner of Tax v Ferera 1976 (2) SA 653 (RAD), 38 SATC 66, 1976 Taxpayer 167 at 241. Also, idem Emslie, Trevor; Davis, Dennis; Hutton, SJ; & Olivier, Lynette *Income Tax Cases & Materials* 3rd Ed (2001), South Africa, p928) case it was stated "*that the avoidance of tax is an evil*", (supra) while on the other hand tax avoidance has been described as "*the only intellectual pursuit that carries any reward*" (Keynes, John Maynard. Available at http://www.quotesandpoem.com/quotes/listquotes/subject/taxes [Accessed 22 January 2007]).

Significant points at issue are implicated by taxation and the virtual world. Pertinent issues encompass tax avoidance, tax evasion and compelling compliance in respect of tax in eCommerce, as well as administrative costs incurred by the taxation of eTransactions versus the benefits of imposition and enforcement of eTax. A significant aspect of eCommerce is that it transacts across borders and a single transaction can engage diverse jurisdictions. To compel tax compliance in such a situation may present a challenge. Therefore, a flexible taxing system operating in combination with an uncontrolled technological environment in diverse jurisdictions is essential.

A critical point at issue is that the Internet facilitates increased 'double non-taxation' transactions consequently potentially expediting tax avoidance schemes. Although it may be argued that VAT does not have unlimited power and influence in respect of anti-avoidance tax measures relevant to the virtual world, it is submitted that VAT more effectively prevents 'double taxation' and 'double non-taxation' in comparison with income tax provisions.

Non-declaration of income, a primary aspect of which may be fraudulent income, is the common symptom of tax evasion. Tax evasion is commonly regarded as illegal and is typically not dealt with in tax legislation but is incidental to the common law of the land.[1] Tax evasion is defined by the OECD as the "*illegal arrangements*

[1]Bardopoulos, A. *UCT P.G.Dip Taxation: International Taxation & Domestic Taxation: Tax Avoidance and Double Tax Agreements* (2007) – material has been extracted from discussion of

A.M. Bardopoulos, *eCommerce and the Effects of Technology on Taxation*,
Law, Governance and Technology Series 22, DOI 10.1007/978-3-319-15449-7_25

through or by the means of which liability to tax is hidden or ignored".[2] Discussion of tax evasion is a study in its own right, however, significant to this paper is the comment that tax evasion may be intensified by rapid globalisation and may, furthermore, find a perfect zone in the virtual world. It is, furthermore, vital to distinguish between tax evasion, which is purely illegal evasion of taxation, and tax avoidance which may be described as the legal organisation of a taxpayer's income affairs in a manner which allows the taxpayer to minimise the total tax payable, and effect such action within the limits of the law.

While a distinction may be made between tax evasion and tax avoidance, the difference between the two may be described as "*the thickness of a prison wall*".[3] Tax avoidance is a highly debatable moral issue, on the one hand in the Commissioner of Tax v Ferera[4] case it was stated "*that the avoidance of tax is an evil*",[5] while on the other hand tax avoidance has been described as "*the only intellectual pursuit that carries any reward*".[6] Several jurisdictional courts have recognised that "*every man is entitled, if he can, to order his affairs so as that the tax attaching under the appropriate Acts is less than it would otherwise be. If he succeeds in ordering them so as to secure this result, then however unappreciative the Commissioners ... or his fellow-taxpayers may be of his ingenuity, [the taxpayer] cannot be compelled to pay an increased tax*".[7]

A further distinction between legal tax avoidance and impermissible tax avoidance should be established by the conclusion which may be deduced by applying the legal precedent:

---

tax evasion and tax avoidance in the cited reference for the purpose of a synoptic (expanded where necessary) scrutiny of such issues in this paper.

[2]South African Revenue Services *Discussion Paper on Tax Avoidance and Section 103 of the[South African] Income Tax Act, 1962 (Act No. 58 of 1962)* Available at http://www.sars.gov.za/AllDocs/LegalDoclib/DiscPapers/LAPD-LPrep-DP-2005-01%20-%20Discussion%20Paper%20Tax%20Avoidance%20Section%20103%20of%20Income%20Tax%20Act%201962.pdf Paper on Tax Avoidance – for comment on or before 31January2006.pdf [Accessed 23 January 2007].

[3]Healey, Denis. Available at http://quotations.about.com/od/moretypes/a/taxquotes2.htm [Accessed 22 January 2007].

[4]Former Rhodesia (Zimbabwean case) Commissioner of Tax v Ferera 1976(2) SA 653 (RAD), 38 SATC 66, 1976 Taxpayer 167 at 241. Also, idem Emslie, Trevor; Davis, Dennis; Hutton, SJ; & Olivier, Lynette *Income Tax Cases & Materials* 3rd Ed (2001) The Taxpayer. Cape Town, South Africa, p928.

[5]supra.

[6]Keynes, John Maynard. Available at http://www.quotesandpoem.com/quotes/listquotes/subject/taxes [Accessed 22 January 2007].

[7]Inland Revenue Commissioners v Duke of Westminster [1936] AC1 at 19 [UK].

Erf 3183/1 Ladysmith and Another v Commissioner of Inland Revenue 1996 (3) SA 942 (A), 58 SATC 299, 1996 [RSA].

idem Emslie et al. p986.

> *There is a real distinction between the case of a man who so orders his affairs that he has no income which would expose him to liability for income tax, and the case of a man who so orders his affairs that he escapes from liability for taxation which he ought to pay upon the income which is in reality his.*[8]

An impermissible tax avoidance transaction, operation or scheme (referred to as 'transaction' hereinafter) may be determined by examining whether the transaction was concluded '*at arm's length*'. '*An arm's length*' transaction connotes "*that each party is independent of the other . . . [whereby each party strives to gain] the utmost possible advantage . . .*"[9] from the transaction. The 'arm's length' principle is applied in transfer pricing determination and has the distinctive qualities pertaining to a jurisdiction's anti-avoidance measures. The 'arm's length principle' is an internationally accepted practice supported by the OECD.[10]

Pre-existing problems in respect of the application of transfer pricing provisions in cross-border transactions are amplified by the virtual world environment, and will be discussed in the next chapter.

A multi-jurisdictional enterprise subject to double non-taxation is readily structured, for example, the Case Study – Software Consulting: New Age Business Structure. Implicit in this genre of Case Study is the inference that income tax provisions are susceptible to double non-taxation. Furthermore, the virtual world facilitates easy access to tax havens. Dr Pinto notes "*the inability . . . to accommodate these situations*"[11] which may only be prevented with "*anti-avoidance measures such as . . . transfer pricing mechanisms to tax profits arising out of transactions conducted from low-tax jurisdictions*".[12] However, Dr Pinto submits that such anti-avoidance measures "*may need to be modified to ensure they can be applied effectively in an electronic commerce*".[13]

VAT/GST, on the other hand, may not be as susceptible to unintentional double taxation or double non-taxation as is income tax in respect of cross-border

---

[8]South African Commissioner of Inland Revenue v King 1947 (2) SA 196 (A), 14 SATC 184 at 237 [RSA].
idem Emslie et al. p902.

[9]Hicklin v SIR 1980 (1) SA 481 (A), 41 SATC 179, 1980 Taxpayer 49 at 243 [RSA].
idem Emslie et al. p902.

[10]OECD *Transfer Pricing Guidelines for Multinational Enterprises and Tax Administrations* (2001), France, p G-1.

The 'arm's length principle' has been incorporated into the OECD Model Tax Convention and may be found under Article 9, which reads as follows:

> *conditions are made or imposed between the two enterprises in their commercial or financial relations which differ from those which would be made between independent enterprises, then any profits which would, but, by reason of those conditions, have not so accrued, may be included in the profits of that enterprise and taxed accordingly.*

[11]op cit Pinto, Dale *E-Commerce and Source-Based Income Taxation* (2003), Netherlands, p189.

[12]supra.

[13]supra.

eTransactions. Dr Rendahl submits that unintentional double taxation may occur but holds that in terms of her comparative study unintentional double non-taxation is less likely.[14] Furthermore, Dr Rendahl endorses the OECD's opinion *"that the risks for non-taxation are as frequent as the risks for double taxation due to the symmetric nature of VAT and GST"*.[15]

Both Drs Pinto and Rendahl proffer meritory points of view worthy of consideration. In terms of the case studies discussed in this paper a supply deemed "taxable" in two countries is generally zero rated in one and subject to VAT at the standard rate in the other. Furthermore, where "taxable supplies" are not taxed in either country it typically pertains to "intentional" exclusion of such supply from the jurisdiction where the supply would have otherwise been subjected to tax at the standard rate. Therefore, it can be argued that it cannot be deemed "*unintentional double taxation*" where jurisdictions exclude non-registered consumers from applying the 'reverse charge mechanism' on account of the administrative cost of enforcing such tax collection outweighing the benefit received.

A critical point at issue is that the Internet facilitates increased 'double non-taxation' transactions consequently potentially expediting tax avoidance schemes. Although it may be argued that VAT does not have unlimited power and influence in respect of anti-avoidance tax measures relevant to the virtual world, it is submitted that VAT more effectively prevents 'double taxation' and 'double non-taxation' in comparison with income tax provisions.

Bibliography

Secondary Sources

Cases

Republic of South African Cases

Erf 3183/1 Ladysmith and Another v Commissioner of Inland Revenue 1996 (3) SA 942 (A), 58 SATC 299, 1996.

Hicklin v SIR 1980 (1) SA 481 (A), 41 SATC 179.

South African Commissioner of Inland Revenue v King 1947 (2) SA 196 (A), 14 SATC 184 at 237.

United Kingdom Cases

Inland Revenue Commissioners v Duke of Westminster [1936] AC1. Available at http://www.google.co.za/url?sa=t&rct=j&q=inland%20revenue%20commissioners%20v%20duke%20of%20westminster&source=web&cd=1&sqi=2&ved=0CCwQFjAA&url=http%3A%2F%2Fwww.law.utoronto.ca%2Fdocuments%2Fconferences%2Ftax_ex_TheDuke.DOC&ei=Pu0bT96dKqjGmQW1krSUCg&usg=AFQjCNG1dtf7Zy6a3p7aT9uOg8ftBuhDVg. Accessed 22 Jan 2012.

[14] op cit Rendahl, Pernilla, *Cross-Border Consumption Taxation on Digital Supplies,* Netherlands, p338.

[15] supra.

Other Cases
Commissioner of Taxes v Ferera 1976(2) SA 653 (RAD), 38 SATC 66 [Rhodesia, presently Zimbabwe].

Secondary Sources

Bardopoulos, Anne. 2007. *International taxation & domestic taxation: Tax avoidance and double tax agreements*. University of Cape Town Postgraduate Diploma in Taxation Dissertation.

Emslie, Trevor, Dennis Davis, S.J. Hutton, and Lynette Olivier. 2001. *Income tax cases & materials*, 3rd ed. Cape Town: The Taxpayer.

Healey, Denis. Available at http://quotations.about.com/od/moretypes/a/taxquotes2.htm. Accessed 22 Jan 2007.

Keynes, John Maynard. Available at http://www.quotesandpoem.com/quotes/listquotes/subject/taxes. Accessed 22 Jan 2007.

OECD. 2001. *Transfer pricing guidelines for multinational enterprises and tax administrations*. Paris: OECD Publications.

Pinto, Dale. 2003. *E-Commerce and source-based income taxation*. Amsterdam: IBFD Publications.

Rendahl, Pernilla. 2009. *Cross-border consumption taxation of digital supplies*. Amsterdam: IBFD.

South African Revenue Services. *Discussion paper on tax avoidance and section 103 of the [South African] Income Tax Act, 1962 (Act No. 58 of 1962)* Available at http://www.sars.gov.za/AllDocs/LegalDoclib/DiscPapers/LAPD-LPrep-DP-2005-01%20-%20Discussion%20Paper%20Tax%20Avoidance%20Section%20103%20of%20Income%20Tax%20Act%201962.pdf. Paper on Tax Avoidance – for comment on or before 31January2006.pdf. Accessed 23 Jan 2007.

Chapter 26
Transfer Pricing Issues and Concerns

Abstract It is the OECD's assessment that "*the transfer pricing problems raised so far are not unique to electronic commerce, [but] the increased speed and mobility of business activities and cross-border transactions may raise new difficulties in the application of transfer pricing methods*". (op cit OECD *Tax Policy Studies E-Commerce: Transfer Pricing and Business Profits Taxation No. 10* (2005) OECD, France, p66).

The point at issue is that problems regarding effective and efficient application of taxation are intrinsic to traditional transfer pricing principles and are not peculiar to eCommerce but are amplified by eCommerce.

Transfer pricing issues and concerns are of significance in that they further demonstrate the impact of technology on taxation. The primary significance of VAT is that in its current form it is a relatively effective tax to apply to eCommerce because it is more flexible than other taxing systems and, therefore, it is more easily adapted to possible variations in business practices caused by technological amelioration. Furthermore, VAT is more amenable than income tax (even if theoretically minimal in comparison) to government application on a global scale and, therefore, to boosting government revenue globally.

Although the primary focus of this paper is the impact of technology on taxation in respect of income tax and VAT, a summary discussion of the impact of technology has had on other spheres of taxation, such as transfer pricing, is necessary as cognisance should be taken of the far-reaching consequences of technology.

It is the OECD's assessment that "*the transfer pricing problems raised so far are not unique to electronic commerce, [but it is, nevertheless, acknowledged that] the increased speed and mobility of business activities and cross-border transactions may raise new difficulties in the application of transfer pricing methods*".[1]

[1] op cit OECD *Tax Policy Studies E-Commerce: Transfer Pricing and Business Profits Taxation No. 10*, p66.

A.M. Bardopoulos, *eCommerce and the Effects of Technology on Taxation*,
Law, Governance and Technology Series 22, DOI 10.1007/978-3-319-15449-7_26

26.1 Traditional Definition of Transfer Pricing

The OECD has published two fundamental characteristics of the traditional approach to transfer pricing containing, as a specified element, the essential condition of a transactional approach and the refinement and improvement of the comparability analysis.[2]

A prerequisite to a discussion of the impact of technology on transfer pricing is a qualified perception of transfer pricing and the concept of the traditional approach to transfer pricing, an intelligible definition of which is:

> *Transfer pricing refers to the pricing policies and practices that are established when physical goods, intangible property, and services are charged between business units within a group. The prices which are established for cross-border transfers should satisfy the 'arm's length principle'. Essentially, this principle requires that intra-group transfer prices should be equivalent to those that are / would have been charged between independent persons dealing at arm's length in otherwise similar circumstances.*[3] [Emphasis Added]

26.2 Issues and Concerns in Respect of the Application of Transfer Pricing Principles in an eCommerce Environment

> *Having analysed the fact patterns of the ... e-commerce business models, the existing guidance on the application of the arm's length principle in the OECD Transfer Pricing Guidelines for Multinational Enterprises and Tax Administrations appears capable of dealing with the transfer pricing issues raised by e-commerce.*[4]

Despite the OECD statement the OECD has acknowledged various points at issue which may occur in eCommerce. Such points at issue are not solely intrinsic to eCommerce but are also evident in traditional application. However, the proliferation of eCommerce has amplified pre-existing issues of concern.

Furthermore, the OECD has also held that issues pertinent to transfer pricing taxation within an eCommerce environment are similar to issues accruing in 'permanent establishment' and 'source basis' taxation.[5] The similarity pertains to the borderless environment within which cross-border transactions occur.[6] However, the eCommerce environment increases the difficulty for jurisdictions to "*identify,*

[2] idem p58.

[3] op cit Lymer, Andrew & Hasseldine, John *The International Taxation System* (2002) Kluwer Academic Publishers, U.S.A, p158.

[4] op cit OECD *Tax Policy Studies E-Commerce: Transfer Pricing and Business Profits Taxation No. 10*, p11.

[5] idem p55.

[6] supra.

trace and quantify cross-border transactions".[7] The significance of this similarity is the 'comparability' of intra-group transactions with third party transactions in order to determine the 'arm's length price',[8] while the cause of the increased difficulty is due to *"[t]he speed, frequency, anonymity and integration of exchanges over the Internet and the development of intranets ... [which facilitate] the use of automated functions, functions become more mobile and able to be 'located' in virtually any place*".[9]

26.3 Impact of Technology on Transfer Pricing

While cognizance has been taken of the impact of proliferating eCommerce on transfer pricing and the measure of effective application thereof, certain academic groups have recommended postponing correction and improvement in respect of application contending that any attempt at adjustment would be premature as eCommerce is still in its infancy.[10]

However, the notion of being in *"an early stage in the development of the business of electronic commerce*"[11] is a debatable point at issue, as is it may be contended that expectation of eCommerce maturity are unrealistic in respect of continuously ameliorating technology.

Therefore, considered in relation to unconstrained technological amelioration recent threshold business practice will become obsolete as it is established generated by a futile pursuit of an unreachable end. However, this contention is in itself a debatable point at issue.

The OECD Technical Advisory Group, while supporting the contention that "*fundamental changes*"[12] are unnecessary at this time, argues the current financial impact of technology on policies such as transfer pricing, commenting that:

> *[A]t this stage, e-commerce and other business models resulting from new communication technologies would not, by themselves, justify a dramatic departure from the current rules. Contrary to early predictions, there does not seem to be actual evidence that the communications efficiencies of the internet have caused any significant decrease to the tax revenues of capital importing countries.*[13] [Emphasis Added]

[7] supra.

[8] idem p60.

[9] supra.

[10] op cit OECD *Tax Policy Studies E-Commerce: Transfer Pricing and Business Profits Taxation No. 10*, p67.

[11] supra.

[12] idem p151.

[13] supra.

This comment by the OECD provokes a reaction in that the OECD has contended that the internet has caused an increased inability "*to identify, trace and quantify cross-border transactions*".[14] Therefore, the question begs as to how it may be reliably held that no 'actual evidence' exists in respect to revenue loss. A further point at issue is that problems regarding effective and efficient application are intrinsic to traditional transfer pricing principles and are not peculiar to eCommerce but are amplified by eCommerce. As with 'source basis' principles, transfer pricing provisions may need to be 'reconceptualised' in order to be effectively applied in an eCommerce environment. Furthermore, current transfer pricing principles may prove to be inadequate and obsolete when pertaining to further development of technology as is the case with 'residence basis' principles.

A protracted analysis of transfer pricing issues and concerns within an eCommerce environment, including possible solutions and recommendations, falls outside the scope of this paper. However, transfer pricing issues and concerns are of significance in that they further demonstrate the impact of technology on taxation and while this paper supports VAT as the eTax solution it does not assert that VAT is a tax system of undisputed power and influence. The primary significance of VAT is that in its current form it is a relatively effective tax to apply to eCommerce because it is more flexible than other taxing systems and, therefore, it is most easily adapted to possible variations in business practices caused by technological amelioration. Furthermore, VAT is more amenable than income tax (even if theoretically minimal in comparison) to government application on a global scale and, therefore, to boosting government revenue globally.

Bibliography

Secondary Sources

Lymer, Andrew, and John Hasseldine. 2002. *The international taxation system*. Boston/Dordrecht/London: Kluwer Academic Publishers.

OECD Tax Policy Studies. 2005. *E-Commerce: Transfer pricing and business profits taxation* No. 10. Paris: OECD.

[14]idem p58.

Chapter 27
Enforceability & Administrative Costs vs. Benefits

Abstract The prime issues in respect of enforcement of VAT/GST are identification and verification of the suppliers' and customers' location and verification of the suppliers' VAT/GST registration status.

A further point at issue is in regard to circumstances where a foreign supplier is required to register for VAT/GST in another jurisdiction. The administrative costs required to effectively and efficiently enforce VAT/GST may, in certain circumstances, outweigh the tax revenue benefits received in return.

Issues of concern relevant to the enforceability of VAT/GST in regard to cross-border transactions have been exacerbated by the proliferation of eCommerce. It has been suggested that a third party should be established for the purpose of imposing, collecting and administering VAT engendered by cross-border transactions. This may prove to be the more effective means of contending with tax revenue received which would not exceed the administrative costs relevant to the enforcement of VAT/GST.

Reference has periodically been made to the enforceability of VAT/GST in preceding discussion in this paper especially in Parts V and VI. This chapter accentuates synoptically crucial points at issue in regard to enforceability. The prime issues in respect of enforcement are identification and verification of the supplier's and customer's location and verification of the supplier's VAT/GST registration status. This has, however, been discussed and it was submitted that practical use of the user's IP address for the purpose of determining location is the most reliable and effective method of identification.

A further point at issue regarding enforcement is in regard to circumstances where a foreign supplier is required to register for VAT/GST in another jurisdiction. The administrative costs required to effectively and efficiently enforce VAT/GST may, in certain circumstances, outweigh the tax revenue benefits received in return. Cognizance of this point at issue by certain jurisdictions is evident in the 'reverse charge mechanism' established in that jurisdiction whereby the supplier will not be required to register for VAT in terms of a threshold, but the customer may have to register where supplies received exceed the registration threshold (for example New Zealand).

A.M. Bardopoulos, *eCommerce and the Effects of Technology on Taxation*,
Law, Governance and Technology Series 22, DOI 10.1007/978-3-319-15449-7_27

While such practice may result in hypothetical loss of tax revenue, the administrative costs involved in the enforcing of foreign suppliers to register for VAT may outweigh the benefits received. Therefore, jurisdictions such as New Zealand opt for the hypothetically lower tax revenue while at the same time minimising administrative costs integral to enforcement. Issues of concern relevant to the enforceability of VAT/GST in regard to cross-border transactions have been exacerbated by the proliferation of eCommerce. Various solutions devised to contend with such problems have been discussed, and it has been suggested that a third party should be established for the purpose of imposing, collecting and administering VAT engendered by cross-border transactions. As previously submitted this may prove to be the more effective means of contending with tax revenue received which may not exceed the administrative costs relevant to the enforcement of VAT/GST.

Chapter 28
Various Recommended Solutions

Abstract A critical point at issue is the impact of technology on taxation and the urgent necessity to devise an effective tax system relevant to this issue. The OECD has discussed the possibility of a 'virtual permanent establishment' which may be applied to eCommerce transactions (Op cit OECD *Tax Policy Studies E-Commerce: Transfer Pricing and Business Profits Taxation No. 10* (2005) OECD. France, p144).

Other OECD alternatives in respect of 'permanent virtual establishment' are acknowledgement of 'virtual fixed place of businesses', (Refer to footnote 2 [p350]) 'virtual agents' (Refer to footnote 3 [p350]) and 'on-site business presence' (Refer to footnote 4 [p350]).

A further alternative is the possibility of the virtual world constituting a jurisdiction in its own right, allowing all taxes to be imposed and collected by an independent third party and then distributed to all participating jurisdictions in accordance with a pre-accepted distribution formula. However, such solutions, including the OECD's proposed alternatives for a 'virtual permanent establishment', require considerable international co-operation and co-ordination. With the proliferation of eCommerce political harmony may be impelled as tax evasion and tax avoidance spiral out of control.

It is futile to implement a taxing system or regime which cannot be effectively enforced, or where the compliance and administrative costs outweigh the benefits received in regards to taxation recovered.

A critical point at issue in this paper is the impact of technology on taxation and the urgent necessity to devise an effective tax system relevant to this issue. The submission that the virtual world should be recognised as a jurisdiction in its own right is controversial and rigorously debated, the political significance of which must, furthermore, be considered. However, the OECD has discussed the possibility of a 'virtual permanent establishment' which may be applied to eCommerce transactions.[1]

The OECD has examined diverse evolutionary alternatives for the idea of 'permanent establishment' from the traditional concept to the reconceptualised idea

[1] op cit OECD *Tax Policy Studies E-Commerce: Transfer Pricing and Business Profits Taxation No. 10*, p144.

A.M. Bardopoulos, *eCommerce and the Effects of Technology on Taxation*,
Law, Governance and Technology Series 22, DOI 10.1007/978-3-319-15449-7_28

of a ‘virtual permanent establishment’, all of which require cognizance of the ‘virtual world’ and the impact it has had on the traditional approach to business. Thorough examination of the various given recommended solutions to the issue of the impact of technology on taxation falls outside the scope of this paper as the solutions are primarily in respect of income tax provisions, however, the alternative solutions are of primary importance in respect of the acknowledgement of ‘virtual fixed place of businesses’,[2] ‘virtual agents’[3] and ‘on-site business presence’.[4] However, these various alternatives remain OECD discussion points which have not as yet been implemented.

Various solutions to the eTax dilemma have been submitted in the course of this paper, including the possibility of the virtual world constituting a jurisdiction in its own right, allowing all taxes to be imposed and collected by an independent third party and then distributed to all participating jurisdictions in accordance with a pre-accepted distribution formula. However, such solutions, including the OECD’s proposed alternatives for a ‘virtual permanent establishment’, require considerable international co-operation and co-ordination which may be, currently, unachievable on account of differing political motives. However, with the proliferation of eCommerce such political harmony may be impelled as tax evasion and tax avoidance spiral out of control.

It is, furthermore, futile to implement a taxing system or regime which may not be effectively enforced or, alternatively, where the compliance and administrative costs, in regard to enforcing certain taxing provisions, outweigh the benefits received in regards to the taxation recovered. This should be a consideration in respect of the implementation of any solution or tax law. Examples of such a situation are VAT/GST jurisdictions which either zero rate certain supplies or cause certain supplies to fall outside the scope of their VAT/GST tax net because of the

[2]According to the OECD *“[t]he ‘Virtual Fixed Place of Business PE’ would create a permanent establishment when the enterprise maintains a web site on a server of another enterprise located in a jurisdiction and carries on business through that web site. The place of business is the web site, which is virtual . . . ”.*

[op cit OECD *Tax Policy Studies E-Commerce: Transfer Pricing and Business Profits Taxation*, p144].

[3]According to the OECD “*‘the Virtual Agency PE’, would seek to extend the existing dependent agent permanent establishment concept to electronic equivalent of a dependent agent . . . ”.*

[op cit OECD *Tax Policy Studies E-Commerce: Transfer Pricing and Business Profits Taxation*, p144].

[4]According to the OECD the “*‘On-site Business Presence PE’ proposes a new threshold for source taxation which does not depend on the existence of a fixed place of business at the disposal of the enterprise or on the traditional view of a business activity taking place within a jurisdiction. Rather, it looks at the economic presence of an enterprise within a jurisdiction in circumstances where the foreign enterprise provides what the proponents of that approach view as on-site services or other business interface (which could be a computer or phone interaction) at the customer’s location . . .*”.

[op cit OECD *Tax Policy Studies E-Commerce: Transfer Pricing and Business Profits Taxation*, p145].

considerable administrative cost and burden fundamental to the enforcement of the imposition and collection of VAT/GST on such supplies. For example, a jurisdiction such as New Zealand enforces the 'reverse charge mechanism' in respect of taxable supplies made to a New Zealand registered, or required to be registered, person.

The reason for limiting the 'reverse charge mechanism' to registered, or required to be registered, persons is because the administrative costs and burden pertaining to the enforcing of the 'reverse charge mechanism' with non-registered customers would most likely outweigh the benefit the New Zealand revenue authority would receive. South Africa has not limited the 'reverse charge mechanism' to registered, or required to be registered, persons, and realistically it is doubtful that SARS enforces the self-assessment and payment of VAT on downloaded software, games, music, movies, etc. by non-registered persons. The administrative cost of enforcing such taxable supplies would be crippling.

Bibliography

Secondary Sources

OECD Tax Policy Studies. 2005. *E-Commerce: Transfer pricing and business profits taxation* No. 10. Paris: OECD.

Part VIII
Conclusion and Opinion Advocated with Regard to the eTax Solution

Chapter 29
Is the Allure of VAT Justified?

Abstract The preeminent points at issue are the application of taxation on eCommerce; the submission that VAT supersedes income tax in flexibility and adaptability in respect of eCommerce; and the espousal of VAT as the most practicable and effective means of application of tax on and implementation of tax in eCommerce. The point in question should not be whether eCommerce should be subject to taxation, but rather the impact of technology on taxation, most specifically in respect of the most effective modus operandi of imposing tax on an eCommerce impelled by proliferating technology. If an activity or income earned or generated in the traditional world is taxable, then it may be argued that taxable activities in the virtual world should be equally taxable.

Notwithstanding administrative problems which impede the effective imposition of VAT in the virtual world, the resolution of which presupposes governmental co-operation across jurisdictions, it is submitted that within the realms of an unbounded environment contingent upon ameliorating technology, the flexible and amenable nature inherent to VAT makes VAT the preferred taxing system to be ardently pursued by jurisdictions as the eTax solution to eCommerce.

29.1 Review of the Argument Within This Paper Supporting VAT as the eTax Solution

Technology has undeniably impacted taxation and the manner in which it is effectively imposed. While this paper is aimed at supporting the contention that VAT is the eTax solution, income tax issues relating to 'residence' versus 'source' have also been addressed in order to provide a comparative analysis of applying income tax and VAT principles to eCommerce transactions. It is submitted that income tax principles may have to be 'reconceptualised' in order to be effectively applied to eCommerce transactions as income tax principles, in their current form, are not conducive to cross-border eCommerce transactions. For example, determining the location of a 'permanent establishment' by determining the location of the server has proved to be ineffective because the rapid amelioration of technology rendered such an application obsolete and out-dated, for example, due to the introduction of load-shedding.

A.M. Bardopoulos, *eCommerce and the Effects of Technology on Taxation*,
Law, Governance and Technology Series 22, DOI 10.1007/978-3-319-15449-7_29

Application of VAT within the virtual world does not differ significantly from traditional application. The primary difference appears to pertain to determining the place of supply, but apart from such determination VAT principles and concepts can be applied with relative ease within the virtual world. Income tax laws, on the other hand, have deemed certain technology to constitute, for example, permanent establishment when required and, furthermore, the conflict in source and resident based systems implemented globally creates further complexities.

It is submitted that the indirect consumption-based VAT system is the most amenable taxation system in respect of effective imposition of tax on cross-border eCommerce transactions. Furthermore, VAT is the most amenable tax system in respect of application in eCommerce, because VAT's inherently flexible nature enables it to adapt to technical amelioration and the undiscovered, borderless terrain of the virtual world. While VAT is not perfect and does require modification if it is to be effectively applied to the virtual world, and although administrative difficulties pertaining to cross-border transactions do require resolution, it is submitted that VAT is, nevertheless, more effective than income tax. This contention is based primarily on the flexibility of VAT principles compared to the inflexible principles of income tax.

A further point of significance in this regard is that VAT is a consumption tax in principle which is, moreover, a transactional tax and systems may be introduced for the collection thereof from either the seller or buyer. Income tax, on the other hand, is naturally more complex with respect to determining, the imposition and collection of tax on cross-border transactions.

Furthermore, while VAT may require amendment to allow for a more conducive global application, the various systems examined demonstrate that:

(a) It is possible for countries to harmonize their VAT systems to allow for a more efficient application and administration of VAT (as demonstrated by the European Union); and
(b) VAT is capable of co-existing with an indirect consumption-based retail tax system as is demonstrated by the USA and also Canada which has implemented both a federal VAT system and a provincial retail sales tax systems.

It is of paramount importance that the retail tax system utilised by the USA, the largest commercial hub, especially in respect of eCommerce transactions, can effectively operate in conjunction with VAT. Indeed, the USA is a critical point at issue when determining an effective global taxing system.

The impact of technology on VAT has not been in regard to the application of VAT, but rather to the determination of the place of supply, enforcement, collection and overall administrative aspects of the imposition of VAT. This is evident from the eCommerce guidelines published by the several jurisdictions (for example, the UK, Sweden, etc.) and the OECD wherein the points at issue are in respect of place of supply and administrative aspects rather than the need to reconceptualise and reformulate the principles of VAT.

Income tax has been examined and debated in detail, and while 'source-based' taxation has been promoted as the best income tax method, application of the 'source-based' method in its current form and in respect of eCommerce and the Internet has proved itself to be ineffectual and problem laden. Application of the 'residence-based' tax system with regard to eCommerce remains problematic as the virtual world has allowed for the manipulation of the place of 'effective management'.

While this paper may not advocate the abandonment of income tax principles in their entirety, upon comparison of income tax based principles and the VAT laws implemented in the various jurisdictions, it is submitted that the virtual world is more amenable to the application of VAT than to income tax principles. Income tax, however, appears to be the primary focus of much research, debate and discussion contingent upon the quantity of tax revenue connected with effective imposition of income tax.

29.2 Conclusion and Opinion Advocated That VAT Is the eTax Solution

An examination of the diverse jurisdictions reveals an urgent need for decisive tax rules. The crucial point at issue is a lack of commonality in respect of income tax jurisdictions which are not in unanimity regarding the adaptation of income tax to technology and the establishing of common decisive rules with regard to cross-border transactions engendered by technology. However, the principles of VAT, and even sales tax, are more flexible and are more amenable to technology and adaption because the consumer bears the tax. Consumption tax, in principle, is levied where the goods or services are consumed. Thus, as a very broad perception and application of VAT, the consumer's location at the time the service or good is consumed is the decisive key factor. This is supported by the far greater commonality which exists amongst VAT/GST jurisdictions, and even indirect jurisdictions as a whole, which demonstrates unanimity regarding the adaptation of VAT to technology and the establishment of common decisive rules in regard to cross-border transactions. However, this does not imply that administrative problems will not be a point at issue. Intrinsic to administrative difficulties is the establishing of globally accepted common rules, definitions, principles and collection methods. The OECD and EU have made considerable progress in the pursuit of this common goal.

If jurisdictions can attain global accord in regard to determining the consumers' location and collection, then, notwithstanding technological amelioration, VAT will more readily adapt to new technology than income tax. It may be argued that if traditional methods of locating the server (which is of primary importance for the purpose of determining the taxing jurisdiction in respect of income tax) prove to be ineffectual, then traditional methodology will prove ever less effective should servers relocate entirely to outer space. As already shown, classical methodology is already obsolete in regard to the current technological development of load-shedding. However, VAT can be imposed where the service is consumed.

Furthermore, deeming provisions, rules or guidelines introduced in regard to income tax are often obsolete by the time such provisions, rules or guidelines are published, for example, the deeming provision that the location of a server may constitute a permanent establishment for income tax purposes. The primary points at issue in respect of VAT may be tendered as place of supply in regard to whether the destination or origin principle should apply, the practicality and efficiency of collecting VAT in regard to cross-border transactions and the administration burdens in respect of the collection and enforcement methods. As previously discussed, an increasing number of jurisdictions espouse the destination based principle. In respect of the destination principle, VAT should be imposed where the goods or services are consumed despite, as previously discussed, the points at issue implicit to such a rule, in respect of which several jurisdictions have introduced a 'place of supply rule' to ensure certainty in the determination of whether a supply is subject to VAT within that jurisdiction.

A point at issue regarding the 'place of supply rules' is that exact certainty is implicit to traditional cross-border transactions. The virtual world has merely exacerbated the need for certainty. Even if tax definitions and principles become congruent with those of the technology industry, and 'place of supply' rules persist in most jurisdictions, place of supply rules, nevertheless, should not be as inflexible as the deeming provisions introduced to income tax.

The deeming provisions in respect of income tax are too closely aligned to current technology which renders such deeming provisions obsolete. It follows that deeming provisions in regard to income tax will have to be continuously amended in respect of application to current technology. Regardless of solutions suggested, tax definitions pertaining to technology should be congruent with those of the technology industry. Furthermore, consultation with the technology industry concerning a proposed amelioration is crucial to effectively taxing eCommerce in that such consultation can prevent adoption of inflexible systems and publication of already obsolete policies.

Furthermore, it is improbable that unanimity in respect of deeming provisions in respect of income tax will be achieved and timeously published to accord with existing and developing technology. It is probable, furthermore, that such deeming provisions will thus become regularly obsolete. For example, the current deeming provision pertaining to 'permanent establishment' for income tax purposes refers to the location of the server, whereas the 'place of supply' rules for VAT purposes routinely refer to the consumer or supplier's residence or location. While the supplier and consumer's location may still have to be determined, not being fixed to current technology permits flexibility of determination and ready adaptability to ameliorating technology. A common example used throughout this paper is determining location of a 'permanent establishment' by determining the location of the server. It is thus crucial that the deciding factor for location is not fixed to current technology because technology is continuously changing and the 'deciding factor' will become obsolete as has happened in respect of income tax principles.

The preeminent points which are cardinal to this paper are thus the application of taxation on eCommerce; the submission that VAT supersedes income tax in flexibility and adaptability in respect of eCommerce; and the espousal of VAT as the most practicable and effective means of application of tax on and implementation of tax in eCommerce. The point at issue should not be whether eCommerce should be subject to taxation, but rather the impact of technology on taxation, most specifically in respect of the most effective *modus operandi* of imposing tax on an eCommerce impelled by proliferating technology. If an activity or income earned or generated in the traditional world is taxable, then it may be argued that taxable activities in the virtual world should be equally taxable.

Traditional taxing principles are rapidly ineffective with regard to effective imposition and collection of tax within the virtual world. However, it is submitted that implicit to VAT is the potential to resist these developments. Notwithstanding rigorous debate regarding the radical hypotheses of collection and monitoring of tax in respect of eCommerce, indirect taxes such as VAT persist in being persistently flexible when applied to eCommerce. Indeed, the submission that VAT is the eCommerce solution is cardinal to the intellectual basis of this paper. VAT's advantage is that it is both flexible and adaptable in respect of eCommerce, and in contradistinction to income taxation can be applied to eCommerce without significant change or amendment. Indeed, amendment, radical change and reconceptualisation of income tax provisions are necessary for effective application to the virtual world. It is submitted that such amendment, radical change and reconceptualization of VAT provisions and principles are not necessary for effective application to the virtual world. Notwithstanding the applicable amendment of relevant general peculiarities of the virtual world which would unequivocally assist in establishing VAT's capacity as an effective eTax, it is submitted that VAT is, not only provisionally, a dependable eTax in respect of eCommerce, but will remain a powerful taxing tool within the virtual world.

A further significant point at issue is the confirmed compatibility of VAT and retail sales tax as is demonstrated by trade interaction between the USA and Canada. Furthermore, retail sales tax and VAT can be concurrently imposed and collected and then redistributed to the relevant governing bodies as is demonstrated by the Canadian Harmonized GST system. Notwithstanding administrative problems which impede the effective imposition of VAT in the virtual world, the resolution of which presupposes governmental co-operation across jurisdictions, it is submitted that within the realms of an unbounded environment contingent upon ameliorating technology, the flexible and amenable nature inherent to VAT makes VAT the preferred taxing system to be ardently pursued by jurisdictions as the eTax solution to eCommerce.

Appendices

A.M. Bardopoulos, *eCommerce and the Effects of Technology on Taxation*,
Law, Governance and Technology Series 22, DOI 10.1007/978-3-319-15449-7

Appendix 1

Jurisdictional Analysis

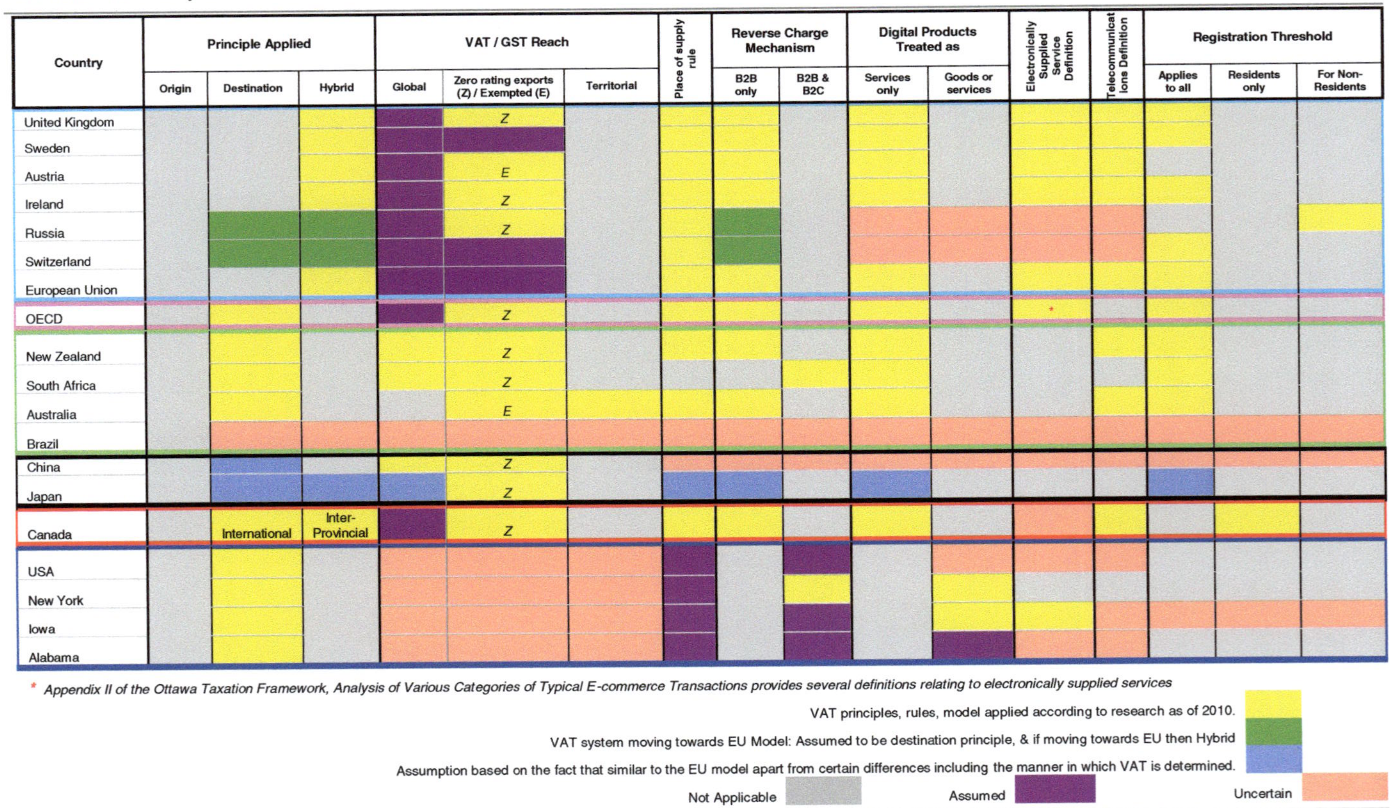

Appendix 2

Table 1 as set out in *HMRC Electronically Supplied Services: A Guide to Interpretation* which is taken from Annex L of the EU VAT on E-Commerce Directive (2002/38/EC)

Annex l reference	*Supplies covered by the legal text*	*Example of a service that is an electronically supplied service*
Item 1	*A. Website supply, web hosting and distance maintenance of programmes and equipment*	*Website hosting and web page hosting*
		Automated, online distance maintenance of programmes
		Remote systems administration
		Online data warehousing (in other words where specific data is stored and retrieved electronically)
		Online supply of on demand disc space
Item 2	*A. Software and updating thereof*	*Accessing or downloading software (for example procurement/ accountancy programmes, antivirus software) plus updates*
		Bannerblockers (software to block banner adverts showing)
		Download drivers, such as software that interfaces PC with peripheral equipment (for example printers)
		Online automated installation of filters on websites
		Online automated installation of firewalls
Item 3	*A. Images*	*Accessing or downloading desktop themes*
	B. Text and information	*Accessing or downloading photographic or pictorial images or screensavers*
	C. Making databases available	*The digitised content of books and other electronic publications*
		Subscription to online newspaper and journals
		Weblogs and website statistics
		Online news, traffic information and weather reports
		Online information generated automatically by software from specific data input by the customer, such as legal and financial data (for example continually updated stock market data).
		The provision of advertising space (for example banner ads on a website/webpage)
		Use of search engines and Internet directories

(continued)

Annex l reference	*Supplies covered by the legal text*	*Example of a service that is an electronically supplied service*
Item 4	*A. Music.*	*Accessing or downloading of music onto PCs, mobile phones, and so on*
	B. Films.	*Accessing or downloading of jingles, excerpts, ringtones, or other sounds*
	C. Broadcasts and events – political, cultural, artistic, sporting, scientific and entertainment.	*Accessing or downloading of films*
		Web-based broadcasting that is only provided over the Internet or similar electronic network and is not simultaneously broadcast over a traditional radio or television network, as opposed to Item 4, Table 2
	D. Games, including games of chance and gambling games.	*Downloads of games onto PCs, mobile phones, and so on*
		Accessing automated online games which are dependent on the Internet, or other similar electronic networks, where players are remote from one another
Item 5	*A. Distance teaching.*	*Teaching that is automated and dependent on the Internet or similar electronic network to function, including virtual classrooms, as opposed to Item 2(b), Table 2*
		Workbooks completed by pupil online and marked automatically, without human intervention
Item 6	*A. Those not explicitly listed in Annex L.*	*Online auction services (to the extent that they are not already considered to be web hosting services under Item 1) that are dependent on automated databases and data input by the customer requiring little or no human intervention (for example an online market place or online shopping portals), as opposed to Item 3(f), Table 2*
Other services included		*Internet Service Packages (ISPs) in which the telecommunications component is an ancillary and subordinate part (in other words a package that goes beyond mere Internet access comprising various elements (for example content pages containing news, weather, travel information; games for a; web hosting; access to chatlines and so on))*

Appendix 3

Table 2 as set out in *HMRC Electronically Supplied Services: A Guide to Interpretation* which is taken from Annex L of the EU VAT on E-Commerce Directive (2002/38/EC)

Example of a transaction not considered to be a supply of an 'electronically supplied service'	*Rationale*
1. A supply of:	*These are supplies of goods*
(a) A good, where the order and processing is done electronically	
(b) A CD-Rom, floppy disc and similar tangible media	
(c) Printed matter such as a book, newsletter, newspaper or journal	
(d) A CD, audio cassette	
(e) A video cassette, DVD	
(f) Games on a CD-Rom	
2. A supply of:	*This is a supply of service that relies on substantial human intervention and the Internet or electronic network is only used as a means of communication*
(a) services of lawyers and financial consultants and so on, who advise clients through email	
(b) interactive teaching services where the course content is delivered by a teacher over the Internet or an electronic network (. . . via remote link)	
3. A supply of:	*These are supplies of services that are not delivered over the Internet and rely on substantial human intervention*
(a) Physical repair services of computer equipment	
(b) Offline data warehousing services	
(c) Advertising services, such as in newspapers, on posters and on television	
(d) Telephone helpdesk services	
(e) Teaching services involving correspondence courses such as postal courses	
(f) Conventional auctioneers' services reliant on direct human intervention, irrespective of how bids are made (for example in person, Internet or telephone), as opposed to Item 6(a), Table 1.	
4. A supply of a radio and television broadcasting service provided over the Internet or similar electronic network simultaneous to the same broadcast being provided over traditional radio or television network, as opposed to Item 4(c), Table 1	*This is a supply of a radio and television broadcasting service, which is covered by the penultimate indent of Article 9(2)(e)*
5. A supply of:	*These are supplies of telecommunication services and are covered by the place of supply rules for such services under the ninth indent of Article 9(2)(e)*
(a) Videophone services (. . . telephone services with a video component)	
(b) Access to the Internet and world wide web	
(c) Telephony (. . . telephone service provided through the Internet)	

Index

A.M. Bardopoulos, *eCommerce and the Effects of Technology on Taxation*, Law, Governance and Technology Series 22, DOI 10.1007/978-3-319-15449-7

MIX
Papier aus verantwortungsvollen Quellen
Paper from responsible sources
FSC® C105338

If you have any concerns about our products,
you can contact us on
ProductSafety@springernature.com

In case Publisher is established outside the EU,
the EU authorized representative is:
Springer Nature Customer Service Center GmbH
Europaplatz 3, 69115 Heidelberg, Germany

Printed by Libri Plureos GmbH
in Hamburg, Germany